WITH MUSKET & TOMAHAWK

With Musket and Tomahawk

The Saratoga Campaign and the Wilderness War of 1777

MICHAEL O. LOGUSZ

CASEMATE

Philadelphia & Newbury

Published in the United States of America and Great Britain in 2010 by
CASEMATE PUBLISHERS
908 Darby Road, Havertown, PA 19083
and
17 Cheap Street, Newbury RG14 5DD

Copyright 2010 © Michael O. Logusz

ISBN 978-1-935149-00-2

Cataloging-in-publication data is available from the Library of Congress
and the British Library.

10 9 8 7 6 5 4 3 2 1

Printed and bound in the United States of America.

For a complete list of Casemate titles please contact:

CASEMATE PUBLISHERS (US)
Telephone (610) 853-9131, Fax (610) 853-9146
E-mail: casemate@casematepublishing.com

CASEMATE PUBLISHERS (UK)
Telephone (01635) 231091, Fax (01635) 41619
E-mail: casemate-uk@casematepublishing.co.uk

Mixed Sources
Product group from well-managed
forests and other controlled sources
www.fsc.org   Cert no. SW-COC-002283
© 1996 Forest Stewardship Council
FSC

Contents

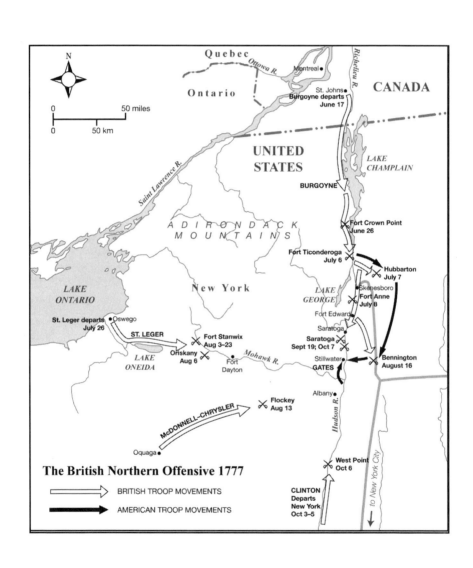

The British Northern Offensive 1777

N

0   50 miles
0   50 km

Quebec

Ottowa R.

Montreal

Ontario

St. Johns
Burgoyne departs
June 17

CANADA

Richelieu R.

UNITED
STATES

LAKE
CHAMPLAIN

BURGOYNE

Saint Lawrence R.

A D I R O N D A C K
M O U N T A I N S

Fort Crown Point
June 26

Fort Ticonderoga
July 6

Hubbarton
July 7

New York

LAKE
GEORGE

Skenesboro
Fort Anne
July 8

LAKE
ONTARIO

St. Leger departs
July 26

Oswego

Fort Edward

ST. LEGER

Fort Stanwix
Aug 3–23

Oriskany
Aug 6

LAKE
ONEIDA

Fort
Dayton

Mohawk R.

Saratoga

Saratoga
Sept 19; Oct 7

Stillwater

GATES

Bennington
August 16

McDONNELL-CHRYSLER

Flockey
Aug 13

Albany

Hudson R.

Oquaga

West Point
Oct 6

CLINTON
Departs
New York
Oct 3–5

to New York City

BRITISH TROOP MOVEMENTS

AMERICAN TROOP MOVEMENTS

Introduction:
The Wilderness War of 1777

1777. In America's history, it was a monumental year. It was the year of the terrible 7's. The year when the tomahawk, musket, rifle, knife, bayonet, war club, and bow and arrow reigned. The year when a vicious struggle was fought throughout the entire frontier wilderness of New York and its adjoining colonies. And it was the year that touched each man, woman, and child living in and around a raging inferno which rightfully may be recorded as the terrible Wilderness War of 1777.

The ideas which led to the American Revolution and thus the events of 1777 had actually been born many decades earlier. Evolving steadily through a difficult process, the origins of these ideas began in two places—in the minds of urban intellectuals and in the free spirits within the wilderness of the northeast.

From the moment the first Europeans stepped onto the shores of the New World, the Old World's conservative attitudes, along with its established way of life, were left behind. Proceeding further inland, as they entered the wilderness region with its massive forests, the men and women of European heritage immediately encountered an entirely new world, and with it a new way of life.

European settlers were especially affected by two factors: the first was the wilderness itself; the second, its original inhabitants, Native American Indians. Between the two, settlers from Europe quickly assumed an entirely new and different character.

In Europe, families typically resided on small plots of land, their lives centered within a village or town. One generation after another lived in small, crowded homes and communities. Within this environment, the Europeans could not elevate themselves. They could neither think nor act freely. Between the combination of an accepted lifestyle (no other was known) and the rules, laws, and regulations imposed and maintained by Europe's kings, queens, barons, princes, and the church, no other social system existed. Even worse, no new way of life could be developed.

They crossed a large ocean, fleeing from Europe's confinement and harsh conditions. Upon arrival in the New World, Europe's authority was left far behind them. Seeking land, the new settlers entered the world of endless trees, virgin streams, and trackless mountains.

For the new settlers it was, of course, a rough life. The death rate was high, especially amongst newborns. But many others survived. As they swung their axes to build homes, cleared fields for farming, and removed the fur of trapped beavers and other animals to be converted into rich pelts, they noted that no one was around within their part of the wilderness to dictate to them where and how they were to establish their farms, what to plant, and how to live. Simultaneously, as they lived and worked among the vast forests, they developed not only physical strength but a strong sense of confidence. From this confidence success was nurtured. In turn, success led to a strong commitment to freedom and independence, especially from any foreign power.

In the aftermath of the French and Indian War of 1754–1763, Britain became the dominant power in the New World. Noting the richness of the wilderness, England's rulers vied with other powers to control it. They also needed to maintain a strong hold on the expanding trade developed by those residing in the new land. But in order to effectively control the wilderness, England not only had to possess the coastal harbors and towns but, just as importantly, the regions adjacent to the wilderness. Via its network of Royal Governors and economic beneficiaries, British rule was imposed and spread inland.

By the mid 1700's the wilderness region of present day New York State, including the greater part of the Mohawk, Hudson, and Susquehanna Valleys, had been transformed into a land where people of various races, national origins, backgrounds, and professions were residing. Here trappers, settlers, and frontiersmen intermixed with farmers and craftsmen. Artists, intellectuals, Mennonites, and newly arrived immigrants, as well as some wealthy farmers and entrepreneurs, dwelled within or near the wilderness. Upon encountering the Native Americans, or Indians, an exchange of cultures took place. Settlers began to eat Indian corn and other foods heretofore unknown. Settlers found Indian footwear and buckskin clothing more comfortable and useful for their needs; in turn, from sheep brought in by the settlers, the Indians quickly weaved new woolen blankets while still retaining their exotic and beautiful native designs. Noting the usefulness of the tomahawk, the settlers improved upon it. It would not be long before the centuries-old tomahawk with its stone head was replaced by the stronger and sharper steel manufactured by Europe's skilled craftsmen residing in and around the forests.

Hand-in-hand with this cultural development, a strong dissatisfaction with British rule began to emerge. Many of those who were living in and around the endless forests professed a strong spirit of freedom. Though by the mid-1700's this feeling had worked its way through each and every colony, it was especially pronounced in the wilderness forests of the northeast and in adjacent New England. With the eruption of the Revolutionary War in 1775, it was now vital for the British to subdue the rebelling colonies, especially those of New England where the intellectual spearhead of rebellion had been nurtured. By severing New England from the rest of the colonies, the revolt could be quelled.

In order to accomplish this, Britain's military would have to undertake a major campaign through a massive wilderness region, largely bereft of roads. As they advanced through the wilderness they would not only need to subdue its inhabitants who were opposing the Crown but also place the richness of the vast territory into their own hands.

For those who planned the 1777 military campaign in England, it was to be a quick, straightforward operation. Looking at the map alone, nothing was deemed as being overly difficult, especially considering that key advantages lay with Great Britain.

The British held most of the major cities. Entire Atlantic coastal regions, along with centers of communications and commerce, were in British hands. They controlled the St. Lawrence River and the eastern Great Lakes. Their armies were composed of crack fighters with years of field experience. Most British commanders had previously served on the North American continent. Many were even familiar with wilderness survival and tactics from their war against the French. Great Britain's well led, armed, and experienced armies were to be reinforced with many loyal American-born sympathizers. British commanders would be operating on inner lines while their opponents would have to shift around the external periphery. The patriots' so-called Northern Army was just a shell, lacking men, materiel, firepower, and training.

Most of the patriot forts were not even completed and those that existed were weakly manned. The patriot supply and support system hardly existed. The British possessed a strict unity of command whereas the Northern Army's command was disjointed. Patriot forces were also loosely organized and scattered. Internal political squabbles within the ranks of the patriots further weakened them. These factors alone should have easily allowed the revolt to be shattered.

With such conclusions, King George III gave his commanders the green light to commence the campaign. And as Britain's forces invaded the wilderness, they triggered a massive and fiery struggle. Suddenly, the peaceful tranquility of the woodland was shattered. No one was safe, and no one could remain neutral. By the time the Wilderness War of 1777 concluded, it would be fought throughout a region comprised of tens of thousands of square miles. From Oswego to New Hampshire, from the Canadian border to New York City, and through parts of Connecticut and Massachusetts, its full fury and impact would be felt by one and all.

In truth, waging war in a region classified as wilderness is a very difficult undertaking. True, a forest has its beauty, but for those committed to a virgin landscape to wage war, the wilderness holds no beauty. Psychologically, a forest exerts a very strong feeling of uncertainty upon an invader. The endless miles of tall trees, many well over fifteen feet thick, interlocked with brush, swamps, bogs, rivers, streams, ponds, lakes, and fields—such terrain affects each and every year-round inhabitant as well as those entering such a region for the first time.

In the 18th century, western and central Europe had its share of forests. But those found in England and France were totally different from the endless primeval forests found on the North American continent. Europe's forests were also cultivated; America's were not. Most of Europe's inhabited centers were close to one another; America's inhabited places were few and far between. In Europe, numerous clearings existed in its forests; in America, few were found. Those which existed were usually located along the rivers and were spaced many miles apart.

American roads were few and in early stages of development. Most were in poor condition and many were seasonal only. Some roads were nothing but sizable trails. During periods of rain or thaw, entire sections were flooded. Once the snows and waters receded, the roads remained as pits of deep mud until they finally dried out. Only then could they be used, especially by wheeled transport.

In addition to the natural dangers of the forest, there also existed human dangers. No one knew when and where danger lurked. A traveler could not know when someone would suddenly fire down from the top of a tree or from behind it. No one knew when a native warrior would emerge with a tomahawk, knife, spear, or war club at a full run towards an opponent or civilian. Every new settler feared the tomahawk and scalping knife of the land's natives.

No matter how strong an invading force, it was still very difficult to completely seal off, surround, and decisively defeat an opponent within a huge forested region. Repeatedly, the British succeeded in driving the patriots into wooded and swampy areas, but they could not destroy them. Another burden the English War Ministry faced was that no matter how well trained and disciplined their troops, they simply could not surpass in fighting skill those who had been born and raised in the wilderness. Many of the patriots had mastered strong natural instincts—critical for survival in a frontier region—long before 1777. They could shoot, move, and communicate with ease. They could quickly cover vast distances on foot. They knew how to live off the land. Many were masters at hunting, fishing, and trapping. And almost all had mastered the use of the rifle and tomahawk. In the end, such forest skills helped the patriots to achieve a victory so crucially needed in the opening stages of the Revolutionary War.

As is always the case in a violent conflict, there is the human factor to consider. Many authors fail to properly cover this area while others cover it weakly or not at all. Yet, it is always the human drama which makes a story interesting. Therefore, I have examined it in depth.

I am including the story of what it was like to live, survive, fight, and die in 1777. One can only imagine what it must have been like to move vast distances through a thickly forested region, especially in pitch-black darkness or to experience hunger while in the field. Imagine what it was like to hear the terrifying shouts of war cries along with the screams of those being scalped, tortured, or mutilated; the sounds of major battles in the vast forests, along with the numerous battles fought in and around private homes, farms, and settlements. The blasts of gunfire, cannons, exploding shells; the hiss of bullets, flying arrows, spears, and thrown tomahawks; the triumphant shouts of raiders and the pitiful moans of the wounded . . . these must be evoked or the human experience is lost, not only to the modern reader but also, most importantly, to history.

Along with the visceral human aspect, I truly feel that to date, no one has ever adequately portrayed the critical military, political, economic, religious, and social events of 1777.

Most who fought in the terrible Wilderness War of 1777 had little to no notion of what the American Declaration of Independence, the Bill of Rights, or the Constitution stood for. Many did not care for any government at all, with its consequent taxation, restrictions, and complex regulations.

Yet they fought. They fought for their families and loved ones, their lands, farms, homes, and their way of life. In many cases their possessions were meager, but for them it was the entire world. Others fought simply to preserve the wilderness they so loved and cherished. Some fought to preserve the fur trade solely for themselves. Others fought because they feared British rule, and whether their fears were imaginary or real does not matter. What matters is that they fought, and the resistance of the wildnerness population, alongside units of the regular Continental Army, made a significant contribution to the victory of 1777.

Historians estimate that during the Revolutionary War approximately one-third of the males residing in the thirteen colonies supported the struggle for independence. Another third supported the Crown, and the remaining third, as John Adams perhaps summed it up best, "didn't give a damn one way or another!"

But among the women, this was not the case. Women, especially those who resided in and around the wilderness, tremendously supported the Revolution. Though a number had husbands, fathers, brothers, and cousins who sided with the Crown, these women not only sympathized with the patriots but also rendered the revolutionary cause important assistance, often in secret. In the end, their efforts helped the patriots to achieve the victory they so desperately needed in 1777.

Yet there was a price to pay for loyalty. For example, with her hands tied firmly behind her back, Jane Campbell stood no more than ten feet in front of her mother when suddenly an enemy raider appeared behind the older woman and drove a tomahawk deep into her head. Desperate to save her mother, Jane cried out to her captors but to no avail. For Jane, this was just one of the many sadnesses she experienced in 1777. Earlier, she had learned that her cousin had perished in the battle of Oriskany. Along with her parents and other family members, Jane had crossed the Atlantic from faraway Scotland to settle in the beautiful

Mohawk Valley. Never would they have imagined that their hopes of living in peace would be shattered by a new and vicious struggle raging around them. Jane Campbell, however, was by no means an exception. By the time the Wilderness War of 1777 concluded, thousands of Jane Campbells would feel its full fury and impact.

There are also the stories of the numerous African-American soldiers who loyally served and fought for the patriot cause during the Wilderness War. Agrippa Hull joined the Northern Army on 1 May 1777. Prince Whipple, always loyal to his master, General William Whipple, also enlisted in the Northern Army. "Colonel" Louie, a trapper of mixed African-Indian heritage, served and fought from Oswego to the Mohawk Valley and the Adirondack Mountains. Volunteers like them were just a few among hundreds of African descent who helped achieve a critical victory in 1777.

This is also the story of Native Americans such as Thomas Spencer, whose Indian name was Ahnyero, and Honyery Thawengarakwen Doxtater, an Oneida warrior, who loyally protected Colonel Samuel Campbell. Along with Honyery served his wife. During the Battle of Oriskany, she fought side-by-side with her husband. Through that entire bloody day of 6 August, both husband and wife played a critical role in achieving a victory for the patriots.

Combat, especially close-quarters combat, is vicious and brutal. In the forests and wilderness of 1777, knives, tomahawks, clubs, spears, and often bare hands, frequently decided an outcome. In the following pages, there will be a number of combat accounts which were obtained from some of the old works written either in the immediate aftermath of the Wilderness War of 1777 or, in some cases, decades later. Commencing in the 1830's and 1840's, a number of Revolutionary War scholars, such as James Phinney Baxter, William Campbell, Benson Lossing, and William Stone laboriously recorded the historical events of 1775 to1783, in the process uncovering a number of firsthand accounts of hand-to-hand combat. It was not an easy task, but through their efforts these authors preserved valuable historical accounts, chronicles, and events for future generations.

Some of the accounts might be difficult to believe; others might question the necessity of including them. But again, I wanted to capture the full human spectrum. One can only imagine what Northern Army scout Frederick Sammons must have felt when, on 7 August, he came across hundreds of bodies lying motionless on the Oriskany battlefield, or the horror young Thomas Mellen experienced in 1777. Eager to go to war, Mellen set off joyfully to what he thought would be a quick military operation with its various adventures. Upon his return, he planned to recall with enthusiasm to anyone who cared to listen his adventures and experiences. Mellen did return but for decades afterward he never uttered a word about the war. He attempted to forget all that he had seen and experienced, but he could not. Until the last day of his life, Mellen would be haunted by the ordeals and experiences of 1777.

Yet as often happens, age has its influence. Along with many others who had remained silent for decades, Mellen, in his senior years, began to speak out. Vividly, he recalled his ordeals in the terrible Wilderness War. A family member wrote down his story, which is now part of history. On both sides, brave soldiers, militiamen, and civilians endured much hardship, horror, and agony.

Generals and staff officers plan battles. They execute the actions needed to conduct a campaign. But in the end, it is the lowly soldiers who win the battles and wars. It will always be that way. And in 1777, among both the vanquished and victors, heroes emerged.

Sergeant Roger Lamb, an Irish volunteer who served in General John Burgoyne's British army, was one such example. Captured in October 1777, he was eventually released and became reunited with his family in his native Ireland. Yet, in the true sense, Sergeant Lamb had never been defeated. He had served nobly, soldiered to the best of his ability, and never disgraced the Crown he so loyally served. But just as important, Sergeant Lamb never harbored any hatred toward his former enemies. Until his death, the sergeant always held his former opponents in high esteem. In a personal journal he carried, the sergeant carefully documented the 1777 campaign as seen through the eyes of an invader who was also an elite warrior.

And then, there was Timothy Murphy, also of Irish descent. Born in the New World, he had never seen the land of his forebears. But he knew who he was. And he was aware of England's unjust policy towards the Irish. Proud of his heritage and determined to live free of English rule, Murphy stepped forward and joined the patriots. In combat he was a hellion. With his rifle, tomahawk, and knife, he killed over forty of his opponents. Franklin Delano Roosevelt served as the governor of New York prior to being elected president, and at the 152nd anniversary ceremony honoring the patriot victory at Saratoga, he stated, "This country has been made by the Timothy Murphy's, the men in the ranks. For it was to them, more than to the generals, that we were indebted for our military victories."

Neither Sergeant Lamb nor riflemen Tim Murphy were exceptions. On both sides, there were many heroes. In the following pages, their valor and deeds will be presented.

In itself, the Northern Army was truly an exotic fighting force. It was initially created in 1776 to contest the British in Canada and to protect and control New York State and New England. At the beginning of 1777, it was still a loosely organized and undisciplined force. At one point, after a disastrous offensive into Canada, the army had almost ceased to exist; yet it survived and grew. By the conclusion of 1777, the Northern Army had emerged as a highly respected and dreaded military force.

One of the army's strengths was that it was solely a volunteer force. Although conscription had been attempted in parts of New England, the draft system never worked. The Northern Army relied strictly on willing volunteers.

Recruitment was open to all males between the ages of 16 and 60. Recruits for the Northern Army were obtained from Canada to New York City, throughout New England, and the entire wilderness in between. The army did not discriminate in its recruitment. Within its ranks, whites, blacks, Indians, and immigrants soldiered side-by-side. The volunteers hailed from many different backgrounds and nationalities. It was an integrated army and a multinational force. In 1777, the Northern Army proved that whites and minorities could co-exist and serve equally. Tolerance was the norm.

The army was composed of regular Continental Army regiments and battalions, various militia units, scouts, and irregular (guerrilla) fighters. Many spies, agents, and couriers, from Montreal to New York City, operated for the Northern Army. In addition to those of Dutch, English, Irish, Scottish, and Welsh descent, there were also various other Europeans found in the Northern Army's ranks, such as Scandinavians from Denmark, Norway, Sweden and Finland, as well as a number of Czechs, Slovaks, Hungarians, Italians, Greeks, Spaniards, and Poles. Also, from distant Eastern Europe, the 1777 roster of names contain volunteers of the Ruthenian-Ukrainian heritage. Jewish personnel also served in the Northern Army.

In my research I have yet to find an author who has compiled a significant list of the different languages that were spoken at this time. It may be safely surmised that if one counted the various European, Native American, and African languages still known and spoken in this region, no less than thirty languages and dialects were used within the Northern Army. In turn, this exotic diversity played a major role in enabling the newly formed army to overcome an adversary whose military possessed a proud tradition stemming hundreds of years.

1777 was a monumental year not only because the victory achieved at Saratoga is regarded as one of the most decisive in military history, but for many other reasons as well. New York State officially came into existence that year. Despite the massive conflict being waged in their midst, New York's delegates, under adverse conditions, achieved a successful free election with many participants. New York state's first governor was elected and a new state constitution was drafted which exists to this day. Needing money, the early politicians of New York State organized and implemented its very first lottery. In 1777, lottery tickets were even sold on the battlefields. Successful at the time, the New York lotto exists to this day.

1777 saw the very early stages of the emancipation of America's black slaves. That year, adjacent to the eastern border of New York State within a disputed area known as the Hampshire Grants, a new entity emerged: Vermont. At first declaring itself an independent republic, in due course, on 4 March 1791, Vermont would join the newly established nation and become one of the United States.

From its inception in 1777, Vermont was a progressive state, and that same year it drafted a constitution. One of the first measures passed into law was an act that banned slavery. Following suit, New Hampshire, Massachusetts, Connecticut, and New York also passed various measures curbing slavery. Though human bondage at this time was not fully eradicated, it was placed on its deathbed. Proud of their status and determined to remain free, many blacks volunteered to serve in the Northern Army.

1777, however, also commenced the tragic end for the Native American Indians of the northeast, amongst whom were the mighty Iroquois. Prior to that year, the Iroquois Confederation had already been weakened. Europe and colonial America's influence was slowly eradicating the power of this once proud and powerful league. During the French and Indian War of 1754–1763, the Iroquois Confederacy had somehow succeeded in remaining neutral. But during the Revolution they were unable to remain on the sidelines. Despite strong efforts by this group to remain together, it was to no avail. In January, 1777, the league held its last Great Conference:

> We, the remaining part of the Onondagas Do now Inform Our Brothers that there is no longer a Council Fire at the Capitol of Six Nations. However, we are determined to use our feeble endeavors to support peace in the Confederate Nations. But let this be kept in Mind that the Central Council fire is extinguished… and can no longer burn.

Even the powerful Council of Mothers could not alter the tragic sequence of events. Divided among themselves, Indian warriors began battling one another. Some fought for the British; others fought for the newly established nation. 1777 was the year when a civil war formally commenced among the Iroquois. 1777 may also be cited as the year when the Iroquois Confederacy formally ceased to exist.

1777 solidified the entire American northeast. Although bloody raids against the patriots would continue until the conclusion of the Revolutionary War in 1783, the patriots could not be overthrown. The new nation remained firmly in place.

1777 also sadly commenced the beginning of the end of the raw American wilderness. Many who fought within and around the wilderness that year did so in order to preserve a certain way of life. Yet inadvertently, their victory helped destroy the life they cherished.

In the aftermath of the war, large numbers of settlers, land speculators, and sizable companies—the forerunners of modern industry—along with the first waves of European immigrants, poured into the wilderness. The huge, majestic trees, which had stood for centuries, were cut down, as economic growth replaced an appreciation of the wilderness. Until 1777 beavers, otters, muskrats, lynx, and other fur-bearing animals roamed the wilderness in large numbers. In the aftermath of the war, they virtually became extinct. What few animals remained retreated deep into the Adirondack Mountains.

No longer would the howl of the wolf or coyote be heard late at night. No longer would an eagle be seen hovering high above. The numerous moose, bears, and deer virtually disappeared. In due time, certain species of animals and birds, such as the passenger pigeon which flew in huge flocks over the British armies and the Northern Army, disappeared completely from the face of the earth. In 1777 a destructive trend commenced that tragically lasted for nearly two hundred years. By the time efforts were taken to reverse it, entire rivers, lakes, ponds, and streams would be dead. No longer would the air be clean and fresh water available for the taking. 1777 marked the end of the wild as it had existed in the American northeast.

1777 did not just destroy the natural wilderness; it heralded the beginning of the end of women's rights for over a century. Under Dutch rule women had a tremendous say in the economic sector. Women were immensely involved in trade and they played a vital role in the economy, especially in wilderness regions. Within larger towns women ran numerous businesses and discrimination was at a minimum. Women dealt with male traders in the hard manner the times called for. Women quickly adopted the style, mannerisms, languages, and the independent spirit of the American Indians. Women of European and African heritage especially admired the Native American Council of Mothers. From this council non-Indian women learned how to involve themselves in political affairs. Prior to the British imposing their rule, wilderness women had a tremendous say in matters pertaining to local and regional politics and economy.

One of the main reasons why so many women supported the Revolutionary War effort in 1777 was to preserve and restore their authority, independence, and rights. Many women also viewed the Revolution as an opportunity to further advance the cause of women's rights. Prior to 1775, the British system had been highly unjust towards women. Women of the time feared, in the event of continued British rule, that they would be reduced to domestic servants, virtually the same status experienced by women residing in England or in regions long under British rule.

America's female patriots played a vital role in achieving the victory of 1777. Yet, in the aftermath of the Revolutionary War, English views regarding the role of women in society not only remained firmly in place but also, tragically, expanded. Women's rights collapsed hand in hand with the collapse of the wilderness. As the endless forests disappeared, so too did a woman's privilege and authority. Equal opportunity, the right to vote, the ability to hold a job or to trade freely all became more of a struggle—one that would not finally triumph, in fact, for another two hundred years. But the women of today, who play such a critical role in our society, owe much to their female ancestors who not only fed, clothed, and nursed the Northern Army, but frequently fought side-by-side with their male compatriots during this monumental year.

1777 proved the value of an armed citizenry. Prior to the conflict, within the wilderness many men and women had sharpened their shooting and survival skills to a razor's edge. Numerous families, farms, and homes were saved as a result of ordinary armed citizens. Crime, especially problematic during periods of chaos, was kept at a minimum. Armed women protected themselves, their children, and their property from roving bands of criminals, loyalists, British army deserters, and Indian raiders.

In one instance, 400 armed women rallied to defend Pittsfield, Vermont. That day the men were off pursuing a raiding party which had previously attempted to attack the town. Warned that another sizable loyalist and Indian force with British advisers was approaching Pittsfield, the women quickly mustered in defense. Throughout the day they successfully battled the enemy force. Of significance is that this was the only time in America's history that an entire battle was fought on one side solely by women. Europe's soldiers quickly learned that their troops could not easily pillage a farm or village to obtain badly needed supplies in America, especially in and around the wilderness, as they might have been able to do in the European countryside. Well before the British campaign of 1777 had concluded, a number of senior ranking British and German officers acknowledged that armed citizens had hampered operations and posed a constant threat to their campaign.

1777 also proved the value of American riflemen, who, with their rifles and tomahawks, were the terror of the wilderness. Although the rifleman is discussed in many books, journals, and magazines, few accounts have portrayed these tough fighters in their true role. In the following pages, readers will become acquainted with the type of rugged forest fighters they were. Additionally, their clothing, weapons, equipment, and tactics will be presented in detail. In the words of Harold Kels Swan, a Senior Historic Preservation Specialist and curator of the Swan Collection of the American Revolution, the American rifleman had "no equal throughout the world during the period [of the Revolution]."

Perhaps British Army General John Burgoyne best summed it up on 17 October 1777, following his capitulation. When introduced by General Horatio Gates, the commander of the Northern Army, to Colonel Daniel Morgan, who commanded the army's rifle unit, Burgoyne, warmly clasping Morgan's hand, exclaimed to him, "Sir, you command the finest regiment in the world!"

1777 tore entire families apart. History records that during the American Civil War of 1861–1865, brother fought brother, families were divided, and loyalties ran in various directions. What many may not realize is that during the Revolutionary War, family loyalties also ran in opposing directions, and in 1777 this was no exception. On many battlefields, family members faced one another.

On the very same day General Herkimer lay wounded at Oriskany, though still commanding his militia force, his brother was directing a loyalist force for the British Army not far away. General Philip Schuyler, who commanded the Northern Army prior to General Gates, had relatives, both close and distant, firmly on the British side. General Benedict Arnold, whose aggressiveness and commitment played a major role in achieving victory in the Wilderness War of 1777, was married to a woman who was deeply supportive of the British. In time she convinced her husband to abandon the patriot cause and switch sides. Also Benjamin Franklin, who in 1777 was overseas seeking European support for the new nation, had a son named William Franklin, who was not only a loyalist but served as England's Royal Governor of New Jersey in 1777.

1777 was seen as a major military and political victory. Militarily, Saratoga is still regarded as one of the most decisive battles in military history. Unlike most other battles where two opposing forces met and fought it out within a confined time and area, what we call Saratoga was really a series of battles, skirmishes, and maneuvers taking place across several weeks and considerable distance. The campaign as a whole lasted the better part of a year until Burgoyne's final surrender at the hamlet of Saratoga (today the town known as Schuylerville).

Politically, the victory achieved in the terrible Wilderness War of 1777 not only raised patriot spirits but added legitimacy to the cause in the international arena. Saratoga went far toward convincing overseas observers that the Americans could ultimately prevail in the war, and withing months of Burgoyne's surrender, France, Spain, and the Netherlands declared war against England. Other European powers, including Russia, although officially not taking up arms, encouraged Britain to withdraw from the American colonies. Even Pope Clement XIV of the Vatican exerted his influence upon the British Ministry and King George III.

On 3 December 1777, news of Burgoyne's defeat reached London.

On that day, the British parliament was in session, and when the surrender was announced, it struck the assemblage like a thunderbolt. Critics of the war demanded an immediate end to the conflict. Prior to 1777 most of England's populace was either supportive of the King's policy in the colonies or did not care. After that year this changed. The northern battles of 1777 helped turn parliamentarians, regional officials, and much of England's populace against the entire effort to maintain rule of the American colonies. 1777 may be cited as the year when the British Empire, which spanned the world and still had its greatest days to come, was briefly rocked to its foundation.

1777 shattered the British high command on the North American continent. Psychologically and morally, the war struck deep, and soon afterward many British officers and officials were dismissed. Among them was Canada's Governor-General Guy Carleton and commander-in-chief of British forces in America, General Sir William Howe. In turn, General Henry Clinton, New York City's commander, was appointed as the commander-in-chief of the British military in both Canada and America. Clinton, however, did not want this assignment. Until mid-1777, he held the view that the colonists could be defeated. By September 1777 Clinton began to confide to close friends that the British campaign of 1777 was not only doomed, but in actuality the British would probably not win the war. 1777 was the beginning of the end of Britain's rule in the New World.

1777 marked the doom of the native British loyalists (also known as tories). Despite the claims of many that "countless thousands will rally around the King's armies," such a widespread uprising of volunteers for the Crown never occurred. Loyalists such as Colonel John Peters, Major Ebenezer Jessup, Major Philip Skene, Colonel John Butler and his son Captain Walter Butler, promised much but produced little. Though in Canada and nearby areas such as Fort Niagara these leaders succeeded in filling their ranks with sufficient volunteers, it was only for the time being. As for those recruited within the regions which fell to the British advance in 1777, many became "loyalist" not out of sympathy, but simply to avoid persecution or to protect their families and property while under occupation. Once the situation shifted, they fled in droves and supported the American patriots.

Despite the efforts, promises, and even threats from loyalist leaders, their support never developed into a formidable force. In fact, in 1777, the loyalists actually weakened the British military and its colonial government. Many weapons, along with sizable amounts of ammunition, equipment, food, clothing and materiel, desperately needed by regular British army units, was instead diverted to irregulars which in the end accomplished little for the British war effort. Following the failure of the British northern campaign of 1777, many of the loyalists fled to New York City or Canada. There they further strained England's limited resources and became a burden for British officials. For the most part, loyalists lost their estates, farms, lands, and possessions. Fleeing to Canada, Colonel Peters continued to agitate for the Crown and recruit loyalists for the British. His efforts, however, were largely fruitless as only a limited number stepped forward.

In the aftermath of 1777, loyalist support diminished considerably. This was evidenced in a letter dated 27 July 1778 by Charles Smith, a New York tory leader, to Colonel Walter Butler. After writing his letter, Smith passed it on to a messenger who, in turn, was to deliver it to Butler in Canada. However, a patriot spy, operating within Smith's circle, reported to Governor Clinton that Smith was corresponding with Butler. The messenger was intercepted and the letter was instead delivered to Clinton. Smith's letter revealed that it was very difficult to obtain recruits. "Men are struck with tarror [terror]. The Northern Army, I understand, having given them a sad stroke in 1777."

1777 resulted in the devastation of the economy in New York and, to a large measure, that of New England. Thousands of acres of cropland were burned. Many thousands remained unplowed as a result of the war or the threat of war. Tens of thousands of head of cattle, goats, sheep, and pigs were destroyed. Many were driven into swamps and forested areas or removed from the region. Thousands of civilians wound up homeless. For those caught up in the terrible Wilderness War of 1777, the fighting was bad enough, but its aftermath was equally harsh.

Food became scarce, especially in the cities. In 1777 and early 1778, hardly any foodstuffs were able to be transported to New York City. Hunger became the norm. Sticks and firewood for heating and cooking became scarce. Inflation skyrocketed. Prices tripled, quadrupled, and eventually rose to five or six times of normal cost.

Following Burgoyne's surrender, it would not be long before the first snow fell. The winter of 1777–1778 subsequently turned out harsh and long. It was brutally cold and a true nightmare, especially for those who resided in New York City. Daily, the cries of "Bring out your dead!"

were heralded through the streets as half-starved horses pulled wagons filled with dead civilians.

There was not enough hay or animal feed. Milk and cheese products were scarce. Civilians suffered from malnutrition. Scurvy set in. Many who survived developed lifetime physical ailments as a result of a poor diet. It was dangerous to walk down the streets with a loaf of bread or a basket of food. Starved and emancipated criminals lurked at street corners. Food riots broke out. The English occupation government could no longer effectively feed its soldiers, the city's numerous civilians, or the thousands of loyalists who, in the aftermath of the Wilderness War of 1777, fled to the city accompanied in many cases by their families.

Horses, dogs, and cats were killed and eaten. Even rats were trapped and devoured. Starvation was not just an urban problem. In the rural and wilderness areas, hunger also struck. Many Indians starved after their warriors went off to war, as few remained behind to hunt, fish, and cultivate crops. The economic consequences were devastating to one and all.

1777 marked the birth of the U.S. Army's Civil Affairs units. Prior to the conclusion of the conflict in October 1777, the Northern Army,, with General George Washington's urgings, designated certain units and specific personnel to assist civilians with relief operations. Civil-military personnel were quite active in the Albany Highlands, New England, and the Mohawk and Hudson Valleys. Relief efforts were undertaken to ease the suffering, in coordination with local civilians and religious groups such as the Mennonites.

1777 was also the very first year when the U.S. Army's regular continental regiments, along with its militia units, were utilized to combat crime and curb the activities of organized gangs.

1777 was also the year when the American flag was first flown in the face of an enemy in combat.

1777 also marked the de facto birth of the U.S. Army's Long Range Reconnaissance Patrols (LRRPs) and other deep-penetration Special Forces. Patrolling was nothing new; it had always been done. But the events of the Wilderness War necessarily elevated patrolling to a much higher degree of sophistication.

For the very first time, individuals, teams, and squads were specifically formed and inserted deep behind enemy lines in wilderness regions to conduct specific missions. The men selected for these difficult assignments had to be professional woodsmen. They had to be tough, both physically and mentally. They had to possess the ability to retain everything they witnessed. The collecting of information reached an entirely new level. For the first time certain individuals (such as scout Frederick Sammons) and various teams were subordinated solely to an army high command. Operating for days deep within enemy territory, the scouts brought back vital information and, on occasion, rescued individuals.

Prior to the commencement of a military operation within a specific region, scouts thoroughly examined the area and brought back vital information pertaining to roads, bridges, terrain, obstacles, enemy units, strength, positions, activities, and so forth. On more than one occasion, the Northern Army conducted successful military operations based on information secured by individuals who, prior to the commencement of the operation, had been patrolling for days deep behind enemy lines.

1777 ensured religious freedom. New York State's legislatures stipulated that the new state constitution guarantee freedom of worship. Along with the newly established nation, New York State supported the notion that church and state were to be separate.

1777 was not just a war fought with guns and tomahawks. It was a war supported by intellectuals such as Benjamin Franklin and the American patriot-poet Philip Morin Furneau. Franklin quickly exploited the wilderness events of 1777 to America's advantage. For the first two years of the conflict it was not easy for Franklin to negotiate. He had nothing in his favor. That changed in 1777, as in the aftermath of the Saratoga campaign Franklin's position, and in fact status, in the eyes of foreign governments improved significantly.

Philip Furneau also strongly supported the patriots. Shortly before he was captured on a ship in the Caribbean and placed into the infamous prison ship *Jersey*, Furneau wrote to commemorate the patriots' Wilderness War victory over Burgoyne:

> Led on by lust of lucre and renown,
> Burgoyne marching with his thousands down,
> High were his thoughts and furious his career,
> Puff'd with self-confidence and pride severe,
> Swollen with the idea of his future deeds,
> Onward to ruin each advantage leads.

Initially, my intent was also to write in detail on what had happened to the thousands of British and German soldiers captured in Saratoga. I chose not to do so because so much detail pertains to this area that an entire book could be written on this topic alone.

Under the "convention" agreed upon by General Gates and General Burgoyne, the surrendered personnel were to be marched to Boston and returned to England after swearing an oath of allegiance that never again would they fight the patriots. America's Continental Congress, however, vetoed this measure. Congress feared that once the British-German troops were boarded on ships, New York or Newport would be their destination rather than Europe. Soon, the released officers and soldiers might once again be committed into combat against the patriots. Therefore, excluding Burgoyne and a small number of others who in 1778 were permitted (under a gentleman's parole agreement) to return to England, the majority ended up staying in America.

It must be noted that General Howe also played a key role in this. Initially, Howe was to immediately dispatch to Boston the transport ships which were to convoy the surrendered troops directly back to England. Instead, he delayed. Afterward, Howe began to negotiate to have the surrendered personnel returned to a port still under British control, such as New York City. To the American Congress, this was perceived as a measure to incorporate Burgoyne's surrendered personnel back into the British army. To prevent this, Congress ordered that the prisoners be held and instead marched down through New York, New Jersey, and Pennsylvania into prisoner-of-war camps in Virginia. Enroute, and in captivity, many soldiers perished while others disappeared. Many were absorbed into various communities through which they passed. In time, these veterans became useful citizens. The ex-prisoners settled down, many marrying local women. Their future kin would fight America's wars. Others returned to their homeland, such as Sergeant Lamb to his native Ireland after the war. His family had feared that he had been killed.

As for the captured enemy wounded, many were returned to New York City in January 1778 under a flag of truce. Among them was Major John Acland. Accompanied by his wife, Lady Harriet Acland, he returned to England that same year. One night shortly afterward, in an officers club in London, Major Acland was horrified to hear a fellow officer, who had never served on the North American continent, viciously denounce, curse, and criticize the fighting capabilities of the patriots.

Major Acland began to argue with this officer. A heated dispute arose and led to a fight. The other officer demanded to settle the affair on the following morning with a duel. Pistols would be used. Major Acland accepted. Though Acland survived the terrible Wilderness War of 1777, he did not survive this duel. In the end, he died defending the character and honor of those whom for months he had been relentlessly battling in a faraway wilderness.

Stories, like the one about Major Acland, are why I wanted to write this book and tell of this incredible moment in history, when courage, bravery, and honor was the norm.

I

The Strategic Dilemma in the Northern Theater

Within months of the "shot heard around the world" at Lexington, Massachusetts in April 1775, the American rebellion against the British Crown, now known as the Revolutionary War, had developed into a serious insurrection. Rather than relying on ad hoc militias, the patriots had begun to field standing armies to vie with the forces of Great Britain, who at that time were considered the best troops in the world. Determined to maintain the rebellious colonies within the fold of the British Empire, King George III ordered the revolt to be suppressed. The king and his supporters knew that if the American colonists succeeded in breaking away, others would surely follow suit. In time, this would lead to a severe decline in British power.

In 1775 Canada's Governor Guy Carleton, along with Generals William Howe and John Burgoyne, concluded that the key to victory lay in suppressing the region of New England. New England was, after all, the wellspring of the American rebellion. Excluding an estimated ten percent of the population which maintained an allegiance to the British Crown,[1] New England was overwhelmingly pro-rebellion.

Assessing how the colonists could be defeated, Major General Sir John "Gentleman Johnny" Burgoyne wrote, in late 1775, a short summary of his observations. Titled "Reflections Upon the War in America," Burgoyne advocated a double thrust against the Colony of New York.[2] Simultaneously conducted, one thrust would be directed from Canada southward and the other, either from the vicinity of New York City[3] or New England, would be directed northward. Somewhere in the middle, the two forces would unite. After isolating New England, a patriot[4] collapse would ensue.

MID-DECEMBER, 1776

Needing some time to take care of personal matters and to secure his seat in England's Parliament, General Burgoyne returned to England. The approaching Christmas holiday also provided Burgoyne the opportunity to visit family and close friends.

Prior to his arrival in London, Burgoyne had been in command of the British Army based in Canada. Viewing the situation to the south, Burgoyne concluded that General George Washington and his fellow rebels, despite their reversals on Long Island, New York City, and New Jersey through the summer and fall of 1776, were still a threat. Unlike most of the other British commanders who were confident that the patriots were so shattered that they would simply melt away during the winter and spring of 1777, Burgoyne's instincts told him differently.

In the late evening hours of 24 December 1776, General Washington began to move the remnants of his battered but proud army eastward. Washington's army was young, very young. Created on 15 June 1775, it was inexperienced in combat and poorly armed, trained, and equipped. It lacked proper supply and support, and needed more leaders, especially at the critical junior officer and non-commissioned (sergeant) level. Yet, despite the army's weaknesses, the men possessed a strong spirit.

After crossing the Delaware River from Pennsylvania into New Jersey, the young army performed superbly in the next ten days. Shattering an entire Hessian Regiment at Trenton, it then outmaneuvered a superior British force at Princeton and recaptured that town as well. In the process, the patriots captured huge amounts of critically needed weapons, ammunition, wagons, horses, and other supplies. Shortly afterwards, in far away Imperial Germany, Frederick the Great classified Washington's winter offensive of 25 December 1776 to 3 January 1777 as one of the greatest maneuvers in military history. Unable at the moment to halt and destroy Washington, the remaining British and Hessian garrisons in western and central New Jersey were ordered to withdraw into New York City proper. The patriots had not only achieved an immense victory but, more importantly, had rekindled the flame of a dying revolution.

Back in London, King George III himself felt the ramifications of Washington's actions. Desperate now more than ever to put an end to the rebelling Continentals, the ruling nobility began to formulate a new battle plan for the late spring and summer of 1777. Among those in

England who heard of Washington's success was British Army General John Burgoyne. As the British proceeded to develop a decisive course of action in order to suppress the rebellion, the "Reflections Upon the War in America" theory of 1775 was revived.

Exactly when General Burgoyne began to formulate his plan on how to defeat the rebelling colonists is not known. Regardless, on 28 February 1777,[5] while still in England, Burgoyne submitted a fairly detailed plan to Lord George Germain.[6] At this time Lord Germain served the King as Secretary of State for the Colonies. His ministry was also responsible for conducting the war in America.

In a paper titled "Thoughts for Conducting the War From the Side of Canada,"[7] Burgoyne proposed such a military operation. His first objective in the campaign would be to secure Lake Champlain. To accomplish this, Crown Point would be seized and utilized as a base of operations. Continuing to advance southward, Fort Ticonderoga, a major obstacle, would be captured sometime in the early summer. Once Crown Point and Fort Ticonderoga were secured, "the next measure must depend upon those taken by the enemy, and upon the general plan of the campaign as concerted at home."[8]

If England's ministry decided that General Howe's entire army should march northward from New York City to conduct an action on the Hudson River, then "the only object of the Canada Army[9] is to effect a junction with that force."[10] Therefore, Burgoyne proposed to advance southward to Albany from Fort Ticonderoga via Lake George to link up with an army pushing northward. The link up would occur in Albany. However, in the event that this would not be the case, General Burgoyne proposed that his army, in conjunction with English forces from Rhode Island, would secure the Connecticut River Valley. As Burgoyne wrote, "Should the junction between the Canada and Rhode Island armies be effected upon the Connecticut, it would not be too sanguine an expectation that all New England provinces will be reduced by their operation."[11]

In support of these plans Burgoyne also proposed a secondary offensive via Lake Ontario and the Mohawk Valley, "as a diversion to facilitate every proposed operation."[12] Basically, Burgoyne's "Thoughts" thesis of 1777 stemmed from his previous 1775 "Reflections Upon the War in America."

Yet, an examination of Burgoyne's "Thoughts" analysis reveals a series of proposals but no precise objectives or military planning on his part. Furthermore, it appears that Burgoyne was possibly anticipating that a higher military-political command (possibly even the King and his ministry) would develop an elaborate plan for the summer campaign of 1777. This is evidenced with the words "... upon the general plan of the campaign as concerted at home." So what exactly was Burgoyne thinking when he wrote at the conclusion of "Thoughts..." is not fully known.

> These ideas are formed upon the supposition that it be the sole purpose of the (British) Canadian army to effect a junction with General Howe, or cooperating so far as to get possession of Albany and open the communication to New York, to remain upon the Hudson River, and thereby enable that general to act with his whole force to the southward.

Was Burgoyne advocating a joint military operation with Howe? If so, how was this to be done? Who, exactly, would get "possession of Albany?" Who would "open the communication to New York?" Did Burgoyne expect to join Howe in Albany or for that matter, St. Leger? Although Burgoyne's "Thoughts" advocated that the Colony of New York held the key to victory, in "Thoughts..." or any of his other writings, Burgoyne is not specific. In fact what Burgoyne expected or wanted to do in 1777 has left historians bewildered to this day.

Meanwhile, as Burgoyne was formulating a loose plan, unknown to him, General Sir William Howe was also formulating a plan. Previously, on 9 October 1776, Howe had written to Lord Germain on the importance of "opening a communication with Canada" via the Hudson River in order to attack New England.[13] In early 1776, Howe had advocated capturing New York City to not only deny the patriots a major port city, but also to use the city as a base for expanding future military operations northward into New England, "the heart of the rebellion."[14] Along with a host of others, Howe had also analyzed the importance of securing the colonies of New York and New England.

SATURDAY, 30 NOVEMBER

On this day, as Washington was retreating, General Howe wrote two letters.[15] Both letters were addressed to Lord Germain. In his first letter Howe reported on the successful British operations in and around New York City.[16] But in his second letter (also dated 30 November, but lengthier), Howe informed Germain that he (Howe) planned to position a large number of troops in New Jersey throughout the winter. Howe also wrote that he expected the Americans to defend Philadelphia, and[17] Howe informed Germain that Carleton had recently abandoned his plans to conduct a southward offensive towards Albany.

Likewise in his second letter, Howe proposed a plan of strategy against the New England region. Howe sincerely believed he could "finish the War in one year by an extensive and vigorous exertion of His Majesty's arms."[18] Although Howe was not specific, he advocated that several military operations be simultaneously conducted. The first one, with Rhode Island as a base, would be launched against Boston; the second would be launched into the Hudson River area, "to attack Albany from New York," and the third called for an attack to commence from Canada toward Albany.

As all of this would be occurring, a smaller military action would be undertaken in New Jersey to check Washington by exploiting American fears of a British occupation of Philadelphia, which Howe now proposed "to attack in the Autumn." Once the patriots were totally obliterated in the northeast, a final mopping-up campaign would be undertaken in South Carolina and Georgia[19] during the winter months.

In order to accomplish this, Howe wrote that he needed a larger naval presence and at least 35,000 troops.[20] Estimating his strength at 20,000,[21] Howe requested a reinforcement of 15,000 troops.[22] Knowing that the additional manpower could not be derived from England proper, General Howe suggested that his majesty recruit troops not only from Germany's Hanover region but also from throughout Germany, as well as other European nations such as Russia. [23]

FRIDAY, 20 DECEMBER

Just five days before George Washington launched his winter offensive, General Howe submitted his third letter to Lord Germain. Convinced that American fighting capabilities had diminished to the point of posing no threat to the Crown, Howe now expressed his belief that the inhabitants of Pennsylvania were turning toward peace, and that their sentiment lay against the newly established nation. As Howe wrote, "… in which Sentiment they would be confirmed by our getting possession of Philadelphia."[24] Howe no longer regarded New York and New England as the key to victory; rather, he was now convinced that the key to victory lay in capturing Philadelphia, the capital of the newly-established American nation.[25] Of interest is that in his 20 December letter, Howe also lowered his troop strength requirements. Whereas on 30 November he stipulated a strength of 35,000, now he cited that 19,000 would suffice.[26] So confident was Howe of Pennsylvania's importance that he even advocated that the New England offensive be temporarily postponed. As Howe wrote, "[so] that there might be a Corps to act defensively on the lower part of Hudson's River to cover Jersey and to facilitate in some degree the approach of the Canada Army."[27]

SUNDAY, 29 DECEMBER

Fueled with more information on what had transpired at Trenton on Christmas Day, Howe, on 29 December 1776, dispatched a fourth letter to Germain.[28] In this letter, Howe provided some detailed information on what had transpired in Trenton and Princeton. Howe was now convinced that Washington was a greater threat than previously envisioned. Therefore, in order to suppress the patriot revolution, it was vital to not only seize Philadelphia but, just as importantly, to destroy Washington's Army. Thinking like a typical European general, Howe concluded that once he and his army approached Philadelphia, Washington would stand and fight for the city. This would enable Howe the opportunity not only to capture Philadelphia but also, in the process, to destroy Washington and his army once and for all.

TUESDAY, 14 JANUARY 1777

On this day, George Germain responded to Howe's letters of 30 November 1776. Informing Howe that no course of action had yet been agreed upon, Germain also wrote, "The King would defer sending you his sentiments on your plan for the next campaign until he was enabled to take the whole into his royal consideration."[29]

SUNDAY, 23 FEBRUARY

Lord Germain received Howe's letter of 20 December 1776. By now Germain had learned—via a number of military dispatches—more about the battles and events of Trenton and Princeton.[30]

MONDAY, 3 MARCH

Lord Germain again wrote to Howe. Prior to responding to Howe, Germain had conferred with King George III. Both Germain and the king were unhappy with the sequence of events which had occurred in late December 1776 and early January 1777. Wanting to extinguish the American Revolution as soon as possible, both agreed with Howe that perhaps a thrust into Pennsylvania was the answer. Therefore, Germain authorized Howe to attack Philadelphia. Germain wrote, "I am now commanded to acquaint you that the King entirely approves of your proposed deviation from the plan which you formerly suggested, being of opinion that the reasons which have induced you to recommend this change in your operations are solid and decisive."[31]

Frustrated that he had not been able to defeat Washington, Howe began to conclude that a military march from New York City through New Jersey and across the Delaware River into Pennsylvania via land was too risky. He feared that a strong pro-American sentiment existed in these areas, especially around the areas previously retaken and briefly occupied by Washington. Strong anti-British sentiment could not only pose a threat to the British Army but, as every commander knows, a lengthy supply and communication line (the distance alone from New York City to Philadelphia is exactly 109 miles) frequently creates hardships for an army. Not only could it be disrupted by patriot guerrillas, but Howe also feared that an overland march would reveal to Washington the British Army's intent and strength. Hence, for security and tactical efficiency, Howe decided to abandon his initial idea of an overland march and instead utilize a sea maneuver.

In the meantime, King George and his ministers were not just concerned about the military events of late 1776 and early 1777. They were especially concerned about the current and future political situation.

Following France's defeat in the French and Indian War, France renounced, on 10 February 1763, in a treaty signed in Paris, its claim to Canada, Nova Scotia, the St. Lawrence River Islands, and all of its territory in America east of the Mississippi River except for the city of New Orleans. Simply put, French rule had come to an end on the North American continent.

Yet, despite this setback, France was still a major power. Many in England knew that France desired to reassert herself once again on the North American continent. France was increasingly favoring the American rebellion. Fearing the possibility of France's intervention on the side of the patriots, England needed to suppress the rebellion as quickly as possible.[32]

THURSDAY, 27 MARCH
General Burgoyne departed for Plymouth, a coastal town in southern England.[33]

WEDNESDAY, 2 APRIL
On this day, Howe sent a fifth letter to Germain.[34] In this letter Howe proposed his sea plan. But Howe's letter also contained a critical note and warning when he wrote, "Restricted as I am from entering upon more extensive operations by the want of force, my hopes of terminating War [by the end of] this year are vanished." [35]
Continuing on, Howe also added that by the end of the campaign he expected to possess the colonies of Pennsylvania, New Jersey, and New York. But he warned, "though that must depend on the success of the Northern [British Canadian] Army."[36]

THURSDAY, 3 APRIL
Burgoyne set sail, boarding the HMS *Apollo*. His destination: Quebec, Canada.[37]
Prior to his departure from England, Burgoyne dropped into the prestigious Brooks Club in London. A hangout for senior military officers as well as the wealthy and prominent, Brooks was also a haven for England's intellectuals, with many opposing England's dominance of the New World. Encountering Charles James Fox, one of the King's critics and an advocate of independence for the American colonists, Burgoyne boasted to Fox, "I will be home, victorious, from America by Christmas Day, 1777." In response, Fox brazenly replied, "General, be not over sanguine in your expectations. I believe when next you return to England, you will be a prisoner on parole."
Because the comments had been made in front of others, Burgoyne realized that he could not just simply walk away from Fox. By doing so, he would not only have been verbally defeated but, but even worse, he would look like a fool who perhaps secretly feared that Fox was right. Therefore, Burgoyne challenged Fox to a hefty monetary bet. Burgoyne offered a bet of 50 Guineas (comparable to today's 522 pounds or approximately 750 U.S. dollars). While it was in those days a substantial amount of money, Fox still took up the offer. Someone retrieved the club's record book and the bet was duly recorded.[38]
Stepping outside, Burgoyne looked up into the dark night sky. He wondered if he had done the right thing. In addition to being tall, quite

handsome, very debonair, and a talented writer who had written several successful plays, Burgoyne was also a fighter. And he was tremendously devoted to his profession, his nation, its army, and the Royal Crown. Burgoyne was determined to succeed.

SUNDAY, 20 APRIL

Writing a sixth letter to Germain, Howe voiced concerns that possibly he would not be able to complete his campaign in Pennsylvania in time to assist Burgoyne advancing down from Canada.[39] It is important to note, at this point in time, that Howe's most recent view was unknown to General Burgoyne.

II

Lord Germain's Proposal

THURSDAY, 8 MAY 1777

Howe's letter of 2 April reached Germain. Prior to its arrival, King George III and his ministers had reviewed Burgoyne's proposals for conducting an attack into the colony of New York; simultaneously, as they studied Burgoyne's plans, the King and his ministry reviewed Howe's plans and letters of 20 and 29 December 1776. Among themselves, it was agreed that in order to secure a victory for the British Empire in 1777, a major military action would have to be undertaken against New York and New England.

Along with the King, Lord Germain and the other ministers, Lord Frederick North[1] also approved of Burgoyne's plans. In the end, London ordered Burgoyne, "to force your way to Albany."[2] To support Burgoyne, the ministers directed that a secondary force be assembled. This force was to be commanded by Lieutenant-Colonel Barry St. Leger and his mission was to advance eastward through the Mohawk Valley to link up with Burgoyne at Albany.[3] By now it was also anticipated that General Howe, advancing northward from New York City, would also be in Albany. Once united with Howe, both Burgoyne and St. Leger were to place their forces under his command. It is not known if at this time the King and his ministers discussed or made any mention of a fourth thrust. Originating in Oquga,[4] a wilderness region just to the north of the Colony of Pennsylvania, a smaller but nevertheless significant force of loyalists, Indians, and British advisors were to proceed northeastwards via the Schoharie Valley to a location west of Albany. Once there, they were to link up with St. Leger's force and together, proceed to Albany. Right from the outset and well before the very first

30

shots of the British 1777 campaign were fired, serious issues arose. Unfortunately for the British ministry, these issues were never properly identified, discussed, or resolved. Soon these unresolved issues would develop into severe problems which only complicated matters and, factually speaking, in the end created numerous and severe problems leading to the British defeat in the upcoming Wilderness War of 1777.

To begin, there was a lack of clear guidance, directives, orders, and messages. Always critical for any type of military operation, especially one involving joint military operations spanning an immense geographic area, the lack of such clear-cut directives doomed the British campaign from the outset.

What further complicated the matter is that neither the King, Lord Germain, Lord North, nor anyone else, had formulated an exact plan. In response to Howe's letter of 20 December 1776 to launch an attack into Pennsylvania with Philadelphia as the main objective, Lord Germain—with King George's consent—approved Howe's plan.[5] With this approval, Lord Germain (whether he realized it or not) immediately approved two very different plans: one into the Colony of New York and the second into Pennsylvania. Worse, Lord Germain not only failed to warn Burgoyne of Howe's new intentions but Lord Germain also failed to subordinate Howe to any specific plan. Such was evidenced on 18 May 1777. After consulting with King George III, Lord Germain responded to Howe about his proposal to attack Pennsylvania by a sea route around New Jersey and Delaware. Germain wrote to Howe that both he and the King were confident of Howe's decision, and they approved of any changes in Howe's plans. But Germain added, "trusting, however, that whatever you mediate, it will be executed in time for you to cooperate with the arm ordered to proceed from Canada [Germain was referring, of course, to Burgoyne's army] and put itself under your command."[6]

Besides allowing Howe far too much leverage, Germain's response did not reach Howe until the general was in Chesapeake Bay enroute to Philadelphia[7] to pursue the "Old Fox." Germain's[8] response, again with the King's approval, created another immense dilemma.[9] And in combat, dilemma leads to uncertainty. Did Lord Germain believe that Howe's campaign into Pennsylvania was only to be a short-lived campaign? Since no time factor was allocated in Howe's 2 April letter, did the possibility exist that Germain believed Howe's operation into Pennsylvania would be quickly concluded? It must be remembered that

Germain's response of 18 May stated such: "…it will be executed in time for you to cooperate with the army ordered to proceed from Canada and put itself under your command." Did the possibility also exist that Germain thought Howe's move into Pennsylvania was only to be a secondary offensive and no more? Exactly what Germain was thinking in 1777 is speculative.

What further complicated the situation in 1777 was that amongst the entire senior British political and military leadership, strong animosities, tensions, ill-feelings, mistrust, and even outright hatred ran rife among the top leadership. Hostilities existed between Generals Howe and Clinton; Governor-General Carleton abhorred Lords North and Germain, and to some extent, Burgoyne. Howe also did not care much for Burgoyne. Also, almost everyone had a low opinion of Lord Germain. In some cases, the origins of these bitter feelings spanned back decades. Though disagreements occasionally will arise in a top command and must even be expected, in the British military and political arena of 1777 it was so bad that it hindered operations.

Thus, through a combination of uncaring attitudes and concerns, personal animosities, misunderstandings, mistrust, no clear-cut directives, and too much freedom provided to military commanders—along with a lack of urgency to respond to critical messages and letters—the British campaign of 1777 was plagued from the onset.

III

General Burgoyne's Plan to Advance on Albany

TUESDAY, 6 MAY

Arriving in Quebec, General Burgoyne was pleased to see that the winter had not been very harsh and that the St. Lawrence River was free of heavy floating ice chunks. As any commander knows, inclement weather can paralyze military operations. With free flowing water minus obstructing ice, river traffic would not be slowed or halted.

MONDAY, 12 MAY

When he arrived in Montreal, Burgoyne immediately met with Governor General Sir Guy Carleton. In 1777 Carleton served in a dual capacity—he was the commander-in-chief of the British Army in Canada and he was the British-appointed Governor of Canada. Prior to meeting with Carleton, Burgoyne had frequently wondered if Canada's governor was receptive to the upcoming operation. But if Burgoyne had any doubts about Carleton's support, those doubts quickly disappeared. Carleton was not only enthusiastic about the operation, he also promised to support it in any way he could. Unfortunately for Burgoyne, Carleton had very little intelligence information. In this area Carleton was very weak.

Burgoyne, however, was especially shocked by another matter. It seemed as if everyone in Montreal knew that a campaign of some sort was underway. Information regarding the campaign was so widespread that all of the officers were aware of it. Even many of the lowest ranking soldiers knew. Burgoyne was so upset about the lack of secrecy, and irritated that no security measures had been implemented, that within a couple of days he formally voiced a strong complaint about it directly to Lord Harvey, Canada's Adjutant-General, and to Carleton. As every commander knows, secrecy is vital to any military operation. Burgoyne feared that with so many people aware of his plan, the Americans must surely be privy to it as well. As it turned out, Burgoyne's fears proved to be unwarranted. The rebelling Americans hadn't caught a whiff of it.[1]

Aside from a lack of good intelligence-gathering, and the lack of secrecy about his own plans, Burgoyne was also hindered by the lack of solid transport.

Regarding transportation, neither Burgoyne, Carleton, nor anyone else could be faulted. The British's Army's transport issue would not finally be resolved until 1799, when the military established its own Royal Wagon Train when at long last, the British Army's entire transport system ceased to be dependent on civilian drivers and managers. In addition to the contracting and sub-contracting problems encountered, civilian drivers (though inserted into army units) were not subject to military law and discipline. Civilian transport drivers could—and frequently did—create problems for army commanders, especially in combat or during other periods of difficulty. On more than one occasion, the civilian drivers proved to be uncontrollable, unreliable, and even downright useless.[2] 1777 would soon prove to be a case in point.

Using animals for power, always critical for an army, was another thorny issue. In order for Burgoyne to march his army, a sizable number of healthy horses were needed to not only move the numerous carts and wagons but especially the numerous cannon and heavy artillery Burgoyne had ordered to be brought along. Writing to Carleton on 12 June, Burgoyne stated, "It also appears to me that seven or eight hundred horses may become indispensably necessary to my purpose."[3]

Burgoyne, however, soon reconsidered his initial estimate. While in Montreal he met and discussed this matter with Nathaniel Day, the Commissary-General of the British Army in Canada. Burgoyne needed to know how many horses and carts would be required to transport thirty days of rations and "about 1,000 gallons of rum" for a force of 10,000 soldiers.[4]

To what extent, if any, Day was able to assist Burgoyne is not known. But the seriousness of animal power was realized when General William Phillips, Burgoyne's second-in-command and a combat seasoned commander who would accompany the force, informed Burgoyne that no less than 400 horses would be required just to pull the artillery with its munitions.[5] Another 2,000 horses would be required to pull the many carts and wagons loaded with the army's baggage, provisions, and equipment.

Exactly how many horses were finally obtained at the commencement of the campaign is not certain; however, it is known that not more than 700 horses were found at the outset of the campaign.[6] While of course this figure would change in the weeks and months to come, it is known that from the beginning to the end, Burgoyne was always in need of additional animal power.[7]

For rapid mobility, no less than 500 light two-wheeled carts were to be utilized, however, as with the horses, problems arose. Unlike heavy wagons, carts are not sturdy, and they lack the space to carry a heavy or sizable load. Normally, four to six horses were required to pull a wagon heavily laden with military materiel or ammunition, whereas a cart, with its smaller and lighter load, required only one or two horses. Despite an initial request for no less than 500 carts, not enough were on hand. Corruption and theft, rife within the British Empire, also took its toll. Prior to Burgoyne's arrival, a number of the carts had disappeared. No one knew were they were, but it was obvious that some had been stolen. To rectify the problem, orders were issued by Carleton to produce new carts, though in order to produce strong ones seasoned wood had to be used. Unfortunately for Carleton, there was a lack of seasoned wood. As with the carts, no one knew what had happened with the seasoned wood previously ordered by the ministry and stored within the supply houses for future usage. Clearly, it too had been stolen. Therefore, unseasoned green wood had to be used, but because it lacks strength and tends to expand as it dries, the drying process tore some of the carts apart while in use.

Likewise, in the upcoming campaign, a number of major rivers, lakes, and sizable streams would need to be crossed or traversed. Therefore, many bateaux along with skilled men were needed to handle them.

Basically, a bateau was a riverboat. In size bateaux ranged anywhere from 18 feet to 50 feet in length. A boat's average width and height varied according to its length, but six feet was usually the average width of a boat measuring 30–32 feet in length. A three-man crew handled a 30–32 foot river craft, hence the term "three-handed" bateau. How much weight a bateau could carry depended on how much water was in a sizable stream or river. In low water, up to 2,000 pounds could be carried in a 30–32 foot bateau; and in ideal conditions up to 3,000 pounds

could be carried in the same bateau. A much larger boat with additional crewmen could carry much more weight. Generally, fir wood was utilized in the construction of a bateau. As for the boats' keel, this was
always constructed of hardwood, usually oak.[8]

In 1777, a sufficient number of bateaux were available; however,
not enough Canadian manpower was around to handle them and some
soldiers were tasked to assist in handling the bateaux.

TUESDAY, 3 JUNE

On this day Burgoyne's army began to move from the vicinity of
the town of Chambly.[9] Located not far from Montreal on the rapids of
the Richelieu River, Chambly also contained a fort by the same name.
Burgoyne's army would reposition itself further to the south in the town
of St. John's, which in 1777 was still known by its old French name as
St. Jean-sur-Richelieu. As for St. John's, it was located about 22 miles to
the southeast of Montreal on the western bank of the Richelieu River. A
sizable and active fort overlooking the river was also in the vicinity. St.
John's was now to be utilized as the army's assembly area.

Once fully assembled, Burgoyne's army would sail directly southward up the Richelieu River into the northern mouth of Lake
Champlain. After navigating down the lake, Burgoyne's plan was to
capture Crown Point and Fort Ticonderoga. With the capture and elim-
ination of these two major obstacles, he would cross over to Lake
George. (Lake George's northern tip was not far from the southwest
corner of Lake Champlain). Sailing southward upon this lake, Burgoyne
would reach Fort George, located on the southern shore of Lake
George. From there, he would continue to move southward overland to
Fort Edward, located on the Hudson River's northern bank. Here, the
Hudson veers sharply in a southerly direction. Via the river and the river
roads adjacent to both sides of the river, Burgoyne's army would
advance southward to Albany.

At this time, besides being a sizable town, Albany was also a critical road and river junction. From the west flows the Mohawk River,
emptying into the Hudson at Albany. In Albany, Burgoyne was to rendezvous with the forces of General Barry St. Leger advancing from the
west, and with General William Howe's forces proceeding northward
from New York City.[10] Once accomplished, the patriot forces in New
York would be shattered, the critical Mohawk and Hudson Valleys
would be overrun, and New England, the main center of patriot activi-

ty, would be completely cut off from the rest of the colonies. With the three armies uniting together into one massive force, a large number of British, German, Canadian, and loyalist soldiers, plus Indian warriors, would be in the vicinity positioned on favorable terrain. In turn, this would force General Washington to march northward with his main Continental Army to rectify the situation. Drawn into battle, Washington would be defeated and the entire patriot revolutionary effort would collapse.

So thought Burgoyne, King George III, Lord Germain, Lord North, and various others within the British Ministry.

IV

The British Army in Canada

Once in St. John's, his first and primary assembly area, Burgoyne's invading army began to take shape as a powerful striking force. The army was multinational,[1] composed of English,[2] German,[3] Canadian,[4] Indian,[5] and American loyalists.[6] From the British Canadian Army the 9th,[7] 20th,[8] 21st,[9] 24th,[10] 29th,[11,] 31st,[12] 47th,[13] 53rd,[14] and 62nd Foot Infantry Regiments[15] were selected. Various artillerymen, naval personnel, supply-and-support soldiers, along with civilian workers and axmen, were also recruited for the army.

The German contingent was organized into two brigades. The 1st Brigade was formed from the von Rhetz,[16] von Specht,[17] and the von Riedesel[18] Regiments; the 2nd Brigade was formed from the Prince Frederick[19] and the Hesse-Hanau Regiments.[20]

The backbone of the British Army was its infantry foot regiments; therefore, it is important to understand what comprised a foot regiment.

Worldwide, the backbone of any army is its infantry—"the Queen of Battle." While, of course, other branches (i.e. artillery, cavalry, and support) play an important role, it is the infantryman—or foot soldier—who, with his personal gun, knife, and bayonet, decides the final outcome of most battles.

Prior to the American Revolution, the British Army maintained a strength of 70 Foot Regiments,[21] and by the end of the war in 1783 it would be expanded to 105 regiments.[22] But at the war's outbreak, Great Britain's entire army totaled 48,647 of all ranks[23] (not counting militias or foreign auxiliaries). Of this strength, 39,294 were infantry, 6,869 cavalry, and 2,484 artillery.[24] This initial troop strength would eventually rise to 110,000 by war's end.[25]

In 1777, every foot regiment had ten companies. Of these, eight comprised the regiment's main body and were referred to as either "Battalion" or "Center" companies. In addition to the eight battalion or center companies, one Grenadier company and one Light company were also included. Grenadier companies were generally composed of the tallest and strongest soldiers of the regiment. As for the term "grenadier," it derived from the past. At one time, certain soldiers, who had the capability to throw a grenade the furthest into a fortifications system while on the attack, became known as "grenadiers" or "grenadiermen." Because the hand grenade of that era was unreliable, difficult to ignite, and especially hard to throw, the hand grenade was eventually eliminated. Though in future years it would again find its place in warfare, the hand grenade had been eliminated from the British Army's weapons inventory prior to the Revolutionary War but the term "grenadier" still clung on. To symbolize the past, grenadiers even continued to wear on their cartridge box slings the brass cases in which they once carried the lit matches needed to ignite a grenade fuse.

For close-quarters combat, each grenadier was also issued a short sword. Tall, black bearskin caps with fancy plates mounted on the front characterized a grenadier soldier's headgear in North America. The grenadier company was regarded as the regiment's "heavy" foot company.

The last company which made up the group was referred to as the "light" company. Composed of men usually smaller in height but very physically fit and agile, the light company was used largely for the purpose of scouting. During a regiment's march, both the "light" and "heavy grenadier" companies were utilized for flank protection.

Each company, whether battalion or center, light or heavy, was authorized a strength of 60 soldiers.[26] Though such a strength was authorized, in that era it was common for a company to be under strength. Desertions, discharges from service, transfers, accidents, and illnesses, along with occasional recruitment difficulties, kept many companies from achieving their full strength. Therefore, each regiment was not the same size. The size and strength of a regiment is often determined by war needs, casualties, and mission demands. For example, in the latter part of the Revolutionary War, extra companies were sometimes inserted into a unit so that some regiments had twelve companies.

The strength of a full regiment comprised of eight battalion or center companies, along with one grenadier and one light company, along with all the officers, averaged approximately 600–650 soldiers.[27] To this strength were added about 20 so-called "contingent" men. Their function was to repair weapons, equipment, and wagons, and assist in the care of the horses.

A foot regiment that contained twelve companies averaged a strength of approximately 811 soldiers.[28] Its personnel strength was organized in the following manner: a colonel, a lieutenant-colonel, a major, nine captains, 14 lieutenants, 10 ensigns, 36 sergeants, 36 corporals, one chaplain, one adjutant, one quartermaster, one medical surgeon with an assistant, two fifers, and 672 privates.[29]

Normally, a lieutenant-colonel commanded a foot regiment of ten companies. A regiment which contained twelve companies was usually commanded by a full colonel, but lieutenant-colonels were known to command as well. If a lieutenant-colonel was not available, a major held command. A captain never commanded in this capacity. Cases did occur where an officer with the rank of general did command, but this was rare and occurred only during an unusual combat situation.

Britain's infantry was armed with the so-called "Brown Bess," a .75 caliber, smooth-bore musket. One version was the 46-inch "Long Land" model, and the other a 42-inch "Short Land" model.[30] Both could mount a bayonet.

"Brown" derived from the brown color of the weapon whereas "Bess" derived from the German word "Busche," meaning a shooting weapon. In accuracy, by the book the weapon was classified as being accurate up to 200 yards; however, it was common knowledge that at best it was accurate to only about 100 yards. Keep in mind that British combat tactics of that era were not based on marksmanship but rather on coordinated, mass fire. Accuracy was not emphasized. On the march into a battle area, the regiment traveled in a column—two or more lines of soldiers. Once the area was reached, the columns immediately deployed into "lines of battle." (Unless if a regiment was held in reserve). The "lines of battle" usually consisted of two ranks facing an opponent with a third reserve line. If "three lines of battle" were utilized, a fourth line would be held in reserve. The reserve could be used to fill any gaps created in the line, to counterattack penetrations, or to exploit success on the offensive.

Another weapon each British soldier carried was the bayonet. Officers and non-commissioned officers (sergeants and corporals) also carried swords, short swords, or pikes. During an offensive action the lines advanced with fixed bayonets toward the opponent. Drummer boys, usually 10 to 15 years of age, beat a marching cadence. Once the lines reached an effective firing range, the infantry musketeers raised upward their muskets and fired. Afterwards, unless ordered to reload and fire, they marched rapidly or charged forward with the bayonet toward their opponents. Once contact was established, both the bayonet and musket stock were used to club, slash, and stab.

If on the defensive outside a fortifications system, the regimental companies would also be deployed into "lines of battle." The soldiers would wait as their opponents marched or charged toward them. Once the enemy was within what was regarded as effective musket range, the command of "Fire!" was shouted. Once the musketeers fired, unless commanded otherwise, they continued to load and fire as rapidly as possible.

After the first volley it was often difficult to see an opponent through the thick smoke, but that did not matter. As mentioned, in the British military system of the era, marksmanship was considered a secondary skill. Since the musket was not very accurate, shooters fired in mass against mass. Whether on the offense or defense, once it was believed an opponent was sufficiently shattered and immobilized by the shock of mass fire, the shooters then attacked or counterattacked with the bayonet.

By 1777 certain British commanders, among them General Burgoyne, began to take musketry shooting more seriously, and they organized a special so-called "shooter's corps." Yet, British tactics were still based on mass fire and close-in combat. Remembering that England's military utilized the "Brown Bess" well beyond the years of the Revolutionary War, this weapon denied Britain's military the ability to possess many crack shooters. This weakness would play a major role in the British defeat in New York's wilderness in 1777.

The four key elements of combat power are maneuverability/ mobility, firepower, protection, and leadership. Of the four, leadership is the most critical.

Born 24 February 1723 in London, Sir John Burgoyne, "Gentleman Jhonny," was a noted general, politician, dramatist, and playwright. Educated at the Westminster School, he joined the British Army at the age of 17. In 1746, he resigned his commission and went to France. With the eruption of the Seven Years War (1756–1763), he reentered the army, rising rapidly to the rank of Brigadier General. In 1762 he was sent to Portugal, an ally of England, to serve as an advisor. From 1768–1774 he served as a member of the British Parliament. An avid writer and theater lover, Burgoyne produced a play titled, "The Maid of the Oaks." It was first featured in London by the great theater actor, producer, and director David Garrick, receiving high reviews.

When the Revolutionary War erupted in 1775, Burgoyne was serving under General Thomas Gage in Boston, but in 1776 was reassigned to Canada where he served under General Sir Guy Carleton. Promoted to Major-General, Burgoyne was soon given command of the British force designated to advance southwards from the vicinity of Montreal to Albany, New York. The fact that Burgoyne himself was an advocate of separating the New England from the rest of the colonies by a three-pronged operation played a role in his being selected to a command position.

As a strategist, Burgoyne was strong. As a tactician, it may be argued that he had his faults. Regardless, he was a courageous soldier who brought great determination to accomplish whatever he set forth to do. Well versed in the art of warfare, Burgoyne also had the trust and confidence of his subordinates.

General Burgoyne's force was created from Britain's so-called "Canada Army." Numerically not a huge force, it was nevertheless powerful, with well-trained and experienced soldiers. Most of the foot regiments were crack outfits with traditions stemming back centuries. Its ranks were filled with men who had made the army their career. Many, such as Sergeant Robert Lamb, were careerists who had served throughout the world.

This army registered a strength of 3,724 British troops[31] and 3,016 Germans.[32] By and large, it was an infantry force. Along with Canadian, loyalist, and Indian auxiliaries, Burgoyne's force maintained a total strength of no less than 7,213 [33] to about 8,000 personnel.[34]

Initially, Burgoyne had requested a troop strength of at least 8,000 regulars.[35] Lord Germain, however, allotted Burgoyne a strength of 7,173 regulars,[36] instructing the general to gather "together as many Canadians and Indians as may be thought necessary for this service."[37]

As is often the case when it comes to deriving an army's exact strength, various other figures have been cited. Reginald Hargreaves cited Burgoyne as possessing 7,399 regulars.[38] This figure does not include the sailors detachment allocated for duty on the rivers and lakes and the irregular fighters. John Luzader cites 4,119 British, 3,217

German, 250 Canadians and loyalists, and about 400 Indians that marched southward into the Colony of New York.[39] Rupert Furneaux provides a strength of 8,300.[40] To this number he added the officers, non-commissioned officers, and musicians for a total of 9,500.[41] In addition to this combat strength, another 1,000 non-combatants such as commissary personnel, transport personnel, and women followers[42] came along. Regardless of the exact figure, it may be correctly stated that at the commencement of his march Burgoyne's entire fighting strength edged close to 8,000 regulars, 800 irregulars, and perhaps another 1,000 non-combatants and camp followers, most of whom were women.[43]

Burgoyne's second-in-command was Major General William Phillips. A career army officer, Phillips had twenty years of army service and was a noted artilleryman.

Burgoyne's advance corps was composed of the entire 24th Foot Regiment. This included the 24th's light and grenadier companies. The flank companies of the 29th and 31st Foot Regiments were also posted to the advance corps.[44] Brigadier General Simon Fraser commanded this corps. Also posted to the advance corps was a scout group composed of loyalists, Canadians and Indians augmented with British advisors. Commanded by Captain Alexander Simon, General Simon's nephew, the group's mission was to probe ahead of the advance corps to obtain information and, if possible, to secure additional foodstuffs.

Burgoyne's right wing consisted of the 9th, 47th, and 53rd Foot Regiments organized into the 1st Brigade. The 20th, 21st, and 62nd Foot Regiments fell into the 2nd Brigade. Brigadier General Henry Watson Powell commanded the 1st Brigade, and the 2nd was led by Brigadier General James Inglis Hamilton. In turn, these two brigades were commanded by Major General William Phillips, who also commanded the entire right wing.

Burgoyne's left wing was dominated mostly by the German contingent, commanded by Major General Baron Friedrich Adolph von Riedesel. Von Riedesel's force was organized into two brigades and an advance corps. The 1st Brigade, commanded by Brigadier General Johann Friedrich von Specht, comprised the von Rhetz, von Riedesel, and von Specht Regiments. The 2nd Brigade, commanded by Brigadier General Walther R. von Gall, consisted of the Prince Frederick and Hesse-Hanau Regiments. The advance corps was commanded by Lieutenant-Colonel Heinrich Breymann. In turn, this corps contained a number of jaeger (hunter) soldiers commanded by Major von Barner, and a horseless dragoon unit commanded by Lieutenant-Colonel Friedrich Baum.[45]

The loyalists fell into a unit called the "Queen's Loyal Rangers." Raised in the spring of 1777 in Canada by Colonel John Peters, the unit was composed of American loyalists who previously had fled to Canada. It was commanded by Major Ebenezer Jessup. Peters did, however, accompany the unit and he played a major role in the campaign of 1777. Despite the promises of loyalist leaders that many more recruits would flock to Burgoyne's ranks once the British army entered the colonies, it did not happen. Although throughout the campaign some additional loyalists were recruited along the way and inserted into the "Queens Loyal Rangers," the promised strengths never materialized.

Another disappointment proved to be the Indians. Initially Burgoyne was informed that 1,000 or more Indians would be recruited. Yet at the outset of his campaign, at best, between 400 and 500 appeared.[46] Although (as in the case of the loyalists) additional Indians would be recruited along the way and others would arrive from Canada in the upcoming months, by and large the Indian effort in the campaign would prove to be disappointing, if not (as we will see) more trouble than it was worth.

What compounded the problem was that the Indians were "commanded" by Chevalier St. Luc de la Corne and Charles de Langlade (whose full name was Charles-Michel Mouet de Langlade). The latter individual had played a critical role in the disastrous ambush of British General Edward Braddock during the French and Indian War. Initially unknown to Burgoyne was the fact that both of these individuals were con men with poor reputations. Although St. Luc hailed from a respected family, he was, at heart, a mercenary. He began his career as a warrior when, in his early twenties, he volunteered to fight the Sauk and Fox Indians. Later on, during the French and Indian War, St. Luc conducted raids into the regions of Albany, Schenectady, Saratoga, and into the Mohawk Valley. He struck as far eastward as Massachusetts.

St. Luc, however, did not only earn his ugly reputation by being a raider. By profession, he was also a thief and con artist. He once ran a "security" company which "protected" fur shipments and fur storage sites. In actuality, his "security men" were nothing more than hired criminals and thugs. St. Luc employed them in self-arranged hold-ups or to pillage a fur warehouse. Of course, any profits reaped from the stolen furs ended up in St. Luc's hands.

Furs, however, were not his main source of income. St. Luc was also a slaver. In fact, his greatest profits were derived from serving as a middleman in the slave trade. By 1777, despite his advanced age of sixty-six, St. Luc's desire to profit from someone else's suffering had not diminished in the least. St. Luc also knew that from the Canadian border southward to Albany there existed a land rich in fur pelts, gold, and silver, as well as free blacks to be captured and resold into slavery.

At the start of the campaign, Burgoyne also expected 2,000 Canadians to appear. Some were to serve as soldiers, others as axmen or pioneers.[47] Yet, despite the promises of a strong Canadian presence in the British Canadian Army, in actuality very few Canadians volunteered. In the end, at best, approximately 200 were recruited.[48] Records reveal that two Canadian light infantry companies served in Burgoyne's 1777 army. Captain René-Antoine de Boucherville commanded one of these units and the other was commanded by Captain David Monin.[49]

Supply, a top priority for any army, was an issue for Burgoyne. In 1777, Nathaniel Day, the commissary general who directed the British army's supply needs, was directed to furnish Burgoyne the supplies required for the campaign. To ensure a close cooperation with Burgoyne, Day appointed two of his deputies, Jonathan Clarke, the assistant commissary general, and Fleetwood Parkhurst, to accompany Burgoyne's expedition. With such units and leaders, General Burgoyne set forth to sever the nascent American nation.

V

The Northern Campaign Commences

FRIDAY, 13 JUNE

Assembling his commanders and many notables, among them Canada's Governor-General Guy Carleton, Burgoyne held a huge pageant-like review of his force. In addition to assembling his ground forces, Burgoyne's entire fleet was assembled in the Richelieu River.[1]

To impress the dignitaries, Burgoyne ordered a massive demonstration of firepower. At a pre-arranged signal, every cannon in the fleet[2] and in St. John's fort fired a tributary salute. The three-masted *Royal George* with its thirty-two cannon and the *Inflexible*, a twenty-eight-gun frigate with powerful 24-pound guns along with some mortars mounted on its deck, were joined by the schooners *Carleton*, *Maria*, and *Thunderer*. Three smaller ships, *Washington*, *New Jersey*, and *Lee*, previously captured from the Americans in the aftermath of the 1776 Battle of Valcour Island, along with the *Loyal Convert*, a vessel abandoned by the Americans upon their withdrawal from Quebec in early 1777, also stood in the fleet and fired. So loud was the thunderous noise that it was heard for miles around. Indeed, so thick was the smoke that the entire fleet was obscured by it.

Amid the jubilation and sending-off ceremony, Burgoyne received his first bad news. Governor Carleton, still fearful of another American attack into Canada, decided at the last moment to keep a number of the troops previously designated for the campaign in Canada proper. Although sympathetic to Burgoyne, Carleton would now retain the entire 34th Foot Regiment along with most of the 29th and 31st Foot and some of the German and independent companies.[3] In addition, some of the supplies had not yet arrived. The delay was caused by the

Americans who had previously retreated from Canada, destroying all of the bridges and some sections of the main roads between Chambly and St. Johns. Because the damage had not yet been fully repaired, supply columns were detoured onto secondary roads which were in poor condition. While traversing these roads some of the flimsy carts, constructed just days before from unseasoned wood, shattered.[4] And most of Burgoyne's dragoons still lacked horses. The horse soldiers disembarking from their boats would have to march until they somehow obtained mounts. Noting Burgoyne's dissatisfaction and concerns, Carleton assured him that additional supplies, horses, and Canadian and Indian manpower would be forthcoming. It may also be worth noting that although many of his mounted troops still lacked horses, Burgoyne made certain that enough animals were still available to pull the carts containing his personal luxuries.

In proximity to Albany, Burgoyne's main objective, St. John's, is almost 180 miles directly north. Once the British exited the Richelieu River, they would enter Lake Champlain. A huge lake, with a north-south length of about 120 miles,[5] its western (left) bank borders on the Adirondack Mountains located in New York State and its eastern (right) bank borders Vermont's Green Mountains. Numerous rivers and streams, such as the Missiquoi, Lamoille, La Platte, La Chute, Otter, Mettawee, Poultney, Mt. Hope, Boquet, Ausable, Salmon, Saranac, and Great Chazy flow into the lake. These rivers and streams originate in the mountains and hills of both the Adirondack and Green Mountains.

To reach Albany from his position at St. John's, Burgoyne would be advancing directly southward. Because Lake Champlain flows in a northerly direction and empties into the Richelieu River which, in turn, empties into the St. Lawrence on its way to the Atlantic Ocean, Burgoyne's army would actually be moving up the lake and into higher terrain in its water route southward.

About three-quarters of the way up Lake Champlain stood Fort Ticonderoga. Here, the army would land and, assisted by navy ships, capture the site. Afterwards, Burgoyne would march to the northern shore of Lake George.[6] To reach Lake George, Burgoyne planned to march on a road adjacent to the La Chute River which flowed from Lake George into Lake Champlain. Upon reaching Lake George, Burgoyne's entire army would be transported by bateau and canoe over the lake to its southern shore where stood an old and uncompleted installation named Fort George. From there, Burgoyne would march via a road through the wilderness to Fort Edward, located on the western shore of the Hudson River. From Fort Edward, utilizing both the river and the roads adjacent the Hudson River, Burgoyne's army would continue to move in a southerly direction to secure Albany via Fort Miller, Saratoga, Stillwater, Half-Moon, and the various towns and settlements existing in between. Once in Albany, he expected to link up with General Howe, coming from New York City, and General St. Leger, advancing from Oswego in the west.

In addition, once Fort Ticonderoga was secured, a smaller force would be dispatched further up Lake Champlain to secure Skenesborough,[7] a settlement located at the southern end of the lake. This would not only secure Burgoyne's left (eastern) flank but would also demonstrate to the "numerous loyalists" residing between Skenesborough and the region of Vermont the Crown's strength and determination. In this area Burgoyne was also to recruit (or so he was led to believe) many armed loyalists.

When in England, as Burgoyne and the others viewed a map of the northern colonies, the route of the offensive appeared to be simple. Through a system of rivers, lakes, roads, and towns filled with British sympathizers, Burgoyne would march straight down to Albany with relative ease. Encountering little if any effective resistance, it would be a quick and easy campaign. So Burgoyne and the others thought.

From St. John's, Burgoyne's first major objective would be Fort Ticonderoga, located almost 115 miles directly south of St. John's. The fort lies on a square-like peninsula, or promontory, on the southwestern edge of Lake Champlain.

A short distance to the southwest of Fort Ticonderoga lies Lake George. In elevation Lake George lies on higher terrain, and at its northern tip is a waterfall. The distance from the base of the waterfall, which empties into the La Chute River, to Lake Champlain is about three-and-a-half miles. As the La Chute flows into Lake Champlain, its waters flow adjacent to the promontory upon which is located Fort Ticonderoga. Many historians believe that it was here that Samuel de Champlain, the "Father of New France," while accompanying a party of Huron and Algonquin Indians from Canada southward into present day New York State to conduct a raid upon the Iroquois, fired his blunderbuss on 30 July 1609. As de Champlain fired on the Iroquois, he officially commenced the beginning of a new era of European warfare on the North American continent which would last for over two centuries.

The patriots referred to Fort Ticonderoga as "Fort Ti." The origins of the fort lay in the 1750s when French army engineers constructed a combined stronghold and fur trading post. Constructed from logs and the local bluestone, the position soon turned into a sizable fortification. Smaller defense positions were also constructed on its two sides or flanks. At first, Fort Ticonderoga was named Fort Carrion in honor of the French fur trader Philippe de Carrion du Fresnoy. Over the subsequent decades numerous fur traders roaming up and down the lake referred to the site as "Carrion's trading post." In addition to the fur trading, supplies could also be purchased at Carrion's post. In a sense it was like a huge modern-day truck stop and shopping center located at a critical junction.

When the French and English began to battle for the North American continent in earnest, additional redoubts and positions, such as the so-called "French Lines,"[8] were constructed around Fort Carrion. During the French and Indian War the English besieged the fort. Deciding not to defend the position, the French burned down as much of it as they could and blew up the rest. The English renamed it Fort Ticonderoga, the name deriving from the Mohawk word meaning "between the two great waters."[9] With the conclusion of the French and Indian War and the shift of the fur trade farther west, the British decided not to rebuild the fort. Until the Revolutionary War, travelers rowing up and down Lake Champlain only viewed the ruins of what was once a major trading post and fortification system.

To maintain firm tactical control of his army, Burgoyne knew that while proceeding up Lake Champlain enroute to Fort Ticonderoga, he would need to make some stops. Therefore, while still at St. John's, he ordered General Fraser to move southward from St. John's just beyond the Isle aux Noix[10] to occupy a place known as Cumberland Head. This encompassed a strip of land jutting into the western side of Lake Champlain just above the present day city of Plattsburg, New York, and directly across from Grand Island. Nearby was also located the Isle la Motte or Motte Island. In the meantime, Burgoyne would follow Fraser's advance and, after rendezvousing with his subordinate, the army would be assembled at Cumberland Head.[11] From there, directly to the south, lies Valcour Island, where in October 1776 the American General Benedict Arnold fought his famous naval battle against Governor General Carleton and General Burgoyne.

Following the gala ceremony of 13 June in St. Johns, Burgoyne's force sailed up the Richelieu River toward Lake Champlain. Approximately 20 miles to the south, the army sailed past the Isle aux Noix. Entering the lake, the flotilla proceeded up Lake Champlain for approximately 20 more miles to Cumberland Head.

Sailing slowly in their ships and bateaux, Burgoyne's soldiers and civilian support personnel were awed by the size of the lake and its many splendors. Huge moose, black bears, beavers, otters, muskrats, and turtles, including giant snapping turtles, were seen. Foxes, bobcats, raccoons, opossums, and skunks were rampant. Wild ducks and geese, along with various species of birds, were plentiful. Huge flocks of passenger pigeons flew over, at times so many that they actually obscured the sunlight and darkened the area.[12] Throughout the day, the wilderness vibrated with the sounds of animals and birds; at night, the howls of the wolves and coyotes were heard far and wide.

Europe's soldiers had seen some wildlife in Europe. But nothing in their homeland compared to what they witnessed on the North American continent. Enroute, some of the men fished. Pike, muskellunge, salmon, and various species of smaller fish were caught. Sometimes a net was torn apart, a line snapped, or a fishing pole was broken in half as a huge thirty-pound or larger northern pike or muskellunge suddenly lunged free.

Despite the beauty of the land, it had its difficulties as well. Huge floating logs—in some cases entire trees—floated ahead and around the sides of the flotilla. Waterlogged, they posed serious obstacles to the moving ships and boats. Herculean efforts were required to clear some of these natural obstacles.

The worst, however, was when the soldiers pulled over to the shoreline, especially at night. As they attempted to prepare their dinner and rest, insects—especially the infamous black fly with its vicious bite—made life miserable for everyone. Even the numerous campfires could not repel these pests. Throughout the night, those who had the misfortune of being positioned on land or on a boat adjacent to the shore were virtually devoured alive. They could not easily find a moment of rest. Doctor Julius Frederich Wasmus, a Brunswick surgeon who served with the German dragoons, recalled Cumberland Head as "a miserable place."[13] Surrounded by swamps and forests filled with insects, Doctor Wasmus suffered like the others. But what especially terrified the doctor were the snakes. Until his arrival in the New World, Dr. Wasmus had never seen a snake, yet now, to him, they appeared to be everywhere.

Not all of the soldiers, however, spent pitiful nights amongst the mosquitoes, flies, and snakes. A firm believer in the finer comforts of life, General Burgoyne spent his nights aboard the ship *Maria*. It was also rumored that he kept a woman on board.[14]

The moment Burgoyne's army proceeded southward from Canada, it entered a wilderness region which in 1777 was not yet formally a part of New York State. That year, the present day State of New York was known as the Colony of New York. In turn, this colony was divided into fourteen counties: New York (encompassing the City of New York on Manhattan Island and its other adjoining islands), Richmond, Kings, Queens, Suffolk, Westchester, Dutchess, Orange, Ulster, Albany, Tryon, Charlotte, Cumberland, and Gloucester.[15] As for the rest of the area that now encompasses present-day New York State (such as the Thousand Islands, the land mass from Buffalo to the Mohawk Valley, the southern area of the state along Pennsylvania's current border, and most of the Adirondack mountain region including the Lake Champlain/Lake George region), it was just one huge wilderness. The Hudson Valley along with the eastern portion of the Mohawk Valley was by and large settled. But the central and western Catskill region was untamed territory.

In the first two years of the Revolutionary War the inhabitants residing in the wilderness outside of the heavily settled areas had not yet been touched by the war. Even the brief combat activity which took place around Fort Ticonderoga and Valcour Island in 1776 had hardly affected the inhabitants of the wilderness. This would dramatically change in 1777.[16]

Simultaneously, as Burgoyne's army entered the wilderness region north of the Colony of New York, it entered an area officially designated by America's Continental Congress as the Northern Department. Established in June/July 1776, the Northern Department encompassed a huge geographic area. Although its borders were never specifically defined, it covered the entire wilderness regions surrounding of the Colony of New York, as well as the populated areas within the Colony including New York City, Long Island, and the regions of Vermont, Massachusetts, and Connecticut. Needing someone to command this huge region, the Continental Congress appointed General Philip Schuyler to command the Northern Department in June 1777.

Born on 20 November 1733 in Albany, General Schuyler began his military career in the British Army during the French and Indian War.

He quickly rose to the rank of major. In 1761 he traveled to England on a military assignment, but while there he studied England's factory methods and canal systems during his free time. Returning to America in 1763, Schuyler constructed the first American flax mill.

Prior to entering the Continental Army in 1775, Schuyler was a successful farmer and lumber dealer in the vicinity of Saratoga and Fish Kill.[17] He was also prominent in politics. From 1768 to 1775, Schuyler served as a representative in the colonial assembly, and in 1775 as a New York delegate to the gathering of the Continental Congress held in May, 1775. A personal friend of George Washington, Schuyler assisted him in formulating regulations for the newly established Continental Army raised on 15 June 1775. On 19 June, Schuyler was commissioned a major general. Because he was well acquainted with the Colony of New York and the rest of the northeast, the Continental Congress ordered him to command the Northern Department and its Northern Army.[18] The army's main headquarters was located in Albany.

Given the looming British presence in Canada, General Schuyler assumed a difficult undertaking. He was responsible for protecting a huge area encompassing many thousands of square miles. Although a number of forts such as the system at Fort Ticonderoga did exist, most others were far from completion. Some of the forts were crumbling from age and non-use. Likewise, an entire army needed to be raised from scratch. Competent commanders, along with leaders on all levels, were needed. An effective supply and support system—crucial to any military organization—had to be established. Military training, vital to any army, also needed to be conducted. There seemed to be no end to the work that lay ahead for the new commander of the Northern Department.

Along with America's Congress, General Schuyler knew that Fort Ticonderoga was a critical position, effectively marking the northern border of the newly established nation. In the event of its fall, serious negative military, psychological, and political repercussions could arise.

Seeking a strong commander for this fort, America's Congress appointed Major-General Arthur St. Clair.[19] A Congressman from Pennsylvania, James Wilson, informed St. Clair of the decision in early June 1777. Prior to receiving the news, St. Clair, a handsome Scot by birth, had commanded a Pennsylvania militia unit within Washington's main Continental Army, and later the 2nd Pennsylvania Battalion which fought in Canada against the British in 1776. Returning to General

Washington's army, St. Clair participated in the ten-day winter offensive of late December 1776 and early 1777 in New Jersey. Saying goodbye to Washington in June in order to take command of an isolated outpost was not easy, but an order was an order. St. Clair's appointment doubtless stemmed from the fact that he had some knowledge of the area, had fought in Canada, was a highly aggressive commander, and was well experienced in commanding both militia and regular army forces.

In itself, Fort Ticonderoga was far from being an impregnable defensive position. Despite its imposing appearance, both the main fort as well as its outer forts and redoubts were in no condition to withstand a major attack. For decades the fort and its outlying defensive system had been in disrepair.

Prior to the arrival of General St. Clair on 12 June 1777, Fort Ticonderoga had been undergoing a major change. It commenced in July 1776 when Colonel Jeduthan Baldwin, an engineer officer who had fought at Bunker Hill in June 1775,[20] arrived to revitalize the old fort. Baldwin's men worked continuously on the site, excluding the period from November 1776 until February 1777 when Baldwin was away on emergency leave due to an illness. By the time Ticonderoga's new commander, General Arthur St. Clair, appeared, a number of enhancements had been made despite a harsh winter with several months of extreme weather slowing down the progress.

Boats and ships were built and repaired. Docks were installed. A sawmill was constructed and was in operation. Two additional guard-houses, a campsite, and a large storehouse with a bakery and a hospital were built. Crops for future consumption were planted. A log barrier to impede the advance of enemy vessels was constructed at a narrow point in the lake just north of the fort. A new fort, named Fort Independence, was being constructed on the opposite side of the lake, and a so-called "Great Bridge," spanning the quarter-mile waterway from the west to the east between Fort Ticonderoga and Fort Independence, was constructed.[21]

As mentioned, to protect this bridge and impede any lake traffic from proceeding southward toward the forts, a major water obstacle was also created adjacent the northern side of the bridge. Basically it consisted of a large number of logs placed side-by-side floating on the water. To keep the logs in place, steel rivets and bolts were driven into the logs, and through the rivets' eyelets a lengthy chain, one-and-a-half inches wide, was inserted. The chain ran the entire length of this barrier. To hold it in place, the ends of the chain were connected to stable features on each shoreline.

Yet despite the best efforts of the patriots, Fort Ticonderoga was still not fully prepared, or fully manned, as Burgoyne's forces proceeded southward toward America's northern bastion. What further complicated the weaknesses in the defensive system was that certain critical terrain features were not yet fortified.

Well before the arrival of Burgoyne's army, various disputes had been raised pertaining to two especially noted terrain features: Sugar Loaf Hill,[22] re-designated in 1777 as Mount Defiance, and Rattlesnake Hill, re-designated that same year as Mount Independence.

Mount Defiance was located approximately 1,400 yards to the south/southwest of Fort Ticonderoga; Mount Independence, upon which stood the newly created Fort Independence, was located approximately 1,500 yards to the southeast.[23] Both of these sizable hills overlooked Fort Ticonderoga. But Mount Defiance, with its 853-foot summit,[24] not only overlooked Fort Ticonderoga but also Mount Independence.

In 1776 Lieutenant-Colonel John Trumbull, a fiery patriot whose father was the Governor of Connecticut, served briefly at Fort Ticonderoga. A graduate of Harvard, Trumbull also had a keen eye for terrain, and he quickly concluded that the key to the entire defense of Fort Ticonderoga lay not in the fort itself but on the hills which, in 1776, were stilled referred to as Sugar Loaf and Rattlesnake. As Trumbull summed it up:

> It will take a lot of work to make the place ready. But when completed, its guns would have a clear field of fire down the lake to the north. Ships attempting to navigate through the narrow neck of water between Rattlesnake Hill and Fort Ticonderoga would be blocked. The cannons would also cover the old fort [Ticonderoga] across the lake.[25]

Trumbull argued that any cannon positioned on Sugar Loaf Hill could effectively cover both Rattlesnake Hill and Fort Ticonderoga. To prove his point and silence his critics, cannon rounds were fired from Fort Ticonderoga towards the summit peaks of Rattlesnake and Sugar Loaf. Needless to say, the cannon balls exploded very close to the hilltops. Trumbull's point was proved.

A fine artist, Trumbull drew some sketches of the area. In turn, these were shown to General Philip Schuyler, the commanding officer of the Northern Army, and his assistant, General Horatio Gates.

In late 1776 Lieutenant-Colonel Trumbull was promoted to full colonel and made the adjutant general of the Northern Army. Whenever any high-ranking officers visited Fort Ticonderoga, Trumbull immediately presented his views to them.

Trumbull said that a fort at Rattlesnake Hill would have the following advantages: It could not only cover the lake and Fort Ticonderoga proper, but its location made it an ideal site to receive troops, equipment, and supplies arriving from southern New York and New England via a road that ran near the hill. Additionally, Rattlesnake and Sugar Loaf, despite their high elevations, had plenty of fresh water.

Yet despite Trumbull's observations and strong arguments for a reorganization and reconstruction of Fort Ticonderoga, his pleas fell on deaf ears. Although he did receive some sympathy (among his supporters was General Gates), in the end Trumbull's views were accepted only to a small degree.

Colonel Trumbull was not the only commander who felt this way about the terrain. Colonel Thaddeus Kosciuszko, a Polish freedom fighter who had emigrated to the American colonies and, in due course, took up the patriot cause, also shared Trumbull's views.

By profession Kosciuszko was an engineer and, like Trumbull, he had a good eye for terrain. Arriving at Fort Ticonderoga, Kosciuszko immediately identified Sugar Loaf Hill as the key to the overall defense of Ticonderoga. Prior to Kosciuszko's arrival, it had been decided to build a new fort upon Mount Independence. Realizing Kosciuszko's abilities, Fort Ticonderoga's commanders tasked him to assist in the construction of this fort. But, whenever Kosciuszko looked up, he saw the domineering heights of Mount Defiance. In his mind, he could see enemy soldiers upon the summit. To prove his point that the summit was not impossible to scale, Colonel Kosciuszko, accompanied by one other soldier, scaled the summit. After reaching the top, the Pole waited for nighttime whereupon, climbing slightly up a tree, he signaled with a lantern to those beneath his position. As did Trumbull, Kosciuszko repeatedly appealed to Colonel Baldwin to construct a blockhouse or at least a redoubt of some kind atop Mount Defiance. But along with Trumbull's previous pleas, Kosciuszko's efforts fell on deaf ears. Fort Ticonderoga's commanders remained convinced that Mount Defiance was impassible because it was too steep, rocky, and covered with heavy vines, thorn bushes, and thickets.

Unfortunately, neither Kosciuszko nor Trumbull could convince their superiors that the summit needed to be fortified. Even with the arrival of General St. Clair nothing changed. Along with Colonel Baldwin, St. Clair also disregarded the importance of Mount Defiance. As for General Schuyler, though the issue was raised to him, the commander of the Northern Army never intervened firmly in this matter. He decided to let the commanders of the fort have the final say.[26] Disgusted with what was going on, Kosciuszko sadly wrote to General Gates, "I say nothing of what unnecessary works have been carried on. You will be a judge yourself, my General. We are very fond of making block-houses but they are all created in the most improper places."[27]

THURSDAY, 19 JUNE

Coming ashore at Cumberland Head, General Burgoyne inspected the regiments not previously inspected in Canada. After conferring with his commanders, he then issued orders for an early departure on 20 June. Burgoyne's next stop would be the mouth of the Bouquet River almost 35 miles further up Lake Champlain, which, just several days earlier on 17 June, had been reached and occupied by General Fraser's advance guard.[28]

Until this time, no contact had been made between any of Burgoyne's units and any of the patriot continental or militia units. Even Fraser's advance guard, operating miles ahead of Burgoyne's main army, had not engaged in any way with the patriots. When it came to the irregulars it was a different story. The Indians, along with some of the Canadians and loyalists attached to Fraser's advance corps, were probing further and further southward by the hour. As they probed, Northern Army patriot scouts from Fort Ticonderoga and as far as Vermont were simultaneously probing northward into the wilderness surrounding Lake Champlain. Both sides were seeking information and intelligence.

In itself, intelligence is a force multiplier. Simply put, if a commander obtains good intelligence, he will be stronger than his enemy; therefore, commanders need accurate intelligence in order to operate effectively. And as scouts from both sides probed aggressively toward each other's army, they began to make contact. By mid-June skirmishing between each side's advance parties had become the norm. Shots were fired, tomahawks shattered skull and bone, and the first scalps were taken. Orders were also issued by both sides to bring in prisoners. In response, two British prisoners, identified as Adams and Amsbury,[29] were among the first to be captured by patriot scouts operating out of Fort Ticonderoga.

Both revealed to St. Clair that a large British army, commanded by General Burgoyne and augmented with Germans, Canadians, other loyalists, and native Americans, was sailing up Lake Champlain to capture Fort Ticonderoga. A British fleet with warships was transporting this force. The prisoners said that initially this army had been assembled at St. John's, but that an infantry advance guard, commanded by an English general named Simon Fraser, was probing ahead. They estimated that in about two weeks the brunt of the English force would reach Fort Ticonderoga. As for Burgoyne, his main objective was Albany.

St. Clair did not know what to make of this intelligence. Also, Amsbury possessed various items such as a British pass, some gold and silver coins, some Continental money, and various letters from some of Montreal's residents to those residing in the American colonies.[30] St. Clair even feared that, perhaps, these two had even been deliberately sent southward in order to be "captured." In the process, the two would not only provide the Americans false information, but simultaneously learn as much as they could about the patriots and their defenses at Fort Ticonderoga.

What also bothered St. Clair was that the prisoners revealed that several days earlier they had overheard an interesting private discussion among some English officers. Between themselves, the officers had discussed how a sizable British force, reinforced with large numbers of Indians and loyalists under the command of Sir John Johnson, was to advance eastward from Oswego, a fort and former town located along the eastern wilderness shoreline of Lake Ontario. Their mission was to advance into the Mohawk Valley, devastate it, and link up with Burgoyne in Albany.

Uncertain about this information, St. Clair ordered that both prisoners be immediately passed on to General Schuyler. Perhaps Northern Army headquarters would be able to figure out just who these two really were, and how much, if any, of their information was factual.

Stepping outside into the fresh clean air gently rising upward from the lake, St. Clair noted the various construction parties still hastily at work on the fort's partially completed defenses. As he stared, Fort Ticonderoga's commander began to worry. "What if . . . they are not lying?"

VI

British Moves and Patriot Uncertainty

FRIDAY, 20 JUNE 1777

The blast of a cannon from the ship *Maria* in the early morning hours signaled that the naval armada transporting Burgoyne's army was to proceed further up Lake Champlain. Departing Cumberland Head, Burgoyne's next objective was the mouth of the Bouquet River, which flows into the western side of Lake Champlain. Here Burgoyne's force was to establish new campsites.[1]

En route to the Bouquet,[2] the British force remained in its original march order. The advance guard, paving the way forward and already at the site, was still commanded by General Fraser. Major General Phillips still commanded the right wing, which was proceeding up Lake Champlain on its western side, and Major General von Riedesel commanded the left wing proceeding up the lake's eastern side. To maintain tactical control, Burgoyne remained on the *Maria* at the center of his army.

In troop strength Burgoyne had the following: British, 3,252; Germans, 3,007; Indian auxiliaries, 500; and Canadians, 145, for a total strength exceeding 6,900.[3] This figure, however, did not include the strength of the American loyalist volunteers, who were primarily serving with Fraser's advance guard due to their familiarity with the area. Also not included were the 670 naval personnel transporting and protecting Burgoyne's army en route. Of course, this strength also did not include the camp followers hitching a ride on whatever ships and bateaux they could. Along with the troops, Burgoyne's army also possessed 138 cannon handled by some 500 British and German artillerymen.[4]

SATURDAY, 21 JUNE 1777

On 20 and 21 June, Burgoyne's fleet arrived at the mouth of the Bouquet River[5] to join General Fraser who was waiting there with his advance guard, having arrived on the 17th.[6] At this time the Bouquet River was also known as Gilliland's Creek.

On the same 20 June that Burgoyne arrived at the Bouquet River and stepped off the *Maria*, General Schuyler, the commander of the Northern Army, arrived at Fort Ticonderoga to personally confer with General St. Clair.[7] Deeply concerned about the fort's defenses, Schuyler wanted to personally access the situation and see what could be done to rectify any critical matters.

When Schuyler arrived at Fort Ticonderoga, the fort's personnel strength ranged from 2,500 to 3,000.[8] The force was organized into four brigades, each with three regiments for a total of twelve regiments.[9] Along with General St. Clair, three other generals commanded: John Paterson,[10] Enoch Poor,[11] and Chevalier Matthias Alexis de Roche Fermoy.[12] All three generals were subordinate to St. Clair. Major Benjamin Whitcomb commanded the scouts, and Major Ebenezer Stevens served as the fort's artillery commander. Doctor James Thacher was the chief medical officer, and Reverend Enos Hitchcock served as the fort's Chief Chaplain, assisted by Chaplain Thomas Allen. Colonel Bellows commanded the militia personnel.

However, none of the regiments were at full strength. Although a few were relatively strong, some were tremendously understrength, consisting of only one or two good companies. Realizing the danger of this, General Schuyler had repeatedly appealed for reinforcements. As early as March 1777, Schuyler had submitted a request to both the American Continental Congress and George Washington for an additional 10,000 troops to defend Fort Ticonderoga, and he asked for another 2,000 to guard the critical Mohawk Valley.[13]

Unfortunately, getting reinforcements was no easy matter, as is often the case in war. This was especially true in the early summer of 1777. America's nation and army had just been born, General George Washington's own troop strength was fluctuating on a daily basis, and America's Congress, despite its best efforts in assisting the army commanders, simply could not meet all the pressing demands.

Yet Fort Ticonderoga, referred to as the "Gibraltar of America" and the "Key to the Continent," was of immense importance to the young nation. Not only for military reasons but also for the new nation's morale. When two years earlier, on 10 May 1775, Colonel Benedict Arnold and Colonel Ethan Allen with his Green Mountain Boys from Vermont had captured Fort Ticonderoga, "in the name of the great Jehovah and the Continental Congress!"[14] the morale of the patriots had soared immensely.

Despite the strong efforts of Colonels Baldwin, Kosciuszko, and a host of others, by mid-1777 Fort Ticonderoga was still far from being ready. To support the project, Lieutenant Colonel Udny Hay, who served as St. Clair's deputy quartermaster general, recruited a number of African-American freemen. Along with the military personnel, these freemen made prodigious efforts to reconstruct Fort Ticonderoga's defense system.

Fort Ticonderoga was a unique structure. Many, however, found it to be very eerie. The fort was, foremost, located deep in the wilderness. Long, harsh winters, lasting up to six months with little sunlight, dampened spirits. The howl of wolves, especially late at night, made many a man shudder with fear. Stories, reinforced by Indian folklore, spoke of huge serpent fish prowling the depths of Lake Champlain. Perhaps General Anthony Wayne, who briefly commanded Fort Ticonderoga, summed it up best when asked what he thought of the place: "A cold, inhospitable region. It appears to be the last part of the world that God made. I have some ground to believe it [Fort Ticonderoga's region] was finished in the dark."[15]

Under St. Clair the work continued. A sizable project was especially undertaken at Mount Independence. Despite the best efforts of the patriots, continuing manpower, equipment, and animal shortages hindered the efforts of its defenders.

Some have also alleged that hunger was rife within the ranks; however, many accounts point to the contrary.

Reverend Enos Hitchcock recorded in his journal that ample amounts of fish such as pickerel, along with venison steaks, roasts, and thick soups were consumed regularly. The post vegetable garden began to produce the season's first vegetables. Captain Moses Greenleaf, a tall, husky 22-year-old, also recorded in his diary how ample meals of duck, beef, and various other wild and domestic meats were available. Large amounts of chocolate, produced within the fort, were consumed.[16] Whitcomb's scouts also helped to keep the fort amply stocked with game. Virtually every day a raft was towed in by two or three canoes upon which lay a moose or black bear.[17] The garrison also had tons of flour.[18] Biscuits and bread were baked daily. Hunger would eventually set in, but this would occur in the aftermath of Burgoyne's capture of Fort Ticonderoga.

Another matter which also plagued operations in the Northern Department was the personal war fought between Generals Philip Schuyler and Horatio Gates. In fact, this conflict, which involved America's young Continental Congress, may be referred to as the "War Between the Generals."

General Gates and General Schuyler's feud started in the summer of 1776. Following the defeat of the American forces in Canada, the Continental Congress, seeking a new leader to rectify the situation, appointed General Horatio Gates to assume command. General Gates was to relieve Brigadier General John Sullivan and take control of the Canadian-based patriot forces.

But as General Gates traveled northward to his new command, General Sullivan was retreating from Canada. Withdrawing southward into the Colony of New York, Sullivan's troops now fell into the area controlled by the Northern Department commanded by General Schuyler. Therefore, Brigadier General Sullivan and his remnants fell under the control of Schuyler, who also held the higher rank, rather than Gates.

Arriving in Albany, General Gates learned that no patriot soldiers remained in Canada. They were now all back in New York under Schuyler's command. Gates, however, began to insist that the troops who had returned from Canada belonged to him and not to Schuyler. In an attempt to resolve the conflict, both generals appealed to the Continental Congress. That body stipulated that General Schuyler was to take charge of the "Canadian" veterans and incorporate them into his Northern Army. Without a command or a practical place to go, General Gates simply lingered around the Northern Army; there, he began to advise, consult, and even in his own way take charge on matters pertaining to the army. Gates even traveled up to Fort Ticonderoga. Needless to say, a number of the senior leaders, especially Schuyler, found this troublesome.

Gates had strong supporters in Congress, however. Among them were Samuel Adams and his cousin, John Adams. In an effort to resolve the issue and satisfy the two generals, John Hancock, the President of the Congress, informed the two quarrelling generals that Congress had approved joint command. Both generals were to command the Northern Army.

While, of course, two or more commanders of equal rank may share a command, in the end only one commander can have the final say. The Congress, as well as Hancock, did not stipulate which commander was to have definitive word.

In the present-day U.S. Army, unless otherwise specified, a date of rank determines who will command. Since America's army had just been born at that time, perhaps Gates (who was older than Schuyler) felt that his age should be sufficient to make the final decisions. Regardless, seeing that the idea of equal rank was not satisfactory to either of the two, Congress informed Schuyler to remain in command and Gates was recalled.

At this time General Gates also fell under the command of General George Washington, the primary commander of all the patriot armies and forces. In December 1776 Gates was recalled by Washington back to the main Continental Army in Pennsylvania. Along with his recall, Washington also ordered the transfer of all the soldiers who hailed from New Jersey and Pennsylvania serving in the Northern Army. Yet, as Gates proceeded back to Pennsylvania, his friends in Congress continued to demand Schuyler's resignation.

In the meantime, General Schuyler dispatched another letter to Congress.[19] Scolding Congress for not being firm on this matter, Schuyler not only angered and upset John Hancock, John Adams, and various other members, but also inadvertently gained friends for those favoring Gates. Likewise, Schuyler was also creating a situation which would soon lead to his downfall.

Arriving back with Washington's army, Gates requested some time off. Granted leave, Gates rushed off to Congress. There, he personally argued his reasons and justifications as to why he should command the Northern Army.

In mid-March 1777 General Schuyler received a Congressional reprimand. About ten days later, Schuyler was relieved of duty. General Gates was ordered to command the Northern Army.

Schuyler, however, also had friends in Congress. Unhappy with Congress's decision, Schuyler journeyed to Philadelphia. Amongst its representatives, Schuyler argued that he was more fit to command. Convinced that perhaps this was the case, on 22 May 1777[20] Congress reappointed Schuyler to command the Northern Army. On 8 June,[21] Schuyler returned to the army's main headquarters located in Albany. As for Gates, he was again recalled to Washington's army in Pennsylvania. Until his next battle with Gates, Schuyler remained in command.

VII

Burgoyne Advances and Fort Ticonderoga Falls

North of Fort Ticonderoga where Burgoyne's army had assembled at the Bouquet River, a troop count was taken. Following the count, Burgoyne's combat strength was recorded as: British, 3,724; Germans, 3,016; artillerymen, 473; Canadians and Loyalists, 250; Indian auxiliaries, 400, for a total of 7,863.[1] This strength, however, did not include sailors of the Royal Navy, the labor personnel, the bateaumen, or the camp followers.

Although impressive in strength, the army's size was considerably less than the 8,000 regulars, 2,000 Canadians, and 1,000 Indians Burgoyne had initially requested prior to his departure, as expressed in his 28 February 1777 thesis titled, "Thoughts For Conducting the War from the Side of Canada." Furthermore, through a combination of accidents, a few desertions, and a handful that had been killed or captured by Major Whitcomb's patriot scouts, Burgoyne's numbers were affected. Hoping to win additional colonists over to his side, and in the process avoid further bloodshed, Burgoyne decided to issue both a proclamation to the colonists of the area and a directive to his Indians and irregulars.

SATURDAY, 21 JUNE 1777[2]

Assembling his Indian force, Burgoyne spoke directly to them. Excluding those who were out scouting, approximately 400 warriors, from the Iroquois, Ottawa, Algonquian and Abenaki tribes, faced Burgoyne. On hand also were Chevalier St. Luc and Charles de Langlade. Standing nearby was Lieutenant Thomas Anburey, one of those who wished that de Langlade had not been brought along. Besides despising de Langlade, the young English lieutenant did not trust him. Anburey knew that de Langlade, who in the past had fought the English, would prove to be a fatal choice for Burgoyne. As he noted in his journal, "The latter de Langlade is the person who, at the head of the tribe which he now commands, planned and executed the defeat of General Braddock."

Performing as if he was an actor on a stage, Burgoyne delivered a lengthy speech in a powerful voice. As he spoke, a translator quickly interpreted. Raising the Indians into a frenzy, Burgoyne shouted, "Warriors! Go forth in the might of your valor and your cause. Strike at the common enemies of Great Britain and America—disturbers of public order, peace, and happiness—destroyers of commerce, parricides [parasites] of the State!"[3]

Suddenly, the stillness of the air was shattered as hundreds of warriors screamed in unison. The shouts of, "Etow! Etow! Etow!" were heard far and wide; simultaneously, as they raved and ranted, hundreds of tomahawks, knives and muskets were raised. Calming the crowd, Burgoyne proceeded with his speech. But it was not without a warning:

> I positively forbid bloodshed when you are not opposed by arms. Old men, women, children, and prisoners must be held secure from the knife or hatchet, even in time of actual conflict. You shall receive compensation for the prisoners you take, but you will be called to account for scalps.[4]

Upon the conclusion of his speech, several of the chiefs who previously had promised the British commander full support in the upcoming war against the "Bostonians" approached Burgoyne. Among them was an elderly warrior named "Old Chief."[5] In front of everyone, Old Chief ridiculed the Bostonians. He promised strong support for, "our great father [King George III] beyond the great lake [Atlantic Ocean]." To show that he meant business, Old Chief raised a tomahawk upward and screamed, "Our hatchets have been sharpened upon our affections!"[5]

SUNDAY, 22 JUNE 1777

Once again acting as if on a stage, Burgoyne issued a second proclamation to other troops.[6] Though presented in front of many of his soldiers, this proclamation was directed to the colonists, and it urged the rebels among them not to resist. Burgoyne, who considered the American colonies and their people solely a part of England, portrayed himself as a liberator sent by King George III to restore order. Burgoyne intended to put an end to what he termed was:

> The present unnatural rebellion... [where] Arbitrary imprison-
> ment, confiscation of property, persecution and torture unprece-
> dented in the Inquisition of the Romish Church. These are
> inflicted by Assemblies and Committees, who dare to profess
> themselves friends to liberty... [and] which was instigated and
> supported for the completest system of Tyranny that even God,
> in his displeasure suffered for a time to be exercised over a for-
> ward and stubborn generation.[7]

Burgoyne urged the colonists to support his army and provide his troops with foodstuffs and materiel. Burgoyne added how he had ordered his Indians to "Spare the knife and hatchet [tomahawk], even in the time of conflict against aged men, women, children and prison-ers." As the day before, he portrayed himself as an individual dis-patched to restore order rather than fight a war.

Burgoyne's proclamation, however, also contained a message of warning. He cautioned the civilians not to resist his advance. In the event of any resistance, Burgoyne would have no recourse but to release his Indian force. "I have but to give stretch to the Indian forces under my direction, and they amount to thousands, to overtake the hardened enemies of Great Britain and America." In his defense, Burgoyne also added, "I shall stand acquitted in the eyes of God in executing the vengeance of the [British] state against the willful outcasts."[8]

Clearly, Burgoyne planned to use his Indians and irregulars as a ter-ror weapon in the event of any colonial resistance. In the aftermath of his proclamation, copies of it surfaced on both sides of Lake Champlain. Initially, these copies were provided to those who happened to be in the vicinity of Burgoyne's army. Once they went out Burgoyne knew that it would not be long before his words reached far and wide.[9]

Suddenly, from the distant sky, a rumble was heard. Within minutes, pitch-black clouds appeared. Concluding his speech, Burgoyne retreat-ed for cover and silence swept the forest as its wildlife sought places to hide.

MONDAY, 23 JUNE 1777

Returning from a one-man, long-range scouting mission, Sergeant Heath arrived with some vital information. An excellent woodsman and tracker, the patriot Heath had been probing far to the north.

He reported that near the eastern shore of Lake Champlain, just south of where Otter Creek spills into the lake, he observed five anchored British ships. On the other side of the lake, adjacent to both sides of the Bouquet River, the scout observed sizable military encampments. Because he had succeeded in approaching very close, Sergeant Heath reported that "...the Indians were as thick as mosquitoes."[10] Undoubtedly, the Indians sighted by Heath were those who had converged upon the site to hear Burgoyne's speech. Heath also reported that he had encountered a civilian who resided in the area. The man claimed that a sizable enemy force had recently floated up the lake, "in a vast number of bateaux and some gondolas."[11] Heath estimated that the British force now stood no more than 42 miles north of Fort Ticonderoga.

Whitcomb's patriot scouts, however, were not the only ones probing far and wide. So, too, were Burgoyne's scouts, especially his native Indians. As they neared the fort, they began to conduct raids in the style of ambushes.

Previously, on 17 June, two soldiers from the 2nd New Hampshire Regiment, John Batty and John Whiting, had headed for Fort Ticonderoga's sawmill. Suddenly, from out of the blue, a sizable Indian force descended upon them. Whiting was killed instantly. Though wounded, Batty was not killed. Pretending that he was dead, he lay motionless as his footwear and pants were removed. Semi-naked, he was delighted to note that nothing else was taken and that the Indians had turned away from him and moved on.

But then it happened. After scalping Whiting, the warriors returned to Batty. They proceeded to scalp him.

How much fiery pain Batty endured as an Indian tore off his scalp could only be known to Batty. As he gritted his teeth behind tightly closed lips and eyes, Batty prayed that his scalper knew what he was doing. The last thing Batty needed was an amateur.

Batty knew that he had to endure the pain. If he did not, the blow of a tomahawk would shatter his head. Worse, he would be rolled over unto his back. Then, as several warriors would hold him firmly in place, a warrior with a knife would first insert the edged weapon into Batty's side. Not too deep but deep enough for Batty to feel its steel blade. Next, he would slowly work the knife upward toward Batty's heart. Once the tip of the knife was near his heart the warrior would quickly cut the cords, reach in to remove the heart and, after pulling it out, he would hold it up for Batty to see. The last thing Batty would view before entering eternal sleep would be his own heart.

Fortunately for Batty, his scalper was a veteran. In lightning quick motions, he tore off Batty's scalp. Holding up the scalp as high as he could for the other warriors to see, the last thing Batty heard prior to the warrior's quick departure was his high-pitched war cry.

Touching the upper part of his head with his right hand, Batty felt no hair or skin. Just blood. Looking upon his blood covered fingers, Batty began to feel intense pain. Suddenly, he could take no more. Screaming and cursing like a demon, he ran as quickly as he could for the main fort. Enroute he left a long trail of blood.[12]

In response to Burgoyne's directive of 21 June and his proclamation of 22 June, various voices began to be heard. In faraway England, Edmund Burke, a leading member of the English Parliament who opposed the war and England's policy towards the colonists, stood up. In a strong voice and with a sarcastic portrayal of Burgoyne's Indian directive, he shouted:

> Suppose there was a riot on Tower Hill. What would the keeper of His Majesty's lions do? Would he not fling open the dens of the wild beasts and then address them thus – "My dear lions. My humane bears. My sentimental wolves. My tender-hearted hyenas. Go forth. But I exhort you as you are Christians and members of a civilized society, to take care not to hurt any man, woman or child."[13]

The Prime Minister, Lord North, after personally witnessing Burke's one-man Parliamentarian show, laughed so hard that he actually began to cry.

There were many different views taken by the Americans who were notified of Burgoyne's proclamation of 22 June. Some looked upon it humorlessly while others dismissed it outright. Some responded to it as did Edmund Burke in England, in a comical way. Among such was Francis Hopkinson, a member of the Continental Congress and one of the fifty-six signers of the Declaration of Independence. Hopkinson's version, widely circulated throughout the colonies, amused many of his fellow patriots.

Others, however, viewed Burgoyne's 22 June proclamation as an act of desperation. America's freedom fighters were quick to point out that this proclamation was issued because Burgoyne—and possibly the King himself—began to sense defeat. Therefore, the British were hoping, via their proclamation, to achieve victory over the patriots by a combination of appeal and psychology. "Arbitrary imprisonment, confiscation of property, persecution and torture... these are inflicted by [American] Assemblys and committees, who dare to profess themselves friends to Liberty, upon the most quiet subjects..." Such high sounding rhetoric, argued the supporters of the Revolution in New York's and Vermont's villages, towns, and cities, is only cited in the hope of attaining a quick and cheap victory.

Angered by the Indian attack upon scouts Batty and Whiting, St. Clair immediately dispatched a pursuit party. They were unable to overtake the attackers. As skillfully as the Indians had struck, they withdrew. Minor skirmishing, however, continued. In another incident a sizable Indian force ambushed a twelve-man scout party commanded by Lieutenant Nathan Taylor. Though greatly outnumbered, Taylor and his men fought off the ambush party, though one scout was killed and scalped and another disappeared. It was feared that, perhaps, he had been captured. As for Taylor, he was slightly wounded.

Soldiers were not just targeted by the roving Indian parties; civilians were placed in harm's way as well. Responding to an order to bring back prisoners, the Indians nabbed a local civilian who, besides residing just north of Fort Ticonderoga, had once soldiered in the British Army.

His name was James MacIntosh, and by birth was a Scot. Though he resided in the wilderness, MacIntosh did not sympathize with the patriots. This was, of course, unknown to the Indians who had captured him. But MacIntosh quickly proved to be of value. He was well acquainted with Fort Ticonderoga.

Because years earlier Macintosh had served as an infantry sergeant in the British army, his eyes caught and his mind registered details that would have been overlooked by a normal civilian. After being discharged from the army, MacIntosh emigrated to the New World and he settled down in the wilderness area near Lake Champlain. Encountering General Fraser, MacIntosh immediately informed the British general that at one time, "I had served under you!"

Still loyal to the Crown, MacIntosh provided Fraser with much information. He estimated Fort Ticonderoga's troop and support strength at 4,000. He described the fort's various defensive positions, and provided information on its strengths and weaknesses. He identified St. Clair by name and cited that he was now the top ranking commander. MacIntosh revealed how, "...right at this moment to the southeast across the water from Fort Ticonderoga a new fort, named 'Fort Independence,' is in the process of being built upon a hill dubbed 'Mount Independence.'" MacIntosh, however, erred when he stated that a French engineer had recently arrived to supervise the work.[14] As for reinforcements, MacIntosh stated that they were trickling in from Fort Number 4,[15] from Castleton,[16] and the town of Skenesborough.[17]

MacIntosh also spoke about the bridge and boom which connected the defense systems across the lake. In the event of a retreat, the Americans found in and around Fort Ticonderoga would have to flee across the bridge toward Mount Independence. Once there, they would head southwards along a narrow road to the above mentioned fort and towns.

But MacIntosh mentioned something else which tremendously interested Fraser. To the immediate west of Fort Ticonderoga stood a high hill, and the hill overlooked the entire defense system. Yet for some unknown reason which MacIntosh himself could not understand, it was not fortified.

MONDAY, 30 JUNE 1777

Fraser now stood no more than 13 miles to the north of Fort Ticonderoga as Burgoyne's army rapidly approached Crown Point.[18] Leading the way was Major Alexander Lindsay, the Earl of Balcarres, who commanded a light infantry unit. Occupying Crown Point, Lindsay stood approximately 10 miles from the patriot positions. The Earl of Balcarres, along with Fraser and Burgoyne, was getting impatient. All of them were seeking to make contact with the enemy and secure, once and for all, the critical patriot position.

Initially, Burgoyne's intent was to advance toward Fort Ticonderoga on 23 June. But from the 23rd to the 29th a massive storm had pounded the entire region. So furious was the storm that tents were torn apart and ships and boats bobbed in the water as if they were tiny toys. Burgoyne could only wait out the fury of nature.

On 30 June Burgoyne's army advanced further up Lake Champlain and by nightfall was positioned at Crown Point.[19] Elements of his army were by now also positioned at Putnam's Creek to the south. As for Crown Point, it had once housed a sizable French settlement and fort called St. Frédéric, constructed in 1731. During the French and Indian War, the settlement and fort had been destroyed. Only the fort's ramparts and some tall, fire-blackened stone chimneys remained standing. Never rebuilt, the ruins served as a reminder as to how a prosperous settlement can be ravished by the cruelty of war.

Worried about Fort Ticonderoga's troop strength, Lieutenant Anburey approached as close as he could without raising suspicion. Through his telescope, he viewed the main fort and its various positions. Pulling out his journal, the lieutenant wrote, "We are now within sight of the enemy, and their watch-boats are continually rowing about but beyond reach of cannon-shot."

That evening Burgoyne issued an order to the entire army, copies conveyed to each unit. Confident of success, Burgoyne wrote like a victorious conqueror:

> The Army embarks tomorrow to approach the enemy. We are to contend for the King and the Constitution of Great Britain, to vindicate Law, and to relieve the oppressed – a cause in which His Majesty's Troops and those of the Princes his Allies, will feel equal excitement. Their services required of this particular expedition, are critical and conspicuous. During our progress occasions may occur, in which nor difficulty, nor labor nor life are to be regarded. This Army Must Not Retreat![20]

Late that evening Captain Alexander Fraser submitted a report to his uncle, Brigadier General Simon Fraser. As they conferred at Putnam's Creek, the young captain gave his uncle some grim news.

> There are no cattle or hogs in the countryside. None around to be caught or bought. The inhabitants of the area have either concealed their animals or driven them deep into the swamps. Also, as for the locals, the greater number are openly resentful of the King. Burgoyne's proclamation did nothing to encourage support for the Crown. Already, my men and I have been fired upon. And the further we push southwards, the worse it gets!

Thanking his nephew for the news, General Fraser returned to his tent. Sitting alone, he pondered what to do. "Should I pass my nephew's information along to the commander? Will it affect us in a negative manner?"

General Fraser knew that this was bad news. But the last thing the general wanted to do was worry Burgoyne. "After all," reasoned Fraser, "so far everything has gone, overall, quite well. And besides, what if my nephew is wrong. Young men. They always jump to some wrong conclusions. Maybe, just maybe, he had one or two bad experiences with some locals and now feels embittered."

Deciding to hold off with the news, General Fraser readied for some sleep. But as he lay down upon his cot, he again began to ponder his nephew's words. "What if he is right?"

TUESDAY, 1 JULY 1777

At 0500 hours, with drums beating, Burgoyne's army of nearly 9,000 boarded their ships, bateaux, and canoes to commence their advance.[21] Their next destination: Fort Ticonderoga.

Despite previous efforts to obtain accurate information regarding the fort's true strength, as Burgoyne's army approached the fort, little actual information was known.

Previously, in Canada, Governor Carleton had informed Burgoyne that Fort Ticonderoga, "was weakly guarded by a sickly, poorly supplied garrison."[22] Although no official figures were provided, estimates of the garrison's strength ranged from 4,000 to 5,000 men.[23] How many of these were actually soldiers versus how many were workers could only be speculated. Others claimed the patriot troop strength stood between 5,000 and 6,000.[24] A captured patriot officer cited a strength of 6,000.[25] An apparently nervous Lieutenant Anburey recorded, "By all accounts that can be collected, the Americans are in force at Ticonderoga, nearly to the number of 12,000 men. And a considerable number occupy Lake George, sustained by a naval power."[26]

Regardless of Fort Ticonderoga's actual strength, Burgoyne knew that he had to take the place. It was, after all, his first major obstcle enroute to Albany.

Sailing southward from Crown Point, Burgoyne proceeded to a prechosen location just three miles to the north of Fort Ticonderoga. There he disembarked the British regulars upon Lake Champlain's west bank and the Germans on the lake's eastern bank. Remaining on the ship *Royal George*, Burgoyne proceeded along with the other ships directly towards Fort Ticonderoga. Burgoyne's plan was to position himself and his fleet just beyond the range of the fort's cannons, remaiing there for the time being to monitor events. From the center the British commander would maintain a firm tactical control of both his left and right flanks. As for General Fraser, his cautiously probing advance troops were only about one mile in front of the American defensive positions.

As Burgoyne approached Fort Ticonderoga, General Arthur St. Clair was still in command, and slightly over 3,000 Americans were positioned inside in the form of ten regular Continental Army regiments, two militia regiments, and support forces.[27]

But as previously mentioned, most of the regiments were far under strength. Detracting from his strength, too, were the ill, the wounded, the young boys, the labor personnel including those of African descent, the wagon men, and the personnel serving the small American naval presence as on the ship *Beatsy*. Some women were also found. Either they had arrived to render support to the patriot cause or, in the face of the British advance, had fled to the safety of the fort. Regardless of their motive, they were now assisting St. Clair's troops. It is not known, however, if the troop defense figure of 28 June included women.

In terms of defense, the fort's positions had not been completed. Ample amounts of food and ammunition were for the time being available. But not enough army personnel were available to withstand a long siege.

Facing northward toward Burgoyne, Fort Ticonderoga's right (eastern) flank was covered by Fort Independence. This fort was located to the southeast of Fort Ticonderoga on Mount Independence.[28] Though Lake Champlain's South Bay separated the two forts, a "Great Bridge" connected them. Besides linking the forts together, the bridge also provided an avenue of escape for those stationed in Fort Ticonderoga.[29]

Alongside the length of the bridge a chain fence was positioned. Facing northward, it was referred to as a boom. To prevent any accidental sinking to the bottom of the lake, this boom was floated and anchored upon a series of rafts and sizable logs. The main purpose of this chain boom was to protect the bridge and halt any watercraft proceeding further up the lake. Once any ships or boats encountered the boom, they would be halted. Afterwards, cannon fire from Forts Ticonderoga and Independence would shatter the halted vessels.

Fort Ticonderoga's left (western) flank was covered by an old position from the French and Indian War referred to as the "French Lines." Located on hilly terrain, the French Lines had in recent weeks been repaired and strengthened.

Additionally, several small redoubts and blockhouses had been constructed both to the north of Fort Ticonderoga and to the west of the French Lines. Besides serving as an early warning system against the approach of the enemy, these positions would be the first to engage an enemy force approaching the main fort via land. A sizable number of mortars and cannon, including some heavy pieces, were also positioned in and around the French Lines. Sawmills, vital for the production of lumber for the needs of the defense system, were located between the French Lines and Fort Ticonderoga. Adjacent to Fort Ticonderoga flowed the large creek known as the La Chute River, originating at the waterfall at the tip of Lake George. The waters of Lake George, via the La Chute River, flowed into Lake Champlain's South Bay.

WEDNESDAY, 2 JULY 1777
8:00 A.M.[30]

With the fog lifting, General Fraser began his advance. Observing some high ground to the west of the French Lines, he immediately pointed his men toward it. Fraser reasoned that once he obtained this terrain he would be able to envelop the entire American left and open the door to Fort Ticonderoga. Noting that this particular terrain feature had no name, Fraser quickly coined it "Mount Hope."[31]

Officially, 2 July is the date when the British commenced their operations against Fort Ticonderoga. Spearheading the assault was the light infantry battalion commanded by Major Alexander Lindsay, the Earl of Balcarres. Because this battalion was comprised of troops from the 24th Foot Regiment, in the annals of military history, the 24th Foot has gone down as being the first English unit to enter combat in the northern wilderness. Simultaneously, 2 July may be cited as the date when the Wilderness War of 1777 formally exploded in full fury.

Atop this terrain feature, which on 2 July became known for eternity as Mount Hope, stood a small blockhouse manned by a handful of Americans. One can only imagine what thoughts must have flashed through their minds as they observed the long lines of professional British infantry, with fixed bayonets and drums beating, advancing in perfect order toward their position. Setting fire to the blockhouse, the

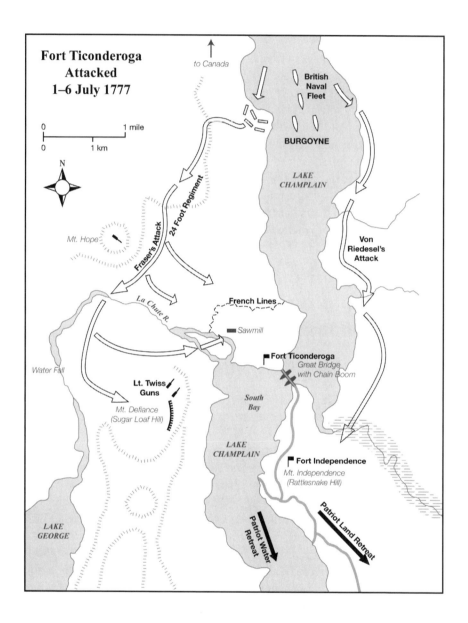

Fort Ticonderoga
Attacked
1–6 July 1777

patriot defenders quickly fled eastward to the former French Lines.

Continuing to advance in unison, the British infantry marched by the burning block-house but then halted less than 100 yards from the French Lines. For the patriot defenders this was, indeed, an awesome sight. Among those who watched was General St. Clair, who had just arrived on the scene minutes before. On that clear day, as the British infantry advanced forward with immaculate discipline and precision, more than one defender was awed by his opponent.

Suddenly, the shout of a command was heard. Immediately, hundreds of Brown Bess muskets rose upwards across the line. Excluding the few Americans who continued to stare in awe before being pulled down, the patriots ducked for cover.

"Fire!" Thick clouds of smoke obscured the infantry as five hundred muskets roared as if in one huge blast. Yet nothing happened. Only an eerie silence pervaded the scene. Ordering his troops to hold their fire, General St. Clair wondered what would happen next.

Suddenly, amid the quietly drifting smoke, one British soldier broke away from the ranks and proceeded forward. Halting halfway between the British and the Americans within the French Lines, midway between friend and foe, he stood alone.

Pointing to this man, Lieutenant-Colonel James Wilkinson ordered a sergeant to shoot him. Taking aim, the sergeant fired. Misinterpreting Wilkinson's order, a few others also stood up and fired; suddenly, many others joined in. Despite the cries of St. Clair and Wilkinson to cease fire, the defenders continued to shoot, reload, and shoot again. In the end, no less than 3,000 shots were fired. As the patriots poured a stream of musket balls against their opponents, the British withdrew. By the time the firing had ceased and the smoke had cleared, the enemy was no longer in sight.

Despite the heavy fire, only four British casualties were noted. Two were wounded and it appeared the other two had been killed. As for the loner who had initially walked out, he lay very still. Feeling sorry for the wounded, General St. Clair ordered that both they and the dead be brought in. But as the patriots approached the loner, they found him completely unharmed.[32]

He was, however, intoxicated. So drunk that he did not even realize that a battle had just taken place. Along with the two wounded, he was taken to the main works of Fort Ticonderoga.

Looking around, General St. Clair shook his head in disgust. Undoubtedly, the general was thinking that never, in a hundred years, would he ever win a war with such marksmen. But British Army Major Alexander Lindsay, for one, was truly grateful. A total of thirty musket balls had pierced his coat and pants, and yet not one had wounded him.

The quiet did not last long. Suddenly, shots were heard from the direction of the sawmill. More shots followed. Soon, a heavy staccato of gunfire was heard and smoke was seen.

In an attempt to save themselves, the soldiers who had been assigned to work in the sawmills retreated into the French Lines. Upon their entry into the patriot position, they reported that a sizable British force, accompanied by some Indian scouts, had attacked the sawmills. Ordered to flee, their withdrawal was covered by a few riflemen. As for the British force which just moments before had been attacking the French Lines, they completely withdrew from sight.

That evening, as General Fraser was finishing a written report to General Burgoyne about the events of the day, General Phillips suddenly appeared. Besides commanding the right wing, General Phillips was also Fraser's superior officer. Concerned about the situation and wanting to speak directly to Fraser, Phillips was upset about the fact that, when earlier in the day he had appeared close to the front to personally assess matters, he had noticed cases of drunkenness. Someone, in total disregard for military discipline, had opened barrels of rum. Alcohol had been issued not only to the troops but to the Indians as well. Under the influence of the "fire water," the Indians had made a lot of unnecessary noise and exposed the positions of the various British units advancing towards the Americans. In an attempt to control the intoxicated Indians a British lieutenant, along with several other soldiers and a loyalist, were injured.

Convinced that the element of surprise had been lost, Phillips ordered a withdrawal. But Fraser differed. Though acknowledging that perhaps the events of the day could have gone better, Fraser asked his superior officer to accompany him over the ground previously secured. Escorting Phillips to a position held by his nephew, Captain Alexander Fraser, General Fraser informed Phillips that the rebel position at the French Lines was less than 1,500 yards away. If these were overwhelmed, Fraser insisted, Fort Ticonderoga could be approached from the west and the entire patriot defense system unhinged. Fraser was also still confident that the French Lines could be taken with minimal loss.

After hearing Fraser out, General Phillips concurred. Thanking him for his efforts, Philips encouraged Fraser to continue the good work, and also informed him that he would bring up the entire 20th Foot Regiment for additional support.

Following Phillips' visit General Burgoyne also appeared, having been briefed by Phillips a short time earlier. Pleased with the events of the day, Burgoyne also thanked Fraser and expressed further encouragement. As he spoke, however, sadness was noticed in his words. Burgoyne recalled how at the very moment when Fraser's soldiers had been engaging the patriot positions at the French Lines, a small group of soldiers had made a dash to secure the sawmills. Their intent was to seize the mills' valuable lumber.

Unfortunately for them, from the upper parts of the sawmills vigilant eyes spotted the approaching group. As some of the patriots torched the sawmills, others, perched high up in the lofts, kept the British and Indians at bay. Accurate long-range rifle fire dropped a number of the raiders. Officers seemed to be specifically targeted. In the process, Lieutenant Haggit was shot right between the eyes and Lieutenant Douglas' heart and lungs were shattered. Unlike the poor marksmanship exhibited by the musket-firing patriots at the French Lines, the riflemen covering the patriot withdrawal from the sawmills fired with deadly accuracy. They protected their fellow soldiers and inflicted the first serious casualties upon Burgoyne's army.

Just before midnight, Burgoyne departed. But in the early morning hours of 3 July, he dispatched a message to Fraser that the rebels were reinforcing the French Lines with artillery and additional manpower. How Burgoyne obtained this information is not known, but he wanted to warn Fraser. For the remainder of the night, a quiet calm settled over the entire region.

THURSDAY, 3 JULY
5:00 A.M.

Dawn. Though it was still somewhat dark, von Riedesel's German soldiers resumed their advance. But as the day before, it would once again be a difficult trek. Swamps, thick brush, huge trees—many no less than fifteen feet in thickness—along with numerous streams hindered their advance. What also made life miserable for the Germans were the ever-present black flies. In vicious droves they continuously sucked the blood of both man and beast. Such insects had no equivalent in Germany. As the Brunswickers struggled their way forward in sheer misery, they cursed those who had recruited them for this God-forsaken expedition.

By now two of the German soldiers had had enough. Defecting to the American side on that day, both were friendly and talkative.

Possessing a fluency in English, the Germans informed their captors that they harbored no ill feelings toward the patriot cause. Grenadier Fassel-Abend was not only especially friendly, but even requested to join the patriot army.

And talk they did. They spoke of British and German strengths, dispositions, and intentions. They identified commanders and their entire chain-of-command, from Canada's Governor-General Carleton down to Burgoyne, Phillips, von Riedesel, and Fraser. Loyalist commanders, such as Philip Skene, were identified. The deserters also provided detailed information on the status of the four German dragoon companies. Though dragoons are horse-mounted soldiers, the deserters reported that since they lacked horses, the dragoons were marching on foot and were hoping to find horses in Fort Ticonderoga. The deserters told how they had disembarked on the east shore of Lake Champlain. Excluding a few of their commanders who possessed horses, everyone else had to march and carry all of their gear, weapons, and equipment. The Germans stated that the dragoons were not the only ones deficient in horses. Burgoyne's entire army had a shortage of animals.

Awakening from his alcoholic stupor, the British grenadier, previously captured in front of the French Lines, found himself sitting alone inside a jail cell located within the main bastion. Loyal to his King, nation, and Burgoyne, and unlike the two Germans, this prisoner-of-war refused to reveal any information. Even after he was provided a good meal, he still refused to talk.

So the Americans came up with a ploy to loosen him up. From among the artillerymen, Captain Johnson was selected to interrogate the Briton. Posing as a captured "loyalist lieutenant" named Andrew H. Tracy, he was ushered into the prison cell. Soon "Tracy" produced a small liquor bottle which, he claimed, had been overlooked by his captors. Taking a sip, the lieutenant exclaimed, "how good it tastes."

By now the imprisoned Briton had been missing his drink and was eager to imbibe. Noting the man's situation, the "loyalist" offered him a sip. "Go right ahead! Take another good swig!" And so it went. In time, the "loyalist" officer had won both the confidence and trust of the Briton. As they toasted one another, the upcoming British victory, and King George, the alcohol produced positive results.

The Briton revealed the strength of Burgoyne's army and navy, how many cannons he had, and how the British planned to secure Fort Ticonderoga. At one point he even bragged how he had helped to kill several patriots who, later, were scalped by the Indians.

On the following morning patriot guards suddenly appeared. Yelling "Lieutenant Tracy, let's go!" they informed the "prisoner" that he was being taken for interrogation. Cursing the patriots, George Washington, and the Continental Congress, "Lieutenant Tracy" wished the Briton godspeed and departed with the guards.

Reporting directly to General St. Clair, Captain Johnson told the fortress commander everything he had learned. Along with the information previously submitted by the two friendly Germans, the British intent had become clear. It was obvious that Fort Ticonderoga was Burgoyne's main objective enroute to Albany.

Thanking Captain Johnson for his invaluable assistance, St. Clair contemplated his situation. He knew he had a very difficult mission. What especially compounded his problem was the lack of troops to effectively defend Fort Ticonderoga. "Should I, or should I not pull out? Can I stand and fight? Will Schuyler assist me in time? Can he?" Such questions undoubtedly went through his mind.

As St. Clair was pondering his next move, the British and Germans were edging closer and closer. As they neared, they spotted a position of value. Looming about 800 feet high, it overlooked Fort Ticonderoga's entire defense system.

FRIDAY, 4 JULY

At the crack of dawn the American defenders at the French Lines saw that the British were constructing a battery in front of their position, consisting of cannon and mortars. Knowing that they had to preserve their combat power, neither Burgoyne nor Fraser would permit a direct frontal attack against the French Lines such as the one undertaken nineteen years earlier, on 8 July 1758, by English General James Abercromby. Failing to bring up his artillery, Abercromby ordered one frontal infantry attack after another, and by the end of the day he had lost over 1,500 men. For this, he was relieved of duty and his military career was terminated.

In honor of the 4th of July and the first anniversary of the birth of the new nation, St. Clair ordered a thirteen cannon salute. One shot for each state was fired. St. Clair reasoned that such a salute would raise morale.

Throughout that day sporadic but ineffective cannon and small arms fire was conducted by both sides. Bored, and seeing that not much was happening, some of the Indians even went off to hunt and fish. Perhaps this explains why the British had no knowledge of the sudden arrival of Colonel Seth Warner along with his second-in-command, Major Samuel Safford, who arrived with 700 militiamen from New Hampshire, amongst whom were nearly 200 "Green Mountain Boys."[33] Along with the troops, eighty head of cattle and sheep were delivered.[34] Needless to say, this reinforcement raised the spirits of St. Clair's force, and the extra food and livestock were greatly appreciated. Just as important, the appearance of Warner demonstrated to Fort Ticonderoga's defenders that they were not forgotten and that the Northern Army was committed to supporting their effort.

As the defenders cheered Warner's arrival amid an occasional cannon blast, both sides continued with their preparations. Delighted with the reinforcement, St. Clair decided to remain in place for the moment.

Reaching the top of the summit with forty light infantry soldiers from Balcarres' unit and a handful of Indians, British Army Captain James Craig and Lieutenant William Twiss were amazed at what they were seeing. Beneath and ahead of them lay the entire defense system of Fort Ticonderoga. In fact, it seemed as if they could see the entire lake. Returning to General Fraser, Lieutenant Twiss reported:

> The hill completely commanded the works and buildings both at Ticonderoga and Fort Independence. [It] was about 1400 yards from the former and 1500 from the latter. The ground might be leveled as to receive cannon, and that a road to convey them, though extremely difficult, might be built in twenty-four hours.[35]

The hill to which Twiss was referring was Mount Defiance.[36] Agreeing with Twiss on its importance, Fraser immediately went to his superior officer, General Phillips.

"So... where a goat can go, a man can go. And where a man can go, he can haul up a gun!"[37] So uttered General Phillips when informed of Twiss' observation. With these words, the order was given and Lieutenant Twiss, a highly competent engineer officer, immediately sprang into action.

SATURDAY, 5 JULY
Midnight. In pitch-black darkness, Lieutenant Twiss moved to the

base of Mount Defiance. Accompanying the lieutenant was a party of four hundred soldiers and axmen.[38] Two 12-pound cannon were brought along from the ship *Thunderer*. Some naval personnel with heavy ropes and block-and-tackle in hand also assisted. To overcome the steepness of Mount Defiance, a sizable path was cut through the brush and the blocks and tackle were put to use. Via the rope and tackle, the cannons would be hauled to the top.

Mount Defiance was steep. As Lieutenant William Digby noted in his journal, "The uphill climb was almost a perpendicular ascent."[39] But it was not impossible, and Lieutenant Twiss knew how the Carthaginian general Hannibal had proven centuries earlier that, "Where a man can put his foot, there he can go." As Twiss pulled, pushed, and tugged on the ropes and cannon, he knew that he would soon have the patriots in his sights. "How foolish they were. Never believing that someone could climb up." Unlike his American opponents who had previously argued that Mount Defiance was "too steep... to thick in trees and brush... impossible... out of range," and so forth, Twiss knew differently. Working steadily through the dark, they inched closer and closer to the summit.

At the same time that Lieutenant Twiss and his men were hacking an artillery trail, many miles to the south General Sir Henry Clinton was disembarking in New York City from a ship which had arrived from England in the early morning hours of 5 July. After stepping onto a pier, Sir Henry would hear two pieces of bad news by the end of the day.

The first was that General Howe had not yet commenced any type of offensive action in order to join hands with Burgoyne. But the second piece of news was even worse. Whereas previously, in late 1776 and early 1777, Howe had been supportive of an offensive up the Hudson towards Albany to rendezvous with an advance from Canada, now, in July, his intent was no longer to conduct any type of offensive to the north. Instead, Howe's plan was to wage a campaign in Pennsylvania. General Washington and Philadelphia were his new objectives.

Since the dual defeats at Trenton and Princeton the previous winter, Howe had become obsessed with Pennsylvania. He firmly believed that if he could capture Philadelphia, the capital of the revolutionary Continental Congress, he would also destroy Washington's army in the process. He felt that Washington would be compelled to defend Philadelphia, and if so, could hardly avoid a pitched battle against the Crown's superior army. Once victory against Washington was accomplished, patriot resistance would collapse in the northeast. Afterwards, a series of mopping-up operations, mostly conducted in the south, would put an end—once and for all—to the American revolt. To Clinton it was obvious that General Howe was thinking in the typical and traditional European fashion: first march against a nation's capital, forcing the enemy's army to stand and fight. Once the enemy is defeated the capital is captured, and afterwards the war or resistance is concluded.

Over the subsequent days Clinton repeatedly attempted to change Howe's mind. He tried to make Howe realize that there was no guarantee that Washington would stand and fight for Philadelphia. "And what if Washington retreats? Are you going to chase him all over Pennsylvania? So Philadelphia falls. We have a city. But victory is not guaranteed." Clinton argued that if the New York City-based army would march northward to link up in Albany with Burgoyne, not only would New England be cut off from the colonies but this would also force General Washington to march north to rectify a critical situation. And somewhere in the Colony of New York, Washington's army could be engaged and destroyed. Afterwards, even during the winter, Philadelphia could be taken. Therefore, argued Clinton, the key to success lay not with the capture of Philadelphia but rather with the town of Albany. But Clinton's argument was to no avail. Howe would not budge from his position.[40]

2:00 P.M.

By now, Lieutenant Twiss and his men were hauling two 12-pound cannon up the steep, nearly 800-foot slope. As expected the block-and-tackle held, and by mid-afternoon the artillery was in place.

By now, far below, St. Clair and his defender's knew that something was up. Several times during the night they had spotted lanterns in the dark. Initially, the patriots had suspected that perhaps it was just an enemy patrol probing its way into the rear of Fort Ticonderoga. When they realized that cannon were now in place, they received the shock of their lives.

Assembling his top commanders, St. Clair presented them the grim news. Along with the general, everyone agreed that a critical situation had developed. St. Clair proposed a retreat.

St. Clair's options were certainly not the best. True, he could remain in place and even dig in deeper. But all of this would now be done under the gaze of British observers and the muzzles of British artillery. Another option would be to launch a surprise attack late at night against Mount Defiance in an attempt to retake it and this time hold the hill. But this would involve a lot of risk with no guarantee. Whether this option was ever proposed or even discussed is not known.

Had the patriots decided to remain in place with Mount Defiance in British hands, they would not have been able to operate effectively. The narrow bridge, for example, which spanned Lake Champlain's narrow neck, would have been knocked down. Once destroyed, it would have been virtually impossible for the patriots to move troops, supplies, and equipment back and forth between Fort Ticonderoga and Mount Independence. With the placement of heavier naval artillery atop Mount Defiance, in time Fort Ticonderoga itself would have been reduced to rubble.[41]

St. Clair also had another critical problem, in that despite Seth Warner's reinforcement, he was still far understrength. Just recently he had cited a troop strength of 2,089[42] with 124 unarmed artificers.[43] Though this figure did not include the nearly 700 who had just arrived, Fort Ticonderoga's garrison was still much weaker than would be required to hold off Burgoyne's entire army. Too, part of the garrison consisted of militiamen who would soon have to return to their farms and occupations.

Outmaneuvered and outnumbered, St. Clair felt that his only remaining option was to save his men and as much of their supplies as possible. He issued the order to retreat. It would be done that night and conducted by both land and water.

A military retreat, especially in the face of enemy pressure, is one of the most difficult—and dreaded—operations to undertake. In order to succeed a unit must leave the false impression that it is remaining in place. It must establish a route or a number of routes to take, hopefully unobserved. The retreating force must ensure that no natural terrain or enemy personnel will intercept, delay, or halt the retreat. Efforts must be made to ensure that roads, passes, and bridges are sufficient in number and strength to support the force and its baggage. Flank and rear guard parties, along with obstacle emplacement personnel, must play a critical role in delaying or halting any pursuing enemy forces. Scouts must be utilized for protection and a strict light and noise discipline must be maintained.

What especially complicated St. Clair's situation is that the British already had two cannon staring down at the patriot positions. Though their fleet was well beyond cannon range, it was still dangerously close to Fort Ticonderoga. From both flanks, the British and Germans were edging closer and closer.

To retreat safely, St. Clair ordered a night movement. No lights were to be shown. To deceive the British into believing that the fort was to be held, some of the heavy cannon were to be fired sporadically. It was also hoped that the sounds of the heavy booming would cover the noise made by the withdrawing troops.

Via the water route, 200 bateaux would be utilized. One hundred wounded and ill personnel, along with all of the women and non-combatants, would travel on the lake. Five armed galley boats: the *Enterprise, Liberty, Gates, Trumbull,* and *Revenge* would accompany the bateaux. As much of the fort's supplies and personnel as possible would be placed upon the boats and bateaux. The waterborne force would sail south on Lake Champlain's s to the town of Skenesborough,[44] located at the base of the lake and the mouth of Wood Creek. Accompanying this group would be the fort's Chief Medical Officer and Surgeon, Doctor James Thacher.[45] Six hundred soldiers, whose task was to provide security and assist with the supplies and equipment, were to accompany the waterborne force commanded by Colonel Pierce Long. Along with the infirm, civilians, and boat crews, Long would be responsible for around 800 personnel.[46]

The rest of Fort Ticonderoga's personnel would retreat by land. After the men on the Ticonderoga side crossed the foot bridge, the columns would assemble behind Mount Independence and proceed in a southeasterly direction to Hubbardton, a hamlet located across the New York border in the present-day state of Vermont. From there the columns would proceed southward toward Castleton (today Castleton, Vermont), approximately 30 miles to the southeast of Fort Ticonderoga. Somewhere north of Castleton the columns would march westward, re-cross the border back into New York, and march southwestward to Skenesborough, there linking with those who had arrived by boat. Once united, the entire force would proceed by land further south to Fort Edward, which lay on the Hudson River about 45 miles north of Albany. At this fort they would rejoin General Schuyler, and a determination would be made of what to do afterward. As for St. Clair, he would remain in overall command of the retreating force and take the land route.

An order of march was quickly organized. General Poor and his brigade would lead the way, followed by Colonel Bellows' militiamen. General Paterson's and General Fermoy's brigades would be in the center, and Colonel Seth Warner would position his militiamen between the center and the rear guard, which would consist of Colonel Francis and about 450 continental soldiers. If Francis needed assistance he was to call on Colonel Warner. Excluding Warner's men, who were regarded as good soldiers, St. Clair knew that, by and large, Fort Ticonderoga's militiamen were unreliable. In fact, many were soon scheduled to return home. In consideration of this, St. Clair feared that should the militiamen be exposed to combat they would flee. By positioning them among the regular Continentals and more or less in the center, a safe check was placed upon their behavior. With such a tactical placement, St. Clair felt confident that he could retreat safely.

Conferring with his quartermaster general, Lieutenant Colonel Udny Hay, St. Clair informed Hay that Fort Ticonderoga had to be evacuated in the early morning hours of 6 July. Hay, however, began to question St. Clair's authorization to withdraw. He wanted to know if the Northern Army's high command or General Schuyler himself were even aware of what was going on.

"If I defend the fort, I save character and lose the army. If I retreat, I lose character but save the army," responded St. Clair.[47] He then ordered Hay to immediately head for the docks to direct the loading of the boats.

As is often is the case in such situations, time raced by. There was no way to halt or slow the clock. Approaching Major Ebenezer Stevens, the fort's artillery commander, St. Clair asked if all of the guns with their ammunition could be removed. "Impossible!" exclaimed the major. There simply was not enough time. However, a strong effort would be made to remove as many of the lighter cannon as possible. To augment Stevens' artillerymen, St. Clair ordered that 500 soldiers and workers be provided to assist the major with the guns. Among the assigned personnel were a number of African Americans. As for the guns, they were to be transported along with some of the horses and ammunition via boat to Skenesborough. The heavier pieces, 18-pounders and up, would be left behind, spiked.

10:00 P.M.

At this time the first bateaux began to row out. It had become apparent that everything could not be taken along as part of the retreat. What further complicated the problem was that although it was quite dark, a fairly strong wind had suddenly blown in. The bateaux, along with the ships, began to bounce in the water. This slowed the boarding, and especially the loading of the boats.

Prior to loading a boat, almost everything had to be transported on a wagon. In turn the wagon, pulled by either horses or oxen, would proceed to the dock. Once there, the wagon would be emptied, and its contents placed either into a bateau or one of the five ships. To save time, the wagon was to be immediately unloaded, and along with its assigned crew, was to turn around and head back where it could obtain more items. Once the wagon was reloaded, it would return to the dock, be unloaded, and return again. By now, those assigned to the task of loading the boats would, hopefully, have the wagon's items upon the boats. But it soon became clear that this would not be the case.

Despite the best efforts of Lieutenant Colonel Hay and the others, ordnance and supplies began to pile up. Crowds of soldiers from various units appeared. More wagons, loaded with supplies, kept appearing. Unable to move up through the piles and crowds of soldiers and noncombatants, they began to back up.

As rapidly as possible, Hay continued with the loading. Mobilizing each and every man that he could, he personally pushed, carried, and shoved items aboard the boats, while he hoped and prayed for the best. "Come on, men. Let's push this barrel on. Let's go. Next wagon!" And so it went. Deep down, Hay knew that he would fail. There simply was not enough time to succeed. Even worse, as he struggled and tried to remain calm and poised, he began to note the first signs of panic among the congested units.

Major Isaac Dunn, General St. Clair's aide, moved rapidly from one position to another. Repeatedly, he ran back and forth across the bridge to supervise and assist whatever needed to be done. To further deceive the enemy, he ordered an officer in charge of a cannon to commence fire upon the enemy battery being constructed near the French Lines.

SUNDAY, 6 JULY
12:00 P.M.

Midnight. By this hour, Fort Ticonderoga's personnel were rapidly preparing for the retreat. After assembling his troops and their tools, Colonel Baldwin began to assist in the loading. Though disgusted that after so many months of hard work everything would now be lost in a matter of hours, Baldwin's biggest regret was that he had not been more persistent in demanding that Mount Defiance be strongly fortified. Regardless, Baldwin knew that it was not his fault.

A factor behind St. Clair's decision to evacuate most of his force by land was that he knew that there would not be enough time for the bateaux and ships to make round trips back and forth to and from Skenesborough. By now it was also apparent to everyone that Fort Ticonderoga was to be abandoned. This realization, in itself, began to create problems.

One of the dilemmas which military commanders face when conducting a retreat[48] is how to maintain a healthy morale when exiting from a position. A retreat or a withdrawal does not necessarily imply that an army has been defeated. If anything, withdrawals are sometimes an integral part of a larger military operation or campaign, simply re-directing strength to more advantageous points of impact. Certain units, for example, might pull back to allow an enemy force to enter an engagement area; simultaneously, as they are retreating they may still be preparing for battle. Once the enemy enters the engagement area and is engaged and destroyed, the forces which had previously retreated may now be utilized in a counterattack role.

In the case of Fort Ticonderoga, General St. Clair actually had no alternative but to retreat. As would be proven in the upcoming months, the forces he saved through his withdrawal, along with the combat activity which occurred during the retreat, played a major role in first halting, and then overcoming Burgoyne's invading army.

Prior to conducting a retreat, it is a good idea to inform soldiers of what is occurring and what is to be expected of them. Unfortunately, a lack of time prevented St. Clair from communicating his full intentions to the men. As the evening wore on and the soldiers toiled into the early morning hours, some of St. Clair's troops began to grumble and curse their general for not, "standing up to the lobsterbacks," or "for not putting up a fight!" Perhaps the words of one volunteer summed up the feelings of many, especially those who were new to the art of warfare: "Such a retreat was never heard of since the creation of the world!"[49]

2:00 A.M.

Initially, 2 a.m. was the hour designated by St. Clair as the time to commence the land march. He had also hoped that by this hour much of the heavier baggage and equipment, along with some food supplies and some cannon, would be on the way via the water route. Yet, despite the best efforts, it was clear that St. Clair's force would not be able to execute its land move at this hour. As for the water route, not much had left by boat either. But it did not matter. In fact, by departing three or four hours later, he would still be able to slip away undetected. And the extra time enabled those loading the boats and wagons more opportunity to evacuate the fort personnel and critical items. Provided, of course, the British did not fire down from Mount Defiance.

Noting that in the vicinity of Mount Independence little was being done, Major Isaac Dunn rushed over to the position. Since the order to abandon Fort Ticonderoga had been issued, General St. Clair's aide had been rushing like a madman from one position to another to ensure that all was going well.

Despite General Fermoy's claims to French aristocracy, in reality he was a terribly incompetent leader. How he had attained the rank of an American army general remains unclear to this day. But history is full of incompetents in high positions, and in a short time Fermoy would be dismissed. Unfortunately for St. Clair and Fort Independence's personnel, however, right at that moment Fermoy was still in charge.

Arriving at General Fermoy's headquarters at Fort Independence, Major Dunn found the commanding officer highly intoxicated. Worse, he was doing absolutely nothing to help organize the retreat. As for his troops, some were milling around while others, mostly on their own, went to the docks in hopes of leaving by boat. Fermoy's soldiers were to be a part of the force retreating by land, yet nothing had been done. This was a critical situation being mishandled. Finding Fermoy intoxicated was bad enough. But what especially angered Major Dunn was his uncaring attitude. As Fermoy's troops cluttered the docks, they only further complicated matters for those such as Lieutenant-Colonel Hay who were working hard on the loading. Unable to accomplish anything with Fermoy, Dunn found some lower ranking officers and sergeants and instructed them what to do. The major then ran off to report to St. Clair on what was transpiring on Mount Independence.

By now the situation on the patriot side was that a strict light and noise discipline was in effect, while occasional cannon shots were fired to muffle the noise of those working on the docks. Bateaux were slowly departing as others were being loaded, and units and personnel were being moved to the southeast to be formed into a marching order.

Colonel Francis, who would command the rear guard, was readying his troops. The rear guard would not only include his own men but several hundred soldiers from General Poor's and General Paterson's brigades. As for General Poor, he was assembling his troops adjacent to Mount Independence. Needing to confer with Colonel Francis, Poor placed his men under the command of his assistant and proceeded to locate the colonel. By now some of the first wagons loaded with supplies and hitched with horses were being positioned to the south of Mount Independence. They would utilize the land route.

3:00 A.M.

As Poor, Francis, and some of the other officers conferred, a massive explosion suddenly burst from the top of Mount Independence. Huge flames rose skyward and immediately a fire illuminated the entire area. Night had turned into day. Whereas just moments before it had been dark, now one could see for many hundreds of yards.[50]

St. Clair was furious. It was bad enough that he had just been angered by Major Dunn's report about Fermoy. But now this. What especially compounded the situation was that many of the troops in Fort Ticonderoga proper, along with all of those defending the French Lines, had not yet withdrawn across the lake to the safety of its eastern shore. From where Poor, Francis, and the others stood, they could see the entire bridge with figures running over it. They also could make out clearly the boat loading area, the soldiers and noncombatants waiting to board, and virtually all of Fort Ticonderoga proper. As the fire lit up the night, those preparing to withdraw from the French Lines, along with those still working within and around Fort Ticonderoga, began to fear that perhaps the bridge might be engulfed in flames.

From his position atop Mount Defiance, British Lieutenant Twiss was truly amazed by what he was witnessing. Although some minor noise had been noted, until now no one had been able to make out what exactly was going on. Especially since just moments earlier the night had been pitch dark. The booming of the cannons had concealed signs of any activity, successfully disguising the patriots' intent. But now that he could see that the Americans were in the process of retreating, the young engineer lieutenant quickly dispatched a messenger to General Fraser and ordered his gunners to get ready.

Demanding to know who set the fire, St. Clair ordered Major Dunn to investigate. Running back to the works at Mount Independence,

Dunn learned that Fermoy had ordered his headquarters to be blown.

Indeed, it was a tragic situation. If the Americans could see all the activity in their camps and at the docks, they knew that so could the British. Fearing a dangerous British reaction, the militiamen began to march rapidly toward Hubbardton. Though they had no orders to do so, they instinctively began to evacuate the area. Some of the more disciplined Continentals began to follow.

Racing past the troops on his horse, St. Clair attempted to stop the exodus. He repeatedly ordered them to halt, but to no avail. Hundreds of militiamen, terrified of what could happen to them, just kept moving. Realizing that he could not halt the raw militia, St. Clair ceased his efforts; however, he did succeed in halting the Continentals. Once order was restored, the regular soldiers proceeded in an orderly march to Hubbardton. St. Clair also reasoned that when the militiamen would be forced to stop for rest, the oncoming Continentals could gather them up.

By now, St. Clair was exhausted. For the last four or five days he had been up virtually day and night. His body screamed for rest. He had not had a proper meal for many hours. Bits and pieces of beef jerky, coupled with an occasional cup of black coffee, comprised his entire diet. Yet he knew that he could not stop, still having a critical mission to fulfill. So he reached for that extra strength. Perhaps the spirit of his ancestral warriors is what kept him going. After all, in faraway Scotland the St. Clairs had been warriors, one generation after another.

As he worked to restore order and halt panic, St. Clair thought how ironic it was that in this wilderness so far away from his ancestral homeland, he was fighting the very same enemy his ancestors had fought for generations. Cursing the thought, St. Clair swore to himself that his son would never be a soldier. But then, in the hills of Scotland, St. Clair's father, grandfather, and great-grandfather had sworn the same.

Returning to Fort Ticonderoga, St. Clair noted that many of the Continentals and militiamen from the fort and the French Lines were now crossing over the bridge. St. Clair was especially delighted to see that panic had not yet set in among these troops and that the British had not yet fired down upon them. As for Hay, he was still working like a dervish to load the boats and bateaux. In a last ditch effort to save the fort's defenders and only their critical items, he was now only loading men, small arms, and all the ammunition, powder, food barrels, and kegs that he could cram on a boat. Everything else was thrown aside.

Realizing that nothing else could be done, St. Clair ordered Hay to cease his loading. As the last boats departed, the general ordered his remaining troops and stragglers to join the ranks of the rear guard. Lieutenant-Colonel Hay also joined the ranks of those retreating via land. Fortunately for St. Clair, Hay had secured St. Clair's vital papers along with some of the maps and documents from the main patriot headquarters. As Hay proceeded down the road, he carried two large suitcases packed with papers.

4:00 A.M.

Slowly, the first signs of daybreak began to appear. By this hour, amid the confusion, the fiery inferno, and the retreating mass, Fort Ticonderoga had ceased to be a patriot stronghold.

VIII

Cries of Retreat and Forest Combats

Far away in Pennsylvania, General George Washington was carefully monitoring the situation in the Northern Department. From the beginning of the Revolutionary War, General Washington had strongly differed with the American Continental Congress which held the view that the British would not attack from the north.

Born with a cunning ability to predict an upcoming action or event, whenever Washington sensed something it usually turned out to be true. Already in early 1775, even before the first shots had been fired at Lexington and Concord, Washington had confided to those around him that in the event of war Albany would be a major objective and that the British would launch an offensive from Canada, New York City, or Connecticut to secure that vital city. Washington also warned that if Fort Ticonderoga fell and the northern frontier collapsed, New England could be cut off, and, in due time, the patriot revolution could be quelled.[1]

To reinforce the Northern Army, Washington dispatched the regiments commanded by Brigadier General John Glover and Brigadier General John Nixon. Washington regarded Glover as a highly efficient officer. A fisherman in civilian life, Glover and his New England boatmen had played an instrumental role in saving Washington's army following its defeats at Brooklyn and Manhattan. Later, during Washington's ten-day winter offensive against Trenton and Princeton, Glover and his fishermen once again played a critical role, especially in the nocturnal crossing of the Delaware that allowed Washington to achieve surprise. Knowing that the Northern Army was operating within a theater filled with massive and numerous rivers, lakes, swamps, ponds and creeks, Washington reasoned that Glover and his men would tremendously benefit the Northern Army in its waterborne operations. In addition to these commanders and their units, Washington also dispatched a number of advisors and staff officers. Amongst these were Major General Benedict Arnold and Major General Benjamin Lincoln, two highly aggressive commanders.

Knowing the critical importance of marksmanship, especially in a wilderness scenario, Washington also dispatched Colonel Daniel Morgan and his brigade of riflemen. He reasoned that Morgan's riflemen would not only play an instrumental role in confronting Burgoyne's main force, but just as important, in engaging Burgoyne's Indians, loyalists, and Canadian irregulars. "I know of no corps so likely to check the enemy's progress in proportion to their number, as the one you command. I have great dependence on you, your officers and men,"[2] so uttered Washington to Morgan.

Morgan's rifle corps was, in fact, an elite unit. It was composed of eight companies. Two other highly competent commanders, Lieutenant-Colonel Richard Butler and Major Jacob Morris, served as second and third in command. The corps registered a total strength of 508.[3]

Morgan's volunteers were strong and hardy frontiersmen. They hailed from various states such as New York, Pennsylvania, Maryland, New Jersey, Virginia, and New Hampshire. Forty-six percent were either born in Ireland or were of Irish descent.[4] Also Scotsman, Scotch-Irish, Germans, Dutch, and English filled the ranks.[5]

Morgan harbored a great deal of affection for Washington. He would never forget the day when Washington, with tears in his eyes, personally thanked him and his troops for their support during the days of greatest crisis. After embracing Morgan, Washington went down the ranks and shook the hand of each and every one of his men.

But Morgan had another reason to go where the fighting was thickest, a personal one: the scars on his back from 499 lashes. Administered years before by the English, the memory of his whipping only intensified Morgan's hatred of the Crown's rule.

Morgan's ill feelings toward England had started years before the French and Indian War. Although employed by them during that war as a wagon driver in the British Army, his resentment of their rule did not diminish. Angered one day by a British officer who dared to physically strike him, Morgan lashed out. A huge man for his times, over six feet tall with a strong build, Morgan flattened the officer with one punch.

Arrested for his actions, the British pronounced a punishment of 500 lashes. Handcuffed to a pole, Morgan was whipped in public. As blow after blow rained upon his back, Morgan quietly counted each and every lash. In the end, they totaled 499.

Most men would have perished from such a beating, but Morgan was not an average man. Placed into the back of a wagon at the conclusion of his whipping by some friends who were forced to witness the punishment, Morgan was delivered home. As his friends carried him into the house, Morgan swore to family members that he would not die until he killed at least 499 Englishmen. Years later, as he packed his bags and readied his troops to move north, Morgan was cheered by knowing that his prophecy could soon be fulfilled.

As Morgan was packing his bags and getting ready, rifleman Timothy Murphy was doing the same. Of Irish descent, Murphy was a young man in his early 20s who craved action and adventure. Enlisting as a rifleman in Morgan's corps, Murphy had already seen some combat but he craved more. Grasping his specially designed, custom-built twin-barreled rifle,[6] Murphy slowly caressed his prized possession.

Murphy loved his rifle. Its shape, length, form, and color intrigued him. In his hands, it was an awesome weapon. The rifle's .58 caliber bullet had tremendous knockdown power. Just as important, it had incredible range. Murphy could fire and accurately strike targets well beyond 300 yards. Momentarily laying the weapon down, Murphy reached for his tomahawk and knife. Along with his rifle, these two weapons were just as lethal in his hands. Continuing to pack, Tim Murphy wondered what new adventures lay ahead.

By now, the word was out in the Northern Department: "The British are coming!" Such cries were heralded throughout each settlement, village, and town. By mid-July, virtually every resident in and around the wilderness was aware of the upcoming danger. The British, augmented with sizable numbers of German, Indian, loyalist, and other mercenaries were on the march. Now, each man, woman, and child was threatened. For most it would be impossible to remain neutral. War had finally come home.

Though some supported the king and opposed the patriots, the greater number of those who resided in and around the wilderness opposed England's rule. All the way from the western fringes of the Mohawk Valley to the present-day states of Vermont and New Hampshire, from the Richelieu River to Albany and beyond to the

Catskills, the region was populated by various inhabitants of Dutch, German, Irish, Scotch-Irish, and Scottish descent. Many had been born in Europe but at the time of the Revolutionary War were still young enough to render support to the American cause. Such was the case of Jane Cannon Campbell, who was born in Ireland. In 1777, as a young woman, she was residing in Cherry Valley, a flourishing community in the Colony of New York. As she documented in her journal, "The inhabitants of Cherry Valley and of other similar Scotch-Irish communities were rebels born. Their forefathers had fled Scotland, and then again Northern Ireland, to escape the British yoke. In addition, the majority of Tryon County's German colonists opposed England and its Germanic King George."[7]

Other settlers were the children and grandchildren of parents and grandparents who, through the early and mid-18th century, had emigrated to the New World. Considering themselves Americans foremost, they would be damned if they would succumb to force to have to live under the British king's rule in the New World. Volunteers began to enlist in various militia, Continental and regional home defense units which, in turn, were either subordinated into the Northern Army or, in some way, rendered it assistance during its battles of 1777.

One such individual was Thomas Mellen, a young man residing in New Hampshire. Excited about the notion of serving, Mellen gathered up some of his personal belongings, and with a bunch of other young men from Francestown marched off to Fort Number 4 where many of New Hampshire's volunteers were assembling. Promising his mother that he would soon return, Mellen wondered what interesting tales he would bring home to tell.

Forty-eight-year-old John Stark was raving to go back to war. A former colonel and hero at Bunker Hill and during Washington's ten-day Christmas offensive of 1776, Stark had served loyally and with distinction. But when in February 1777 the American Continental Congress promoted a number of colonels to the rank of Brigadier General but excluded Stark, he was so angered and humiliated that he resigned his commission and left Washington's army. Returning to his home and wife, Elizabeth "Molly" (née Page) in New Hampshire, Stark swore to her that he would never again serve. Molly Stark, however, would have the final say.

Unlike Stark, who possibly had very little concern for the patriot cause, Molly was a fiery patriot. In fact, had it not been for Molly, Stark would probably have been an unknown in American history. After all, it was Molly who back in 1775 had convinced Stark that the fight for independence was a noble act.

Molly knew that her husband was upset and angry, but she continued to strongly influence him. Shortly after his return, Stark, heeding her words, stepped forward and began to organize a unit. Though no one had formally elevated Stark to the rank of general, he pinned upon the front of his hat the star provided to him by Molly and referred to himself as a "general." And Molly had no qualms about that. She always knew that it was just a matter of time before her husband would soon be formally promoted to the rank of general.

For Stark, no assignment or mission was impossible. On more than one battlefield, his mere presence had made the difference.

With Burgoyne threatening Vermont, New Hampshire's leaders held a special emergency meeting in Exeter, a town located on the Exeter River in southeastern New Hampshire, not far from the Atlantic Ocean. In July 1777 Vermont (formerly known as the "Hampshire Grants") declared its independence, but its eastern border with New Hampshire was not yet clearly defined. Now, with the British pushing into Vermont, New Hampshire's leaders felt endangered. Did Burgoyne's plans actually include an invasion eastward through both Vermont and New Hampshire to reach the Atlantic? After all, the English had always coveted New Hampshire's rich coast with its numerous fishing and trading facilities. By securing the few coastal towns left remaining to the patriots, the cause could be severely endangered.

Unfortunately, New Hampshire was not in a position to arm and equip its own massive force. It was a sparsely populated state, was largely poor, and it had its share of loyalists. But it had its patriots as well. Among them were men such as William Whipple, a young merchant who was one of the signers of the Declaration of Independence and a Revolutionary War General, and also John Langdon, a prominent and wealthy businessman and a member of New Hampshire's General Court. Realizing the need for a sizable unit with a strong leader, Langdon supported the idea of raising a professional force and he urged that John Stark be appointed its commander. As Langdon stated, "We can raise a brigade, and our friend Stark, who so nobly sustained the honor of our arms at Bunker Hill, may safely be entrusted with the command, and we will check Burgoyne."[8]

Confident that Stark was fit to serve with the rank of general, New

Hampshire's General Court voted to promote him from colonel to brigadier general. Molly's predictions began to reach fruition. New Hampshire's decision to raise a fighting force under General Stark was based on urgent military, political, and psychological needs.

Militarily, with the fall of Fort Ticonderoga and Burgoyne's further advance into Vermont proper, many in New Hampshire became disillusioned with the performance of the Northern Army. They were also unhappy with the Continental Congress and its generals. Fearing that New Hampshire might be invaded, and no longer confident that the Continental Congress could defend it, New Hampshire's patriots concluded that they themselves would now have to undertake a larger role in their own defense.

Politically, though a number of New Hampshire's men and women were already serving in the Northern Army and in the other Continental armies, the raising of a large self-defense force would demonstrate to America's newly created Congress that New Hampshire would continue to support the overall effort but would retain a strong hold on its own internal affairs, amongst which was self-defense.

Psychologically, a self-defense force would raise the morale of not only its troops but also its civilian populace. Simultaneously, an internal force would check the activities of New Hampshire's loyalists and counter crime and other acts of lawlessness.

To maintain full authority and sole control over General Stark's force, New Hampshire's legislators stipulated directly to their newly appointed general that he (Stark) was solely to adhere to New Hampshire's authority. In the event that he had to operate against Burgoyne (or, for that matter, against any other enemy forces) Stark would operate when, where, and however he pleased. Graciously accepting New Hampshire's generosity, General Stark swore an allegiance to his state.

6 JULY
6:00 A.M.

Dawn. As the early morning sun arose, two major events were occurring in and around Fort Ticonderoga. The remaining Americans were pulling out and the British, now fully aware of what was happening, were pushing rapidly forward. And the fire started by the incompetent General Fermoy was still burning. Yet, in the final analysis, 6 July would prove to be one of the most decisive days of the entire Wilderness

War of 1777. For it was on this day that a number of major and minor events occurred which greatly influenced its final outcome.

By now, whatever had not been removed would remain at the fort. Among some of the last troops to depart were General St. Clair and his aide, Lieutenant-Colonel Hay. Both St. Clair and Hay were headed to Skenesborough via the land route. Because St. Clair expected Colonel Long to arrive to Skenesborough prior to his arrival, he also instructed Colonel Long that upon reaching Skenesborough he was to wait for the force coming in by land. In the meantime, he was to prepare to travel overland to Fort Edward because General St. Clair had no intention of staying in the town. The general also made it clear to Long that the moment the disparate retreating forces merged they were to immediately proceed to Fort Edward. There they would rendezvous with the commander of the Northern Army, General Philip Schuyler.

One of the last to depart Fort Ticonderoga was Major Whitcomb, the scout leader. Whitcomb knew that he couldn't tarry much longer. Especially since Canada's Governor-General Guy Carleton had recently placed a reward on Whitcomb's head for the sniper killing of British Brigadier General Patrick Gordon. The Indians wanted Whitcomb, too, for the killing and scalping of one of their top chiefs just several days earlier to the north of Fort Ticonderoga.

Whitcomb, however, would be damned before anyone would torture him, hang him, remove his heart or scalp, or attempt to collect the reward put on his head. Shouldering his rifle and rucksack, Whitcomb also made sure his tomahawk and knife could be extracted in a split second.

The scout leader's task, however, was not yet over. Excluding the few scouts who went along with Colonel Long by boat, the majority of Whitcomb's men would proceed on foot with St. Clair's troops. Some were positioned ahead of the march, some covered the flanks, and others covered the rear guard. Despite the retreat, Whitcomb knew that his days of scouting were far from over.

His English accented with Italian, Pascal de Angelis was also glad that the patriots were pulling out. During the previous year, Pascal had fought at Valcour Island on Lake Champlain with General Benedict Arnold. Emigrating to the British Colony of New York from his native Italy prior to the Revolutionary War, with the eruption of hostilities Pascal quickly adopted the patriot cause. He was one of the first to join the Northern Army. But Pascal was not worried. Despite the reversal, he was still confident that in the end the patriots would win. Shouldering his musket and firmly gripping his tomahawk, the exotic weapon of the wilderness, Pascal marched out.

Shortly after de Angelis' departure and Whitcomb's remaining scouts fanned out to follow the American rear guard commanded by Colonel Francis, British troops began to pour into Fort Ticonderoga. By now the French Lines had been overrun and British troops were approaching the bridge and boom. Among them was a young Irish soldier loyally serving his king, Sergeant Roger Lamb.

Burgoyne's troops were now conducting a three-pronged attack against the remainder of the fort. Units from the west, commanded by General Fraser, were already within the defense system. Ships filled with troops and naval personnel were sailing directly toward the boom and bridge, and von Riedesel's Germans were inching closer and closer from the northeast to overrun Mount Independence. The Indians, loyalists, and Canadian mercenaries were accompanying the ground troops.

Riedesel was pushing especially hard. His objective was Mount Independence. If he could secure the patriot defense positions on Mount Independence, he would not only cut off and capture any remaining patriots still lingering, he would also capture much needed materiel. Perhaps he might even overrun and capture the patriot rear guard, provided, of course, they had one. Riedesel hoped to capture the bridge and boom in one piece. Yet, despite his best efforts, this would not be the case. Exceptionally rough terrain, numerous streams, and swampy areas coupled with the thick brush and the ever-present black mosquitoes continued to slow Riedesel's advance.

When Whitcomb's scouts pulled out with the mission of screening Colonel Francis, they left behind one final rear guard. Composed of only four men and one cannon, their mission was to cover the bridge and boom spanning the neck of the lake. Loaded with grapeshot, this cannon was positioned in a shoreline battery at the rear base of Mount Independence, and it was aimed right over the bridge toward Fort Ticonderoga.

The gunners were ordered not to fire until the British began to cross over. Once fired, the blast would not only destroy those first attempting to cross but the blast would warn Colonel Francis and his rear guard that the British had finally reached the bridge. After firing, the four were to spike the cannon and flee.

Unfortunately for Colonel Francis, the four had somehow secured a bottle of Madeira wine. Rapidly consuming it, they quickly fell under the influence of the alcohol's effects. Having fallen asleep, they awoke to the sight of enemy bayonets pointing down at them. Among the British soldiers who ran across the bridge to where the four lay was Sergeant Lamb.[9] The four sodden patriots ended up in captivity. They joined those who somehow had not received the word to flee, or had deliberately remained behind to loot abandoned supplies before the British took over the fort.

Shortly before noon, General Burgoyne entered the main bastion of Fort Ticonderoga. With limited casualties the "Gateway to the North" had fallen into his hands. Delighted with his performance, he strutted like an actor upon the stage as he surveyed the scene. For Burgoyne it was an awesome victory. In actuality, the campaign had only begun.

By the end of the day von Riedesel's Germans, cursing their way through the rough terrain, finally captured Mount Independence. By now, several of the British ships had pulled up to the bridge and boom and immediately proceeded to breach the obstacle.

Storming the fort's prison, Fraser's troops freed those previously captured by the patriots; simultaneously, as the British prisoners were being released, into the cells went the patriots captured during the day. Until their rescue many weeks later, they would experience a very difficult and cruel fate. They would be overworked with no consideration made for inclement weather or difficult labor. And with food running out, they would experience bouts of starvation. Congratulating Generals Fraser, Phillips, and Riedesel for their successful effort in securing Fort Ticonderoga, General Burgoyne surveyed the scene.

Within and around the fort, especially around the docks, lay a considerable amount of baggage and equipment: suitcases, rucksacks, clothing, and here and there a knife, tomahawk, and musket. Many barrels were left behind. Of various sizes, they were filled with food such as salt, dried pork jerky, biscuits, and flour, including many gunpowder barrels. Initially brought over either from Fort Ticonderoga proper or from some other position, these barrels were to be loaded onto the boats departing for Skenesborough. But a combination of not enough time and chaos prevented the removal of many of these important stores and other items.

Among the debris of the fleeing army, British soldiers and Indians rummaged for food or valuables. The fire previously started by Fermoy by now had largely burned itself out and was smoldering.

But the captured loot found within the fort system yielded far more than scattered rations or baggage: eighty large cannon, many not spiked; 10,000 pounds of flour; huge quantities of dried meat, fish, and other edibles; and about 200 oxen.[10] Various weapons, with large amounts of ammunition, baggage, and tents, were also secured.[11] Some horses were found as well. Perplexed that the Americans left behind these items, von Riedesel recorded in his journal: "Great fright and consternation must have prevailed in the enemy's camp. Otherwise they would have taken time to destroy the stores and save something."[12]

Though much was captured, the patriots themselves were still slipping away. Determined to annihilate those fleeing by both land and water, Burgoyne took immediate action. He ordered General Fraser to pursue the patriots by land and that the bridge and boom be immediately breached so that a water pursuit could be undertaken. In response, Commodore Lutwidge brought up a few of his gunboats and at point blank range fired a handful of cannon shots directly against the chain. After collapsing a section of the chain, Lutwidge's seamen pushed a water path through the bridge. Through this opening went the *Royal George*, a ship that Burgoyne had been using for a headquarters, the *Inflexible*, and a number of gunboats.[13] For infantry support, Burgoyne ordered that three crack foot regiments: the 9th, 20th (minus one of its infantry battalions), and 21st, accompany Ludwidge's seamen.

As Burgoyne's ships commenced a rapid pursuit of Colonel Long's waterborne force, the American vessels were slowly pulling into Skenesborough. By now Long's flotilla had been on the water for about twelve hours.

In Skenesborough there was a blockhouse, but Long knew it was in no condition to be held. Besides, St. Clair's orders were specific: after unloading his force, Long was to prepare to march on a moment's notice; therefore he had no time to fortify the blockhouse or prepare a defense. Long knew that he had a critical mission to perform. Unknown to him, however, was that the British were rapidly closing in. Just three miles to the north of Skenesborough, Ludwidge had disembarked all three of his infantry regiments. Their mission was to envelop Skenesborough from the east and capture the retreating force.[14]

3:00 P.M.

With guns bellowing death and destruction, Commodore Lutwidge's ships moved in rapidly for the kill. Well versed through many hours of combat drill, British naval gunners struck with skill and precision. Within minutes the *Enterprise, Gates,* and *Liberty* were ablaze. Noting their precarious position, the *Trumbull* and *Revenge* quickly hoisted white flags of surrender.[15]

When Ludwidge's ships made their sudden appearance, Colonel Long was far from unloading the cargo he had evacuated from Fort Ticonderoga. With cannon balls and shot flying amid numerous explosions, his personnel began to flee in haste. Some, such as Reverends Allen and Hitchcock, quickly reboarded their bateaux and fled further up Wood Creek, while others fled via the narrow road linking Skenesborough to Fort Anne. Many others, however, simply melted into the forest. Quickly gathering up what medical tools and supplies he could carry, Doctor Thacher fled on foot. He had to leave behind his main medical chest.

When the patriots arrived in Skenesborough, most of their bateaux and ships were docked side by side. After quickly eliminating the five ships, British gunners redirected their fire on the bateaux. Striking gunpowder barrels, ammunition, and other flammable items on the boats, the crowded craft began to burn. Set alight by heavy British firepower, the burning *Enterprise, Gates,* and *Liberty* drifted against the bateaux. Fueled by many secondary explosions, flames spread quickly and consumed the numerous craft. A fairly strong wind blowing inland from the lake further fanned the fire, and within minutes a massive inferno consumed the entire site. Nearby buildings began to burn, trees caught fire, and loud blasts were heard far and wide as gunpowder barrels and ammunition boxes exploded. From where they marched, the 9th, 20th, and 21st Foot Regiments not only heard the blasts but also saw smoke rising hundreds of feet.

Yet the British troops advancing southward could not imagine the panic of the patriots fleeing before them as they were forced to hear and see their supplies, ships, and weapons stores going up in flames. Disgusted, his eyes filled with tears, Colonel Long ordered everyone to flee to Fort Anne. In the true military sense his force was entirely shattered. Until he could somehow recover, Colonel Long could do no more.

NEW YORK CITY

In the meantime, as men perished in droves while others were fleeing or advancing, many miles farther to the south on Manhattan Island, General Clinton was meeting with General Howe. Though he had arrived on 5 July, Clinton had not yet met with the British army commander. In fact, it had been months since the two had seen each other. Yet, when they finally met at Howe's headquarters on 6 July, their meeting quickly devolved into a tense and argumentative affair.

Clinton was angry about Howe's refusal to assist Burgoyne. He was also angry about Howe's accusations of Clinton's incompetence on Rhode Island. In turn, Howe demanded to know why Clinton had been ridiculing his 1776 campaign against the patriots. Though Howe refused to cite from whom he had obtained this information, he lashed out at Clinton for not being more candid and forthcoming.

Clinton was not inclined to tolerate Howe's criticism. Though Howe was his superior, Clinton faulted him for his performance at Throggs Neck, White Plains, and Rhode Island. "I cannot serve with pleasure, [being] liable to such unexpected and undeserved attack!"[16] Before Howe could respond, Clinton added, "I want to resign as soon as the campaign is over!"[17] To this, Howe immediately responded, "We never had agreed upon any sizable question,"[18] and he informed Clinton that he would indeed be able to resign, but only "once I get back from Philadelphia!"[19]

Despite their mutual rancor on that day, some positive discussions were held. But in the end, everything remained the same in terms of the army in New York City refusing to coordinate with the thrust from Canada. Howe set sail for Pennsylvania. So, as the confident Burgoyne pushed further into the wilderness, unknown to him was that on this monumental day major decisions were made which soon altered the entire strategic nature of the campaign.

ALBANY

In Albany, at the confluence of the Mohawk and Hudson, Northern Army General Philip Schuyler informed his staff that he needed to see for himself what, exactly, was happening at Fort Ticonderoga. Accompanied by a small staff and a security detail, the general rode out.

For his part, Burgoyne, concluding accurately that Fort Anne was Colonel Long's destination, issued orders to intercept the shattered patriot force. By finishing off the patriots who had retreated by water, St. Clair with his land force would be further isolated and weakened. Burgoyne also reasoned that at this point it really made no difference whether he finished off the rebels in mass or piece by piece. He would soon make his way toward Albany.

Despite his best attempts, Burgoyne's plan fell short, the failure largely due to the difficult wilderness terrain. The thick forest, immense brush, and confusing trails tremendously hampered the efforts of the 9th, most of the 20th, and the 21st regiments of Foot. Perhaps had the British naval contingent attacked Skenesborough just a short time later, the British regiments might have had time to cut off Long's force. Since the patriots were totally unprepared, the British might have been able to march right into Skenesborough and capture everyone. As it turned out, as Ludwidge's cannoneers were pounding patriots into smithereens and scrambling others into a southerly flight, the British infantry regiments were still a short distance away. The British spearheads and what rightfully may be called a fleeing mob had just missed each another. Entering Skenesborough, the British regimental commanders linked up with Ludwidge and everyone was amazed by the vast destruction.

Yet as is often the case in warfare, leaders emerged from moments of crisis. No matter how battered a unit is or how much defeat has been inflicted upon it, some still refuse to give in. Quickly forming order from the chaos, such men by their actions frequently alter a situation or sequence of events. Among the tall trees on 6 July, one such leader emerged. A captain in rank, his name was James Gray. Despite the debacle at Skenesborough, Captain Gray succeeded in not only maintaining firm control of his company but also began to gather up stragglers. Attaining a troop strength of 220,[20] Gray moved his men during the evening hours into the thick forest and allowed them to rest, knowing that by the next day the British would be upon them.

MONDAY, 7 JULY

Realizing that at Skenesborough Colonel Long had evaded their planned pincers of naval power and three regiments of infantry, the British revised their plan. In an attempt to surround the surviving patriots the 9th Foot Regiment, commanded by Lieutenant-Colonel John Hill, would proceed directly via a road march to Fort Anne. Hill was to overcome any patriots enroute, take Fort Anne, and hold it until relieved. In the meantime, the 20th and 21st Foot would proceed down Wood Creek to a point further south but very close to Fort Anne. To accomplish this, they pulled out of Skenesborough's harbor some of the charred but still usable bateaux. Removing some of the cannon from their ships, the British repositioned them on some of the bateaux. As some of the soldiers would float down the creek, others would march alongside it on a small road. Once they neared the fort, the two British regiments would link up with the 9th Foot and destroy any patriot forces still surviving and operating in the area.

Awakening his men early in the morning, the patriot Captain Gray proceeded to Fort Anne, where he noted that everything was chaotic, "and [there was] nothing to eat."[21] Fearing that disorder and confusion would demoralize his men, and concerned about the reports of "approaching Indians," Gray quickly exited the fort and reestablished his men in a defensive mode approximately half a mile to the north. To protect his force, he also positioned some picket personnel around his perimeter. In the event of the enemy's approach, the observers were to commence fire and warn Gray and the others of any incoming threat.

As Captain Gray was setting up this perimeter around Fort Anne, British Lieutenant-Colonel Hill was on his way to capture the fort. Once again the exceptionally rough wilderness terrain and the exceptionally narrow road slowed his men. Though he was pushing hard, Hill also knew that he had to be careful. His men had not had a warm meal or proper rest since 5 July, and for the last two days amid the wild, they had been pushed hard.

At Fort Anne, meanwhile, some 400 patriot militiamen, commanded by Colonel Henry Van Rensselaer, had emerged from the woods to reinforce the garrison. Their appearance raised morale and strengthened Colonel Long's depleted forces. Initially, Van Rensselaer had been stationed in Fort George at the base of Lake George. Why he chose to move slightly to the northeast toward Fort Anne is not known. Possibly, the fact that Fort George itself was far from completion played a role, or perhaps Colonel Van Rensselaer feared that if he remained there he would be cut off from the rest of the Northern Army. In any event, with Burgoyne now advancing on Fort Anne, his switch of position was a welcome development for the patriots.

Among Captain Gray's 220 soldiers, there were 17 rangers, whom he dispatched forward as scouts. As his rangers probed, not far from Fort Anne they encountered Lieutenant-Colonel Hill's leading element. Immediately, shots were fired and a brisk firefight ensued with the 9th Foot.

Hearing the shots in Fort Anne, Colonel Long conferred with Colonel Van Rensselaer. Both agreed that Van Rensselaer's unit was to march immediately to the scene of the fighting. When the battle commenced between Captain Gray's men and Lieutenant-Colonel Hill's regiment, the bulk of Hill's 9th Foot was spread out along the difficult route of march so at that moment he had fewer than 200 soldiers at hand.[22] With the quick arrival of Van Rensselaer's militia, Hill was heavily outnumbered. For the next four hours both sides skirmished with much vigor and intensity. Seeking reinforcement, Hill dispatched messengers not only to his subordinates to hurry up but also to both the 20th and 21st Foot Regiments. Under heavy patriot pressure, Hill slowly began to backtrack, constantly worried about his flanks.

General Schuyler was enroute to Fort Ticonderoga when he met Lieutenant-Colonel Udny Hay, who informed him that the fort had fallen. Schuyler received the news with much sorrow. Informed too that General St. Clair was retreating to Fort Edward, Schuyler decided to proceed to that location, hoping that somewhere in the vicinity he could rendezvous with the surviving garrison.

SKENESBOROUGH

General Burgoyne arrived in Skenesborough that evening. He was accompanied by the loyalist landowner, Major Philip Skene. Delighted that the British had recaptured the area, Skene immediately moved back into his mansion. Though it had been looted and his wife's grave had been desecrated,[23] neither his home or any of the other buildings had been torched. Immediately, Skene invited Burgoyne and a few of the higher-ranking officers into his residence.

Accompanying Burgoyne into the comfortable home was Captain Sir Francis Carr Clarke, his aide. But the captain did not stay long. Seeking information, Burgoyne ordered Sir Francis to ride into the vicinity of Fort Anne, obtain as much information as he could, and report back as soon as possible the following day. Captain Clark immediately set forth in the gathering dark.

Burgoyne, however, was not the only one seeking information. So, too, was Colonel Long. By now, Long had managed to get a grip on his tactical situation. Shattered units were being reformed, stragglers were being gathered up, and order was being restored. Though informed that the spearhead of what appeared to be an entire British regiment had been repulsed, Long still needed to know more. Asking for a volunteer who would pretend that he wanted to "desert," the man would enter the British side, obtain as much information as possible, and afterwards exit from their ranks and return to Colonel Long. The volunteer was also to also provide the British false information which Long hoped would hamper their operations. This was a dangerous mission.

With darkness setting in, this was the situation. Nearby at Fort Anne, Captain Gray and Van Rensselaer's Continental soldiers, rangers, and militia were still probing around Hill's leading troops of the 9th Foot and would continue to do so through the night in an attempt to thoroughly encircle them; St. Clair was retreating south in the territory of Vermont via land; Sir Francis was having an exceptionally hard time getting through the wilderness in order to accomplish his reconnaissance mission; Burgoyne, following a warm bath, was enjoying another glass of wine; and deep down in New York City, Sir Henry Clinton was thinking about the upcoming meeting he was going to have with Howe on the 8th of July. "Perhaps," thought Clinton, "I'll change that bastard's mind yet."

TUESDAY, 8 JULY
6:00 A.M.

Prior to the first shots being fired, an American "rebel deserter" approached Lieutenant-Colonel Hill's position. After being secured, the prisoner was immediately brought before the officer.

Though the deserter stated that the Americans had been weakened and many had fled in panic, he added that no less than 1,000 men were assembled in Fort Anne.[26] Concerned about this strength and convinced that it was accurate information, Lieutenant-Colonel Hill immediately dispatched a messenger with this news to Burgoyne. In the meantime, the deserter succeeded in slipping away through the thick forest. As Sergeant Lamb soon recorded in his journal:

> Not many minutes after the message was sent off to Burgoyne, the pretended deserter disappeared; he had viewed the situation and seen the strength of the British, which did not amount to above one hundred and ninety men including officers. It was soon found that he had made a faithful report to his friends, for in less than half an hour they came out of the fort with great fury. The British outlying sentries received them with great bravery and steadiness, and obliged them to retreat; they then returned again and came on with redoubled violence.[27]

Buoyed by the information that the 9th Foot was weak and that the other British regiments were still some distance away, Colonel Long ordered that Lieutenant-Colonel Hill's force be destroyed. Long knew that if this could be accomplished the victory would be a tonic to patriot morale throughout the Northern Department—a much-needed development during those days of constant retreat.

10:00–11:00 A.M.

After crossing Wood Creek, the patriots fanned out and succeeded in flanking behind Hill's position. Though the small advance band of the 9th Foot could not see the patriots through the thick woods and brush, they could hear them. Here and there, some were momentarily spotted as they leapt from behind one tree to another. And then, suddenly, it happened. Heavy gunfire began to pour into the British position.

Not far away, the remainder of the 9th Foot could hear the gunfire. So, too, did soldiers of the approaching 20th and 21st Foot. Informed by Hill's messengers that a large rebel force was operating in the vicinity of Fort Anne, the British regiments began to move as rapidly as possible toward Hill's position.

Unable to hold his position, Hill moved his troops onto a heavily wooded hill. From its summit, the British could at least temporarily hold off the flank attacks and maintain their ground. Unable to bring along his fourteen wounded soldiers, however, Hill was forced to leave them behind at the base of the hill. Among the wounded were thirteen privates and one officer, Captain William Montgomery. To assist them, Hill ordered that Doctor Shelly, the 9th's Regimental Surgeon, along with Lieutenant Richard Westropp, Sergeant Roger Lamb, and one private remain behind. Opening a medical chest just recently acquired, Doctor Shelly and his assistants proceeded to treat the wounded.

Sergeant Lamb, however, did not stay long at his post. With "the rebels pouring upon us like a mighty torrent,"[28] Lamb, along with the lieutenant and private, fled up the hill. Though Lamb made it, the other two did not. As musket and rifle rounds flew past Lamb, Lieutenant Westropp, running close by, fell. A musket round struck him in the back and tore through his lungs. The young private never made it either. Struck in the back of the head, he also collapsed into eternal rest. Doctor Shelly, Captain Montgomery, and the rest of the wounded were removed by the patriots.[29] Glancing downward as he ran for cover, Sergeant Lamb noted that the Americans had reached the wounded, and a few were reloading their weapons. Establishing contact with his fellow soldiers, Sergeant Lamb was issued a musket and proceeded to assist in the defense of the hill.

NEW YORK CITY

As Sergeant Lamb and Lieutenant-Colonel Hill were defending their critical hilltop position, in Manhattan, General Clinton and General Howe were again discussing the campaign of 1777. Acknowledging that Clinton's force garrisoning New York City and Long Island would be weakened with his departure, Howe now permitted Clinton to attack northward to support Burgoyne if he chose to do so. Howe added, "And if I succeed in Pennsylvania more quickly than expected, half the army will be sent back to New York City."[30]

Perhaps Howe said this simply to please Clinton. Yet, had Howe received Lord Germain's critical letter of 18 May 1777 instructing him to cooperate with the army marching south from Canada, Howe might have had to go along with Clinton. As it was, despite the heavy fighting raging far to the north, he continued to prepare for his upcoming operation into Pennsylvania.[31]

FORT ANNE

Running low on ammunition, Lieutenant-Colonel Hill began to contemplate surrender. Though he was unaware of it at the moment, however, Burgoyne was fully aware of the 9th Foot's situation. Earlier, Burgoyne had conferred with Captain Clark, who had delivered an accurate report after returning from his reconnaissance. Now determined to extricate Hill from a difficult situation, Burgoyne ordered Brigadier-General Powell, who commanded the 1st Brigade, to assist in solving his spearhead's dilemma.

For Hill, the end was near in sight. But suddenly Captain John Money, an officer from the rest of the 9th Foot, appeared. Accompanied by a party of Indians, Money and his warriors filled the woods with war cries. By now, the British were not the only ones running out of ammunition; so were the attacking patriots. And believing that a sizable British-Indian force had appeared on the scene, the patriots began to withdraw. Perhaps this was for the better because just at that moment General Phillips himself, along with an advance force of 520 soldiers and two cannon, was quickly approaching.

Withdrawing to Fort Anne with the prisoners,[32] Doctor Thacher noted a familiar looking medical chest. It was his. He was delighted to get it back. With more tools, bandages, and medication, the doctor was better prepared to treat the wounded and injured, among whom was Colonel Van Rensselaer, whose hip had been shattered by a shot. Though Doctor Thatcher succeeded in removing the musket ball, the colonel would experience hardships from the wound for the rest of his life.

Inside Fort Anne, Colonel Long conferred with his officers. It was agreed that Fort Anne would have to be abandoned. Though no one wanted to leave the stronghold, and the patriots regarded the battle fought in the nearby woods as their victory, it was still decided that a withdrawal was in their best interest. A severe ammunition and gunpowder shortage had set in, and, the patriots had learned that General Phillips was rapidly approaching, followed by several regiments with a strength of around 2,000 soldiers. Fearing also the Indian threat, the patriot commanders issued orders to gather up all the arms and ammunition that could be carried, place the wounded on stretchers, and form up into columns to commence a march to Fort Edward.

Some of the men who knew the trail system would retreat through the forests. But the bulk of the Continentals and militiamen would retreat via the road leading to Fort Edward. As for the road, it was nothing but a narrow track crossing over numerous creeks largely surrounded by swamps with high hills in the background.

Unlike on 6 July, Colonel Long now had a strong rearguard. Augmented with militiamen and armed civilians who had no desire to remain in the area, the mission of this rearguard was not only to protect Long's force but also to tear up the road system leading to Fort Edward. Every bridge, no matter how large or small, was to be destroyed. Culverts were to be torn up and, here and there along the way, trees were to be felled. Orders were issued for Fort Anne to be torched.

Simultaneously, as Colonel Long and his command were withdrawing to the south, Lieutenant-Colonel Hill and his survivors, accompanied by Captain Money, were retreating northward back to the vicinity of Skenesborough. After two days amid the thick brush, tangled vines, and near-constant musket-fire, Hill's men badly needed a respite.

As often is the case in warfare, there was the issue of what to do with the wounded. During the Wilderness War of 1777 this was especially a problem as there was a lack of medical facilities, doctors, and medical support personnel. Most settlements or towns stood miles apart, connected by roads that were difficult enough for able men to traverse, much less stretcher bearers. Wounded and injured personnel had to be transported slowly over rough terrain, hampering their recovery, only to find treatment that was rudimentary during that era in any event.

Fearing that a strong patriot force would soon be upon him, and knowing that the wounded would slow his escape, Lieutenant-Colonel Hill decided to leave them behind, albeit hoping to return and recover them as soon as possible. Hill selected Sergeant Lamb to remain with the injured until a British force could appear to gather them up. In the event the patriots should arrive before the wounded were retrieved, the British commander provided Lamb a letter. Specifically addressed to the patriot commander, Hill's letter asked for kindness and proper treatment for the wounded.

For one full week Sergeant Lamb, along with a woman servant,[33] took care of the wounded men. It was no easy task. What really compounded the problem was the lack of medical supplies due to the patriot recovery of Doctor Thacher's medical chest. Finding a small cottage about two miles from where the battle had been fought, Sergeant Lamb, along with the woman and the wounded who could assist, brought everyone to the site. Although they found some shelter, they still experienced a difficult time until their rescue. As Sergeant Lamb recalled in his journal:[34]

It was a distressing sight to see the wounded men bleeding on the ground; and what made it more so, the rain came pouring down like a deluge upon us. And still, to add to the distress of the sufferers, there was nothing to dress their wounds, as the small medicine box, which was filled with salve, was left behind with Surgeon Shelly and Captain Montgomery at the time of our movement up the hill. The poor fellows earnestly entreated me to tie up their wounds. Immediately, I took off my shirt, tore it up, and, with the help of a soldier's wife (the only woman who was with us, and who kept closely by her husband's side during the engagement), made some bandages, stopped the bleeding of their wounds, and conveyed them in blankets to a small hut about two miles to our rear. Our regiment now marched back to Skenesborough, leaving me behind to attend the wounded, with a small guard for protection. I was directed, that in case I should be either surrounded or overpowered by the Americans, to deliver a letter, which General Burgoyne gave me, to their commanding officer.

Here I remained seven days with the wounded men, expecting every moment to be taken prisoner. Although we heard the enemy cutting down trees every night during our stay, in order to block up the passages of the road and river, yet we were never molested. Every necessary which we wanted was sent us from the camp at Skenesborough, and all the wounded men (except three who died) were nearly fit for duty when we arrived at headquarters.

There was one additional matter of interest that occurred in the vicinity of Fort Anne: the capture of what appeared to be an American flag adorned with thirteen stars in a blue constellation with red and white stripes.

This incident was described by Lieutenant James Hadden, a British army officer. If correct, then this would be the first time in America's military history that the "Stars and Stripes," the formal national flag of the newly born nation, was ever flown in combat.

Yet Lieutenant Hadden was not in the vicinity of Fort Anne. In fact, he was about 25 miles away to the northeast of the fort, across the border in Vermont where he had fought in the Battle of Hubbardton. Does the possibility exist that Lieutenant Hadden erred in his location of the find? Was the first flag actually captured at Hubbardton but confusion arose as to where it was initially found? At the time, of course, the British would have been unaware of the significance of their find.

Unfortunately, no formal records or documents exist to verify if a flag was flown in the vicinity of Fort Anne or, for that matter, at Hubbardton. However, the possibility exists that either a continental soldier or militiamen did carry a flag. Either it was found on his body or was taken away from him if he was captured. If this is the case it refutes the argument that the "Stars and Stripes" was first flown in the western theater at Fort Stanwix. Regardless at which exact site the new nation's flag was first flown in combat, it is known that the "Stars and Stripes" was, in fact, first unfurled and flown in the face of the enemy during the Wilderness War of 1777.

On 8 July, Burgoyne formally established his headquarters in Skene's mansion near Skenesborough. As the top British commander reviewed the various situations and combat reports, he once again glanced over at a letter delivered earlier to his headquarters. Addressed directly "To General Burgoyne," the letter had initially been found by British troops posted on a tree on the road leading to Fort Anne, not far from where the patriots had battled it out with Hill. Somehow, the letter had worked its way up the chain of command all the way to the general.

Burgoyne shuddered. There was something very ominous about its words:

TO GENERAL BURGOYNE!

IT AIN'T OVER YET!

Burgoyne did not like it. In fact, he felt that the words forecast a sense of doom.

IX
_____

The Battle of
Hubbardton

_____

The fighting that took place at Fort Ticonderoga and in the region between Skenesborough and Fort Anne during the period 6–8 July between the patriots and General Burgoyne's advance guard was not the only confrontation of those days. While Burgoyne pursued the Americans who had retreated by water, his most able lieutenants, Brigadier Simon Fraser and Major General Friedrich von Riedesel, were pursuing General St. Clair and the bulk of the American army which had retreated by land. While Burgoyne's focus had been on taking Fort Ticonderoga, other battles and significant events were taking place. In order to better understand the overall picture, it is important to analyze the events that occurred in and around the soon-to-be-declared "Republic of Vermont" during 6–8 July.

6 JULY

After retreating from Fort Ticonderoga, St. Clair rounded the northern shoreline of Lake Bomoseen, crossed a creek named Sucker Brook, and entered the settlement of Hubbardton.[1] Located across the border from New York, Hubbardton was almost 20 miles, straight line distance, to the southeast of Fort Ticonderoga. In consideration of the weaving road system, each Continental and militiaman probably marched closer to 25 or 30 miles.

In itself, Hubbardton was just a tiny settlement named after a local farmer. Had it not been for the Wilderness War of 1777, the village would have remained an insignificant place, known today only for its nearby lakeside vacation spots. As often happens in warfare, however, battles suddenly erupt in places where no one expects to fight, and the last place anyone expected a battle was at Hubbardton.

When St. Clair, leading the column of patriots retreating by land from Fort Ticonderoga, marched into Hubbardton during the early evening hours of 6 July, the general just wanted to bivouac for the night. When informed that perhaps as many as 500 loyalists and Indians were in the vicinity, he decided to continue on to Castleton, about 6 miles further ahead. While it is now known that during the day a party of a few dozen loyalist and Indian raiders had passed by, St. Clair was unaware of their true strength. Concluding that his men were still capable of marching, he continued on. The extra miles would also put more distance between the patriots and any pursuing British forces.

Before proceeding with the main body of troops, St. Clair ordered Colonel Seth Warner, who commanded the Green Mountain Boys, and Colonel Nathan Hale (no relation to the famous patriot spy), who commanded the 2nd New Hampshire Regiment, to remain in Hubbardton. The 2nd New Hampshire, with a strength of 360 soldiers,[2] was also given charge of over 100 stragglers who were gradually arriving at the hamlet.[3] Along with Warner's 173 Green Mountain Boys they were,[4] for the time being, to remain in place at Hubbardton to await the arrival of Colonel Ebeneezer Francis' rearguard 11th Massachusetts Regiment with its 420 Continental troops.[5] Because Colonel Warner was the senior ranking officer, St. Clair instructed him to assume overall command upon Francis' arrival and, with the entire force, to proceed immediately to Castleton. Once reunited, everyone would then receive further orders.

The Continental units that Colonels Hale and Francis commanded were not ragtag outfits. Both the 2nd New Hampshire and the 11th Massachusetts were well trained and disciplined. Their volunteers were ardent patriots who, despite their recent reversals, were still confident of success. Colonel Warner and his Green Mountain Boys were also a formidable force. Prior to the Revolution, due to a land dispute between New Hampshire and New York, Ethan Allen had put the men through formal military training. Tough mountain men augmented with skilled artisans, the unit traced its origins back to about 1770, and at one point the Royal Governor of New York had put a price on Allen's head.

In 1771–72 Warner had served as a captain under Allen, who was his cousin.[6] The Green Mountain Boys first achieved great fame when, on 10 May 1775, under Ethan Allen and accompanied by Benedict Arnold, they caught the British garrison at Fort Ticonderoga by surprise and captured that critical site for the patriots. The fort's cannon were subsequently transferred to Washington's army and were instrumental in forcing the British to evacuate Boston.

Two days later, a detachment under Warner captured Crown Point, though a subsequent attempt by Allen to take St. John's misfired. The unit also participated in the failed Canada invasion of winter 1775–76, though by this time the men had elected Warner as their commander, and Allen, in a side operation against Montreal, had been captured by the British.

Despite the travails of the patriots' Canada campaign, the Green Mountain Boys performed well, and Seth Warner had proven himself an aggressive and exceptionally tough leader, devoted to his troops. The Boys themselves were proficient with rifles and every man carried a tomahawk, some able to throw it with lethal accuracy. Free men who despised any kind of authority, especially a foreign one, the unit did not discriminate in its recruitment. African-American mountain boys volunteered for the unit, among whom were Lemuel Haynes, Primus Black, and Epheram Blackman. All three had participated in the May 1775 capture of Fort Ticonderoga, and at Hubbardton were still present in the ranks.

4:00 P.M.

Once the 11th Massachusetts had marched into Hubbardton, Colonel Francis encountered Colonels Hale and Warner in the cabin home of a man named Selleck. What exactly was discussed in the cabin is not known, but the decision was made, for the time being, to stay in place. Remembering that Colonel Warner was a highly audacious commander, and senior among the three colonels, the possibility exists that he might have wanted to engage the approaching British force; or possibly he just wanted to give the troops additional rest. In either event, Warner's decision was in violation of General St. Clair's specific order that the men were to proceed immediately to Castleton.

Though unsure of the exact proximity of the pursuing British, Colonel Warner posted his three units in a careful defensive manner. Hale's 2nd New Hampshire, along with the sick and stragglers who had been scooped up, occupied the ground along Sucker Brook. To the east of this creek and north of Hale's position was a saddle ridge around which he positioned Francis' 11th Massachusetts. The Green Mountain Boys camped a short distance behind Hale's regiment, to the left of

Francis' men. From there, Warner would not only be able to defend a sector but also be able to support both Colonels Hale and Francis.

Sucker Brook flowed from the northeast to southwest. As the patriots retreated, they marched on a road—actually little more than a wagon track—which took them in a southeasterly direction. Approximately three-quarters of a mile beyond the brook the road came to an intersection with the main Castleton Road. If a traveler turned left, he would proceed north to Crown Point; turning right, he proceeded directly south to Castleton.

Around this intersection was the tiny settlement of Hubbardton. As for Sucker Brook, it was not deep. Depending on the time of year, its depth ranged anywhere from about six inches to a couple of feet. Its waters, however, were very clear and a traveler crossing the brook could see the numerous stones underneath.

North of the saddle ridge—which after the fighting would be known as Monument Hill—were two expansive heights called Sargent Hill and, to the east, Pittsford Ridge. South of the saddle and overlooking the Castleton Road was a formidable height called Zion Hill. This was the highest of all the hills in the area, rising to 1,200 feet. The moment the patriots crossed Sucker Brook, they saw this dominating feature to their right. Zion Hill was also very steep and thickly covered with trees. Its trees stood so tall that they actually shaded much of the valley.

Warner knew that he lacked the strength to occupy Zion Hill. Besides, it was so thickly forested that in order to use it effectively, here and there some trees would have to be cut down. And there was no time for that. Therefore, he reasoned that, for the time being, he would just use Zion Hill as a massive obstacle. He extended Hale's left flank to the base of this hill so that, including the saddle, Warner's entire front line ran about 3,000 feet.[7] In total troop strength, he had just shy of 1,000 effectives, plus anywhere from 100 to as many as 300 sick and stragglers.[8]

By such a placement, Warner was protecting the entire valley. Though not a very large area, if successfully held it would bar anyone from attempting to advance eastward or southward. Warner concluded that he would not only be able to defend the valley and its road intersection if attacked, but if necessary he would also be able to maneuver around any approaching enemy force with the 11th Massachusetts. Both Colonels Francis and Hale concurred.

After positioning the troops, Warner told them to rest. He knew that they would need it. As it turned out, for many it would be the last time they slept.

Not far away, General Simon Fraser also halted for the night. He too needed to give his troops some rest. Fraser's force consisted of light infantry, grenadiers, and his own 24th Foot, now commanded by Major Grant. Along with a contingent of loyalists and a few Indians he had some 850 men. General von Riedesel with 1,100 Germans followed several miles behind. Plopping down on the ground, Fraser's exhausted personnel lay with their muskets, other weapons, rucksacks, and equipment at their sides.

As for General St. Clair, after reaching Castleton, he also halted for the night, though two of his patriot regiments encamped on the road between Castleton and Hubbardton.

MONDAY, 7 JULY
3:00 A.M.

After sleeping for about five hours, Fraser awakened his troops, wanting to get an early start. By now, his loyalist Jessup Corps, commanded by Major Ebenezer Jessup[9] and uniformed in red coats with green lacings, was enroute to Hubbardton, with some Indian scouts probing ahead of the loyalists.

4:00 A.M.

Well before the sun began to rise, St. Clair was already up. A messenger had arrived informing him that the British fleet had gotten through the boom at Ticonderoga and had descended on Skenesborough, causing the patriot fleet and supplies there to be put to the torch. Now determined to march out of Castleton to Fort Edward as soon as possible, St. Clair did two things: he began to awaken his force and he dispatched a rider to Colonel Warner with a new message. Instead of linking up with St. Clair at Castleton, Warner was instead to follow St. Clair's main body, via Castleton and Rutland, directly to Fort Edward.

Despite the treacherous road, rough terrain, and little rest, Fraser was pushing his British advance troops hard. Unknown to him, the patriots were just a few hills away. Probing ahead were the loyalists and Indians, who encountered patriot pickets about a half mile from their camp. At least one shot was fired, although the patriots remained unaware that a heavy British force was less then three miles away, on the march and bearing down on them.

Riding into Hubbardton, the mounted horse messenger immediately found Colonel Warner, who at that moment was conferring with Francis. Informed of St. Clair's message, Warner stated that he would comply and he instructed the man to return. As the messenger rode off, Colonel Francis rushed back to his regiment.

5:00–6:00 A.M.

On reaching the woods above Sucker Brook, Major Grant at the head of the 24th Foot was both surprised and excited to encounter a large patriot force, many of the men still cooking their breakfasts. General Fraser was hesitant whether to attack a force of unknown size without waiting for von Riedesel to come up, but Grant successfully persuaded him to pitch in. Immediately, the British infantry formed into line and fired a volley into the 2nd New Hampshire and its accompanying clumps of sick and stragglers who had encamped along the stream. Continentals collapsed into eternal silence while others scattered or surrendered to the oncoming British.

But other patriots did not panic or flee. Taking cover behind trees they poured fire back against the British. Warner, hearing the sounds of battle, rushed his Green Mountain Boys to the scene. Spreading out in support of Hale's stalwarts, they waited for the British to come near and unleashed a volley of their own. Twenty-one British fell, including the impetuous Major Grant, who had stepped atop a tree stump to better direct his attack. Now leaderless, the 24th Foot fell back through the woods, though around Sucker Brook many of the stragglers were grabbed up as prisoners while the 2nd New Hampshire itself had been thrown into confusion.

Simon Fraser had no way of knowing whether he had run up against the entire patriot force or just a rearguard; in any case, he correctly assumed he did not have an advantage in numbers, and sent couriers back to von Riedesel to hasten his advance.

For his part, Seth Warner temporarily dropped his plan to march on to Castleton since it was apparent he had a battle on his hands where he stood. By holding the British he would allow more time for St. Clair to safely withdraw; and if the British had just pitted a small advance force against him, he might even defeat it. Colonel Francis' 11th Massachusetts had already been drawn up into march formation and was now ready to meet the threat. They were just in time because Fraser

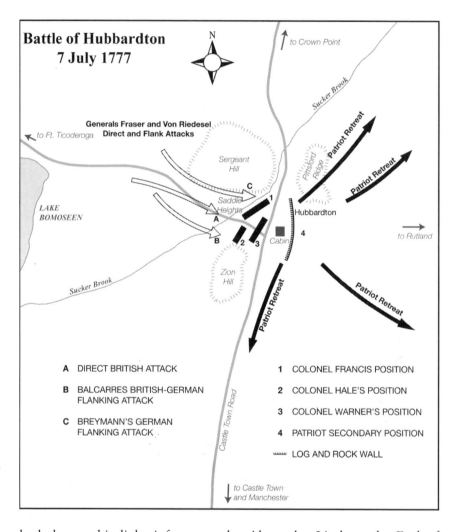

Battle of Hubbardton
7 July 1777

N

to Crown Point

to Ft. Ticoderoga

Generals Fraser and Von Riedesel
Direct and Flank Attacks

Sucker Brook

Sergeant
Hill

Patriot Retreat

Patriot Retreat

Pittsford Ridge

C
Saddle
Heights
A
B

LAKE
BOMOSEEN

1

Hubbardton

2 3
Cabin

4

to Rutland

Zion
Hill

Patriot Retreat

Sucker Brook

Patriot Retreat

Patriot Retreat

A   DIRECT BRITISH ATTACK

B   BALCARRES BRITISH-GERMAN
    FLANKING ATTACK

C   BREYMANN'S GERMAN
    FLANKING ATTACK

Castle Town Road

1   COLONEL FRANCIS POSITION

2   COLONEL HALE'S POSITION

3   COLONEL WARNER'S POSITION

4   PATRIOT SECONDARY POSITION

〰   LOG AND ROCK WALL

to Castle Town
and Manchester

had thrown his light infantry under Alexander Lindsay, the Earl of Balcarres, against the patriot right. They were heading for Monument Hill (the saddle ridge) but Francis' men rushed for the same spot, atop which stood a stone wall. Reaching it first, the 11th Massachusetts fired a volley into Balcarres' climbing British troops and knocked them back down the hill.

Awakening early in the morning, the settler woman residing near the intersection of Castleton Road was surprised to find so many soldiers clustered around her cabin home. From a few she learned that they were members of various patriot units retiring from Fort Ticonderoga. Unsure of what to do, she decided to stay in place for the moment.

Hearing heavy volleys of shots, the woman grabbed her baby and a blanket. Opening the entry hatch which led down to a small storage space beneath her cabin, where jugs of milk and other food items were stored in its cool foundation, the woman placed her child upon the ground and lay beside it. Covering herself and the child with the blanket, her nightmare was about to begin.

Observing the full field, General Fraser correctly concluded that the rebels were tucked in between the two sizable hill masses.[10] He could attempt to flank the patriots by moving across Zion Hill, or by somehow working his way through the saddle ridge to cut off the road to Castleton. But this would take time and before it would be accomplished, the patriots might either disappear or be reinforced. Fraser desperately wanted to finish off the rebels that he had been pursuing so hard.

Concluding that he had no choice but to advance rapidly forward, Fraser ordered his grenadier battalion of the 20th Foot,[11] commanded by Major John Dyke Acland, to climb Zion Hill to outflank the patriot left, whereupon they would command the Castleton Road. At the same time Balcarres' light infantry, supported by the 24th Foot, renewed their assault against the 11th Massachusetts on the saddle. Fraser also sent another messenger to urge the German contingent that was following up his force to hurry.

The 24th and Balcarres' light infantry charged again, hoping to come within bayonet range of the patriots behind the stone wall, but Francis' men unleashed a tremendous volley, cutting down dozens of British soldiers.[12] Among the wounded was the Earl of Balcarres, who was nicked by a bullet in the shoulder.[13] Advancing forward, Lieutenant Digby was certain that he would soon see his creator. As he neared the patriots, Digby could feel the, "showers of balls mixed with buck shot."[14]

Despite the patriot firepower from Colonel Francis' Continentals, the British continued to press forward. In disciplined fashion they halted no more than sixty yards in front of Francis' regiment.[15] Raising their Brown Bess muskets, they awaited their next command.

"Fire!" A wall of smoke rose from the British line as the men blasted the patriot position in unison.

"Re-load! Fire at will!" Men were now falling on both sides, and

Colonel Francis was hit in the arm, though refused to leave the field.

With his light infantry stymied, the key to British success was to now to flank the American left by surmounting the commanding height on which it rested. As the sun came up on that July day, Acland's grenadiers laboriously pulled themselves up Zion Hill, grabbing tree roots and branches to gain precarious footholds. Some of Hale's 2nd New Hampshire had fallen back near the height and they, together with the Green Mountain Boys, fired into the climbing British. Major Acland was hit in the thigh and could not continue, but his men kept going.

Though bold, Fraser's decisions were also dangerous. To begin with, he still had no idea as to the true strength of the patriots in the vicinity,[16] or their true dispositions and intents. By shifting the bulk of his strength from the vicinity of the saddle toward Zion Hill, Fraser was taking a dangerous risk that the patriots would turn his own left. He was, however, counting on the German support.

Prior to the British reshifting their strength and effort, the fighting against Colonel Francis and his 11th Massachusetts, bolstered by some of Colonel Hale's troops, had been brief but vicious. On both sides brave men had collapsed in droves. Despite his bleeding arm, Colonel Francis remained in command of his troops.

Seth Warner's immediate problem was the inexorable advance of the grenadiers on his left. At one point about 60 patriot soldiers approached the British with their muskets reversed, their stocks up in the air. In this era of warfare, such was the internationally accepted sign of surrender. Assuming the patriots had given in, the British held their fire. Some of the patriots even shouted, "I surrender!" as the British halted in place and waited for the Americans to come near.

Suddenly, the patriots committed an ugly deed. Coming within about 30 feet of the British, they quickly raised their rifles and fired. British regulars fell. So shocked were the grenadiers that before they could respond, the patriots hightailed out of danger. Seeking safety behind and amidst the nearby trees, they reloaded and continued to fire.

Needless to say, the American trickery was a violation of a rule of warfare established decades before. In the aftermath of the Battle of Hubbardton, Lieutenant Thomas Anburey was correct when he recorded in disgust, "a breach of all military rules."[17] But, in the vicious Wilderness War of 1777, rules of warfare were frequently violated. Before the madness of 1777 would finally conclude, Anburey would not only hear of other atrocities but would witness a number himself.

Despite Warner's efforts, the advance of the grenadiers could not be stopped. A vicious struggle ensued, as angry about their losses and the patriot trickery which resulted in more deaths, the British gave no quarter. Rifles and muskets were swung like clubs. Steel blades and wooden stocks shattered skull and bone. Bayonets tore deep into human flesh and ended lives. Tomahawks, either swung or thrown, penetrated deeply. By now, the entire valley was filled with thick smoke and blood. Amid this hell, men fought with a viciousness and savagery not previously witnessed in this wilderness. As for Sucker Brook, its waters were no longer clear. The entire steam flowed in a reddish crimson color.

Under tremendous pressure, Colonel Warner finally ordered his remaining 2nd New Hampshiremen and Green Mountain Boys to withdraw. They were to run back to a position east of Castleton Road where lay a long log and rock fence. At the expense of taking a few British bullets in their backs en route, Warner's marksmen would then continue to inflict damage upon the grenadiers who would have to cross the same open terrain to come to close grips. And if they decided to charge across the field, Warner's frontier marksmen would rain accurate and heavy firepower upon them. In a maneuver known as "refusing the flank" Warner's men quickly dashed over to their new position to continue the battle.

With a rifle in his left hand and a bloodied tomahawk in his right, Lemuel Haynes galloped back, wondering just how much more of this he could take. Haynes had experienced some combat in the past, but nothing like this. And Major Samuel Safford, who until now had been all over the battlefield, quickly reached the log and rock fence and helped ensure that the withdrawal did not turn into a panicked flight.

Back on the patriot right, noting that the British to his front were weakening and that their main effort had shifted toward Zion Hill, Colonel Francis sensed a moment of opportunity. His 11th Massachusetts, together with some of Hale's men, was still well in hand and defiant. Despite his wound, Francis ordered them to advance forward. Instead of waiting for another British attack he would deliver his own. If successful he could turn the British flank, press them from the rear, and shatter them.

Miles away in Castleton, General St. Clair could hear the noise of the battle. He dispatched two of his aides, Lieutenant-Colonels Henry Livingston and Isaac Dunn, to return to Hubbardton and assess the situation. En route, they were to inform Colonel Bellows to turn his militia around and return to Hubbardton as rapidly as possible in order to assist Warner. The aides were also to inform both Bellows and Warner that St. Clair himself, accompanied by the main force, was returning to Hubbardton immediately.

Noting the new course of events, General Fraser began to fear defeat. The British general knew that if the patriot advance against his left flank was not checked, the enemy would encircle the British force from behind. Trapped between Warner and Francis at the base of Zion Hill, his defeat would be ensured. What further complicated the situation for Fraser was that he still could not determine the total American strength or what reinforcements were on the way. For Fraser, it was obvious that everything now hinged on the arrival of von Riedesel and his German troops.

Galloping northward, Livingston and Dunn immediately ordered whomever they encountered to return northward. Establishing contact with Colonel Bellows, they informed him of St. Clair's orders. But it was to no avail. Despite Bellows' best efforts, he could not turn his force around. Their fears aroused by the sounds of heavy gunfire, Bellows' militiamen continued to surge southward to join St. Clair's main force. Warner's rearguard was on its own.

Earlier that morning, von Riedesel had set off with 180 light infantry and grenadiers in advance of his main force. Arriving at the battlefield on the same road Fraser had taken, the veteran German quickly assessed the situation. The battle had come to resemble a pinwheel, with the patriots falling back on their left but advancing with their right, the latter movement threatening to cut off the entire British force. Unlike General Fraser, who had begun to fear the worst, von Riedesel believed that the patriots were actually on the verge of defeat. He issued orders to his Brunswick light infantry, under Captain Karl von Geyso, to fall in on the left of Balcarres' men to strengthen the British flank. Then he ordered his grenadiers, commanded by Captain Maximilian Schottelius, to maneuver even farther to the left to gain the patriots' right rear. While the British and Germans held Francis' men in front, the grenadiers would smash in their flank.

Fixing their bayonets, the Germans pressed forward. To disguise their small numbers, von Riedesel ordered his musicians to play and the men to sing, so to give the impression that his entire force had arrived. Indeed the psychological tactic must have been effective, as above the din of battle the patriots suddenly heard the strange sounds of foreign voices and instruments suddenly closing in on them. The same sounds raised the spirits of the hard-pressed British troops who realized that their reinforcements had finally arrived.

Prior to attacking, the Germans first had to cross Sucker Brook. As they marched through the creek, each and every one noted the crimson color of the water. Bodies lay here and there either directly in the brook or on its banks.

As Generals Fraser and von Riedesel were hammering away, Colonel Warner's Green Mountain Boys, from their new position across Castleton Road, were pouring devastating fire into the advancing British grenadiers. Though it was difficult to see through the thick dust and smoke, Warner's men blasted away at the 20th Foot and the companies of the 24th Foot that had come up on their left. From behind his new position, riflemen Joseph Bird fired no less than twenty bullets into the advancing British and German grenadiers.

On the patriot right the indefatigible Colonel Francis refused to yield. He rallied his men against their foes in front as well as against the Brunswick grenadiers methodically stalking up the hill on his flank. "Fire!" British and German muskets roared in unison. Another mass plume of smoke rose upwards. Musket balls tore deep into the patriots. Among those who fell was Colonel Francis, a German bullet through his heart.

For Sir John Harrington it was indeed a brutal day. Despite years of service in the British army, until this ugly day in 1777 Harrington had never killed anyone. Observing a rebel aiming directly at his head, Harrington reacted quickly and shot. The patriot collapsed. Overcome with remorse, Harrington quickly ran over and actually asked the dead man if he was all right.

With Hale's 2nd New Hampshire ineffective and Colonel Francis dead, the 11th Massachusetts could no longer hold. Weakened by heavy casualties, the 11th could no longer halt the combined British-German thrust. Colonel Hale was out of the picture, cut off with about 70 of his men who were all later captured in the woods.[18] As survivors dashed back, Colonel Warner knew that he had to call it quits. It was imperative for him to save the remainder of his command for another day. Spotting the German force which had worked its way through the saddle and now was successfully flanking the surviving patriots, Warner also knew that within a matter of minutes they would be behind him. If trapped in the center, no one would escape alive.

As he stood in the thick smoke, massive dust, and deafening noise of the battle, Warner momentarily thought about the possibility of an organized retreat. Suddenly, he realized there was no time for that. Another musket ball whizzed by his head. Facing his men, Warner waved his left arm backwards and yelled "Meet me in Manchester!"

Warner's message was clear—pull back. Hoisting some of their wounded upon their shoulders, Warner's Green Mountain Boys, along with the survivors of the 2nd New Hampshire and the 11th Massachusetts, scattered through the woods or along roads to the north and east, the Castleton Road to the south now being occupied by British grenadiers. As they fled, shouts of "Meet me in Manchester!" were continuously heralded both far and wide by the retreating survivors.

9:00 A.M.

Well before the last puffs of smoke had cleared and the final dust had settled, an eerie silence prevailed over the landscape. Emerging out of her hiding place with her baby, the young woman immediately noted the hundreds of musket and bullet holes in the four walls. Slowly pushing open the wooden door, also riddled with bullet holes, she stepped outside and immediately came face to face with a horror that would haunt her for the rest of her days.

It was the sight of bodies. They lay all around, sometimes on top of one another. Dozens of them. A few had their eyes open as if they were just staring off into space. Blotches of blood seeped through shirts, uniforms, pants, and buckskin jackets. Here and there a body that was seemingly dead would suddenly quiver. Quickly gathering up a few of her belongings, the woman fled. Never again would she return to this ghastly place.

Cautiously returning to the scene after fleeing, a lone patriot rifleman concealed himself somewhere in the trees and brush near the saddle ridge. His day of warmaking was not yet over. He was still going to have the final say or, better yet, the final shot.

10:00 A.M.

After regrouping their forces, the combined British-German force began to review the results of their victory. For Lindsay, the Earl of Balcarres, it had indeed been a fortunate morning. In addition to be slightly wounded, the Earl counted ten bullet holes through his clothes. His personal weapon had been hit twice. Shortly afterwards, Lindsay would write to his sister Margaret to inform her that July 7th had not been his day to die.

Colonel Francis was found among the fallen. Among those who viewed the tall and eloquent patriot leader was Lieutenant Digby. "Even in death, he made me regard him with attention,"[19] noted the young Englishman in his journal. By now, a number of British officers were standing over Colonel Francis. One of the items removed from the fallen patriot was the watch given to him by his mother.[20] After removing the letters and papers from a shoulder bag which had been draped around him, the officers began to study them.

As they were reading his papers, unknown to them was the rifleman lining them up in his sights. The shooter knew that it would be a long shot. Aiming at a group of individuals bunched up, the sniper reasoned that his bullet would strike someone. Taking into consideration the distance factor and allowing for bullet drop, the sniper kept his sights slightly higher. Noting no wind, he exhaled half of his breath and slowly, slowly, pulled the trigger.

Crack! With tremendous force, a bullet tore deep into the heart and lungs of Captain John Shrimpton. An officer from the 62nd Foot, Shrimpton had been attached to Fraser's staff. As for the sniper, he got away. More sadness filled the air among the British officers witnessing the incredible shot.

The bullet that killed Captain Shrimpton was the very last shot of the battle. The Battle of Hubbardton was now history.

No one, including Burgoyne, St. Clair, Fraser, von Riedesel, nor anyone else had expected a battle in the wilderness just one day after the fall of Fort Ticonderoga. Although some fighting had taken place at Fort Ticonderoga, Skenesborough, and Fort Anne, Hubbardton was the first major battle of the Wilderness War of 1777.

On 7 July, elements of the Northern Army fought full-strength European units with centuries old traditions and well-trained professional soldiers. Yet at Hubbardton, the young and largely inexperienced patriot Continental and militia units commanded by Colonels Hale, Francis, and Warner demonstrated true professionalism, bravery, and a strong elan in combat against elite forces. Prior to Hubbardton, both the Germans and the British in the northern theater didn't have much respect for the Americans. After Hubbardton, that changed.

Tactically, the Battle of Hubbardton was a British victory. They had driven the Americans from the field. They did not, however, succeed in destroying the patriot force, and had suffered heavily themselves in the attempt. As for the patriots who fought that day, they eventually reorganized and returned to fight another day. Even the actions of the lone sniper demonstrated loyalty and the determination to succeed.

Some have alleged that by disobeying St. Clair's orders, Warner actually saved, in the long run, St. Clair's main force.[21] Had the battle not been fought, Fraser, pursuing rapidly, might have marched directly into St. Clair's main body and, supported by von Riedesel's full force, destroyed it. In turn, this would have comprised a crippling blow to the Northern Army and opened the road to Albany.

On the contrary, the Battle of Hubbardton halted the British. Weakened by heavy casualties, uncertain of the American strength, curious what patriot forces lay ahead, and fearing that more patriot forces were en route,[22] Fraser decided to no longer pursue. He was also too far away from Burgoyne's main body to risk another battle. As Digby wrote, "Not knowing, but the enemy might be reinforced and come again to attack."[23]

On the following day, Fraser withdrew. It must be noted that during this time, he had been operating in the dark. Colonel Jessup, along with the other loyalists and Indians attached to Fraser, had consistently failed to support the British general with information pertaining to the strength and locations of the patriot forces. The knowledge that he could no longer count on his irregulars also compelled Fraser to withdraw.

Casualties on both sides were horrible. This is especially so considering the sizes of the forces involved and the battle's short duration. Excluding the skirmishing, the entire battle raged for no more than forty-five minutes. Within these short minutes both sides sustained most of their casualties.

According to Cobb, 324 Americans were killed, wounded, or captured,[24] while the British suffered 198 dead or wounded.[25] Thus, over a quarter (27%) of those committed became casualties.[26] These are heavy losses, comparable to the casualty percentages of some of Europe's largest land battles, such as the 1815 Battle of Waterloo[27] or the American 1863 Battle of Gettysburg. The tally among commanding officers may be especially indicative, as among the British, Major Grant was killed and Balcarres and Acland wounded; whereas of the three patriot colonels, Francis was killed and Hale was captured.

According to Furneaux, the British incurred 50 dead and 100 wounded.[28] The Germans suffered 10 dead and 14 wounded,[29] for a combined total of 174.[30] Though Furneaux is not explicit on how many casualties the American's suffered, he cites the British and Germans as capturing 288 patriots.[31] Most of these were captured when the British mopped up the area within hours after the battle.[32] And Ketchum cites a total of 230 American prisoners of whom 17, including Colonel Hale, were officers.[33]

11:00 A.M.–12:00 P.M.

General Fraser, however, did not withdraw immediately. He was not in a position to do so. After establishing his pickets and dispatching a scouting party to check on the road leading southward to Castleton, Fraser began to deal with the numerous urgent matters that such an intense battle presents.

Utilizing Hubbardton's cabins for the treatment of the wounded and injured, throughout the entire day and long into the night the incapacitated were brought in, laid upon a table and treated as best as possible by medical personnel. By and large the medical aid was rudimentary at best, and a number of the wounded perished. Organizing the captive Americans into a work detail, the prisoners were forced to dig long trenches. Into these went the dead.

That afternoon, it began to rain. At first, it rained on and off. But in the late evening hours, the rains turned into a downpour.[34] Also when it rains in northern New York or Vermont, temperatures plummet, even in the summer. The cool evening turned into a cold night. This only further exacerbated everyone's misery. Especially those who were wounded. Dispatching parties to search the countryside for any food, Fraser was disappointed when they returned empty handed. No food was found. Worse, additional prisoners had been secured. Now there were more mouths to feed.

As they encountered officers and continentals fleeing from Hubbardton, St. Clair's aides learned that the battle was over. Noting that the massive distant noises and rumblings had ceased, Dunn and Livingston turned their horses around and raced back down Castleton Road to report their findings to St. Clair. Based on their information, St. Clair reversed his decision to return to Hubbardton. But he also decided not to proceed to Castleton. Instead, St. Clair issued the order to retreat to Rutland, which was located about seven miles to the east/northeast of Castleton.

Meeting with von Riedesel late that night, Fraser informed the German general that sometime in the morning, they would return to Skenesborough. Hopefully by then, the rain would lift. Fraser also cited that they were too far away from the main army. Though confident that for the time being the patriots posed no immediate threat, he felt remaining in place would be suicidal. Von Riedesel agreed.

There was more. In a soft tone for only von Riedesel to hear, Fraser confided to the German commander that he was no longer confident that England could secure a victory in the wilderness. "Jawohl!" was the German General's response.

TUESDAY, 8 JULY

Though he had initially wanted to leave on the morning of the 8th, numerous problems kept Fraser in place. For one thing, it was still pouring. The wounded continued to die. More prisoners were secured, and the doctors needed more time. Fraser also hoped that, perhaps, Burgoyne might appear with some new orders or a relief force of some sort would arrive to assist.

En route to Rutland, St. Clair decided instead to head for the town of Dorset, located approximately 25 miles further to the south. St. Clair wanted to distance himself further from the British. Concluding that Dorset, and not Fort Edward, would be the ideal site to rest and reorganize, St. Clair also dispatched a small force to Rutland to establish a straggler control point in that town. In the event that Warner and any of his men or any stragglers from whatever unit should appear, they were to be immediately redirected to Dorset.

WEDNESDAY, 9 JULY
4:00 A.M.

Departing Hubbardton, Fraser's force at first actually proceeded southward into the direction of Castleton. As for the more seriously wounded, they were left behind with one or two doctors and some assistants along with a small number of soldiers. The soldiers were to assist the medical personnel with the wounded and protect everyone from any bandits or Indians bent on looting, killing, or scalping. However, in the event that any patriot militia or continental force should appear, they were to surrender to them. Prior to his departure, Fraser assured them that an effort would soon be made to recover them.[35]

Arriving in Dorset, St. Clair immediately began to reorganize and rest his force. After marching and fighting for several days, St. Clair needed to halt for a while. From here, he also dispatched a series of letters to General Schuyler, various regional commanders, and to Vermont's leaders. In his letters St. Clair explained why Fort Ticonderoga had to be abandoned, why the Battle at Hubbardton had been fought, and why it was important to defend the Hudson. St. Clair also emphasized the importance of obtaining supplies and ammunition. Though acknowledging that losses had been suffered, St. Clair added that his strength was rising daily because more and more men previously feared to have been lost were returning from the wild.

Late that evening Generals Fraser and Von Riedesel finally returned to Skenesborough. It had not been an easy march. Cold rains had soaked them to the bone. Swamps, with water up to their waists, had to be crossed. Because the bridge crossing the Poultney River had been destroyed, a hastily constructed bridge needed to be built. For both Fraser and von Riedesel, the war in the wilderness had been a very difficult and trying ordeal.

What doubtless disturbed them most was that after their dogged pursuit of the supposedly beaten rebel army, they had not been able to finish the job against a ragtag force of amateur militia. Instead they had caught a wolf by the tail and been bitten badly. As the weary British and German soldiers finally got some rest they, were left to contemplate exactly how formidable a foe these roughhewn patriot backwoodsmen had turned out to be.

X

Fighting Off Marauders and Raiders

As St. Clair continued his retreat toward Fort Edward, the British-German force at Hubbardton was retiring, and while Lieutenant-Colonel Hill was withdrawing westward from his engagement near Fort Anne, another kind of retreat was also taking place. It was the flight of the refugees.

Terrorized by marauding Indian and loyalist bands, frequently augmented by Canadian mercenaries, and fearful of what might happen to them should they find themselves under British occupation, civilians began to flee en masse ahead of Burgoyne's army as it slowly proceeded southward. Perhaps Benson J. Lossing, the noted Revolutionary War historian, described it best: "As Burgoyne approached, the people fled, in terror and dismay, toward Albany, leaving the ripe harvest fields and pleasant homes to be trodden down or burned by the enemy."[1]

Suddenly, vicious raiders were everywhere. They struck far and wide rendering no place or person safe. Farms, homes, and settlements were specifically targeted. Raiders were encountered from Fort Chambly north of St. Johns to the outskirts of Albany, deep into Vermont and western Massachusetts, and through the entire Mohawk and Schoharie Valleys.

It would not be long before such news began to make the front pages of newspapers. In August, the *New Hampshire Gazette* reported that many of Albany's residents, terrified of the marauders, were leaving their town and fleeing southward. Citing how cruel the raiders could be, the New Hampshire newspaper reported how two little girls, innocently picking berries, were murdered and scalped.[2] Another pro-patriot newspaper, *The Massachusetts Spy*, reported that in the vicinity of

Saratoga, Indians were not only killing and scalping men, women, and children, but were also "making no distinction between [pro-patriot] Whigs or [pro-British] Tories."[3] Atrocities occurring in Pennsylvania, Maryland, Virginia, Rhode Island, and other colonial states were reported by other presses. Even the pro-British newspaper, *The New York Gazette*, published by James Rivington,[4] ran articles on atrocities.

Clearly, some of the newspaper accounts were inflamed and others were great works of propaganda. Yet tragically, there was much truth to the reporting.

Around Hubbardton, Skenesborough, Rutland, Castleton, Fort George, Fort Edward, Fort Anne, Oswego, Fort Stanwix, Rockingham, Bennington, Pawlet, and numerous other towns and settlements, the killing was rampant. Raiders struck as far east as Pittsfield and Peru in Massachusetts. Countless numbers of mini-battles were fought in and around inhabited areas, trapper cabins, and on private farms. On wilderness roads and trails private citizens and wagon drivers were ambushed. How many such private battles were fought cannot be known. In actuality, if one counted all of the numerous private battles which raged through the entire terrible Wilderness War of 1777 from Oswego to Massachusetts and from Canada to the outskirts of New York City, surely the violence included hundreds of incidents. These conflicts characterized the harshness of the Wilderness War.

Despite Burgoyne's explicit orders to refrain from unnecessary killing and scalping, and to spare women, children, and prisoners, his orders were largely ignored. The fate of John Allen was one such example. John and his entire family, along with three free African-American employees, were murdered by rampaging Indians serving as British auxiliaries. Afterwards, everyone was scalped and the entire farm was burned to the ground.

Torture was also rampant, as evidenced in the vicinity of Fort Miller. Here German soldiers recovered the body of a patriot officer who had not only been scalped but an examination revealed that the soles of his feet had been sliced off with a knife. After examining the dead man, Doctor Wasmus concluded that he had been tortured prior to dying. By now, Wasmus was fully aware that savagery and viciousness had been given free rein across the wilderness. Once again, in disgust, the chief ranking German medical officer voiced another strong protest not only to his commander, General von Riedesel, but directly to Burgoyne as well.

Most of Burgoyne's British and German army regulars observed his orders and, by and large, acted with civility. The fact that the European units had chaplains attached tremendously helped to reduce brutal incidents that would be known in future years as "war crimes." A number of the higher ranking British and German commanders of aristocratic background also regarded themselves as true gentleman and would not tolerate excesses. If a soldier was caught committing an offense, punishment was meted out. By the time Burgoyne's campaign terminated with his surrender in late October 1777, a number of British and German soldiers, accused and found guilty of crimes, had been punished. Although the lash was commonly used, cases of execution were known to have been meted out. Even Burgoyne himself was reported to have intervened to prevent an atrocity. Such was the case one evening when the general ordered that three captives, selected by his auxiliaries for torture, "were not to be roasted and eaten."

However, when it came to the likes of Chevalier St. Luc, Charles de Langlade, "Captain" Colin Campbell, and the Jessup brothers, different standards held sway.[5] They never had — nor cared to have — firm control of their Indian, loyalist, and mercenary personnel. Released into the wilderness, they acted with little civility; in fact, from the beginning many of them had volunteered solely to plunder, caring little for British strategic goals in the campaign of 1777. Loot was their only concern. And Barry St. Leger, a British army general pushing eastward from Oswego to link up with Burgoyne, was known to encourage scalping, and he did allow some captured military personnel to be tortured. Surrounded by vicious personnel such as Colonel John Butler, his son, Captain Walter Butler, and other members of the Johnson clan,[6] St. Leger frequently looked the other way when excesses were committed. His offer of monetary payment for scalps did not help either. A simple review of some of St. Leger's directives shows that terror against the civilian populace was meant to be one of his tools of warfare.

> Marauding parties fell upon isolated families like lighting bolts from the clouds, and the blaze of dwellings upon the hills and in the valleys nightly warned the yet secure inhabitant to be on the alert. Their dwellings were transformed into blockhouses. The women were taught the use of weapons and stood sentinel when the men were at work. Every man worked armed in his field.[7]

The marauding situation worsened when Burgoyne's army, after penetrating deeper into the wilderness, began to run out of supplies, especially food. As the British supply line lengthened and shortages consequently intensified, stronger efforts were made to secure foodstuffs from the local populace. But when the irregulars failed to produce enough foodstuffs, hungry soldiers took over the mission of procuring sustenance. And with hunger gnawing at their insides, whenever they encountered resistance, ugly incidents were bound to occur. Prolonged hunger could drive even an innocent soldier to the edge of barbarity.

By the time Burgoyne surrendered, stories of British-sponsored atrocities, murder, and torture had made their way all the way to England. Disgusted with such horrors, those in the British Parliament and press who resented and opposed the war and King George III's colonial policies, used the atrocities as fuel in voicing their resentment against the war. "We employ the savages to butcher them, their wives, their aged parents and their children."[8] So screamed Edmund Burke in the Parliament.

Yet for the marauding parties, raiding was by no means an easy undertaking. Unlike in Europe where marauders and requisitioning parties could secure whatever they desired by simply appearing at a docile town or farm, in frontier America there existed a force that was unknown in Europe—the armed citizen.

Frustrated, angered, and determined to survive and protect what they regarded as theirs, armed citizens struck back. Many succeeded in defending their homes and farms. Here and there, entire settlements and towns successfully held off raiders or requisitioning parties.

Among themselves neighbors organized various defense measures. When neighbors heard shots and the noise of a nearby battle, they rushed in with guns to assist.

Entire communities established defense perimeters. People slept at night in designated cabins and barns while others stood guard with guns. Many cabins were turned into blockhouse positions. As verified by an old account, "The inhabitants throughout this part of the country having been much harassed by the Indians and Tories, and in constant danger of their lives, were consequently under the necessity, for their own safety, of building, at different stations, what they termed block houses."[9]

Dried meat, fish, and various foods, along with extra guns, bullets, and gunpowder, were stored within each blockhouse. Holes were cut into the sides from which the tip of a rifle or musket barrel could be expended outward. Barrels and pails of water for drinking and fighting fires were placed inside. Sand was strewn on the top of cabins and buildings to extinguish fire arrows. In some places towers were also erected from which riflemen could fire down on any opponents. During nighttime hours armed civilians patrolled designated areas.

Armed civilians shot and killed not only British and German regulars but also many loyalists, Canadian mercenaries, and Indian raiders. Crime, always problematic during periods of chaos, was kept to a minimum due to the number of armed and active citizens. Years later, James Madison, one of the authors of the famous eighty-five letters which became known as "The Federalist Papers," would recall those days of 1777 when armed civilians successfully protected themselves and inflicted heavy causalities upon Burgoyne's army. As Madison wrote, "Those who are best acquainted with the late successful resistance of this country against the British arms will be most inclined to deny the possibility of it. Besides the advantage of being armed, which the Americans possess over the people of almost every other nation..."[10]

Well before the battles of Bennington and Saratoga had been fought, armed citizens succeeded in creating tremendous hardships for General Burgoyne. Besides inflicting casualties upon his army, armed citizens also defended numerous farms, ranches, and settlements. They denied his army vital foodstuffs and other critically needed items. Frequently, when Burgoyne's soldiers or irregulars were dispatched with wagons to secure supplies from local inhabitants they not only returned empty handed but also with their wagons piled with their own dead and wounded.

The fighting that took place in these countless "private battles" was often harsh. Patriots, too, could be both vicious and brutal. Besides their personal guns, they utilized various other types of weapons to include spears, knives, and the favored weapon of many wilderness families: the tomahawk. Considering that most did not know the rules of warfare (and even if they did might not have adhered to them), private citizens frequently lashed out furiously.

Wounded or unwounded enemy personnel captured on private farms in the aftermath of a "private battle" were usually shot or hanged from the nearest tree. Sometimes, scalps were taken.[11] Cases occurred where commanders were known to have had their hearts cut out as they lay on the ground. Amid the endless forest battles and small skirmishes, savagery and brutality became the norm.

Besides the human story found within the massive cruelty of the endless forests, there is another story which must be told: the importance of the dog. To this day it remains virtually unknown, but in 1777 dogs, too, played their role.

From the very first moment when settlers entered the wilderness lands, they brought dogs with them. Dogs served as companions, protectors, and were used for hunting. Strong dogs were preferred, so that virtually every canine was a large-sized animal. Some of the dogs were even intermixed with wolves and coyotes. Amid the toughness of the frontier region, wilderness dogs were a breed unto themselves.

Animals that were known to be excellent watchdogs were frequently positioned hundreds of feet from a dwelling to provide the first warning. Unfortunately, this frequently exposed such a dog to danger. When marauders approached, the dogs barked and growled. Sometimes the very first fired shots were directed against a watchdog. In the Wilderness War of 1777 many a loyal dog perished saving the life of its owner.

Knowing the threat wilderness dogs posed, raiders killed each and every canine they encountered. Loyal dogs defended their masters and cases occurred where they died beside them. In turn, dogs bit and tore apart enemy soldiers, loyalists, mercenaries, and Indian warriors. Many a bandit or deserter bent on looting was forced to flee after encountering a vicious farm dog. Indian raiders were also superstitious about bells, so whenever they encountered a farm animal with a bell around its neck the animal was immediately shot or killed with an edged weapon.

Ironically, one of the main reasons the British launched the campaign of 1777 was to secure the patriot food base. Vital to the mission were the areas located in the Mohawk, Schoharie, and Hudson Valleys. Then they hoped to starve the patriots into submission. Though they succeeded in creating ample food shortages for the patriots, in actuality, by their actions, the British only created for themselves a much larger shortage.

By the late summer of 1777, in British-occupied cities and towns such as New York City, food shortages had become commonplace. By early 1778, the situation had only worsened. Food shortages, coupled with increasing prices, even reached England proper.

Yet, unlike the British who continued to experience food shortages, the patriots recovered much sooner. By late 1778, or within a year of the

Wilderness War of 1777, the patriots had succeeded in restoring to a large degree their food base. Though shortages were still known to exist, and occasionally food items were difficult to deliver to the Continental armies, by and large the patriots had it well under control. For the British, who occupied population centers more than the countryside, this would not be the case. The British army, along with the civilians found living within the areas of its jurisdiction, endured far wider and harsher food shortages.[12]

XI

Samuel Kirkland: Chaplain and Intelligence Agent

Despite its setbacks, the Northern Army was still in the field, and even growing. Volunteers, many angered by the real and, in some cases, imagined atrocities, continued to join. Weekly, shattered units regained strength with fresh volunteers, and additional units were raised. From out of nowhere, entire forces even appeared. Ably led and well-armed, they continuously strengthened the Northern Army. Though battered and still retreating, the army was surviving and resisting.

Noting that chaplains were needed, America's Congressional Congress began an effort to secure them for the Northern Army. One such person selected was Reverend Samuel Kirkland, who would become the army's Chief Chaplain.

Reverend Kirkland harbored a great deal of affection and respect for Native American Indians. He had spent much of his life living and working among the people of the Iroquois Confederacy. Fluent in their language, he was also an expert on their arts, culture, and customs.

Kirkland was also a well known and highly respected man amongst the settlers and trappers. Frequently, he served as an unofficial negotiator and translator between the Indians and whites.

When the Revolutionary War erupted in 1775, Kirkland was residing with the Iroquois. In May of that year, an Oneida chief who was one of Kirkland's former pupils wrote, in the English language, a work titled "Declaration of Neutrality." In front of a large number of chiefs and representatives from each of the tribes plus some white settlers, the Oneida read the proclamation in English. As he read, Reverend

Kirkland translated his words into the Iroquois language.

Despite the best efforts of Kirkland, the Iroquois Nations' Council of Mothers, and various chiefs to maintain Iroquois neutrality, it was to no avail. Within months of the Declaration of Neutrality, the Iroquois Confederacy began to split in different directions. Some sided with the patriots and others with the British. Tragically, the neutrality could not be honored.

Reverend Kirkland, however, strongly sympathized with the patriot cause. Kirkland knew that Europe's powers wanted to exploit the American continent and the rich resources of America's wilderness as well as its inhabitants—whether Indian, white, or black. An opponent of British rule, Kirkland also held the view that if royal rule could somehow be removed, the newly established American nation would be able to co-exist in harmony and economic justice with the Native Americans. In July 1775, Kirkland departed his beloved Iroquois Confederacy and wilderness to offer his services to the patriot cause.

Traveling to Philadelphia, he met with members of the Continental Congress such as John Adams. The Congress was keenly interested in keeping the Native Americans neutral, or if possible, to somehow win them over to the side of the patriots. America's Congress was also interested in the Indians' own concerns, to the point that in July 1775 it established an Indian Department. Congress also awarded Kirkland a sum of several hundred dollars for his previous Indian activities.[1] Prior to departing Philadelphia, Kirkland was formally tasked by Congress to urge the Iroquois Confederacy to remain neutral.

The Congress knew that if anyone could succeed in this endeavor, it was Kirkland. The Presbyterian Minister had already demonstrated competence and experience in this area as previously evidenced in Virginia in 1775. The Shawnee Nation, enraged by the continuing encroachment of white settlers and the killing of some of some of its members, sought to go to war against the whites. Seeking support, they approached the Iroquois in hopes of swaying them into a war. Kirkland, who at this time was residing among the Oneidas and Tuscaroras, convinced these two tribes within the Iroquois Confederacy to remain neutral. In turn, the Cayugas, Senecas, Mohawks, and Onondagas not only followed suit but succeeded in convincing the Shawnees to settle for a compromise with the Virginian settlers. Thus, a major war had been prevented.[2]

In January 1777, in the Onondaga Indian region, a Central Council was held. Representatives from all six tribes of the Iroquois Confederacy came to this council.[3] Unable to arrive at a solution, the Council declared that, "As of this moment, each nation would decide its own path." Excluding the Oneidas and Tuscaroras, who sided with the American cause, by and large the Cayugas, Senecas, Mohawks, and Onondagas supported the British.[4]

It is not known if Reverend Kirkland was present at this Council. It is known that in 1777 he joined the Northern Army. Possibly he did so at the urging of the Congress.

Kirkland also knew many of the hunters and trappers who roamed through New York's wilderness. Aware that they often came across information which could benefit the American cause, Kirkland undertook the mission of tapping them for this information. Grateful for his loyalty and assistance, America's Congress extended another $300 to Kirkland for his new services as a military chaplain and intelligence agent. Assigned to Fort Stanwix, deep within New York's wilderness, Kirkland served as an army chaplain for this outpost, while continuing to gather intelligence, and also performing his vital missionary and pro-American proselytizing among the Iroquois.

XII

Burgoyne's Plan to Reach Fort Edward

THURSDAY, 10 JULY

On this day General Burgoyne decided, through Philip Skene, to address the inhabitants of the region. During his association with Skene, Burgoyne had been constantly assured that, "The region is rife with those loyal to the English Crown." Skene, however, was not the only notable saying this. Others also assured Burgoyne that, "Masses will flock to you!" Realizing the vital importance of a solid loyalist backing, Burgoyne decided to issue another public statement in addition to his previous of 20 June. He figured that perhaps some of the inhabitants had not yet heard of his earlier proclamation.

In order to reach the populace, Burgoyne stipulated that on 13 July a delegation of ten representatives was to appear at Castleton to meet with Philip Skene. These representatives were to appear from each nearby settlement and town. Skene, in turn, would inform them as to what advantages lay in siding with the British, and he would attempt to recruit more loyalists for Burgoyne's army. After receiving Burgoyne's message through Skene, the representatives would return to their respective settlements and towns to deliver Burgoyne's message to their fellow neighbors and townsmen.

Burgoyne was hoping that a good dose of propaganda would work. A sinister message, however, was also included. Though it was not to be delivered immediately, Burgoyne informed Skene that should he encounter pro-patriot sentiment or any unruly citizens, he was to immediately warn them that any resistance to the Crown was not only futile but could result in a cruel fate.

During this time General Burgoyne also repositioned his forces. He needed to rest his army, bring up units and supplies still in the rear, and develop a new course of action. Three large assembly areas were established. Around Skenesborough was positioned a corps of British troops. Twelve miles to the east, in and around Castleton, von Riedesel and his German troops were posted, while General Fraser's corps encamped in the center between the two towns.[1]

Whenever an army advances a large distance, units have to be positioned along the way to maintain a solid communications and supply line. In Burgoyne's case he needed to maintain his ties with Canada. Because of the extensive distance, the entire 62nd Foot Regiment, commanded by Lieutenant-Colonel John Anstruther, along with the German Prinz Friedrich Regiment, commanded by Colonel Christian Pratorius, were positioned at Fort Ticonderoga. General James Hamilton was in charge of the whole, although in due course Hamilton, along with the 62nd Foot and most of the other German soldiers, would be recalled to Burgoyne's army where they would see much action in the vicinity of Saratoga.[2]

As for the various loyalist units, irregulars, and Indians, they were posted within the various corps, from which, on a daily basis, they conducted missions deep outside their assembly areas. Burgoyne also positioned his forces in such a manner as to confuse the patriots. "Will he advance down the Hudson or strike into New England? Will Connecticut be his true objective?" Such questions were raised in the Northern Army's high command.

By now rumors pertaining to the fall of Fort Ticonderoga were rife and flying far and wide. There were rumors of treason: that General St. Clair was actually nothing but a British agent in American uniform. It was said that St. Clair and Schuyler engineered the defeat to better themselves; stories that St. Clair was a coward were making the rounds. Perhaps the best one was how the British fired gold and silver coins from their cannons into Fort Ticonderoga. After filling his pockets with British gold and silver, St. Clair "sold" the fort to the enemy.[3]

Totally disgusted with what had occurred, Abigail Adams, John Adams' wife, wrote to her husband, "How are all our vast magazines of cannon, powder, arms, clothing, provision, medicine, etc., to be restored to us? But, what is vastly more, how shall the disgrace be wiped away?"[4]

In response John Adams wrote back: "I think we shall never defend a post until we shoot a general and this event in my opinion is not far off. We have suffered too many disgraces to pass unexpiated."[5]

To counter such criticism and prepare himself for a possible Congressional review, St. Clair wrote a number of letters to various officials explaining why he had authorized a retreat and what had been done since.[6] Fortunately for St. Clair, despite the heavy criticism, many soon came forward to support him.[7] And as more military events unfolded, it actually became evident that despite the loss of Fort Ticonderoga, the patriot position was better off as a result of St. Clair's retreat.[8]

Though Burgoyne had positioned his army into three major assembly areas, he knew that he could not sit very long in Skenesborough. Now, he was faced with the critical dilemma of how to reach his next objective: Fort Edward.

Constructed on a series of British works built between 1709–1757, Fort Edward was located where the Hudson River takes a sharp 90-degree turn as it flows south. Initially built on an island known as Roger's Island, by 1777 a part of the fort and its troop barracks were also established on the eastern bank of the Hudson.[9] It is also in this location that Wood Creek flows into the river.

In 1777 a small settlement[10] with one particularly prominent structure, referred to as the "Old Fort House," stood adjacent the fort.[11] Several small but critical roads went through this site as well. Therefore, it was a hub for both river and road travel. By advancing southward and capturing Fort Edward, Burgoyne would secure another vital position and additionally position his army no more than 45 miles directly to the north of Albany.[12]

The distance from Skenesborough to Fort Edward was about 23 miles.[13] En route to Fort Edward lay Fort Anne, where Burgoyne's spearheads had already battled it out with patriot forces. Fort Anne lies approximately 12 miles south of Skenesborough and about 11 miles north of Fort Edward.[14]

Previously in England, when Burgoyne had conferred with Lord Germaine, Lord North, and various other high-ranking political-military leaders about the upcoming campaign, a map was on hand. In faraway England, everything looked so easy. A series of water routes with land connections would be utilized. Across a series of water and land bridges an army of 10,000 would move easily to its main objective of Albany. Though problems might be encountered, by and large the plan appeared to be reasonable and even simple. In reality, the opposite was true.

To begin with no one, either in England or Canada, made a formal or proper terrain study. Armies of that era generally did not acquaint themselves with extensive terrain studies as they do today. But if someone on Burgoyne's staff had made a cursory study or received a proper briefing of the reality on the ground, perhaps, the entire campaign might have been addressed differently. But no such study was ever made. Soon, it would be proven that the wilderness terrain played a major factor in the British defeat of 1777.

In his pursuit of the patriots and through a combination of military actions, General Burgoyne found himself in Skenesborough. Now, he was faced with a serious dilemma: which route was he to take to Albany?

Initially, Burgoyne had not planned to head all the way down to the base of Lake Champlain. After capturing Fort Ticonderoga, his plan had been to cross over to the northern part of Lake George. This would be accomplished by utilizing the water route with its adjacent road. As previously mentioned, in England it all looked so simple.

Yet this water route, referred to as the La Chute River between Lake George and Lake Champlain, was nothing more than a narrow, rock filled creek with little depth. Here and there, trees collapsed in storms lay across the creek. Furthermore, in elevation, Lake George actually overlooks Lake Champlain by 200 feet, and its northern terminus consists of a waterfall, which is the source of the La Chute River which flows between the two lakes. The waters which feed the La Chute tumble from Lake George down a very steep slope, which of course needed to be bypassed by an army and its transport.

Adjacent to the tumbling waters a sizable path existed, though there was no formal road. Furthermore, this trail was exceptionally steep. In fact, it was so precipitous that if a man utilized the trail to reach the top, he had to walk bent over. As one proceeded upward to reach the top of this waterfall and Lake George, the trail became increasingly steep, and the slope around the waterfall was heavily forested with thick trees and heavy brush on both sides.

From Fort George, at the northern edge of Lake George, to Fort Edward located on the Hudson River, the distance was about 12 miles. It's important to note that a fairly good and sizable road existed between the two. And once Fort Edward was reached, the most difficult part of the wilderness crossing would be overcome.

In order to revert to his original plan, Burgoyne would first have to return to Fort Ticonderoga. To do so, he would have to recall his soldiers from Castleton and the various other locations back to Skenesborough and then proceed—traveling by boat—about 25 miles back down Lake Champlain to Ticonderoga. Once there, via the creek and the narrow trail linking the two lakes, the army would make its way to Lake George. Though not impossible to do, this would entail certain issues.

First, the trail between Lake Champlain and Lake George would have to be expanded. After that, adjacent to the steep waterfalls which tumble from Lake George into the La Chute River, the British would have to haul all of their troops and equipment, which included everything from heavy cannons to gunpowder barrels, up the steep terrain into Lake George. This would be an extremely difficult task.

Complicating the march would be the lack of horses, oxen, harnesses, pulleys, and heavy ropes needed to pull the bateaux and other equipment up the fairly steep incline.[15] Additional ropes and pulleys could be obtained from naval boats and ships, but this would still not be enough. Furthermore, Burgoyne's deputy quartermaster general, Captain John Money, warned Burgoyne that between 300 to 400 bateaux would be needed to ferry the army in a reasonable period of time over Lake George.[16] If the army was transported across the lake to Fort George, the lack of horses and oxen would prevent the army from moving swiftly the approximately 12 miles to Fort Edward on the upper Hudson.[17]

And of course there was Burgoyne's friend, the loyalist leader, Philip Skene. Possessing over 56,000 acres of land,[18] Skene was already eyeing the future. Convinced that the British would win in 1777, Skene firmly believed that King George III would reward him with additional land and money for supporting Burgoyne. Possibly, the King would even appoint him to be the next Royal Governor of the Colony of New York. Skene was delighted that Burgoyne had advanced so far because this enabled Skene to recover his personal estate.

Skene, however, had another plan. He wanted to enhance the value of his property. In order to do this, one of the things he needed was a good road, running from Skenesborough to the Hudson River, on which he would be able to exploit his land much more. He would be able to easily transport lumber, produce, animal and fish products, and also iron ore from some deposits found in the vicinity.

To what extent Skene played a factor in convincing Burgoyne to construct a road is not known.[19] But it is known that he did play some role in it. Perhaps most influential was his claim that "many loyalists abound in the region." Already, Skene was visualizing how a newly constructed road, with an entire British army marching upon it, would rally more individuals to support the King's effort.

Burgoyne could wait no longer before making a decision. So he issued two orders. The first was that a road was to be built from Skenesborough through the wilderness to Fort Edward. But not totally swaying from the original idea of a Lake Ticonderoga-Lake George-Fort George-Fort Edward route, Burgoyne also stipulated that a large part of the army's personnel and materiel was to be transported via the originally planned route.[20] General Phillips was ordered to immediately proceed with this secondary project.

Simultaneously, Burgoyne put in an urgent request to Canada for more horses and wagons. To emphasize the importance of this matter, he wrote directly to Governor-General Carleton. In his letter Burgoyne requested that some of the British-based troops in Canada proper be dispatched into the Lake Champlain area. He was becoming increasingly concerned about his troop strength and the ever-growing supply line with his base in Canada.

As for the roads to be constructed, Burgoyne ordered that each army corps was to dispatch a number of soldiers, along with most of the Canadians and loyalists, to work on the project. Virtually every engineer officer and sergeant was tasked to assist. In the meantime, amid Skene's comfortable accommodations, Burgoyne would take it easy and wait for his reinforcements. Perhaps soon, he would even receive some news from General Howe in New York City or from Barry St. Leger pushing in from the west. Of course, there was also that sizable loyalist-Indian force augmented with British army advisors which was to appear from the southwest via the Schoharie Valley. Once strengthened with more men and materiel moving along on two newly constructed routes via Lake George and the new road through the wilderness, it would not be long before Burgoyne would, once and for all, finish off those dammed rebel patriots who were virtually on the edge of collapse.

Or so Burgoyne thought.

XIII

Bolstering Forces on Both Sides

Though he was far from where the action was taking place, General George Washington was carefully monitoring the events of the Wilderness War. Fully aware of the numerous problems and demands that a general has to contend with, Washington strongly sympathized with General Schuyler. Via numerous dispatches and letters, he kept in close touch with the Northern Army commander.[1]

Somehow, by mid-July, Washington had begun to sense that Burgoyne was actually headed for defeat. Washington also knew that if the British campaign of 1777 could be defeated in the wilderness, no matter how many reversals the patriots would suffer in the central and southern theaters of war, the ramifications of a defeat in the north would be disastrous for Great Britain, not only regionally but worldwide. As Washington wrote to Schuyler:[2]

> Though our affairs for some days past have worn a dark and gloomy aspect, I yet look forward to a fortunate and happy change. I trust General Burgoyne's army will meet sooner or later an effectual check and, as I suggested before, that the success he has had will precipitate his ruin. From your accounts, he appears to be pursuing that line of conduct that of all others is most favorable to us. I mean acting in detachment. This conduct will certainly give room for enterprise on our part and expose his parties to great hazard. Could we be so happy as to cut one of them off, supposing it should not exceed four, five or six hundred men, it would inspirit the people and do away with much of their present anxiety.

Washington, however, was not just sending messages. As mentioned previously, he was also assisting the Northern Army with its needs as best as he could. Besides dispatching two able generals, Benedict Arnold and Benjamin Lincoln, along with various advisors, Washington also sent a few units. Along with the famed rifle corps commanded by Colonel Daniel Morgan, Washington also dispatched General Glover's 21st Massachusetts (sailor) Regiment, 1,200 strong,[3] and General Thomas Nixon's 6th Massachusetts Regiment with a strength of 581 soldiers.[4]

Washington was not the only one reinforcing Schuyler. By now, the word was out, "The British Are Coming!" Largely motivated by fear and the horror stories of brutality, patriot militiamen and volunteers began to pour in from various corners of the New York wilderness, New England, and Vermont. With their arrival, they began to bolster the understrength continental units requiring additional manpower and the existing militia units grew larger and stronger. Even regional governments got involved, such as Vermont's and New Hampshire's.

Within days of the Battle of Hubbardton, Vermont's officials not only urged its citizenry to assist the Revolutionary War effort but also called upon neighboring states to assist in the struggle as well.

Concerned with events, New Hampshire's Legislature voted to raise an independent brigade.[5] Unanimously, the legislature also voted to appoint Stark as its commanding officer with the rank of general. Within a week, General Stark recruited a contingent of nearly 1,500 men.[6] In consideration that Stark "had had enough of both the Continental Congress and the Continental Army," New Hampshire's Legislature also authorized General Stark to act independently. In his operations against Burgoyne, he could operate as he saw fit.[7] Stark did have to answer to a superior command, but it was solely the New Hampshire Legislature.

New York, Vermont, and New Hampshire were not the only ones recruiting personnel. In early August, the Massachusetts General Court ordered one-sixth of its able-bodied men to report to the Northern Army.[8] By and large, the months of July and August may be characterized as a period undertaken by both sides to build up their forces, regain their strength, and prepare for the upcoming battle.

SUNDAY, 13 JULY
NEW YORK CITY

Once again, Generals Clinton and Howe met. Immediately, the northern campaign became the main discussion. As previously, when the two conferred about what course of action should be taken regarding the campaign of 1777, strong differences of opinion arose.

Howe argued that if he sailed southward, Washington would be faced with one of three options: engage him (Howe) directly, move northward into the Colony of New York toward Burgoyne, or directly attack New York City. Howe insisted that by forcing Washington into any one of these three options the British would prevail.[9]

Clinton, however, reiterated that the only justification Howe sought for going to Pennsylvania was to have a decisive battle. "But the rebels will be too wise to offer such a battle and we are powerless to force. Only territory would be gained." As for the British Army, Clinton insisted that "it would be tied down, holding on to this territory." Though acknowledging that some loyalists would be recruited, Clinton doubted their value when he added, "The territory could not be held by any quickly raised body of loyalists."[10] Though both commanders presented what, for them, was the most important course of action to take, in the end no agreement was made. Howe was still convinced that the key to victory lay in Pennsylvania.

Miles away, in Philadelphia, John Adams was reevaluating his former position regarding the fall of Fort Ticonderoga. Adams now concluded that, perhaps, the patriots would actually benefit from the seeming disaster. Writing to his wife Abigail, he elaborated:

> Discipline and disposition are our resource. It is our policy to draw the Enemy into the country, where we can avail ourselves of hills, woods, rivers, defiles, etc, until our soldiers are more inured to war. Howe and Burgoyne will not be able to meet this year, and if they were met, it would only be better for us, for we shall draw all our forces to a point too. If they were met, they could not cut off the communication between the northern and southern states. But if the communication was cut off for a time, it would be no misfortune, for New England would defend itself, and the south States would defend themselves.[11]

THURSDAY, 17 JULY

In the vicinity of Skenesborough no less than 500 Indian warriors suddenly appeared. For Burgoyne, this was a relief because his Indian reserve strength—through casualties and desertions—had decreased. The reinforcements would not only raise his Indian strength and bolster the morale of the other warriors, but also that of the loyalists and regulars. The greater number of these warriors hailed from the Canadian tribes,[12] however some Iroquois were numbered among the group. Along with the existing Indians, the new arrivals would also be utilized for scouting, reconnaissance, and ambushing.

Unfortunately for Burgoyne, these new Indians had been recruited by Chevalier St. Luc's and Charles de Langlade's agents who promised them loot and scalps. Such promises, of course, would soon cause both Burgoyne and the British high command immense problems.

In addition, some loyalists appeared at the British camps. But to what extent they were motivated by "loyalty to the King" could only be surmised. From the outset, the loyalists frequently argued among themselves. They quarreled about their command make-up, who was to do what in combat, various pay issues, what role they were to undertake, and how long they were to serve.

Some of the loyalists even demanded pay that was considered by many as outrageous. It is also now known that a number of the "loyalists" appeared simply to protect themselves and their families by currying favor with the invaders. They may have had no desire to serve the Crown, and in some cases were not only sympathetic with the patriots but were spying for them. Moving freely through the camps, they gathered up information, disappeared into the wilderness, and returned to the patriots with vital information.

Throughout July and well into August, combined bands of Indians and loyalists attacked indiscriminately. Though their raiding had commenced weeks before, by mid-July it had reached a new high.

Some of the raiders would be gone for days. On other occasions, the bands were under orders to secure only items (such as food, horses, and oxen) needed by Burgoyne's army. In such cases, the raiders could be accompanied by either British or German troops.

More often, however, the raiders spread throughout the wilderness region and New England attacking vulnerable settlers or small groups while under little or no discipline. It would not be long before Burgoyne was accused not only of employing vicious fighters but also of condoning their murderous activities.[13] Tomahawks were especially utilized. In his journal, Lieutenant Anburey described the weapon as, "this terrible implement of warfare."

As the threat of raiding parties increased, so did the defensive measures of the colonists; ambushes, for example, could be sprung by both sides. As the hardy people of the frontier geared for self-defense, easy targets became fewer and the hunters could become the hunted. The colonists' self-made blockhouses also proved to be of exceptional value in resisting raids. As noted, "Although often attacked, and sometimes with considerable force, [they were] attacked without much success, though with some loss to the assailants."[14]

And it would only get worse for Burgoyne.

XIV

Burgoyne Hacks His Way South

When the British began to construct their road to the Hudson, Burgoyne quickly learned that this would be a much larger and complex task than he had initially believed. From Skenesborough, bateaux and canoes could negotiate a short way southward along the narrow waterways of the Mattawee and Halfway Creeks which flow northward into and through Skenesborough en route to the base of Lake Champlain. But this was only for a short distance. The bulk of the move would have to be done overland and virtually through uncharted wilderness.

The closest straight-line distance from Skenesborough to the Hudson River bend, where a settlement by the name of Half Moon stood, was 20 miles.[1] In itself, 20 miles is not a difficult march for an army, but is a considerable distance to make passable against the accumulated strength of nature. And after reaching the Hudson River, there were another two miles of straight-line distance south to Fort Edward.

True, some trails and one very narrow seasonal road did exist. Other than that, there were no formal routes. As for the narrow road that connected to Fort Edward, it traversed hills, ravines, and creeks. Numerous small lakes, ponds, streams (some sizable), and huge swamps bordered both sides of this road. Thick trees, interlocked with tremendous amounts of brush and vines, filled the region. No fields or natural cleared areas existed along the route. In the true sense, it was nothing but an untamed wild.

At this time Schuyler knew that he could not halt Burgoyne completely. Knowing, however, that Burgoyne was making an attempt to reach the Hudson, Schuyler attempted to impede his effort. During this period when the Northern Army was gradually gaining strength, he concluded that if Burgoyne could at least be slowed, then much would be gained in the long run.

To impede the invaders' approach, Schuyler tasked Brigadier General John Fellows, the commander of a Massachusetts militia force, with the mission of creating obstructions. In support, Fellows also received the nearly 600-strong regiment commanded by General Nixon. Initially, Nixon's unit was based in the New York Highlands at Peekskill. On 12 July it arrived in Albany, and within days, it was ordered further north to Fort Edward. Side-by-side with Fellows' militiamen, Nixon's men worked hard to slow Burgoyne's efforts.

In warfare there are two main types of physical obstacles—man-made and natural—and Fellows' command incorporated both. Starting at Fort Anne, the road was torn apart. Every bridge was burned. Huge trees were dropped into the narrow road and creeks. Frequently, two or three trees were dropped together, and as they fell their branches interlocked. Most of the time the trees were dropped so that the tips of the branches would face outward. Those tasked to clear away the trees were forced at first to cut and pull away the branches prior to chopping away at the main trunk. Hours could easily be spent just clearing the branches, a tiresome and frustrating job. Once the branches were removed, the main trunks still remained, an even bigger task.

Aside from dropping trees, trenches were dug. Connected to nearby creeks and swamps, their waters flooded any dry land adjacent to the route and weakened the banks of the dirt road. Even if just six inches of water covered the ground next to the road, the wetness would prohibit anyone from utilizing the ground to camp, erect a tent, graze animals, or park a wagon with supplies. Wherever a stream flowed adjacent to the road, it was dammed up. Once a dam was created, the water would flow over and flood a portion of the road and any flat land near it. As more and more militiamen appeared, they too, were inserted into the project. Among the ax men and ditch diggers were a sizable number of African Americans.[2] They, too, had a stake in halting the British offensive.

Along with the obstacle building project, patriot patrols were dispatched to warn the populace, gather food, monitor and counter British, loyalist and Indian activities, to confiscate items from known loyalists, and to assist regional farmers in driving their farm animals to the safety of distant pastures or nearby swamps and forests. Many acres of wheat, barley, and corn were burned. Adhering to her husband's orders, Mrs. Schuyler torched the rich wheat fields she had planted ear-lier that year. As the fields burned, she drove her cattle into the nearby swamps and chopped down every fruit tree. The patriots were waging a type of warfare which in the future would be known as "scorched earth."[3]

As difficult as it was for the patriots, it was even more difficult for those assigned to the task of clearing the obstacles and developing the shattered and flooded road into a system to support the movement of large numbers of troops, wagons, artillery, and heavy equipment.

Around the clock, vicious black flies, known as "punkies," devoured Burgoyne's troops and laborers. The summer days were exceptionally hot. Nights were very cool, if not cold. July was also a very rainy month. Whenever the rains fell, temperatures plummeted. As the rain poured, water levels rose behind the dams created by the patri-ots. Frequently, before continuing on a stretch of road, the British first had to dismantle or, with explosives, blow up a dam to lower the water level.

Soldiers and laborers began to suffer from colds, fever, dysentery, and various other illnesses. Scurvy set in. Heavy work demands were placed upon the horses and captured oxen. Overworked, hungry, and thirsty animals collapsed. Whenever that occurred, a party of men would have to drag the carcass off the road and bury it to preserve hygiene. It was more work. And dozens of bridges had to be construct-ed during this long trek.[4]

Hunger, for the first time, set in. Burgoyne's supply line of 200-plus miles with Canada began to collapse.[5] As for the military hospital estab-lished in late June at Crown Point, it began to fill with the seriously ill and, for the first time, combat casualties. As the clearing crews slaved away, they cursed the patriots. Lieutenant Anburey noted in his journal:

> You would think it almost impossible, but every ten or twelve yards great trees are laid across the road! It was with the utmost pains and fatigue we could work our way through them. Exclusive of these, the watery grounds and marshes were so numerous that we were under the necessity of constructing no less than forty bridges to pass them. And over one morass there was a bridge of near two miles in length.[6]

In the meantime, as the British inched their way forward through the hellish wilderness, the Indian-loyalist raids continued on a large scale. Examining some of their victims, Doctor Wasmus was horrified to see that torture was still occurring. Again and directly, he voiced another strong protest to Burgoyne.[7]

Civilians, however, were not the only ones targeted. Patriot soldiers, militiamen, and their laborers also felt the fury. To travel alone was an invitation for death or capture. Supply personnel, especially those in small groups, were repeatedly struck. To counter these attacks, convoys were organized with scouts probing ahead and flanking the wagons. Extra gunmen were posted to each wagon. Upon his arrival with the Northern Army, Glover and his 21st Regiment were positioned near Saratoga. By the time the unit would depart the area, raiders had inflicted no less than fifty to sixty casualties upon it.[8]

Desperate to repel the raiders, Glover launched what in modern warfare would be regarded as an anti-guerrilla/partisan operation. Targeting a forested area not far from Saratoga, one late night Glover dispatched hundreds of his troops to first surround the woods. At the crack of dawn, the troops carefully swept the entire forest for any enemy personnel, though on that occasion none were found.

Realizing that Fort George and Fort Edward were not very strong positions, General Schuyler ordered that both be abandoned. He then ordered the army to retreat to an area dubbed Moses Kill, located about four miles south of Fort Edward and four miles north of Fort Miller on the Hudson's eastern bank. Initially built as a blockhouse by Colonel Samuel Miller, the fort stood about 47 miles northeast of Albany. To the south of the fort flowed the Batten Kill River, which emptied into the Hudson. The Batten Kill originates further to the east in the high hills and mountains near Manchester and flows westward into the Hudson. Immediately across the Hudson, about 12 miles directly southward stood the small town of Saratoga.

Fort Miller, unfortunately, was another weak position. General Schuyler quickly concluded that he could not make a stand at Fort Miller either, and his move to the area of Moses Kill was undertaken for strictly tactical reasons. The time to fight would be later, and farther to the south. Riding out of Fort Edward at the head of his troops, General Schuyler was followed by almost 3,000 Continental soldiers and about 1,500 militiamen.[9] This strength, however, did not include those still obstructing the road, those further to the west at Fort Stanwix, those assembling in the Mohawk Valley, those found further to the east in

Manchester, and those organizing or reorganizing new and old units in various regions of Vermont and New Hampshire.[10] The number also did not include those in and around Albany, or in the Schoharie Valley and the Highlands. Once finally assembled, the Northern Army's strength would rise significantly. Many months later the British high command would acknowledge that it had seriously underestimated the colonial capability to amass combat personnel. For the time being, however, Schuyler had to make do with what he had.

THURSDAY, 17 JULY

From his headquarters in New York City, General Howe dispatched a letter to Burgoyne. Though acknowledging that his intent was not to move immediately northward, Howe assured Burgoyne that in the event Washington decided to move northward, "I shall soon be after him to relieve you."[11] It would take several weeks before Burgoyne would receive this letter.[12]

SATURDAY, 19 JULY

As Howe prepared to sail on his expedition against Philadelphia, a man suddenly appeared at the British headquarters in New York City. Claiming that he had vital information, he reported seeing Burgoyne's troops on 10 July near Fort Edward. Howe was immediately notified of this.

By now both Howe and Clinton were fully aware that Fort Ticonderoga had fallen. But surely, they felt, this man must have erred. Fort Edward was some distance from Ticonderoga. Under no circumstances could Burgoyne have been able to move so fast. Or could he? Likewise, this man did not belong to any unit. Was he a patriot? Was he possibly passing on false information?

MONDAY, 21 JULY

A messenger runner appeared in New York City. After speaking with Howe, he was brought to Clinton. Of significance is that this messenger was the first one dispatched by Burgoyne to arrive safely through patriot territory. The messenger provided details of Burgoyne's capture of Fort Ticonderoga and how a road was presently being constructed through the wilderness to reach Fort Edward.

After speaking with the messenger, Clinton was convinced more than ever that Burgoyne's efforts needed to be supported. Perhaps the messenger was more candid and honest with Clinton than with Howe. Regardless, Clinton immediately dispatched a quick letter to Howe in which he proposed another plan, "Why not bypass the Highlands by advancing up the Connecticut Valley, while Burgoyne moved into Massachusetts for a junction east of the Berkshires? Such things may be at this instant done there as will decide the war. Forgive me if I give my opinion freely."[13]

WEDNESDAY, 23 JULY

Howe's first ships sailed away early in the morning. By the end of the day, the bulk of the fleet had departed. By midnight, messengers had been dispatched to both Washington and Schuyler to keep them informed. New York City's highly effective spy agency, which for days had been monitoring British activity, came through once again. Correctly, they reported that the British had boarded ships for their journey to Pennsylvania[14] and that the bulk of the fleet had sailed away.

That evening Clinton sat down and in disgust wrote a letter to his close friend, Lord Hugh Percy, Duke of Northumberland. He stated, "I fear it is elsewhere; I fear it bears heavy on Burgoyne. If this campaign does not finish the war, I prophesy that there is an end of British domination in America."[15]

XV

The Tragic Case of Jane McCrea

After reaching the ruins of Fort Anne, General Burgoyne's army painstakingly proceeded to work its way toward Fort Edward on the Hudson. They were not the only ones experiencing hardships, however. Farther to the north, at the Lake George-Lake Champlain waterfall portage, General Phillips was also having a hard time. Despite a virtually around-the-clock effort, it was slow going. Hauling up the bateaux, cannons, ammunition, gunpowder barrels, wagons, and various other supplies proved to be an extremely difficult task. Desperate for labor, the British even forced their captives to work.

Worn out ropes began to snap. Pulleys released. Whenever this happened, a bateaux or wagon would come crashing down. Sliding downwards and often loaded with supplies, it would strike rocks, boulders, and tree stumps. In most cases, the boat or wagon would shatter. Soon, bits and pieces of vehicles, along with wooden barrels, boxes, and other items were seen floating in Lake Champlain proper as the waters plummeting from Lake George's falls pushed the wreckage and lost items down the La Chute River into the lake itself.

Once a boat was somehow dragged over the portage and launched upon Lake George, it had to be loaded. Afterwards, it was floated for over 35 miles south to Fort George. There the bateaux was unloaded and its contents transferred to a wagon or cart. Then the boat was returned to its initial point. As for the wagons, carts, and the horses and oxen required to pull them, these had to be transported across the lake. Under such difficult conditions, troops, laborers, and prisoners sweltered throughout July.

Once a wagon was loaded, it had to travel over land about twelve miles from Fort George to Fort Edward. Again, this was straight-line distance. As for the road that weaved through the wilderness connecting the two forts, here and there it needed to be improved. Bridges needed to be reinforced or built, and thickets and brush growing upon the road had to be cleared. The nasty black flies constantly gnawed at the men and animals. Soon Phillip's men, like those hacking out a road further to the east, began to suffer from various illnesses including dysentery and scurvy. And the first complaints of "not enough to eat" were voiced as well.

While in Castleton, von Riedesel, the German commander, began to receive reports from scouts and loyalists that numerous supplies existed to the east in the Connecticut River Valley. Horses, along with "fat cows" and much grain, were reported to be in abundance. Experiencing his first shortages and knowing that the entire army was in the same position, von Riedesel concluded that Burgoyne's army could replenish its needs from raids in this area.

From the outset of the campaign, von Riedesel's dragoons, or mounted troops, had been without horses. What few they possessed were mainly large draft or work horses relegated to pulling the Germans' supply carts and wagons. But when orders were issued to dispatch even these horses to assist in the Lake George-Fort Ticonderoga work project, the proud, elaborately uniformed dragoons found themselves in more forlorn shape than before.

Since disembarking from their boats at Lake Champlain, the Germans had been moving on foot. Dressed in stiff leather breeches and clumsy leather boots adorned with spurs which caught on the thick brush, the Germans had found it exceptionally difficult to march. Whereas before at least their saddles and equipment had been placed into a cart or wagon and had been pulled by some draft horses, now each dragoon had to carry most of his equipment. Besides carrying his carbine, heavy sword, and the various bags which should have been slung over a saddle, they also had to pull and push along by hand the carts which contained their extra equipment, weapons, ammunition, and saddles. Concerned for the welfare of his troops, Von Riedesel concluded that the only way to mount his dragoons and obtain the extra horses needed for the entire German force (and English units) was by conducting a sizable raid into the Connecticut River Valley. Von Riedesel decided to approach Burgoyne with the idea of a large-scale raid.

In the present-day state of Vermont, after organizing his brigade, patriot General Stark moved to Charlestown during the last week of July. Charlestown was located in western New Hampshire on the eastern edge of the Connecticut River.[1] Acquiring additional volunteers at Charlestown, Stark commenced a vigorous training program. Though mostly from his home region in New Hampshire and the Hampshire Grants (Vermont), the volunteers came from various states such as New York, Massachusetts, and Connecticut. Among them was John Hakes, who hailed from Stonington, Connecticut, who would go on to distinguish himself in the battles to come.[2]

SUNDAY, 27 JULY

Another ugly incident occurs which involved a civilian: the killing of Jane McCrea. What, exactly, happened to Jane on that brutal day is still unknown and, practically speaking, will never be known. Various accounts exist. Although possibly there is a degree of truth to all of them, the entire truth is still not clear.[3]

Jane McCrea was approximately 20 years old. All accounts describe her as being exceptionally beautiful with long, flowing hair. Her family supported the patriots, and in fact her oldest brother, John, was a colonel in the Northern Army. But Jane was deeply in love with a young man named David Jones, who was a loyalist. In 1777 he was serving in Jessup's Corps with the rank of lieutenant.[4]

When Burgoyne's army approached Fort Edward, Lieutenant Jones, noting the danger and anarchy all around, and concerned for Jane's safety, decided to stash her away. On the other hand, Jane knew that the British army was approaching and, unlike many others who had fled, decided to remain near Fort Edward.[5] She reasoned that it would not be long before she and Jones could rendezvous. In the meantime another local woman, Mrs. McNeal, moved in with Jane. Though Mrs. McNeal harbored pro-patriot sentiments, she happened to be General Fraser's first cousin.

Supposedly Lieutenant Jones had dispatched a few Indians to pick up Jane to escort her back to the camp where he and many of the soldiers and loyalists were staying. On this particular day, both Burgoyne and Fraser happened to be there as well. Possibly the Indians who were directed to return with Jane were not properly briefed as to whom she really was and why she had to be escorted back. Therefore the Indians might have regarded her as just another prisoner to be secured.

Not far from the house where Jane and Mrs. McNeal were staying, Lieutenant Tobias Van Vechten, along with a sergeant and about twenty soldiers, had been manning an outpost which had been heavily attacked on that same day. The lieutenant, his sergeant, and a number of the others had been killed. One of the soldiers, Samuel Standish,[6] was slightly wounded and captured.

Jane McCrea knew that Jones was planning to come get her. When a number of Indians appeared instead, perhaps she offered some resistance. Since the Indians probably did not converse well in English, a further misunderstanding may have occurred. Forcefully grabbing Jane and the other woman, the Indians proceeded with them through the wilderness back to Burgoyne's camp.

En route to the camp, the Indians escorting Jane and Mrs. McNeal came in contact with another Indian party who had just been battling the patriots. According to Standish, these Indians were very angry and disgusted with the losses they had incurred while battling Van Vechten and his men. They began to argue over the prisoners. As the argument intensified, the Indians began to shove and strike one another. Suddenly one of them aimed his musket at Jane. Pulling the trigger, he killed her instantly.[7] Within moments, an Indian warrior named Wyandot Panther[8] ran up and, in a fury, scalped her. As for Mrs. McNeal, though she was not raped, most of her clothing was ripped off as she was forcefully stripped and battered.

When the party returned to the British camp, a wave of commotion was unleashed. A very large woman, Mrs. McNeal was viciously cursing her captors, the King, General Burgoyne, and everyone in sight. At that very moment both Generals Burgoyne and Fraser were conferring nearby. Hearing the ruckus, they rushed over to where the Indians and the prisoners were standing. Immediately, both generals noted that Panther was holding a scalp in his hands.

Burgoyne was furious! The sight of the very long, beautifully tended hair attached to the bloody scalp repulsed him. Worse, at this very moment, Lieutenant Jones also arrived. Spotting the hair, he just stood motionless. As Burgoyne raved and Mrs. McNeal cursed, Jones just stared at the hair of the woman who was soon to be his bride. In the meantime, General Fraser placed a cape over his cousin, Mrs. McNeal, and proceeded to remove her from the scene as she continued to scream vulgarities about how her friend Jane had just been murdered. It was an awful scene.

Indeed, a truly explosive situation had developed. If not immediately controlled, it could easily escalate into a large-scale fight between erstwhile allies with guns, knives, and tomahawks.

Cursing the Indians, Jones threatened to kill them. Grasping his tomahawk in his hand, he moved toward them. Some of his loyalist friends inched closer in support, realizing a fight might break out. Mrs. McNeal's harsh tongue only further flamed a very volatile situation. Realizing the danger, Fraser ordered his cousin to be immediately escorted to a tent. Refusing to budge, Mrs. McNeal had to be physically carried from the scene by several soldiers. As they carried her off, her repeated shouts of "Goddamn your bastard King!" were heard far and wide.

Somehow, Burgoyne succeeded in separating the two groups and restoring calm. He assured Jones that the matter would be thoroughly investigated and justice would prevail. He also ordered that Chevalier St. Luc and de Langlade along with various Indian chiefs were to meet with him early in the morning. The other patriot prisoner, Private Standish, was secured by the British.

MONDAY, 28 JULY

Still angry and upset over the previous day's murder, Burgoyne appeared for the meeting. Though St. Luc and some of the Indian chiefs appeared, de Langlade did not. This further angered Burgoyne, for the British general had ordered him to appear as well.

Burgoyne demanded a sentence of death for McCrea's killer. The other Indians in the party were also to be punished. Burgoyne declared that the killing was uncalled for and its perpetrators had to answer it.

Needless to say, the assembled Indians voiced strong resentment. St. Luc was especially argumentative. St. Luc argued that if the warrior was sentenced to death and the others were punished, this would not only lower the morale of the Indian contingent but could induce them to desert en masse. Several of the chiefs requested that the warrior be pardoned. In turn, they promised to curb their killing and scalping.

After conferring again with Fraser, Burgoyne recanted his order of a death sentence. He could not, after all, afford to lose his Indian warriors. However, not to be outdone and determined to get in the last word, Burgoyne stipulated that from now on each raiding party would have at least one British officer attached to it, and the officer would be in command of the raiding party. Otherwise, the Indians and loyalists would not be permitted to raid. Burgoyne needed to reestablish control.

Yet in the end, the deceased Jane McCrea struck the final blow.[9] Within days of her murder, Lieutenant Jones and his captain brother approached Colonel Jessup and even Burgoyne himself, requesting to be dismissed from the unit. Though their request was refused, the brothers deserted regardless and traveled to Canada.[10] Several other loyalists, disgusted by the events, went with them. And some of the Indians, angered by Burgoyne's directive and feeling that the British failed to appreciate their efforts, departed as well. Of historical significance is that in the latter part of July, the first sizable desertions among the irregulars occurred.

For the patriots, however, the killing of Jane McCrea developed into a major triumph. Patriot propagandists and storytellers had a field day. Though many other innocents had been killed and scalped, the killing of Jane McCrea was somehow different. The mood on the frontier took a final turn against the British as the story of Jane's murder spread like wildfire. Soon her name had become a household word. Presses ran articles about her murder and recruitment drives heralded her name. Eventually, even across the ocean, members of the English Parliament expressed shock and outrage at her fate. The British public was equally repulsed. All around the New England area hundreds of men shouldered muskets and rifles, drew knives and tomahawks, and sped off to join the war effort to avenge her. Very soon Burgoyne himself would feel the full fury of her murder. Near the bodies of fallen loyalists and English or German soldiers were found pieces of paper with a message. Scribbled upon them were words such as, "For Jane McCrea!"

TUESDAY, 29 JULY

On this day, Burgoyne finally reached Fort Edward.[11] Other than its ruins and some dilapidated buildings, nothing stood. But it did not matter. The important point was that Burgoyne was now on the Hudson only about 50 miles to the north of Albany.[12] At Fort Edward, he would wait for the remainder of his army to catch up, especially the vital cannons, equipment, and soldiers soon to arrive from Fort George. Burgoyne also decided to rest those who had toiled and marched through the wilderness from Skenesborough via Fort Anne to Fort Edward. After all, it had been a nightmare. During his trek through the wilderness, his army had moved only about one to one-and-a-half miles per day. In the meantime, Burgoyne developed some ideas on how to take Albany, but most importantly he needed to rectify his supply situation. And von Riedesel's request to raid the Connecticut River Valley looked more and more appealing. In the meantime, always seeking comfortable surroundings, Burgoyne moved into the home of William Duer.[13]

Just four miles to the south of Fort Edward at Moses Kill, General Schuyler was conferring with his staff. It was decided to retreat once again. The army would withdraw to Stillwater in the early morning hours of 30 July because Burgoyne's spearheads were just a short way up the road. In the event Burgoyne attacked, Schuyler felt he would be unable to fight off the British with the Northern Army's troop strength as it then stood. It must be remembered that during this time, General Schuyler lacked vital information as to Burgoyne's true personnel strength as well as his intentions as he took hold of Fort Edward.[14]

The fort itself, ringed by high terrain, had not been considered defensible, thus Schuyler's decision to abandon it was legitimate. The big question now was where the British would move next.

WEDNESDAY, 30 JULY

With a strength of approximately 4,000 men, Schuyler retreated further south, his rearguard torching everying in his wake, including Fort Miller. In the vicinity of where the Batten Kill flows into the Hudson, Schuyler crossed the river and assembled his troops on the so-called "Old River" or "River" Road. To his immediate south lay the hamlet of Saratoga. By crossing the Hudson, Schuyler placed a natural obstacle between the patriots and Burgoyne's army. Continuing to march south, the troops passed through the Bemis Heights. These were named after Jotham Bemis, a local farmer who also operated a tavern at their base. As some of Schuyler's troops marched past the tavern, Bemis, an ardent pro-patriot sympathizer, provided them with free food and spirits. Bottles of wine were passed out and canteens were filled with rum. Soon, joyous laughter and songs filled the air.

En route to Stillwater, small bands of loyalists and Indians continuously stalked the columns. Hiding on the eastern bank of the Hudson, they would snipe at the retreating columns from across the river. Finally patriot marksman Dirk Van Vechter had enough. Armed with both a musket and rifle, he slipped up to the bank and crawled to the edge of the river. Positioning himself among the trees and brush, he scanned the other side.

With eagle eyes, spotting an enemy positioning himself for a shot, Dirk drew a bead on him and fired. His opponent collapsed into the water and his lifeless form floated slowly downriver.

Dirk was an excellent shot. He knew his rifle and could hit targets well beyond 300 yards. He also had an amazing sense of where a loyalist or warrior would be attempting to hide. Positioning himself not far from where an opponent would appear, Dirk successfully hunted down a number of those attempting to snipe at his patriot friends. Within a short time, enemy snipers were no longer harassing Dirk's column, instead prudently deciding to stay a safe distance away.

At the end of the month General John Stark was still in Charlestown, New Hampshire. In addition to acquiring volunteers, he continued to train his men, with a strong emphasis on moving units through wooded and brushy terrain. To communicate effectively, Stark and his commanders developed an ingenious system using a combination of turkey, crow, and bird calls. A certain call, such as a double "Gobble, gobble!" meant the enemy is near. "Cluck! Cluck! Cluck!" meant to position a unit to engage the enemy. A sharp crow or raven call signified, for example, to withdraw or to move around a flank. Hand signals along with designated runners were utilized as well. Charlestown's citizens warmly welcomed Stark. Various foodstuffs, high grades of gunpowder, bullets, and musket balls were amply provided to the patriot brigade. Most of Stark's men carried the highly-prized weapon of the wilderness...the tomahawk.

SUNDAY, 3 AUGUST–THURSDAY, 7 AUGUST

Though elements of his army had already reached Stillwater in the late evening hours of 1 August, by the third of the month Schuyler's entire force was in position there. He now stood about 24 miles north of Albany.[15] During the withdrawal he had been forced to leave behind his private estate which was currently deserted.[16] Soon it would be used by General Burgoyne for his residence and headquarters. As for Mrs. Schuyler, she had been removed to Albany.

In Stillwater, General Schuyler rendezvoused with Colonel Thaddeus Kosciuszko. An emigrant from Poland who had adopted the American revolutionary cause, Kosciuzko had just recently been dispatched to the Northern Army once again. The Pole was familiar with the army because he had served at Fort Ticonderoga the previous year. Though Kosciuszko had strongly advocated the importance of fortifying Sugar Loaf Hill (Mount Defiance) overlooking Fort Ticonderoga and its defense system, unfortunately no one had heeded his warnings.

At Stillwater, Kosciuszko was constructing some defensive positions. But several days later, on 6 August, Schuyler issued an order to retreat further south and across the Mohawk River. Since commencing his retreat from the Moses Kill on 30 July, Schuyler's army had retreated about six miles to Saratoga, another 12 miles to Stillwater, and then another 12 miles to where the Mohawk River empties into the Hudson River right below the village of Half-Moon. It was a retreat of no less than 30 miles. Numerous streams and small creeks were crossed, and a number of crumbling old forts and blockhouses were passed as the men marched south. Throughout this time, Schuyler's rearguard continued to destroy every bridge they crossed and further obstruct the road. By now there was plenty of ground between Schuyler and Burgoyne, providing the patriots time to gather additional forces.

In the first days of August, General Stark crossed the Connecticut River and marched about 40 miles west to Manchester, Vermont.[17] En route, he crossed through what in future years would be known as the Green Mountain National Forest. Outside of Manchester, at the base of Big Equinox Mountain, which towers nearly 4,000 feet alongside the Batten Kill, Stark established his camp. Here, he also rendezvoused with Colonel Seth Warner who had reorganized his Green Mountain Boys after the Battle of Hubbardton. Warner and his men were now ready for another fight.

General Schuyler was not only concerned with the front immediately to his north but also with the immense area that spanned west to Oswego on Lake Ontario. The New England states also fell under the jurisdiction of his Northern Army.

To maintain proper command and control of this vast region, Schuyler dispatched Major General Benjamin Lincoln to take command of all the forces within New England. Schuyler knew that General Washington, the commander-in-chief, held Lincoln in high esteem, having once stated, "He [Lincoln] had proved himself on all occasions, an active, spirited, and sensible man."[18]

Noting Manchester's key location, General Lincoln established his regional headquarters there. He also attempted to place Stark under his command, incorporating his brigade into the Northern Army, but Stark would have none of it. He argued that he was a general by virtue of a decision by New Hampshire and not the Continental Congress.

Therefore, insisted Stark, "I and my men fall solely under the authority of New Hampshire's General Court. We are not under the Continental Army, the Continental Congress, Washington, Schuyler, the Northern Army, or anyone else. And that is that!"

Unable to persuade him, Lincoln immediately reported Stark's stance not only to General Schuyler but to the Continental Congress. Meantime, until otherwise dictated, Stark would be on his own.

This was very bad news for Schuyler, for it was he who had initially advocated placing troops in Vermont's border region to harass Burgoyne's left (eastern) flank. After hearing Schuyler's plan, General Washington fully agreed to it, but if Schuyler failed to maintain full command and control on that sector of the front, his operations could be jeopardized.

Schuyler, however, was not the only one receiving bad news in early August. On the third of the month, Burgoyne received Howe's letter of 17 July informing him that the British army in New York City had moved against Pennsylvania rather than north to join forces at Albany. Burgoyne and his army would be on their own.

FRIDAY, 8 AUGUST

On this day, Stark marched his force from Manchester to Bennington. Located about 22 miles to the south/southwest of Manchester, Bennington was also in Vermont but just several miles east of the New York border. From where Stark was now positioned, Saratoga lay 30 miles to the northwest and Albany some 30-plus miles to the southwest.

Stark knew that Bennington contained a vital military depot. Additionally, he sensed an opportunity to strike Burgoyne's left (eastern) flank as he continued to march southward. In fact, though Stark refused to acknowledge the Northern Army's authority, he did inform Lincoln that his intent was to attack Burgoyne's left flank. Although Stark did not get into any specifics as to how, where, and when this would be accomplished, his words assured the patriot commanders that a planned action was pending. In the meantime, Colonel Warner was instructed by Stark to remain behind in Manchester.

Upon arriving in Bennington and being informed that Indian and loyalist raiders were in the vicinity, Stark dispatched a force of 200 men under Lieutenant-Colonel William Gregg to proceed nine miles northwest across the New York border into the vicinity of present-day North

Hoosick, which in 1777 was called Sancoick.[19] Their task was to repel any raiders, obtain fresh intelligence, and warn Stark and his main body of approaching enemy forces. Among those who set out with Gregg was a young volunteer names Eleazur Edgerton.

Near the settlement of Sancoick a series of rivers and creeks converged, one of which is called the Hoosic River. Originating in the high terrain of southwestern Vermont and northwestern Massachusetts,[20] this river flows northwest until it empties into the Hudson. Another river is the Walloomsac which, weaving westward, flows into the Hoosic. Another stream, known as Little White Creek,[21] flows southward into the Walloomsac less than a mile from where it joins the Hoosic. And just slightly to the north of this entire river junction stood a bridge, which in 1777 was known as St. Luke's.[22]

Though not very long, St. Luke's Bridge spanned a deep ravine, through which flowed Little White Creek en route to the Walloomsac. The bridge was part of a thoroughfare known as the Great Market Road, which connected to an intersection located just to the west but within eyesight of the bridge. Around this intersection stood the small settlement of Sancoick, which was bisected by another creek known as the Owl Kill. A small bridge, located within Sancoick, spanned the Owl Kill, which in turn flowed into the Hoosic River.

The Great Market Road continued westward beyond the intersection all the way to the Hudson River, Albany, and other sites. The other roads that passed through this intersection led eastward to Bennington; northwesterly to such centers as Cambridge, Batten Kill, Fort Edward, and Skenesborough; and southward into Rensselaer County.

Near the St. Luke's Bridge stood a mill, which in 1777 was fully operational. After securing the bridge and mill, Lieutenant-Colonel Gregg moved his force to Sancoick, from which he dispatched some patrols further out into the countryside. Noting the importance of the St. Luke's Bridge, the patriot commander positioned a handful of men to guard it and the valuable mill. Among those positioned to guard St. Luke's Bridge was Eleazur Edgerton.

Despite his recent Indian reinforcements, Burgoyne's force was still far from being sufficiently manned. Supplies were barely trickling down along his supply route from Canada, and Howe's letter of 17 July caused further worry. True, the forces of Barry St. Leger, Chrysler, and MacDonell were yet to link up with him; but these forces, largely comprised of loyalists, had limited British-German army personnel.

Burgoyne knew that, sooner or later, he would need sizable reinforcements. But that was still down the road. Perhaps, by then he thought, the situation would improve.

One advantage that Burgoyne enjoyed was that his guns and transport moving along the Lake George-Fort George route and the wilderness road were beginning to arrive. And, of course, additional supplies would soon be forthcoming from Bennington. Once properly provisioned, the British army would be strengthened. So, for the time being, Burgoyne would remain in William Duer's home, enjoying rare comfort, and planning for further actions.

SATURDAY, 9 AUGUST–SUNDAY, 31 AUGUST

For quite some time, Schuyler had been envisioning ways to conduct sizable long-range raids deep into Burgoyne's rear. He especially wanted to wreak havoc on Burgoyne's lines of supply and communications. A strong tactician, Schuyler concluded that one of the keys to a patriot victory lay in isolating Burgoyne as much as possible.

Though large forces had not yet been committed to that purpose, Schuyler did have teams and individuals probing deep into Burgoyne's rear areas. One such team, headed by a scout named John Benson, whose nickname was "Barefoot Benson," traveled far beyond Crown Point. Benson's mission was to ascertain if the British high command was moving any fresh forces into the region to assist Burgoyne. To accomplish their mission, "the scouts proceeded through a dense howling wilderness as far as Schroon Lake."[23]

Late one night, as they lay a short distance apart in the very cool night and slept, they were suddenly awakened by a commotion. Someone was approaching...very slowly. After one or two light steps, they halted. And so it went. As the form neared, Benson and his partner took aim and fired.

There was a groan, followed by the noise of a collapse and something momentarily struggling on the ground. Then only silence. Fearing the approach of an enemy force, both scouts remained vigilant. At the crack of light, they approached their victim. To their surprise, it was a huge deer.

Fluent in Dutch, English, and French, and posing as a pro-British wine salesman, Colonel Cochran was sent directly to Canada on a spy mission. In the area around Montreal he obtained valuable information pertaining to General Burgoyne and the British campaign of 1777. The patriot spy network was yielding results.

Initially, Colonel Cochran was to return on a ship bound for New England. Because his identity was revealed in Canada, however, he was forced to flee across the St. Lawrence River. Then he had to undertake a long one-man wilderness journey in order to reach Schuyler's headquarters in Albany. In consideration of his age and the fact that he was not an outdoorsman, the trek was exceedingly difficult.

Frequently he had to avoid roads and trails for his own safety. Cold night rains drenched him. Hunger and malnourishment set in. Danger lurked everywhere. And the closer he neared the British lines, the chance of death or capture rose.

In the vicinity of Half-Moon, he spotted a log cabin and proceeded to it. Exhausted, he collapsed to the ground and had to crawl on his hands and knees. Approaching the rear of the cabin, he heard voices. At that very moment, several men were discussing how a handsome monetary reward was being offered for a spy fleeing from Canada. As they conversed, the colonel realized that they were actually talking about him. Comments were even made about the colonel's physical description which fit perfectly. Someone added that such a man had just recently been seen in the area.

To Colonel Cochran, it was obvious—they were loyalists. As they conversed, the colonel sneaked away and hid in the nearby woods. Soon the three departed. Desperately seeking some food and drink, Colonel Cochran entered the cabin. His intent was not to stay but only to find some food.

Unknown to him, there was a woman inside. To her, it was obvious that he was the man her husband and her two brothers-in-law were seeking. Begging for help, Colonel Cochran suddenly collapsed before her.

Though the woman's husband was a loyalist, her sympathies lay with the patriots. In the back of the cabin's fireplace was a small storage room that also contained a bed. Helping him into the bed, for the next several hours the woman nursed Colonel Cochran and was eventually able to revive him. She also informed him to remain absolutely quiet should her husband reappear.

That evening a meeting was conducted in the cabin. A discussion arose on how to find the spy-colonel and divide the reward money. From where he lay, Cochran heard everything. As for the woman, she positioned herself in such a way that in the event her husband needed anything from the storage room she could just stand up and say, "I'll get it."

The next morning, the woman escorted Colonel Cochran into a nearby forest. For nearly a week, she continued to nurse him until he regained his strength. With fresh, warm clothes and a package of food, he succeeded in reaching the Northern Army's headquarters in Albany with his vital information. The newly appointed commander of the army, General Horatio Gates, was tremendously pleased to hear that in Montreal many had already written off Burgoyne and the entire campaign of 1777 as a failure.[24]

By the end of August, the Northern Army had scouts ranging far across the wilderness. But they were not just bringing back information. Many of them were also stalking Burgoyne's men. Loyalists and Indian raiders were especially targeted and taken down. Knifed, shot, and tomahawked corpses lay all the way from Fort George to Fort Edward. Oftentimes a piece of paper invoking the memory of Jane McCrea would lay upon a corpse. Snipers thinned Burgoyne's ranks and stories of ghoulish devil forest fighters appearing from out of nowhere filtered through the ranks.

They always struck swiftly and with skill. Rarely, if ever, did they belong to a regular Continental or militia unit. Usually operating alone or in small groups, they waged their own kind of war in the wilderness. To the British and their allies, they were truly demons of the forest. Amid the wooded hills they maneuvered with ease, targeting everything from deserters to columns. And they did not take prisoners.

Proficient with a rifle, bow and arrow, knife, or tomahawk, a "devil fighter" would cautiously stalk a target. Suddenly, from out of nowhere, a rifle would crack or an arrow, its tip frequently drenched in human or animal waste for extra lethality, would be released. As a victim collapsed dead or mortally wounded, an eerie silence followed.

But not for long.

Another shot or arrow would come flying in, followed immediately by the sharp bark of a wildcat, bear, wolf, or other frightening creature. Its pitch would be heard far and wide, its cry chilling in nature. It was not the scream of an Indian, for Indian war cries were emitted from a human. Out here, there was no human.

Stories of werewolves, brought over from Europe, raced through the minds of those who were exposed to these nocturnal attacks. Tightening their grips on their weapons as eyes searched through the brush and forests for a target, the invading forces braced for more.

Then it happened! The sudden scream of a charging madman, his face and neck painted entirely in blue or black, riddled with colored stripes or spots. A black or dark bluish cape of some sort adorned the demon. Moving swiftly in moccasins, the demon would dart in and out amid the trees and brush like a lightning bolt. Always at hand was a tomahawk.

Raising their weapons, the soldiers or loyalists attempted to take aim. But it was to no avail. In a flash the forest fighter disappeared. The blast of a volley would be heard rocketing through a forest. Yet, mass firings rarely, if ever, brought down such a hellish fighter.

Sheer terror continued to grip those being stalked and word of harsh attacks spread. For those caught up in this madness, such sounds and sights would be the last that many would hear or see prior to being shot, knifed, or tomahawked.

Of course, it made no sense. But in the Wilderness War of 1777, many things made little or no sense.

XVI

The Battle of
Bennington

MONDAY, 11 AUGUST

Prior to this date, a group of approximately 200 Rangers had suddenly reported to Colonel Warner's regiment in Manchester and requested to join his force. Excellent woodsmen, all were proficient with rifle and tomahawk. And in central Massachusetts, from the town and county of Worcester, a former British army officer, Major John Rand, organized a force for Schuyler's Northern Army. Though getting on in years and a retired former British army officer, Major Rand sympathized with the American cause. Organizing a force of nearly 100 fighters, he drilled and trained them in the art of warfare. Knowledgeable about how a battle must be fought in forested terrain, Rand emphasized the importance of rifle and musket shooting and how to rapidly deploy into a line of defense when riding or marching forward and suddenly encountering an enemy.

An emphasis was also placed on skirmishing, firing from behind cover, and withdrawing while under fire. Though they would fight mainly on foot, each soldier was mounted on a horse for mobility. Extra packhorses, carrying supplies and ammunition, were part of the unit. In the meantime, more and more individuals appeared at the recruiting offices of the Northern Army to add strength to the various existing units. Among them were a sizable number of former military and militia servicemen. By mid-August, General Schuyler's army was not only growing numerically but also qualitatively.

Early that morning a force from Burgyone's army under a German officer, Lieutenant-Colonel Friedrich Baum, departed from Fort Miller.[1] Baum's mission was to secure the patriot supply depot reported to be at

Bennington, and to requisition horses, cattle and foodstuffs from the surrounding area. To accomplish his mission, Baum was provided a mixed force of Germans, British, Canadians, loyalists, and Indian warriors.[2] Of the 374 Germans, 250 were dismounted dragoons and were Baum's own troops.[3] The remaining 124 Germans, provided by General von Riedesel, were the Brunswicker light jaeger (hunter) infantrymen.[4] For extra firepower, he was provided two 3-pound cannons.[5] Because the dragoons lacked horses they marched with the rest of the column; other than Baum and a few others, the force moved on foot.

Captain Alexander Fraser commanded the British company. Colonel St. Luc's son-in-law, Captain Charles-Louis Tarieu de Lanaudière, and a Captain Colin Campbell commanded the Indians. Baum spoke no English, making him a rather odd choice to command an expedition into the patriots' civilian rear areas. He was given three officers for assistance, however: British army Captains Laurentius O'Connell and Desmaretz Durnford, an engineer expert, and one loyalist officer, Captain Samuel MacKay. And Phillip Skene, newly promoted to colonel, also came along. It appears, however, that Skene did not command the loyalists.

Since it is known that prior to 11 August, Skene had been assuring Burgoyne that the country to the east, "is swarmed with men who wished to take up arms for the King,"[6] and he claimed to have a strong knowledge of the region, Skene was probably posted to serve as both an advisor and a recruiter of additional loyalist manpower. Other loyalists who accompanied Baum included Colonel John Peters, who marched with his Queen's Loyal Rangers unit, Captain Justus Sherwood, and Captain Ebenezer Jessup, whose unit was also committed.[7] Doctor Julius Wasmus was assigned to serve as Baum's chief medical officer.

Initially, when von Riedesel had proposed to strike eastward into the Connecticut River Valley, he only wanted to conduct quick hit-and-run types of raids with a small force. But in time, Burgoyne developed von Riedesel's proposal into a much larger operation.

Burgoyne was possibly even thinking of shifting his entire operation away from Albany and into New England proper. The thousands of British troops occupying southern and eastern Rhode Island could participate in such a thrust.[8] Originally, in his "Thoughts," Burgoyne did advocate a conquest of the New England states by gaining control of the Connecticut River Valley. He wrote, "Should the junction between the [British] Canada and Rhode Island armies be affected upon the

Connecticut, it would not be too sanguine an expectation that all the New England provinces will be reduced by their operations."[9]

By dispatching a large force, Burgoyne might have been speculating that its appearance would demonstrate British strengths and, psychologically, induce New England's populace to rally to the Crown. Perhaps Skene was correct after all.

On approximately 8 August, Lieutenant-Colonel Baum received Burgoyne's instructions on how he was to conduct the operation. The plan called for Baum, after departing Fort Miller, to cross through the pass between the Batten Kill and Hoosic Rivers in the vicinity of Cambridge and proceed eastward into Vermont. Once there, he was to proceed to the town of Arlington, located on the Batten Kill, where he was to await a detachment of regional loyalists. These men belonged to a unit commanded by Captain Justus Sherwood who, at the moment, was serving with Burgoyne and was posted to Baum.

Once the two forces rendezvoused, they were to proceed north for about nine miles to Manchester. Then Baum was to dispatch a force of Indians and light troops[10] northward into the Otter Creek area and also directly eastward to Rockingham. In the event that "no enemy is in force in the neighborhood of Rockingham," Baum was to cross over the Green Mountains toward that town which was located nearly 30 miles almost directly east of Manchester near the Connecticut River's western bank. "There, you are to remain as long as necessary to fulfill the intention of the expedition from thence."

From Rockingham, Baum was to march southward for about 30 miles along the western bank of the Connecticut River to Brattleboro, also in Vermont but adjacent the Connecticut River and about 9 miles from the Massachusetts border. From Brattleboro, Baum's force was to march westward through southern Vermont via the Green Mountains to re-enter New York, thence directly westward to Albany where he was to link up with Burgoyne. In terms of distance, Brattleboro to Albany was about 60 miles.[11] Baum was to continue his mission of gathering supplies and loyalists while enroute. By now, it was anticipated that Baum's dragoons would be fully mounted, with extra horses secured for the entire army. As Burgoyne stipulated, "The number of horses requisite, beside those necessary for mounting the regiment of dragoons, ought to be 1,300. If you can bring more for the use of the army, it will be so much the better."

An emphasis was also placed on securing cattle. As Burgoyne also pointed out, "The object of your expedition is to try the affections of the country, to disconcert the councils of the enemy, to mount von Riedesel's dragoons, to complete Peters' corps, and to obtain large supplies of cattle, horses and forages."[12]

After reviewing the plan, von Riedesel strongly opposed it. The German general argued that it was just too dangerous to travel such a huge distance. In all, easily over 200 miles of road needed to be traversed. The Green Mountains with its high terrain would have to be crossed on two occasions. Much of the march would be conducted through wilderness and forested regions. And the German general seriously doubted that the country, "swarmed with men who wished to take up arms for the King." Yet, despite the German commander's objections, Burgoyne stated that his instructions would remain.

As Baum was undertaking his final preparations in Fort Miller just before his departure, General Burgoyne suddenly appeared early in the morning. Informed just hours before by Captain Sherwood that Bennington was richly stocked with supplies and was lightly guarded, "at best, no more than several hundred rebels on hand," and confident that this was the case, Burgoyne wanted to personally pass this information on to Baum.

Burgoyne, however, did not just present Baum the new intelligence. Citing that Bennington was now to be his main objective, the general also slightly altered his plan. Though basically it would remain the same, Baum was instructed to completely avoid Arlington, Rockingham, and Manchester. Instead, he was to march directly to Bennington to secure its valuable supplies. As for Bennington, it was located approximately 30 miles to the southeast of Fort Miller, right across Vermont's border.

To get to Bennington, Baum would first march directly to Cambridge, New York. From Fort Miller to Cambridge the road distance was approximately 17 miles. But in those days, roads were generally poor, which meant long and tedious travel. Loaded down with packs, plus many with heavy broad swords weighing 14 pounds, the troops marched slowly. To protect his front and flanks, Baum dispatched some of the loyalists and all of his Indians far ahead. Heeding Burgoyne's previous order that English officers were to accompany the Indians, Baum placed English personnel among them.

En route to Cambridge, a loyalist force of approximately 150 was encountered[13] and joined Baum's force. The loyalists were commanded by Captain Francis Pfister[14] and Captain Simeon Covel.[15] Noting the new contingent, Skene became highly jubilant. After embracing them, Skene began to boast that many more would yet appear. "Believe me, the country is rife with King's men!" Augmented with these loyalists, Baum now possessed a strength of over 800.[16] His force, however, continued to move slowly, and it took them over twelve hours just to reach Cambridge. Since it was now late in the evening, the German commander decided to stay overnight. During the remaining hours of the day, additional loyalists appeared. Because they lacked arms, equipment, and training, their effectiveness was questionable.

During the day, as Baum's soldiers inched their way forward, the Indian and loyalist scouts were operating far ahead. They ambushed individuals on the road and attacked homes and farms. Because the Indians regarded cowbells as a bad omen, any cow with a bell attached was immediately killed. Guns and tomahawks shattered lives, scalps were taken, and homes and farms were torched. Despite Burgoyne's strict order to Baum that, "all possible means are to be used to prevent plundering,"[17] this activity occured anyway. Arson, looting, and murder characterized the behavior of the day.

TUESDAY, 12 AUGUST–WEDNESDAY, 13 AUGUST

Departing from Cambridge late in the morning,[18] Baum resumed his march to Bennington. He now had less than 15 miles to go on the road. But as during the previous day, the force continued to move slowly, inadvertently providing the patriots ample warning of its approach. True, the road was in poor condition and the troops were heavily loaded. But an effort could have, and actually should have, been made to move faster.

What exactly, occurred on the 12th and 13th of August is uncertain. The record is not clear. It is, however, known that Baum's army not only continued to move very slowly but also, during these two days, he encountered his first opposition and other problems.

South of Cambridge, Baum's advance guard skirmished with a force of approximately forty to fifty patriots.[19] These men were protecting a sizable herd of cattle. In the ensuing firefight it appears that Baum's side did not take any casualties. Although they succeeded in capturing five of the patriots, the remainder escaped with their cattle. Shortly afterwards, Baum's main force came under additional fire. A force of approximately fifteen patriots sniped at Baum's troops from hidden positions, at one point causing the entire column to halt. And unlike before, Baum now took his first casualties.

Interrogating the five prisoners, Baum learned that in Bennington the patriots had amassed a strength of at least 1,500 men.[20] He also learned that their commander was John Stark. When informed that Stark was in the vicinity, a number of Baum's German and English officers became apprehensive. They knew that Stark was a hellion, as his reputation achieved with the Continental Army during the war's first year preceded him. If it was true that Stark was waiting for them, then Baum's force was headed for trouble.

After skirmishing with Baum's troops, the patriots guarding the cattle and the sharpshooters who had held up the force disengaged from the battle and fled southward. Upon reaching General Stark, they warned him that a sizable enemy force was headed his way. In response, Stark issued a warning order to his troops to be ready to march on a minute's notice, and he dispatched a runner to Manchester to inform Colonel Seth Warner of what was happening and to ready his Green Mountain Boys for an immediate march.

Informed that his unit might soon be in action, the patriot Thomas Mellen became very excited. So far, he had enjoyed soldiering. He had made new friends and he also admired his commanding officer, Colonel Thomas Stickney.

Miles away, Eleazur Edgerton was sitting comfortably and enjoying his lunch on the bridge spanning Little White Creek to the west of Bennington. Along with some other men, Edgerton had been positioned there earlier to protect the bridge and mill. Bored, Edgerton wished for some action. Once in a while a horseman would come galloping up the road and across the bridge carrying a message, but they could not stop to inform anyone of what was transpiring. Munching the beef jerky, bread, and home baked apple pie provided to him by some local residents, Edgerton actually began to worry that he would miss the action.

To the west in New Hampshire, Molly Stark was working virtually around the clock. Dried fish, meat, and various other food items along with medical supplies, clothing, gunpowder, and ammunition had been gathered up, and an army of women was busily loading wagons and preparing to move out. They knew that the Northern Army needed more supplies.

Meanwhile, Baum's effort to gather horses, cattle, and provisions had run into difficulty. "Mein Gott! What is the matter with these people?" Shouting in German, Baum demanded answers. He was furious. It was bad enough that he had been taking casualties and Stark's men were supposedly nearby. But now, Baum wanted to know why the Indians were troubling him as well.

Besides killing and looting indiscriminately, the Indians demanded immediate payment in gold or silver for what few animals they did bring in. Since Baum had not brought along a pay chest, he was unable to pay them. Angry that they could not be paid, the Indians killed several of the horses before driving the remaining animals away.

THURSDAY, 14 AUGUST
6:00 A.M.

As Baum's column inched forward, by now the entire countryside was aware of the invaders' approach. Local inhabitants began to drive their horses and cattle in various directions. Standing on his bridge, Edgerton noted the fleeing populace driving various breeds of animals to safety.

Other people, however, grabbed their guns. That morning, in the vicinity of modern day Eagle Bridge and White Creek, Baum's spearheads tangled with what appeared to be a small local militia force. Armed citizens also resisted. From behind trees, rock walls, buildings, and from rooftops and barn lofts, snipers raked Baum's main body with gunfire. Even females took up arms. From where he stood, Edgerton could hear shots in the distance. Then, suddenly, it became quiet. An eerie silence set in.

But not for long.

9:00 A.M.[21]

Approaching Sancoick, Baum's troops moved rapidly forward in their attempt to secure the settlement and its bridge over the Owl Kill. With banners unfurled, bayonets fixed, and screaming high-pitched battle cries, the Germans surged forward. Behind them, their two cannons lobbed shells into the village.

Encountering Colonel Gregg and most of his 200 militiamen, a bitter fight ensued. For Baum it was a monumental day because this was the first time that he had ever battled an organized American force.[22]

From where he stood on St. Luke's Bridge, Edgerton could actually see the battle, just a short ways down the road. He was amazed. It did have an ugly beauty to it, but as musket balls, bullets, and cannon shot whizzed by and screams filled the air, reality struck. Unable to hold, Colonel Gregg ordered a withdrawal from Sancoick.

Retreating eastward, his troops crossed St. Luke's Bridge. Continuing to hold his position, Edgerton watched as they ran right past him in their flight. The young patriot noted how one trooper, clasping his musket in his left hand, used his right arm to carry the body of a friend slumped over his shoulder. The man was not going to leave his friend behind, even though he appeared to be dead.

Initiative, always a critical factor, is especially important in combat. And on that ugly day, it was of the utmost importance. When the remaining soldiers of Colonel Gregg's force crossed over, Edgerton finally joined them. Then, he realized that the bridge was still intact. Somehow, no one considered destroying the St. Luke's Bridge, including Colonel Gregg. Immediately, Edgerton said that he would go back. He asked if anyone would join him. Two others volunteered.

Approaching the bridge, the threesome noted that it was still unoccupied with no enemy personnel in sight. Quickly rushing the bridge, they removed a wide plank and, climbing onto the timbers, set fire to them. This was very dangerous because in this particular location, the bridge spanned a deep chasm.

Suddenly, from a distance, they were spotted. As they worked, they came under fire, and "British musket balls were whizzing about their ears."[23] By now, others had moved up to assist the three, and a brisk firefight ensued between those attempting to destroy the bridge versus those attempting to capture it. Once the timbers were alight the three escaped.[24]

Approaching the smoldering bridge, Baum immediately ordered that it be repaired. Fortunately for Baum, the entire structure had not collapsed. Disgusted with what had occurred so far, the German dispatched a quick letter to Burgoyne. He reported that five prisoners had been taken, and had revealed that in Bennington, a troop strength of 1,500 to 1,800 men were assembled. Regarding the Indians, Baum added, "The savages cannot be controlled; they ruin and take every spoil they please."[25] Baum also reported that he was continuing pursuit of the patriots he had met and expected "to fall on the enemy tomorrow."[26] He did not yet request reinforcements.

As Baum's men waited for the bridge to be repaired, Stark, fully aware of what had been happening, dispatched a sizeable skirmishing party of riflemen to oppose the oncoming force.

1:00–2:00 P.M.

At some point in the early afternoon, Baum began to cross over Little White Creek. Initially, his intent was to pursue Colonel Gregg's force and reach Bennington, but the delay at the bridge had been a critical setback. In the long run, it would prove to be one of the fatal factors in the eventual destruction of Baum's force.

To reach Bennington quickly, Baum's men marched east on the road. To his right weaved the Walloomsac River. Almost three miles ahead there was a fairly sharp bend in the Walloomsac where they came upon a small unnamed bridge which spanned this bend of the river. It was in this location that "the two forces met a few miles west of Bennington."[27]

Establishing contact with Baum's leading elements, Stark's riflemen immediately swung into action. Accurate rifle fire reached out and struck targets up to and beyond three-hundred yards. Unlike the American riflemen who possessed superior weapons, the German grenadiers, armed mostly with carbines and muskets with limited range, could not fire back as effectively. Without losing one soldier, Stark's skirmishers killed and wounded no less then thirty of Baum's personnel. With darkness setting in and uncertainty up ahead, the German commander decided for the time being to stay put. He issued an order to dig in. Whereas previously he did not request reinforcements, now Baum quickly dispatched another letter to Burgoyne asking for help.

Baum, however, was not alone in requesting reinforcements. So, too, did Stark. Sensing a major battle in the making and confident that Baum's force could be destroyed short of Bennington, Stark dispatched a quick note to Seth Warner. Colonel Warner was ordered to move southward as rapidly as possible in order to join the fight.

Baum concluded that he held a critical position. It would be imperative for him to retain the little—but very significant—bridge. Deciding on an all-around defense, he began to position his troops on both the eastern and western sides of the Walloomsac River.

Not far across the bridge was a large and fairly steep hill that overlooked both the bridge and the road leading to and from Bennington. Baum quickly fortified the hill, which was dubbed the "Tory Redoubt." A 3-pound cannon was brought up. Positioned about halfway up the hill, it quickly proved its value. Within sight of the hill and bridge stood some homes and log cabins. From a few of them, snipers directed their fire upon Baum's mostly loyalist force occupying the hill. Wheeling the cannon into action, the 3-pounder blazed away. The patriot snipers ceased their firing and fled.

During the early evening hours, Stark's force ceased engaging Baum's troops. In the meantime, Baum's force began to entrench. Trees were felled, log walls went up, and positions were dug. Another sizable position, dubbed the "Dragoon Redoubt," was established to the west of the Tory Redoubt and about three quarters-of-a-mile over the northern side of the Walloomsac. This position was the strongest. Here, Baum positioned his second cannon, most of his dragoons, and some of his English and Brunswick troops.

Aside from the Tory Redoubt with its 300 or so loyalists,[28] three smaller redoubts were also established to support the main position.[29] These were manned primarily by the German and English troops. All of the Canadians and the remaining loyalists not positioned in the Tory Redoubt occupied the nearby cabins and houses from which earlier the snipers had fired. A small party of loyalists was also positioned to guard the bridge. Teams of German grenadiers and loyalists were positioned around the entire area of defense. As for the Indians, they were placed on a plateau behind the main Dragoon Redoubt. In all, Baum's force occupied an area almost a mile in length.[30]

To maintain tactical control, Baum positioned himself in the center of the Dragoon Redoubt. Within such a tactical defensive area Baum felt, for the time being, both safe and secure. Now, all he had to do was await the arrival of his reinforcements. Then he would deal with the patriots once and for all.

Or so Baum thought.

FRIDAY, 15 AUGUST
3:00 A.M.

Stepping out of a cabin converted into a medical station, Doctor Wasmas encountered Captain Samuel MacKay. For the doctor, it had been an exceptionally long day. For over twelve straight hours, he had been operating and removing bullets from various wounded soldiers. He was also saddened that he was unable to save the lives of several of his patients.

MacKay was both angry and totally disgusted by the events of the previous day. He was also upset with the way Lieutenant-Colonel Baum had been directing the operation. MacKay faulted Baum for his lack of aggressiveness, which was essential in a wilderness fight. He also criticized von Riedesel, Burgoyne, Carleton, and the entire British high command based in Canada. As for Baum, MacKay grumbled that he "is so course and rude and despises the counsel of those who had been sent along for guidance, assistance, and advice."[31]

MacKay was not just venting frustration. The loyalist officer also predicted that while Baum was sitting still, the rebels, "will gather by the thousands during the night."[32]

Captain MacKay was largely correct. Throughout the day of 14 August and into the night of 15 August, the patriot troop strength continued to rise significantly as more and more volunteers appeared. Stark was gaining manpower by the hour.

One man who showed up with a contingent of militiamen was a minister, Thomas Allen. A native of Pittsfield, Massachusetts, and a veteran and critic of the Ticonderoga fiasco, Allen went right to the cabin which Stark was using for his headquarters. Upon entering, Parson Allen demanded that an immediate attack be launched against the enemy, but right at that very moment a heavy rain was pouring down. Lightning bolts boomed for miles and flashes lit up the countryside.

"Would you go out on this dark and rainy night?"[33] asked Stark. Without waiting for a response, Stark told the minister to return to his men, get some rest, and, "if the Lord gives us some sunshine, and I do not give you fighting enough, I will never ask you to come out again."[34]

6:00 A.M.

At about this time General Burgoyne was roused and informed that a messenger from Baum had just arrived. As the general clambered out of his warm, comfortable bed, he noted the heavy rain which had been falling all night. After reading the message, Burgoyne ordered his aide, Captain Sir Francis Clarke, to inform von Riedesel that he was to immediately deploy another German unit toward Bennington. He stipulated that Colonel Heinrich von Breymann was to command the reinforcement.

9:00 A.M.

With a strength of approximately 650 troops,[35] mostly German, von Breymann marched out. Two heavy 6-pound cannons were also brought along.

Von Breymann's force, as Baum's did previously, moved very slowly. For starters, the weather was against them. Throughout the 15th, it rained continuously, making the already poor road a quagmire. One group of soldiers took a wrong turn, and after approximately a mile realized they had separated from the column. They had to turn around and march back to the right road. What also affected the march was that von Breymann, a strict disciplinarian, frequently halted to dress his troops into proper ranks. He never took into consideration that the roads were slippery and that his soldiers, carrying heavy loads, were soaked to the skin cold rain. Every time he halted, more time was lost. In von Breymann's mind neither Baum nor the mission was the priority; rather, his emphasis was on strict discipline.

Throughout the 15th, as Baum awaited his reinforcements, his troops continued to work on their defensive positions. By now, he was both disillusioned and upset with Skene and his promises. It was also noted that a number of the "loyalists" who had previously appeared on the 12th, 13th, and 14th, were no longer around. Some of the Germans began to suspect that in actuality they were nothing but spies. Additionally, the first Indians began to depart. To counter the desertions, Baum issued an order that no one was to break ranks. Deep down, he knew that his order was fruitless. As for Colonel Peters, he was suffering from a fever.

Despite the heavy rains, thick fog, and mist, General Stark was not sitting idly by. Teams of his men were probing on either side of Baum's force. Using the harsh weather to their advantage, they carefully plotted the various locations of the enemy positions. Stark also learned much from the "loyalists" who had deserted Baum's force. Based on the information he gathered, he began to formulate a plan.

That day, Colonel Warner appeared. Though he was accompanied only by his younger brother Jesse and a small number of soldiers, the mere appearance of this dynamic patriot leader raised spirits. Most of his regiment, though it was still en route, was not far away. Reinforced with rangers, Warner now possessed a fighting strength of no less than 350 men. Major Samuel Safford commanded the main body. A competent officer and combat veteran of Fort Ticonderoga and the Battle of Hubbardton, Safford was quickly marching in from the northeast. And unknown to Stark and Warner, Major Rand was on his way from the southeast. All were converging upon Bennington.

SATURDAY, 16 AUGUST

Shortly before midnight, in a driving rain, Colonel Warner's regiment arrived in Bennington.[36] Unlike the Germans who had marched slowly, Warner's troops had made good time. They quickly set up camp outside the town and bedded down for the night.

Across the Vermont border in New York, von Breymann's corps had not yet reached Cambridge. Unable to continue through the remainder of the night, they halted about seven miles from the town. As von Breymann later testified: [37]

> I started, therefore at 9 o'clock; and there not being any teams, I had two ammunition boxes placed upon the artillery wagons. Each soldier carried with him forty cartridges. The crossing of the Battenkill consumed considerable time, for the men had to wade through the water. The great number of hills, the bottom-less roads, and a severe and continuous rain, made the march so tedious that I could scarcely make one-half of an English mile an hour. The cannons and the ammunition wagons had to be drawn up hill one after the other. All this, of course, impeded our march very much; and I was unable to hasten it not withstanding all of my endeavors. The carts loaded with ammunition upset, and it caused considerable trouble to right them.
>
> To this, also, was added another difficulty. Our guide lost the way and could not find it again. At last, Major [von] Barner found a man who put us back on the right path. All these unexpected mishaps prevented me from marching on the enemy on the 15th, as far as Cambridge, and, I, therefore, found myself obliged to encamp seven miles this side of that place.
>
> Before reaching that place, however, I wrote to Lieutenant-Colonel Baum notifying him of my arrival, and sent Lieutenant Hageman with the dispatch.

Though one can sympathize with his difficulties, von Breymann was still 17 miles away from Baum. As for Lieutenant Hageman, he did succeed in reaching the advance force. Unhappy upon hearing the news that von Breymann was still some distance away, Skene proposed to immediately depart to hasten on the reinforcements. Baum agreed and ordered the lieutenant to accompany Skene. Hageman was to personally emphasize to von Breymann the importance of arriving quickly.

Through the remainder of the night and into the morning, it continued to rain and thunder.

3:00 A.M.

After conferring with his commanders, Stark opted for an offensive action. He concluded that the only way to destroy the enemy was by attacking them. Stark's commanders agreed.

Stark, however, was not going to launch a direct frontal attack under any circumstances. He fully knew the dangers of conducting such an assault. During the French and Indian War at Fort Carillon, Stark had nearly been killed when English General Abercromby launched one frontal attack after another. Vividly recalling that tragic day with its huge losses, Stark was unwilling to repeat such a performance.

He had also participated in General Washington's Christmas attack on Trenton. Although Washington struck the town with his main force, he employed two groups of soldiers to flank the town and a third group to secure a position behind Trenton to cut off any fleeing Hessians. With such a pincer movement, Trenton had fallen rapidly with few casualties; at Bennington, Stark opted to attack the enemy in a similar fashion.

His plan called for Colonel Moses Nichols, with 300-plus New Hampshire troops, to attack Baum's left (northern) position, including the Dragoon Redoubt and Baum's rear; Colonel Samuel Herrick, with about 100 Vermont rangers and local militia, was to attack the right flank; and Colonels David Hobart and Thomas Stickney, with at least 200 troops, were to attack the Tory Redoubt established in front of the bridge spanning the Walloomsac River. Another 100 men were to demonstrate by the side of the river against the Dragoon Redoubt to try to deceive the enemy as to what the patriots were really up to. Stark himself, with the main force of 1,200–1,300 soldiers, would position himself on the road leading to the bridge. For the time being, he would be standing nearby but out of sight, waiting to attack over the bridge.

Once Nichols and Herrick's troops engaged the enemy, the other colonels were to take out the Tory Redoubt and secure the bridge. Then General Stark would immediately charge over the bridge and attack the enemy from within.[37] As for Hobart's and Stickney's troops, along with those conducting the demonstration, once their initial tasks were accomplished, they would be held in reserve to be utilized wherever a need would arise. By now, Stark possessed a fighting strength of well over 2,000 well-trained troops augmented with local militiamen and armed citizens.[38]

Stark informed his commanders that he planned to attack at three o'clock that afternoon.

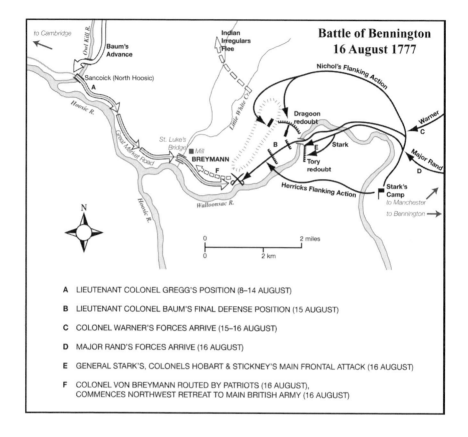

A   LIEUTENANT COLONEL GREGG'S POSITION (8–14 AUGUST)

B   LIEUTENANT COLONEL BAUM'S FINAL DEFENSE POSITION (15 AUGUST)

C   COLONEL WARNER'S FORCES ARRIVE (15–16 AUGUST)

D   MAJOR RAND'S FORCES ARRIVE (16 AUGUST)

E   GENERAL STARK'S, COLONELS HOBART & STICKNEY'S MAIN FRONTAL ATTACK (16 AUGUST)

F   COLONEL VON BREYMANN ROUTED BY PATRIOTS (16 AUGUST),
      COMMENCES NORTHWEST RETREAT TO MAIN BRITISH ARMY (16 AUGUST)

11:00 A.M.

At approximately this time, Colonel Nichols and Colonel Herrick began to move out. They would circle wide of Baum's position and then, using the forest for concealment, they would approach cautiously. Colonel Herrick not only had to swing wide but also move toward a site previously identified as a good place to ford the Walloomsac River. Stark gave them plenty of time. All of the commanders were utilizing the teams which had previously been probing the enemy positions. By now the rain had ceased, the sun was out, and it was turning into a warm day. With tremendous excitement, Thomas Mellen positioned himself with Stark's main body just a short distance to the east of the Tory Redoubt.

At the very same moment that Stark's troops were circling around Baum's mostly dug-in force, and as they were slowly moving into position, several other events were underway: Colonel von Breymann's force had just passed by Cambridge en route to Bennington, Colonel Seth Warner's regiment was approaching to reinforce the patriots, and Major Rand's riders were also nearing the battle.

3:00 P.M.

"Fire!" With the shout of this one-word command, the stillness of the forest was shattered as hundreds of rifle and musket rounds poured into the German, British, loyalist, and Indian positions. As lethal rounds tore into the enemy, Stark's 100-man diversion force immediately moved into action. They not only fired but yelled such boisterous battle cries that it sounded as if countless hundreds were out there.

Within minutes, two of the Indian chiefs were dead and Baum's Canadians and Indians had collapsed. So terrified were they of the incoming attack that the survivors fled. As the patriots stormed the Tory Redoubt, the mostly loyalist force held at first but then began to cave in. Charging over the breastworks, Stark's fighting chaplain, Thomas Allen, screamed, "I demand you surrender in the name of Congress!"

The loyalists fired another volley. But it was ineffective. Though charging uphill, the patriots could not be stopped. Prior to leaping into the loyalist position, a number of the patriots would momentarily stand on the edge of the breastwork, aim downward, and fire. Then, they would jump inside the works. Once inside, they fought with bayonets, swung their weapons like clubs or pulled out a knife. Many, however, used the prized weapon of the wilderness—the tomahawk. Swinging and throwing their tomahawks, they began to shatter the loyalist force. One of the patriot officers who charged forward was Ebenezer Webster, whose son, Daniel, would later be known for creating the famous dictionary.

In this hellhole, loyalist Colonel Peters attempted to hold firm. But it was to no avail. His ranks were rapidly crumbling. Turning around, he spotted a musket, tipped with a bayonet, being aimed at him. There was a blast and puff of smoke, but the round barely missed. Jumping down from the breastwork, Peters' opponent began to reload rapidly. As he reloaded, so did Peters.

Once again, the patriot aimed and fired. Standing beside Peters was a loyalist sergeant. He died from the shot. "Peters! You damn Tory! I have got you!" Looking up, Peters spotted a man charging at him; with a bayonet fixed to the tip of his musket, he was coming in fast.

Peters knew that he had to move. Dropping his ramrod, he raised his musket halfway up to counter the incoming threat. Suddenly, he felt the tip of the bayonet inside his left breast. But before the blade could penetrate any deeper, Peters fired. Captain Jeremiah Post, a former schoolmate and friend, was shoved back by the blast of the musket. He was dead before he hit the ground.

Captain Post was also the husband of one of Peters' cousins, and several years earlier Peters had been a guest at their wedding. By his actions, Peters had just turned his cousin into a widow.

In the meantime, General Stark sensed that the moment to launch his main attack was nearing, and he moved his command closer to the Walloomsac bridge. Ordering his men to stay put, Stark rode his horse a little closer. Dismounting, he approached on foot and watched the progress of his flank attacks. Progress was good, but capturing the bridge would be the key to victory.

Using the wooded terrain to their advantage, the 600 plus troops flanking Baum's various positions would fire from behind a tree, reload, rush forward to another tree, fire again, and repeat the process. Though they were attacking uphill, they were able to take aim at a fixed position, whereas the defenders could only fire at elusive, moving targets. Nearing the main Dragoon Redoubt, Colonel Nichols' men continued to pour a stready stream of fire into the German dragoons and English and loyalist soldiers.

Realizing that the Tory Redoubt could not be held, both Peters and Pfister ordered a retreat. With a double-barreled pistol in his hand, Pfister shot a patriot trooper directly in the face at point blank range. Sensing someone behind him, he quickly turned. A huge man was towering over him. Holding up a bloodied tomahawk, he was about to plunge it into Pfister's head. Leaning quickly to his right to avoid the strike, Pfister fired his second barrel right between the man's eyes.

Though Peters and Pfister escaped by running westward across the bridge, most of the loyalists were not so fortunate. The greater number had been killed or captured. As the survivors of the Tory Redoubt fell back and raced for safety, the small loyalist guard detail positioned to guard the bridge fled with them.

From where he stood, Stark could see the bridge. It was still intact! The small enemy guard had fled pell mell. Mounting his horse, Stark waved to his men and ordered the entire force, including many of those who had stormed the Tory Redoubt and the 100-man diversion force, to charge forward across the bridge. With a massive battle cry, nearly 1,500 men, amongst them John Hakes, surged across the Walloomsac River.

Galloping across the bridge, Stark quickly dismounted and tied his prized horse to a fence rail. Screaming, "We'll beat them today or by night Molly Stark's a widow!" and "Boys, tonight our flag floats over yonder hill or Molly Stark is a widow!" Stark charged forward. From now on, he would command and fight on foot.[39]

With patriot troops pouring in from all sides, Baum's Dragoon Redoubt, along with the other posts, could no longer hold. Taking aim, Jacob Onderkirke, who resided just down the road in Hoosick, fired, killing a German. Lieutenant Spagenberg, who commanded the two artillery pieces, was struck by a bullet in his right arm. Well aimed rifle shots dispatched all of Spangenberg's German gunners.

By now the battle had reached its apex. "It was the hottest I ever saw in my life. It represented one continued clap of thunder!" Stark reported afterwards.[40]

When the shooting commenced, Colonel Seth Warner's main body was still on the march. They were now about five miles to the northeast. Hearing the sounds of the battle, Major Safford urged the men to quicken their pace. Everyone knew that their colonel, along with his brother and a small contingent, were already involved.

Warner's troops, however, were not the only ones to hear the sounds of the battle. As they rode their horses to the northwest, Major Rand and his company noted a rumble. At first, they could not make out what it was. Possibly a storm up ahead? Major Rand's intent was to reach the headquarters of the Northern Army in Albany, but as they neared, it became obvious that this was not the rumble of a storm. Somewhere up ahead, a massive battle was underway. Major Rand ordered his force head for the sound of the guns.

Shortly before the battle had erupted, Philip Skene had returned from his visit to von Breymann. On checking the situation, he retraced his steps and positioned himself at the bridge spanning the Owl Kill in Sancoick, there to await von Breymann's force. Skene also dispatched a couple of loyalists to seek out the German colonel and urge him to hurry.

By now Thomas Mellen, who had formerly been excited by the prospect of battle, had had enough of soldering. He wished that he had never been exposed to such hell. Along with a number of others, he had just been ordered to bring the cannon captured in the Tory Redoubt, along with its ammunition and powder, across the bridge. As they pushed and pulled the gun, Mellen noticed the dead and dying all around. Bodies were floating in the river. Heavy smoke and dust filled his nostrils and entered his lungs. The heat was intense. Sweat poured from every pore of his body. He felt tired... hot... sick... His throat burned from the smoke and his head rang from the noise. Tears filled his eyes. He thought of fleeing, but could not. Morally, he was tied to those around him. As he struggled and pushed amid the shouts of orders and the screams of those fighting, a lieutenant appeared and ordered the gun to be pushed faster. Mellen wondered how much more of this he could take. It was insane. Like a bad dream.

Suddenly, Seth Warner appeared on horseback. Someone from the edge of the bridge informed the colonel that his brother had been killed and was lying by the road. Warner asked, "Is it Jesse?"[41] When informed that it was, Warner was crestfallen. Then he regained his composure. He still had a battle to fight and win. Mellen witnessed this exchange of words. He felt sorrow for the colonel's loss.

Hauling the cannon into position, the patriots attempted to fire it, but there wasn't a trained artillerist among them. Noting the problem, General Stark himself ran up. Stark was all over the battlefield that day. Quickly, he turned the cannon toward a number of Germans. Loading the barrel with grapeshot, he fired. Stark had learned how to handle a cannon during the French and Indian War. Like a blast from a giant shotgun, iron balls tore into the Germans. Following their commander's example, his men reloaded the cannon and repeatedly fired. In the meantime, Stark's men overran another position.

Realizing that his force would be lost if he stayed in place, Baum ordered a breakout. With their ammunition running out, the Germans fixed bayonets and charged. Some of the dragoons unsheathed their heavy swords as they sought to break through the patriot ring.

The battle devolved into a confused melee. Determined to hold the Germans in place, the patriots refused to give ground. Many of Stark's men, especially those who were armed with rifles, did not have bayonets. Lacking time to reload in the close-quarter fighting, they swung their rifles and muskets like clubs. Those who were armed with a bayonet-tipped musket used it; others reached for their swords and tomahawks, while others, from behind cover, reloaded rapidly and continued to pour fire into Baum's men. Some patriots even clambered up into the trees to fire down at the enemy. Though the Germans continued to struggle to open an escape route, the stiff resistance of Stark's men prevented a rapid breakout. The Germans paid dearly for every yard they gained.

Farther west, the two loyalists dispatched by Skene established contact with von Breymann's force. Still moving at a snail's pace, the column was still some distance from the battle. Possibly, von Breymann did not care much about the situation. It is known that he loathed the British, the patriots, the loyalists, the Indians, Burgoyne, King George III, Carleton, Skene, and just about everyone else. Von Breymann had never had a good relationship with Baum. However, now hearing of the desperate situation, he dispatched an entire company to move rapidly forward. Commanded by Captain Gottlieb Joachim von Gleisenberg, the company possessed a strength of 80 soldiers.[42] Dropping their heavy packs, von Gleisenberg's men quickly marched off. Somewhere, in the vicinity of Sancoick, they were to link up with Skene and with as many loyalists as Skene could provide. Once von Gleisenberg's company was reinforced, the combined German-loyalist unit was to march rapidly forward to assist Baum.

Prior to dispatching von Gleisenberg, von Breymann had dispatched Major von Barner to Sancoick to secure some horses. The colonel had reasoned that once his force obtained some fresh mounts, they would move faster.

Back near the Walloomsac, desperate to break out, Baum's group continued to fight its way rearward against swarms of patriot. Suddenly, a powerful round struck the German commander. Collapsing to the ground, he was unable to move. As Baum lay dying, the German effort to break out began to lose its impetus.

At his post by the Sancoick bridge, Phillip Skene spotted a loyalist volunteer fleeing westward and halted him. From the fugitive, Skene learned that his unit had been shattered, the Germans were surrounded, and that they were now being cut to pieces. "As for me," the man said, "I am fleeing for my life!" Refusing to believe him, Skene continued to wait.

4:30 P.M.[43]

Rendezvousing with Major von Barner and Skene at Sancoick, von Gleisenberg had begun to assess the situation when a loyalist officer suddenly appeared. It was Captain Colin Campbell.

Campbell was asked if it were true that the patriots were over-whelming Baum's force and that the loyalists had been shattered. Though acknowledging that a difficult situation had risen and that he himself had barely escaped, Campbell sounded more positive. He assured Skene and the two other German officers that "things were not so bad."[44] Skene then urged the two assembled leaders to wait until von Breymann showed up with the main body.

5:00–6:00 P.M.

As Skene and the others were conferring, Stark's troops were pursuing the survivors of Baum's shattered force. In fact, to Stark and his men, the battle appeared to be over. Excluding a shot here and there, its fiery tempo had abated. The enemy force had been routed, if not obliterated. Baum was dying, Pfister lay dead, Colonel Peters was wounded, two Indian chiefs were dead, and Doctor Wasmus, along with many other Germans, was captured. He would not return to his homeland until 1783. As the patriots chased the survivors in various directions, Stark began to lose the critical element needed for successful combat—command and control.

Arriving at the battle area with his mounted troops, Major Rand could not make out what was happening, what had transpired, or even who was fighting whom. Suddenly, Seth Warner rode up. Introducing himself to Rand, Colonel Warner briefed the major as to what had transpired and what was currently taking place. As for Warner's regiment, it was now about two miles away and, following a brief rest, was marching rapidly forward.

Within minutes of Rand's appearance, Colonel von Breymann finally arrived at the Sancoick Bridge where he linked up with von Gleisenberg, von Barner, Skene, and Campbell. Noting some armed men coming in from the northeast, Skene announced, "They are a loyalist force!" But he was incorrect. The moment Skene and the German force proceeded to cross the Sancoick Bridge, they came under fire from a group of patriots.

Sensing that if he could secure St. Luke's Bridge he would be able to cut off some of the mass of troops fleeing westward, Colonel Herrick, whose initial task of striking Baum's right flank and rear had been successfully accomplished, began to dispatch some of his troops toward Sancoick. As the patriot force advanced, they marched right into von Breymann's incoming force at the St. Luke's Bridge.

After one of the first volleys at the bridge, von Breymann's horse was struck and collapsed. Cursing the patriots in German, the colonel stood up and began to scream orders. He also ordered his two 6-pound cannons to be brought up. Noting that the German force was considerably larger and stronger than they, the patriots began to fall back toward the main battlefield.

But they did not retreat all the way to where Stark's troops were now mopping up and searching for loot. Following their first exchange of fire, they ducked behind trees and rock walls, and backed into higher terrain. A running gun battle ensued. Leapfrogging backwards, they continued to put a steady stream of fire on the Germans. And a horse-mounted messenger was sent back to Stark warning him of the new and fresh incoming German force.

Colonel Herrick's troops, who were battling the new force, proved to be excellent marksmen. Unlike the Germans, who had limited range with their muskets and heavy carbines, Herrick's riflemen could extract a deadly toll at a distance. The rifle once again proved its value that day, as officers and sergeants were specifically targeted. More and more of von Breymann's soldiers collapsed into eternal silence. Desperate to fend off the patriots, the Germans repeatedly halted to fire mass volleys and blast away with their cannons. In the aftermath of the Bennington battle, Skene would openly criticize von Breymann for moving too slowly as he approached Stark's force and for wasting too much ammunition in useless volleys.

Standing on a field adjacent to the road, Stark wondered what was going on up ahead. As he pondered, the messenger sent by Herrick came riding up, shouting, "Where is General Stark?" The general motioned for the rider to come over. Upon receiving the message about the new Hessian force, Stark was shocked. The patriot victory could now be turned into a defeat. Immediately he began to gather up his scattered forces.

Unfortunately for the patriots, the immediate aftermath of the battle was still marked by confusion. Worse, Stark no longer had a firm grip on his units. In addition to the chaos produced by dozens of disparate firefights across the hills, many of Stark's men were looting the enemy's baggage and the fallen. Others were escorting prisoners while still others had advanced further to battle von Breymann. Units had become intermixed. Though he had not taken too many casualties in his force as a whole, some of Stark's officers and key leaders had been killed or wounded. Most, however, were simply not available at the moment. Some were tending to their wounded, others trying to find or gather their men, and some of the local boys, who had appeared in the last day or two with a gun, were actually now heading back home.

Seeing what was happening and fearing that a defeat could yet result, Colonel Seth Warner stepped in. He recommended that Stark gather up whatever troops he could and organize a skirmish line. Galloping over to the left, Warner found Major Rand and ordered his unit forward. Warner also dispatched a messenger to Major Safford with the rest of the Green Mountain Boys to move with all speed.

Stark was, indeed, a very lucky man. Within minutes, Rand's mounted horse soldiers appeared and spotted the cautiously advancing German force. Immediately, both groups commenced firing at each other.

At the beginning of the fight, two musket balls tore into Rand's horse, yet the animal held and did not collapse. Ordering his men to dismount, Rand's highly disciplined force went into action. As every third trooper gathered up the reins of several horses and pulled them backwards to safety, others sought cover. Aiming their weapons toward the incoming Germans, they awaited Major Rand's command.

"Fire! Fire at will!" The crack of rifles and muskets filled the air as patriot lead tore into the German ranks. Several rounds flew through von Breymann's hat and cape; another one struck him in the leg. As Rand's troops battled the Germans, some of Stark's soldiers came rushing in to assist. Whereas just minutes before a somewhat brief calm had set in, now the battle was resumed in full fury.

Conferring with Stark, Warner pleaded with him to hold on. "My men are en route. They'll be here any moment!" Because Stark feared that his force was in no condition to battle it out with a fresh German force, he hoped that Warner's assurances would prove to be correct.[45]

But Stark had no intention of giving way. The moment he gathered up some troops, he fed them into the battle. Though they arrived piecemeal, they reinforced and strengthened those fighting von Breymann. As more and more of his men appeared, Stark continuously steered them toward the new fight.

Von Breymann dispatched Major von Barner to turn Stark's right flank. But right at that critical moment, Major Safford came on the scene with the rest of Seth Warner's command. In addition to bringing up some 130 Green Mountain Boys, he appeared with over 200 rangers.[46] Noting what was happening, Warner committed half of his force to flank and counter von Barner's force and the other half joined Major Rand's and Stark's troops.

The rangers proved to be especially destructive. Deadly, long-range rifle fire dropped many of the German troops. As previously, officers and sergeants were especially targeted. Struck right between the eyes, von Barner collapsed. In the rear, one of the German ammunition wagons suddenly exploded into smithereens. Thousands of sparks, like miniature rockets, flew skyward. Whooping like Indians, the rangers, militiamen, Continentals and Rand's horse soldiers rained death and destruction upon their foes.

8:00 P.M.

By now, von Breymann had had enough. Wounded, his leadership shattered, ammunition running low, incurring heavy casualties, and knowing that it would soon be dark, the German ordered a retreat. As the men fell back, they left behind their two cannons, all of their carts, and much equipment. Some of the wounded were also left behind. But most importantly, as the German survivors fled, the Battle of Bennington was entering history. In the end, von Breymann, who had marched into the battle with an exhausted force, accomplished absolutely nothing. In the following days, he would blame his defeat upon Skene. The German commander would claim that had he known Baum had been defeated, he would never have even marched in. Because of Skene and his cohorts, von Breymann had been urged to walk straight in to a superior and victorious patriot army.

Von Breymann did have much to complain about. Within two hours he had lost a third of his force.[47] No less than 160 of his men had been killed or captured, a figure that did not include the walking wounded who had fallen back with the force. And virtually all of the Germans' equipment was left in the field.

Tragically, at Bennington, some of Stark's men did not know that when a drum parley is beat, it means that a force wants to surrender. As some of the Germans attempted to give up, they were still fired upon. Noting this and fearing for their lives, they began to resist while others fled into the woods. Undoubtedly, some of the casualties Stark incurred arose from the fact that as some of the German, English, and loyalist personnel saw that prisoners were not being taken, they continued to resist. Though Stark's losses were not significant, additional lives—on both sides—could have been saved. It must be noted, however, that once a German and British soldier was taken prisoner, the Europeans were neither violated nor killed, though some robbery did occur.

The Battle of Bennington was a huge disaster for Burgoyne. Besides securing none of the critically needed cattle, horses, and food he needed, the British general suffered an immense loss in both personnel and prestige.

On the following day, 207 German soldiers were found dead on the battlefield.[48] This figure, however, did not include the dead soon to be found in the surrounding forests and hills in the upcoming days and weeks. No less than 700 men were captured[49] including 30 officers.[50]

Of Baum's 375 German troops, only nine escaped.[51] Among them was Lieutenant Spangenburg. Unfortunately for the lieutenant, though his wound was not serious, poor treatment by English doctors resulted in eventual paralysis of his arm. In the aftermath of Bennington, the Germans cited a loss of no less than 596 killed or missing.[52] Indian losses were never accurately reported, but the other contingents of the force had also suffered heavily.[53] Excluding the attached Indians, the British soon cited that if one tallied all of the casualties incurred by the Germans, loyalists, Canadians, and English, the overall loss was over 900 dead or captured.[54] In the end, of an overall strength of nearly 2,000 committed, nearly fifty percent was lost, a proportion indicating disaster. In one day, no less than a sixth of Burgoyne's entire army had been destroyed,[55] casualties that he could ill afford.

In addition to the lost personnel, four cannons and ammunition were abandoned. Also lost were over 700 muskets, and a tremendous amount of equipment—knives, bayonets, swords, pistols, headgear, uniforms, wagons, and valuable horses. What was to be an easy resupply mission not only failed but, in the end, actually cost Burgoyne more men, materiel, and horses than he could have imagined.

And for the patriots, Bennington was not just a physical triumph; it was a major psychological victory. Soon, throughout the colonies, spirits rose. As for the surviving loyalists, their morale fell to a crippling low.

Francis Pfister's unit had been annihilated.[56] So too, effectively, was the Queen's Loyal Rangers. In the ensuing weeks and months of 1777, very few men stepped forward to fight for the loyalist cause. As for the few Tory survivors, more and more of them began to desert.

Loyalists, however, were not the only ones deserting. Sensing that ultimate defeat was inevitable, Canadians and Indians also began to leave.[57] Individually, or in small groups, they disappeared into the wilderness. Even de Langlade himself soon ditched Burgoyne and returned to Canada. Though St. Luc and Burgoyne succeeded in convincing a number of the Indians to stay on for the time being, by and large Bennington marked the true beginning of the end of the Indian participation in the British campaign of 1777.[58] Likewise, in the aftermath of Bennington, desertions among the Germans and British soldiers rose. As for Philip Skene, though he had emerged physically intact, he had lost his reputation. From here on, Burgoyne held Skene in low contempt, and as his campaign deteriorated, their relationship grew worse. In fact, it was soon so bad that in front of others Burgoyne began reprimanding Skene for helping to create such an inferior situation, saying, "You have brought me to this pass. Now tell me how to get out of it!"[59]

There was, of course, a price to pay on both sides, even the victorious one. In all, the patriots lost 30 men killed with at least 40 others wounded.[60]

9:00 P.M.–9:00 A.M.

In the remaining hours of 16 August and through the night hours of Sunday, 17 August, many things occurred.

Totally exhausted from the day's activity, Thomas Mellen, along with many others, simply plopped down on the ground and slept through the night. As hard as he would try to forget that awful day of 16 August, Mellen would never be able to remove it from his mind. Fortunately, for the veterans sleeping on the fields and in the woods, it did not rain.

Stark, on the other hand, was raving mad with anger. During the battle, as he fought, someone had stolen his favorite horse. Along with the horse, the beautiful doe skin-covered saddle had disappeared. His wife Molly's parents had presented it to him as a gift on his wedding day. Cursing the horse thief, Stark swore that if he ever caught the bastard he would have him hanged from the nearest tree. Shouldering his rifle, he re-crossed the bridge and headed to his command post on foot.[61]

In the immediate aftermath of the battle, the wounded were gathered up and transported to a site previously designated as a medical center. Through the long night, American, German, and English personnel labored hard to bring some relief to the wounded. Among the caregivers was Doctor Wasmus. By now, some local civilians had also appeared on the scene and they, too, rendered assistance.

As he treated the wounded, Doctor Wasmus learned that his nephew, a member of von Breymann's force, had been seriously wounded. It did not look good for the young German grenadier.[62] Doctor Wasmus was also saddened to hear that some of the German and English prisoners were being abused.

That night a patriot major appeared, checking up on his wounded and injured men. Informed that Doctor Wasmus had been robbed when captured, the major departed and then shortly afterwards returned. Suspecting that someone from his command was the culprit behind the theft, the major recovered most of the doctor's items. Returning to the cabin being utilized for treating the wounded and injured, he not only returned the doctor's belongings but also politely apologized for the theft.[63]

Yet unfortunately and tragically, as efforts were being taken to save the wounded, killing was still going on. Violence directed against captured or fugitive loyalists occurred, and little, if anything, was done to stop it.

Surely, Stark must have known what was happening within his command; or if he didn't, he surely should have. Possibly Stark did know, but since he also hated the loyalists and regarded them as nothing but common criminals, he chose not to intervene in the bloodlust that ensued.

Revenge, always an ugly matter but especially so during times of civil conflict, ran rampant that night. As already stated, British and German personnel were not badly mistreated. But when it came to the captured loyalists, their fate was harsh and often brutal.

In one instance, approximately 170 loyalists were tied up in groups of two and three. In turn, each group was tied to a long rope pulled by a trooper on horseback. They were pulled to Bennington in such a manner. Those who fell were dragged along the ground, as stones, rocks, and roots tore deep. The men of Jessup's Corps were especially brutalized. One loyalist, already half dead from a musket ball which had torn through his left eye and lodged in his head, was slung upon a captured horse which also had its left eye shot out.[64] Then, the loyalist was led around in a circle until he died. Prior to dying, he was mocked, taunted, and cursed. Others were also humiliated and killed. A report later disclosed that some had even been branded with red-hot irons.[65]

Deep in the wilderness, Catherine Esther Montour, "the Witch of the Wilderness," was having a momentous time. Half intoxicated and armed with a tomahawk, she danced around a circle of sixteen prisoners who lay on the ground with their hands and feet bound firmly with rope. Nearby lay her son. Shortly before, he had passed out from the massive amount of alcohol he had consumed. Laughing insanely and chanting a weird sort of death song, she hopped and skipped around the condemned.

Then it began. With a ferocious scream, she drove her tomahawk deep into the skull of her first victim. Proceeding down the line, she continued to kill. Those who begged for mercy were immediately informed that they would perish. Some were tomahawked but others were shot in the back of the head with a pistol. Between each victim she skipped, hopped, danced, and sipped more alcohol.

Somehow during this gruesome ordeal, two of her victims managed to "escape." But that had been previously arranged by Catherine. She wanted them to get away. After running wild-eyed in terror through the woods, they would eventually return to their unit or area of residence. There they would spread fear while recalling in horror how "the Witch of the Wilderness" slaughtered those whom she regarded as traitors.

Arising in the morning, Thomas Mellen began to move around. He noted numerous dead bodies nearby. Along with some others, he began to search for his unit. Entering the forest, they groped their way forward. It was here that Mellen and the others came across the bodies.

What Mellen had witnessed the day before was gruesome enough, but this was insane. The sight of men lying still with their feet and hands tied behind their backs and the backs of their heads shattered from blows and gunshots sickened the young man.[66]

17 AUGUST
NOON

Along with a number of other officers, Doctor Wasmus was placed in a food line. From where he stood, he saw several other lines of prisoners nearby. Most were German but some English were among them as well. No loyalists, Canadian, or Indians were seen. Doctor Wasmus was provided a decent meal of bread, hard boiled eggs, pork, and potatoes. All of the prisoners, regardless of rank, were provided the same meal. Doctor Wasmus and some of the other officers were also joined at their table for lunch by Seth Warner, who was accompanied by a soldier fluent in German. At this time Colonel Warner returned to the doctor his diary and a box which at one time contained twelve double edged knives. Oddly, Warner stated that he would keep six of them. As for the diary, the colonel informed Doctor Wasmus that it had already been reviewed and, though interesting, was of no military value.

Shortly after lunch, General Stark spoke. All of the prisoners were assembled for his speech. Standing beside Stark was a female translator. Though she was dressed in frontier clothing and wore pants, Doctor Wasmus could not fail to note her delicate features and long hair. She was also fluent in German.

Doctor Wasmus had already noted that among the so-called Americans, there was a strong sense of unity. Whether white or black, native born or immigrant, they got along well. What especially struck the doctor was the informal relationship that existed between the patriot officers and their men. Although the soldiers were respectful of rank, it was obvious that among them there existed a much closer harmony than that found within the German or English armies. Doctor Wasmus noted how when the patriot soldiers went through the food lines, General Stark and his colonels joked and spoke with them. But they did not touch a bite until each of their troops had first received a meal. Furthermore, the officers ate the same food as the men. Stark even ensured that his civilian and female support personnel were fed prior to him sitting down and eating. This was a custom completely different from what Doctor Wasmus had witnessed in his own army. The doctor had seen that while hungry English and German soldiers had been slaving through the wilderness constructing a road, Generals Burgoyne and von Riedesel were surrounded by private servants serving them luxurious meals at Skene's private estate.

As Stark spoke, Doctor Wasmus carefully studied him. Though in his late forties, the patriot general looked much younger. Ruggedly built, he had a strong body as well as mind. He did not wear the tall, black, tight-fitting leather boots customarily worn by most of Europe's officers. Instead, Stark wore a pair of light moccasin ankle-high boots with woolen socks. As he stood in his deerskin smock and pants, he radiated confidence and strength. The only thing that distinguished his rank was the one brass star worn on the front of his sizeable floppy hat.

Through the German-speaking female translator, Doctor Wasmus learned that the prisoners would soon be moved to Bennington proper, and from there they would be escorted to Boston. Stark assured them that no one would be harmed, but he also asked the captured soldiers to cooperate with his men. Stark also informed them that an effort would be made to recover their personal items.

As he stared at this no-nonsense commander, Doctor Wasmus knew right then and there that the British would not only lose this campaign but also the war. Even if the British king sent every soldier that he had, he would still not win. There was just something unique about these wilderness people.[67]

Of importance is that despite Stark's anger and dissatisfaction with the newly established nation and its Congress, when his brigade marched to Bennington, his men proudly carried a flag. Its background was green (possibly to commemorate the green mountains of New Hampshire) and a circle of thirteen gold stars which commemorated the new nation's thirteen colonies. General Stark truly regarded himself and his volunteers as being Americans.[68]

On 4 October 1777, John Stark finally received his recognition. The American Continental Congress, via John Hancock who served as the Congress' President, formally thanked Stark for his services at Bennington and commissioned him to the rank of Brigadier General in the United States Army.[69] His wife Molly, of course, always knew this would happen.

XVII

Schuyler Is Relieved of Command

MONDAY, 18 AUGUST

Eight miles to the north of Albany, where the Mohawk River flows into the Hudson, there are a few small islands. In themselves, the islands are referred to as the Sprouts. Three larger islands—Green, Van Schaick's, and Haver,[1] largely encompass the Sprouts. Within the Sprouts, a fordable area also existed where it was relatively easy to cross the river. Seeking to block this passageway and wanting to construct another defensive position to defend the area north of Albany, General Schuyler ordered that a strong fort be constructed upon Van Schaick's Island where, just recently, he had also established his forward headquarters. The Northern Army's main headquarters, however, still remained in Albany.

Despite the retreats and reversals, General Schuyler did have a firm grip on the situation. British General St. Leger had been held up at Fort Stanwix to the west while patriot reinforcements had been dispatched to confront him; the MacDonell and Chrysler loyalist force had just been solidly defeated in Schoharie County; and a major victory had been won against Burgoyne's men at Bennington. Schuyler knew that as Burgoyne's main army advanced farther south, he would only be weakening himself further. Schuyler was, after all, carefully monitoring Burgoyne's communication and supply line. With the information he had been receiving from his long-range teams operating deep in Burgoyne's rear, he knew that the British were vulnerable. Therefore, to further discomfit his enemy, Schuyler was making plans to attack these supply lines through a series of major long-range operations. In fact, Schuyler was even planning to attack Fort Ticonderoga.

Schuyler also had another major advantage. Daily, the Northern Army was growing in strength. Generals Nixon's and Glover's regiments had arrived, along with Colonel Morgan's elite rifle brigade. Major Henry Dearborn, who hailed from New Hampshire, arrived with five companies of light infantrymen. More and more independent militia companies kept appearing and, weekly, hundreds of individual volunteers appeared as well. They arrived from throughout New York and New England, as well as from New Jersey and Pennsylvania and some even from distant Virginia. By mid-August, Schuyler's Northern Army registered at just over 9,000 men.[2] This strength, however, did not include those serving in the Highlands north of New York City, nor did it include the strength of some of the independent units such as General Stark's brigade, and those serving in Fort Stanwix and in the Mohawk and Schoharie Valleys. And with the arrival of Colonel Warner and Major Rand, General Schuyler's strength rose further.

Though their numbers were not included in the formal mid-August strength figure, also serving with the Northern Army were sizable numbers of women, older men, and some very young boys. These male civilians and women were directly assisting the Northern Army by cooking, baking, and gathering food for the various units. They cleaned pots and pans, sewed and repaired torn uniforms and clothing, repaired weapons and equipment, drove supply wagons, nursed the sick and wounded, delivered dispatches, translated captured documents and orders, spied on the British, cleaned army barracks, assisted in refugee control, and virtually ran the Northern Army's main hospital in Albany, among other vital services.

Many of the women bound to the Northern Army were initially refugees who had fled in the wake of Burgoyne's and St. Leger's advances. By mid-August a number of New York counties were either totally or partially under British occupation. Other counties adjacent to the occupied ones were in shambles out of fear because their menfolk had left to join the patriots' main forces. Settlers who were fleeing their homes, farms, and lands with no place to go, found themselves in the Northern Army. Many others joined up because they supported the revolutionary cause; and yet others simply tagged along with their husbands, sons, or fathers.

Like most commanders, neither Generals Washington nor Schuyler were fond of the idea of women serving with an army. They regarded an army as traditionally a man's place. But, since many women were caught up in the terrible Wilderness War of 1777, at the moment, the Northern Army did offer the benefits of escape and safety in numbers. Therefore, for purposes of morale and because their support was needed, the women were kept in place for the time being. It is, however, important to note that Washington, Schuyler, and many other commanders did, in due course, acknowledge that women played a vital role in helping achieve for the patriots' victory in the northern campaign of 1777.[3]

TUESDAY, 19 AUGUST

Unknown to General Schuyler, as he was working virtually around the clock to defeat the British offensive, a number of key individuals within the Continental Congress were plotting to relieve him of command. Some of these members were still angry about the loss of Fort Ticonderoga and were holding Schuyler personally responsible for it. Not understanding the true nature of Schuyler's withdrawals, they convinced their fellow congressional members that if Schuyler was not replaced, he would lead the army to defeat in the northern theater.

To a large extent, Schuyler may have been at fault. Despite the fact that he did have a firm grip on the situation and was slowly bleeding the British campaign into defeat, Schuyler frequently expressed sentiments of doom in his letters and dispatches to the Continental Congress. And, as often is the case in such situations, politics played a role in determining who should be in command.

Some perceived that General Horatio Gates would relate much better to New England's populace than would Schuyler. John and Samuel Adams especially preferred Gates. The President of the Continental Congress, John Hancock, also supported the move to relieve Schuyler. Hancock was especially frustrated with the constant retreats and Schuyler's repeated requests for supplies and assistance. Hancock insisted that unless a new commander was inserted, defeat was imminent.

Attempting to shift the responsibility of relieving Schuyler directly to General George Washington, the commander-in-chief, Congress requested that he appoint a replacement.

Washington, however, declined. Though acknowledging that he was the top ranking officer of all the Continental armies and forces, he cited that in the case of the Northern Army he had never wielded full command. At best, he stated that he had only nominal powers. Though he advised, supervised, and supported it as best as he could, unlike with his other forces, this particular army was not under his full authority.[4] In fact, as Washington pointed out, when he had previously raised the issue to Congress on whether he was to hold supreme authority over the Northern Army, the Congress failed to respond.

Washington informed Congress that to the best of his understanding the Northern Department, along with its Northern Army, was a separate command solely under the jurisdiction and control of Congress. Washington also stipulated that he had not appointed Schuyler to be its commander; therefore, he was in no position to relieve him. When previously the Gates-Schuyler controversy had risen, Washington had not been consulted. Congress had taken up the matter on its own. Noting Washington's position, Congress opted to replace General Philip Schuyler with General Horatio Gates.

On 14 August, General Gates learned that he was to be the new commander of the Northern Army, and on 19 August, he reported to its headquarters in Albany. Informed that General Schuyler was on Van Schaick's Island, Gates proceeded to that location. Upon meeting with Schuyler he presented to him the Congressional order appointing him (Gates) as the new commander of the Northern Army.[5] Not wanting to create a scene in front of his troops, General Schuyler humbly resigned.[6] On the following day he set out to his home in Albany where his wife, Catharine, was residing. As for Schuyler's estate further north, nearby a hamlet that in the near future would be designated Schuylerville, it stood deserted. Soon, this house would be occupied by General Burgoyne.

Upon learning of Congress' decision, many of Schuyler's officers were disgruntled. Unlike the Congress, they were on the front lines. They knew and understood the true picture, and by and large were supportive of their general's actions. As one of Schuyler's officers summed it up, "The foundation of all the Northern success was laid long before Gates' arrival there. Gates appeared just in time to reap the laurels and rewards."[7]

General Gates, however, was not a lax commander and possessed talents of his own. He immediately attacked the problems associated with the army's strategic position. Gates improved the supply situation and developed an efficient mess feeding system. He expanded the medical service, organized an effective system of rotating men back to their homes and farms to harvest their crops, and he inserted a vigorous training program. Such measures bolstered spirits and troop morale.

After viewing the terrain around the islands at the mouth of the Mohawk and concluding that it was too level to be easily defensible, Gates also began to search for a more favorable landscape.

WEDNESDAY, 20 AUGUST

As Gates was acquainting himself with his army, further to the north General Burgoyne was writing a letter. The words "It ain't over yet!" that had been found posted to a tree weeks earlier, addressed directly to Burgoyne, were haunting him more and more. Though the words were seemingly unimportant and even initially dismissed, following the disaster at Bennington they re-emerged as an ominous warning. Burgoyne could not get these four words out of his mind.

In front of his troops, the fiasco at Bennington was simply downplayed. A minor setback with no significant loss. But deep down, Burgoyne knew differently. Anticipating a possible defeat, he wrote directly to Germain to prepare him for the worst.

A careful review of Burgoyne's lengthy letter does not indicate that he thought disaster was imminent; but it does specify that problems and situations had arisen which, if not rectified, could result in a British defeat. And in clear terms, Burgoyne's letter appealed for assistance.[8]

Regarding the food and communication situation, Burgoyne wrote, "... in all parts the industry and management in driving cattle and removing corn [away from the British] are indefatigable and certain. [Another problem is:] The want of communication with Sir William Howe. Of the messengers I have sent, I know of two being hanged, and am ignorant whether any of the rest arrived."

Burgoyne also warned that "Washington has detached Sullivan with two thousand five hundred men to Albany; that Putnam is in the Highlands with four thousand men."

Evidently Burgoyne was also seeking new orders or more freedom of movement when he wrote, "Had I a latitude in my orders, I should think it my duty to wait in this position, or perhaps, as far back as Fort Edward...; but my orders being positive to force a junction with Sir William Howe, I apprehend I am not at liberty to remain inactive longer than shall be necessary to collect twenty-five days' provision."

But Burgoyne's strongest warning was doubtless the following:

The great bulk of the country is undoubtedly with Congress in principle and zeal; and their measures are executed with a secrecy and dispatch that are not to be equaled. Wherever the king's forces point, militia to the amount of three or four thousand assemble in twenty-four hours; they bring with them their subsistence, etc, and the alarm over, they return to their farms. The Hampshire Grants [9] in particular, a country unpeopled and almost unknown in the last war, now abounds in the most active and rebellious race of the continent, and hangs like a gathering storm on my left...

After producing a copy for his own records, Burgoyne sealed the letter and ordered it to be immediately carried to Montreal. From there a ship would take it across the ocean to England. If everything went well, Germain would receive it in about six weeks. Provided, of course, the runner was not intercepted or killed.

The moment Burgoyne's army emerged from the thick wilderness and approached the Hudson River, it entered a region inhabited by various settlers. This, in itself, would impact negatively upon Burgoyne's army and its goals.

Though many people fled the areas of intense fighting, others remained, especially those who lived around the periphery of his army. Within these regions also resided a number of colonists of German descent who now regarded themselves as Americans.

Von Riedesel's German soldiers were confused by the irreverent attitude of these German-Americans. Teutonic settlers in the New World were just as strong in their opposition to the English king as they were of soldiers recruited in Germany by the British to fight for him. Though born in America, many were still thoroughly fluent in German. "What harm have we done you? You have come here to ruin us!" So uttered an older woman of German heritage one day to Captain Gerhardt Enwald. Another officer, referring to Germans he encountered in Pennsylvania, expressed a view which applied to most of the Germans residing in America: "They are steeped to the American idea of liberty and are unbearable."[10]

Though courageous, the Germans serving in Burgoyne's army began to increasingly view the campaign with uncertainty. By August many, if not most, harbored doubts about it. This was especially true among those forcibly pressed into service,[11] those who were lured to the New World by false promises, or those who had always viewed enlistment as a chance to escape to America.

Knowing of their tenuous loyalty to the British crown, throughout the Revolutionary War the patriots constantly agitated the Germans to desert and join an American army. Various leaflets, written in German, were circulated among the invaders. The leaflets promised freedom, land, a pension, and various other benefits. In its search for skilled soldiers, the Northern Army also did its share in agitating German personnel to desert.

The best agitators were girls and young women of German descent. They were very effective, especially late at night when loneliness and homesickness set in. Approaching a solitary picket post hundreds of yards from a camp, a woman would gently and softly call out in German, "Brother, please. Don't shoot. Come here, please." Emerging from cover, she might cautiously proceed forward while continuously engaging a soldier in dialogue. The sentry would note the cleanliness of the girl or how pretty she looked. Her beautiful smile, coupled with the smell of perfume, eliminated all fears.

The women always knew what to say. "What have you got in Germany?" Before a lonely soldier could respond, she would provide the answer, "Nothing! So come with me. Do not be afraid. We will not harm you. The Americans will be kind to you. Freedom and land await you." She would put out her hand. He would reach for it. Shouldering his musket, he might depart with the girl. His days of service in a German unit within the British army were forever over.

Angered that his Germans were beginning to desert, Burgoyne verbally assailed von Riedesel and a number of the other senior ranking German officers. It was bad enough that the Indians, Canadians, and loyalists were fleeing. But now, the Germans!

To halt the exodus, Burgoyne issued a reward of twenty dollars to anyone who captured and brought in a deserter. He also gave his remaining Indians authority to intercept any men attempting to leave their colors. If they wanted to, they could even kill and scalp them. This way, they would not only earn a twenty-dollar reward but would make additional money later on when selling the scalp.

To show that he was serious, Burgoyne ordered that a German grenadier named Fassel-Abend was to be executed. Previously, Fassel-Abend had defected to the patriots near Fort Ticonderoga, thus being one of the first Germans to do so. Shortly afterwards, along with a group of fellow patriots, he was recaptured near Skenesborough while serving in the Northern Army. Along with the other prisoners, he was initially taken to Fort Ticonderoga where prisoners of war were kept prior to being transported to Canada.

Brought back to the army, the young grenadier turned Northern Army patriot faced a firing squad near Fort Edward. Per Burgoyne's orders, witnesses from each German unit were to be on hand for the execution. Even von Riedesel was ordered to attend. Following the execution, Burgoyne ordered the Indians to hunt down and bring back any German, British, Canadian, or loyalist deserter. Afterwards, a deserter received a public whipping. Up to one thousand lashes were administered, enough to kill the hardiest soldier.

Yet despite Burgoyne's efforts, the desertion rate did not plummet. On the contrary, "Gentleman Johnny's" punishments actually lowered morale, and worse, Fassel-Abend's execution angered many of his fellow Germans. They even faulted von Riedesel for not standing up to Burgoyne. The young grenadier's execution only exacerbated the deterioration in German-British relations, as arguments, thievery, and even open fighting between the two groups became more commonplace.[12]

THURSDAY, 21 AUGUST–SATURDAY, 6 SEPTEMBER

Skirmishing, patrolling, and bringing in supplies by the wilderness road and from the base of Lake George to Fort Miller continued. It was also during this time that Burgoyne received, via an Indian messenger, General St. Leger's letter written in Oswego informing Burgoyne that he had been forced to retreat from Fort Stanwix and would now return to Canada. In an effort to at placate Burgoyne, St. Leger assured him that upon his return to Canada he would immediately assemble another force and would soon link up with him at a later date via Lake Champlain.

For Burgoyne, this was devastating news. If he could not link up with Howe, he had at least been counting on the arrival of St. Leger. Though he knew that St. Leger's force was not very powerful, the addition of 2,000 to 3,000 soldiers from the west would have improved his situation considerably. And after all, St. Leger's mission had included the recruitment of loyalists residing within the Mohawk Valley. The morale and psychological rewards would have been just as great as the gain in manpower. For the time being, Burgoyne decided to keep St. Leger's failure a secret. Other than informing a few key officers, no one else was to know.

The lack of reinforcements however, was not the only problem. By

1 September many of Burgoyne's Indians had departed. As more and more left, it became increasingly difficult for Burgoyne to properly screen and protect his army. It was also becoming increasingly easier for individuals to approach, snipe, observe, and harass his force. Such was the case near Saratoga Lake in early September.

Conducting a three-man patrol for the patriots, Captain Durham, accompanied by Daniel Spike and an unidentified African-American, neared the British army. East of the Wagman Farm, they observed five loyalists. They were resting with their guns stacked, and several of them appeared to be sleeping. Seeing a moment of opportunity, the three rushed the loyalists. Captain Durham and his men seized their guns and captured all five. After binding and gagging them, the loyalist prisoners were brought to the patriot camp. Amongs the five was a known spy named Lovelace. This man was tried in a court martial presided over by General Stark, and he was found guilty and hanged. As for the other four, they remained as prisoners of war in Albany until their release in 1783.

Around Albany, General Gates had concluded that he was sitting on unfavorable ground and, knowing that to the north of him the elevated terrain offered an advantage, he decided to proceed to it.

His action was based on a combined offensive-defensive strategy. He was also confident that at long last the Northern Army could successfully engage Burgoyne's force because it had significantly improved in strength and quality. By the end of 6 September, Gates had over 10,000 troops assembled in the Albany area and the strength was rising daily.[13] Included within the army was an effective engineer force commanded by Colonels Thaddeus Kosciuszko and Jeduthan Baldwin. Several artillery pieces had been secured and a small cavalry force was also structured.[14]

SUNDAY, 7 SEPTEMBER
General Gates issued the army an order to prepare to march. Expecting to move once again southward, many were amazed that they were actually heading north. Their destination was Stillwater.

TUESDAY, 9 SEPTEMBER
On this day, the first advance patriot units reached Stillwater and immediately began to dig in. Previously, Kosciusko had begun construction of some fortifications. But when Schuyler issued the order to

retreat, the work had ceased. Returning to the site with the advance guard, Kosciuszko renewed his efforts.

But the patriots did not stay in Stillwater very long. They realized that better terrain existed even further to the north; also, General Gates wanted to position himself closer to Burgoyne. This higher ground, through which Schuyler's troops had recently marched, was known in 1777 as Bemis Heights.

Considering that perhaps the Heights would be an ideal site, Gates dispatched two of his aides, Colonel James Wilkinson and Colonel Udny Hay, along with Colonel Kosciuszko, to check out the area. Upon their return, they informed the general that the terrain was better suited for defense than Stillwater. Wanting to see it for himself, Gates, accompanied by the trio, returned to the Heights.

Gates liked what he saw. He was confident that from here, his Northern Army could effectively engage Burgoyne. In the event that the British decided to retreat to Fort Ticonderoga, or even retreat to Canada itself, the Northern Army would be closer and in a much better position to pursue.

En route to Bemis Heights, General Gates traveled north on a road along the Hudson known as the River Road. It took a traveler either directly south to Albany or north to Saratoga and beyond. Traveling northward, Gates noted that with the river on his right he could not be outflanked on that side. Approaching the Bemis Heights from behind he came to an intersection where stood an enterprise known as the Bemis Tavern. From this intersection the main River Road continued directly northward; however, another road veered to the left or westward. Known as Wagon Trek Road, it spanned the entire rear base of Bemis Heights.

Several hundred yards to the right of this intersection, the Hudson River flows through a narrow defile. Here the western bluffs of the river rise more than 100 feet. If someone stood on these bluffs and looked westward, they would immediately see River Road, the intersection, the tavern, flat ground, and, just slightly beyond the road, the base of Bemis Heights.

The Heights themselves stretched east and west, thus forming a natural obstacle to any force approaching from the north. They also overlook the River Road, Wagon Trek Road, and the Hudson. The Heights are not superbly high. However, since they lie at the peripheral edge of the Adirondack Mountains, which lie not far to the west and north, some of the western portions of the Bemis Heights reach elevations of up to 300 feet. And in 1777, both slopes of the Heights were heavily wooded.

Immediately to the north of Bemis Heights are some ravines traversed by streams and larger creeks. Most of them empty into the Hudson; some flow year-round while others are intermittent. In 1777, most were unnamed but one of the larger creeks was known as Mill Creek. This creek in turn was fed by a series of streams of which the most prominent were the North Branch, Middle Branch, and South Branch. North of Mill Creek lay the so-called Great Ravine. A sizable stream also flowed through this ravine. Most of the watercourses interlaced one another. Along with the several swamps positioned in between, this terrain formed a number of natural obstacles, especially in the late fall and spring when the rains fell or the snows melted.

Though the terrain was mostly wooded, here and there some fairly large farm fields existed. Early settlers, seeking to carve out a livelihood from the difficult wilderness, had painstakingly cleared plots of land. By 1777 many of these farms had been abandoned, but some barns and cabins were still evidently in use. The farms of John Freeman, John Neilson, Asa Chatfield, and a Mr. Barber were some still being worked.

Another advantage Gates noted in the terrain was that about five and a half miles directly to the west of the Hudson River and virtually adjacent the western edge of Bemis Heights lay a sizable lake. Known in the aftermath of the Revolutionary War as Lake Saratoga, it was no less than five miles in length stretching primarily north to south. This lake would serve as a huge natural obstacle. It was also visible from the western and central portions of Bemis Heights; therefore, if Burgoyne's army continued to advance southward, as predicted by Gates, his army would be funneled directly toward the Bemis Heights by the Hudson on his left and Lake Saratoga on his right. And here, within this huge engagement area, Burgoyne's army could be halted, engaged, and possibly destroyed.

Once the decision was made to fortify Bemis Heights, fighting positions had to be constructed. But in order to construct anything, man-made items such as boards, wooden planks, tools, nails and similar items, are needed. If an army does not possess such items, it cannot dig itself in effectively.

Fortunately for the patriots, on the very same day that the Battle of Bennington was being fought, Colonel Baldwin, with 280 soldiers from the 7th Massachusetts Continental Regiment,[15] had arrived in the

Stillwater-Saratoga area. Some of Baldwin's troops traveled up the road on horseback but most traveled in bateaux northward on the Hudson River. Baldwin's mission was to destroy any remaining bridges and roads. Locating several saw mills within the area and knowing that the Northern Army would need barrier and construction material, Baldwin and his men removed 40,000 planks and boards, numerous boxes of nails, crates of tools, tar pitch barrels, wagons, and other items. These were shipped back down the river on the bateaux. En route downriver, they also noted two individuals with supplies crossing the river to a small wooded island. Because it appeared to be suspicious, a check of the site revealed it to be a hiding place for loyalists and their families from the Stillwater area. Some were even "persons of wealth," and all were awaiting Burgoyne's arrival. Securing them as prisoners, the patriots took them downriver. Colonel Baldwin's effort was productive because the lumber and construction material could now be utilized in the construction of fortifications, buildings, troop housing billets, and for reinforcing and building additional bridges on and behind Bemis Heights.

WEDNESDAY, 10 SEPTEMBER

On this day Burgoyne's army moved to the vicinity of the Batten Kill River[16] where it flows into the Hudson from the east. As anticipated by Gates, Burgoyne would cross the Hudson in order to reach Albany. Throughout the 10th, 11th and 12th, his army constructed a bridge.[17]

Prior to resuming his march, Burgoyne had remained in place for over three weeks as his army struggled to bring in enough supplies, cannons, ammunition, wagons, carts, horses, and such other items as it could gather. After accumulating enough materiel, Burgoyne decided to resume his movement southward. Although his food situation had not yet reached a critical level, he knew that he could not wait much longer. He was not certain he could count on a major resupply from Canada, and it was also nearing mid-September. The nights were becoming increasingly cooler, and the first snowfalls were just around the corner. So Burgoyne had to make a command decision—either march to Albany or retreat back to Canada. He opted to capture Albany.

Burgoyne had to choose one of two routes in order to reach Albany, each with its advantages and disadvantages.

The first option, after crossing the Hudson River, was to advance southward along the river's western bank toward Bemis Heights.

Though Burgoyne's scouts and Indians reported that the Heights were being fortified, the patriots' effort was concentrated toward the east, nearer the river. The western portion, though steeper, was passable. High terrain alone was not daunting to Burgoyne, and his men had already negotiated steep hills at Mount Defiance near Ticonderoga and at Zion Hill at Hubbardton.

The second option would be to head down the Hudson River on its eastern side. But somewhere in the vicinity of Albany, which lay on the west bank, it would have to be crossed. This would be a far more complicated task because there the river is much wider and flows at a much faster pace. Furthermore, the Northern Army would not remain idly in its positions at Bemis Heights. After noting Burgoyne's army marching southward from across the river, Gates would simply march alongside it from the other side, prepared to contest a crossing. And to construct a bridge across from Albany in the face of a large patriot force would have been extremely difficult, if not impossible.

After analyzing his two options, Burgoyne opted to cross the Hudson at its more northern point to utilize the River Road in his southward march to Albany. Just as the patriots counted on the Hudson protecting their right flank, Burgoyne would use it to protect his left. By crossing the Hudson and destroying all of its bridges, Burgoyne would be isolating any patriot threat from the east. In turn, this would enable him to position many more of his soldiers, along with much more firepower, directly to his front. Determined to destroy the Northern Army once and for all, Burgoyne opted for an uncontested crossing of the river followed by what surely would be a set-piece battle against the patriot force defending Albany.

During the time that Burgoyne had paused, he did receive a reinforcement of about 300 to 350 fresh German soldiers; additionally, extra supplies, horses, and ammunition arrived from Canada. Burgoyne also ordered General Powell, Fort Ticonderoga's commander, to send down most of his German troops along with as many of the British soldiers and all of the supplies that he could muster. Powell complied.

Burgoyne knew that the patriots were growing stronger by the day. But he was confident that his European soldiers were still, man-to-man, better fighters, or at least more disciplined in battle. At last, he was going to have a showdown with the patriots' main force. With the summer about to end, it was now or never.

FRIDAY, 12 SEPTEMBER

On this day, General Gates issued the order to occupy the heights and prepare them for defense. Colonel Kosciuszko immediately began work on the fortifications.

Prior to moving out, Gates received a visit from the Chief Chaplain of the Northern Army, Reverend Samuel Kirkland.

Though he had been assigned to Fort Stanwix, Kirkland happened to be somewhere else just prior to its encirclement by St. Leger. As the army's Chief Chaplain, Kirkland was monitoring many sites within a huge region; therefore, he was not caught up in its siege. Traveling around exposed the chaplain to the various horrors of the Wilderness War and he was totally disgusted by it.

Of course, Kirkland knew that warfare is brutal in and of itself. But the battles fought on Long Island and New York City in 1776, including the winter battles in New Jersey into early 1777, had been conducted with a certain humanity. By and large the civilian populace was left alone, prisoners were not violated,[18] torture was unheard of, and property damage was kept to a minimum.

The wilderness war was totally different. From Oswego to Vermont, across the region of Lakes Champlain and George to Albany, and southward into and through the Highlands, there existed brutality, savagery, and viciousness virtually unknown in any of the other theaters.

Innocent men, women, and children were slaughtered. Scalping, the pulling out of an enemy's heart as he lay held down by others, was rampant. Prisoners were known to be abused or slaughtered. Torture was commonplace. Entire farms, settlements, and villages were burned down. Even several sizable towns were razed into non-existence. Crops were destroyed and farm animals slaughtered. Physical beatings were routine and rape occurred.[19] War crimes had been committed by both sides in the fighting in the Mohawk and Schoharie Valleys. Kirkland also noted that in the aftermath of the Battle of Bennington, most of the British and German prisoners had been robbed. Though acknowledging that in general they had not been physically violated, when it came to the loyalists, murder, torture, and abuse was part of their fate. As proof of the insanity going on, Kirkland cited in disgust how just several streets away from the Northern Army's Albany headquarters, a scalp-buying business was "right at this very moment conducting a lucrative business."

General Gates sympathized with the chaplain. As General Schuyler previously had done, Gates took steps to halt the brutality. Part of the problem stemmed from the fact that the Northern Army was operating in a region encompassing tens of thousands of square miles. Mercenaries and irregulars, combined with common criminals, also posed problems. Whether these brutalities were also attributable to the wilderness temperament of its inhabitants can only be surmised.

General Gates, however, assured Chaplain Kirkland that he would continue strong attempts to curb the excesses and that he would attempt to establish a dialogue with the British commanders to reduce them. As for the scalp-buying business, it was shut down on that very day.[20]

Concerned about its northern theater, America's Continental Congress decided to thoroughly investigate the region. Congress was fully aware of the thorny issues such as certain units operating independently, while others had refused to be subordinated into the Northern Army, along with Vermont's refusal to join the newly born nation. Other important issues and pressing matters existed and, on occasion, it seemed as if no one had full authority or control of what was going on. Even General Washington himself had expressed concerns over the northern theater. Therefore, that summer Congress decided to conduct a formal fact-finding mission. Timothy Pickering, a Boston intellectual who hailed from a prominent family, was designated to head the investigation.

After traveling through various towns and settlements, Pickering was truly amazed at what he saw. Especially in the wilderness settlements, he encountered a type of civilization completely foreign from the kind which existed in the coastal areas or major cities.

Out in the wilderness the gun and tomahawk ruled. By and large, its populace resented any type of rules and laws. Many refused to adhere to any kind of authority. Disputes could be settled violently. Robbers and thieves were administered a public whipping. In the event that this was to occur, a public announcement was made. People would even show up with picnic baskets and turn the occasion into a family outing. Among the onlookers, traders sold guns, fur pelts, and war booty. Wrestling matches, especially with black bears, drew crowds.

Unlike in Boston, where education was emphasized and an intellectual respected, little of this existed in the wilderness. Many people could not read or write. What schooling existed was largely confined within the larger towns such as Albany. The world of art was foreign to most. Beyond a beautifully created rifle, pistol, or tomahawk, little else of artistry mattered. Contracts were totally unknown, as deals were settled by one's word and a handshake. And woe be to any individual who broke his word. Lawyers were few and far between, and most of the inhabitants steered away from them.

As for what the Constitution, the Bill of Rights, self-rule, and equality represented, most of the region's inhabitants had little or no understanding. That was all fine for the intellectuals living in the big cities, but the forest inhabitants didn't care one way or another. They did, however, resent the King and English rule. As Pickering wrote, "The inhabitants appear to be a wild ungovernable race, little less savage than their tawny neighbors."[21]

SATURDAY, 13 SEPTEMBER

Burgoyne's army began to cross the Hudson River, continuing the process over the next two days.[22]

The first to cross were the English regiments. Then came the Germans; simultaneously, a fleet of about 200 bateaux, loaded with supplies, floated slowly downriver alongside the army.

MONDAY, 15 SEPTEMBER

By mid-day Burgoyne's army had completed its crossing. Always a dangerous affair, the river crossing was conducted with no serious incidents. That same day, the bridge was dismantled. As its pieces floated downstream, Burgoyne cut his last link with Canada. He was now operating alone. His men moved for the remainder of the day, "with drums beating and colors flying."[23] Burgoyne's army marched southward to a location known as "Dovecote" or "Dovegat."[24]

TUESDAY, 16 SEPTEMBER

Throughout the day, Burgoyne organized his forces for the continuing march south. Scouts were also dispatched ahead to probe for patriot positions. Here and there sections of the road previously torn apart by the patriots were repaired and some small bridges were built. The British reached General Schuyler's estate, through which flowed the Fish Kill Creek. They couldn't fail to note the burned fields and chopped down fruit trees, though most buildings had been left intact. After noting Schuyler's beautiful home, Burgoyne immediately moved in.

WEDNESDAY, 17 SEPTEMBER

After crossing the Fish Kill, Burgoyne's army marched another three miles south to a farm known as "The Sword." Now they stood about four miles directly to the north of Bemis Heights and the patriot positions. It would not be long before a battle would begin.

Although Burgoyne had not yet formally engaged Gates, skirmishing was rampant. In one instance, a party of British soldiers and loyalists had been dispatched to dig up potatoes on a farm to the west of present-day Victory Mills. Encountering armed citizens, a gun battle ensued. Hearing the shots, a sizable patriot force patrolling in the area rushed in. Several enemy soldiers were killed, twenty others were captured, and their horses and wagons were secured. Brought to Bemis Heights, the prisoners revealed vital information.

During this entire time, the patriots had been working around the clock. By 17 September, they had largely completed their project. Nearly 10,000 soldiers, augmented with civilians, toiled at the project. The patriot defense system stretched for almost four miles from the western bank of the Hudson River. Where the Mill Creek flowed into the Hudson, a strong battery was constructed. A number of support batteries were also erected along Mill Creek.

A huge trench, nearly a mile in length, was dug eastward from the base of Bemis Heights to the cliffs overlooking the Hudson. This trench also cut through River Road, though the patriots constructed a movable bridge to cross over the trench when utilizing the road. Wooden planks, nailed on two long logs, were placed right over the trench. With ropes attached to each end, horses or men could quickly tow the makeshift bridge back and forth across the trench. In the event the enemy approached, it would simply be pulled back. Additionally, a huge three-sided, or U-shaped, position with cannons facing outward from all three sides[25] was erected just a short distance to the north of the trench. Anyone coming down the road to breach the trench would first have to overrun this redoubt.

Other positions were erected both to the north of Bemis Heights and upon their crest. In one case a barn was converted into a strong defensive position. Owned by a local farmer named John Neilson, the farm lay virtually on the base of Bemis Heights' northern slope. Reinforcing the barn with lumber and burlap and canvas bags filled with sand, it became known as Fort Neilson. Among the soldiers proudly serving in the Northern Army and manning the fort was Mr. Neilson himself.

Realizing the importance of maintaining troops across the Hudson River in order to secure and patrol the river's eastern bank, a floating bridge was also constructed across the river. Once again, General Glover's fishermen-turned-soldiers, along with some of the engineers, played an important role in the construction of this bridge.

Regardless how strong a position is, it is useless if not manned and protected by soldiers; therefore, various units were positioned from the edge of the Hudson River westward into Bemis Heights.

General Glover's brigade was positioned closest to the river. His troops manned the positions adjacent to Mill Creek's southern bank, and they defended the area between the River Road and the Hudson. They also protected the trench and the intersection where the River and Wagon Trek Roads converged, and where the Bemis Tavern was located. Glover established his headquarters near Bemis Tavern.

To the immediate left (or west) of Glover was General John Nixon's brigade. Nixon's troops defended the terrain to the west of River Road and secured the eastern slope of Bemis Heights overlooking the River Road. General John Paterson's brigade was positioned to Nixon's left. These men defended a large portion of the eastern section of Bemis Heights. Because General Gates regarded the entire right sector as his most critical area, all three commanders fell under his direct control.

Colonel Daniel Morgan, along with Lieutenant-Colonel Henry Dearborn's light New Hampshire infantry, were positioned to the immediate left of Paterson's brigade. On Morgan's left was the brigade of General Enoch Poor. General Ebenezer Learned was positioned next to Poor's left flank and General Abraham Ten Broeck, with nearly 2,000 militiamen, was posted to Learned's left. Both Ten Broeck and Learned were to defend the entire defense system from any attack coming from the west and rear. Major General Benedict Arnold held overall command of the left sector.

Various other commanders were also in place. Colonels Joseph Cilley, George Reid,[26] and Alexander Scammell commanded, respectively, the 1st, 2nd, and 3rd New Hampshire Continentals. These three regiments comprised Poor's brigade.

Militia General William Whipple, along with militia Colonels John Bailey, Thaddeus Cook, Philip Van Cortlandt, Henry Jackson, Jonathan

Latimer, Henry Livingston, James Wesson, and Lieutenant-Colonels
John Brooks, and James Brickett were positioned with their units to the
rear, but were to be ready to reinforce the center or any position at a
moment's notice. Colonel James Wilkinson served as adjutant to
General Gates. Major Griffith Williams, an artillery officer, commanded the Northern Army's cannons.[27] Colonel Van Vechten, who directed
operations and served as a liaison officer between the militia and the
Northern Army for General Schuyler, did the same for General Gates.
Doctor James Thacher, who was based in Albany, served as the chief
medical officer. Reverend Enos Hitchcock was still the Chief Chaplain.
Excluding Generals Gates and Arnold, who both held the rank of Major
General, all of the other generals were Brigadiers. Major General Gates,
however, was the senior ranking officer.

By now General Gates had a combat strength of over 11,000 men.[28]
According to various sources, "they were well fed, confident, and determined."[29] And the army was still growing stronger by the day. Unlike
Burgoyne, who was losing strength through casualties or desertions,[30]
the Northern Army was rapidly gaining strength.

Militiamen and Continentals were not the only ones to appear.
About 150 Native American Iroquois warriors reported to the Northern
Army on or about 15 September. [31] These warriors hailed from the
Seneca, Cayuga, Onondaga, Mohawk, Oneida, and Tuscarora tribes.
General Gates gladly welcomed them and gave them the following mis-
sion: they were to seek out enemy positions and screen the western flank
of the Northern Army on both sides of Saratoga Lake.

Within the ranks of the Northern Army whites, blacks, and Native
Americans soldiered side-by-side. Americans know that during the
Revolutionary War men and women of European heritage from the
Scots, Welsh, Irish, German, and English, along with Frenchmen and
Poles, fought for the patriot cause. But from Lake Champlain to the
Highlands in the Catskills, foreign personnel of various other national-
ities also served and fought in the Northern Army.

Kosciuszko was not the only Pole present with the patriots. And
along with the Polish soldiers, Czechs and Slovaks manned cannons up
and down the Hudson River. Hungarians served on horseback and foot.
Pascal de Angelis, who hailed from Italy, was now manning a position
on Bemis Heights. A soldier by the name of M. Hussack is registered in
the 1777 Northern Army record book. He cited his birthplace as
Eastern Galicia, although Hussack is a common Ukrainian name.

Dutch names are widely registered on the rolls, not surprising because they comprised many of New York's (or New Amsterdam's) original settlers. Many Germans, including those born in Germany, served in the Northern Army. Greek seamen manned bateaux and river boats, delivered supplies via water routes, constructed water obstacles, and fought both on water and land. In the aftermath of the Revolutionary War, when the patriot prisoners were released from the cruel prisons and prison ships located in New York City, six of the survivors were Greek. Several had been captured in the Hudson River area during 1777.

Scandinavians, especially Danes and Swedes, participated. Jewish males also served. Born in 1759, Isaac Franks was a poor Jew, but he could read and was fond the Declaration of Independence. He too, joined the Northern Army.[32] Others, fearing arrest because they spoke out against England's policies as they resided under British rule (such as in New York City), had no choice but to flee. With nowhere to go and being supportive of the cause, they ended up in the Northern Army. Among such was Rabbi Gershom Mendes Seixas. Quickly gathering up his family, the Torah scrolls, certain holy objects, prayer books, and candlesticks, Rabbi Seixas fled as General Washington was retreating from the city. Fleeing to Stratford, Connecticut, the rabbi continued his spiritual work and rendered support to the Northern Army.[33] And Haym Solomon, who was born in Poland but arrived in America as a young man, poured thousands of dollars into the patriot cause. His efforts helped achieve victory in the Wilderness War of 1777.[34]

Each continental regiment, militia unit, and guerrilla group had men and women of African descent. Loyal to both his master and the cause, young Prince Whipple marched off to war with General William Whipple. He was but one of many blacks who served from Oswego to Vermont and from the Canadian border to New York City. Black patriots were found wherever the fighting raged. Though no precise figure exists on how many blacks served in the Northern Army in 1777, it may be surmised that nearly 1,000, if not more, were on hand.[35]

THURSDAY, 18 SEPTEMBER

Early in the morning, Burgoyne's army probed slightly southward. He positioned himself in a place presently known as Wilbur's Basin. By moving forward, Burgoyne now stood no more than two miles from the American front line.[36] His chief British commanders were Major

General William Phillips of the artillery; Brigadier Generals Simon Fraser and James Hamilton, who commanded the grenadiers and light infantry; and among his Germans were Major General Friedrich Adolph von Riedesel and Colonels Johann Specht and Walther von Gall.[37]

It was unknown to Burgoyne, as he advanced southward and made preparations to attack, that other critical events were unfolding in the theater. Though limited in scope and conducted far behind in the rear, these events would nevertheless play a significant role in the British general's demise.

Colonel Seth
Warner's Green
Mountain Boys
battling with
advancing
English-German
forces at the
Battle of
Hubbardton,
7 July 1777.
*Painting
by Ihor
Korotash;
author's
collection.*

Tight Spot. A Patriot rifleman scout hiding from a loyalist patrol on the northern front, 1777. *Oil on panel by H. David Wright ©2002*

American Rifleman. *Acrylic painting by H. David Wright ©1986*

One of Washington's
Men. *Pencil drawing
by H. David Wright
©2004*

Sizing Up The Enemy.
*Pencil drawing by
H. David Wright ©2006*

Aim Small.
*Pencil drawing by
H. David Wright ©2002*

A Patriot firing line during a re-enactment of the Battle of Hubbardton, on the actual site in west-central Vermont. *Photo courtesy of the Vermont Division for Historic Preservation.*

The heights at Hubbardton were key factors for both sides during the fighting. *Photograph courtesy of the Vermont Division for Historic Preservation.*

The British were repeatedly repulsed at what today is known as Monument Hill, before finally seizing the position. *Photo courtesy of the Vermont Division for Historic Preservation.*

British troops fought the initial battle until German reinforcements arrived. *Photo courtesy of the Vermont Division for Historic Preservation.*

Patriot re-enactors at Hubbardton, with not only genuine period costumes but authentic weapons. *Photo courtesy of the Vermont Division for Historic Preservation.*

Hubbardton was not just the only battle of the Revolution to take place on Vermont soil, it was one of the bloodiest of the war in terms of numbers engaged. *Photo courtesy of the Vermont Division for Historic Preservation.*

British Camp. After the battle was over the British kept the field and were busy taking care of the wounded. The majesty of the battle's setting is apparent in this photo. *Photo courtesy of the Vermont Division for Historic Preservation.*

Breymann's Redoubt—Battle of Saratoga. *Painting by Don Troiani; reproduced with permission from the artist.*

XVIII

The Patriots Raid Fort Ticonderoga

For many weeks, scout teams and long-range patrols had been operating deep behind Burgoyne's army. Some of these teams had even been reconnoitering Fort Ticonderoga and the surrounding area. Vital information had been brought back, and occasionally scouts had made life miserable for those left behind to man the long communication and supply line from Canada.

In Pawlet, Vermont,[1] located on the Mettawee River, Major General Lincoln was commanding a strength of about 2,000 troops.[2] Initially, one of the reasons why Lincoln had been dispatched in July from Washington's army was to organize forces to attack Burgoyne's left (eastern) flank. Because of certain issues, other than launching teams to probe Fort Ticonderoga, no sizable raiding missions had been undertaken. However, by early September, Lincoln had finally organized a sufficient strength of ex-Green Mountain Boys, militiamen, and rangers to conduct some significant raids.

Lincoln learned from his scouts that most of the patriot prisoners in British hands had been moved from the main fort at Ticonderoga to the area of Lake George, where they had been used as slave laborers in harsh conditions to haul the British army's goods. For some unknown reason, the prisoners were still being kept there. Lincoln reasoned that if he could free these men, lives would not only be saved but it would raise the patriots' morale. Lincoln also wanted to cripple as much of Burgoyne's supply line as possible. Lincoln was not just thinking in short-term military goals. He also wanted to demonstrate to Canada's Governor General Carleton that patriot forces still retained the capability to operate close to Canada. Besides releasing prisoners and further

227

hindering the enemy's communications, a large raid would also demoralize the enemy—particularly the loyalists—counter British propaganda claims of victory, and possibly induce Carleton to recall Burgoyne completely out of New York and back to Canada.

In order to conduct the raid, Lincoln divided his attacking force into three groups, each consisting of 500 volunteers commanded by a colonel. Lincoln carefully selected the leaders and their men. Each raider had to be tough both physically and morally. Because vast distances would have to be covered on foot through mostly uncharted forests, each raider had to possess the ability to move rapidly and survive in the wilderness environment. Older men, along with those who were known to possess physical problems or handicaps were excluded. Each man had to be proficient not only with his rifle or musket but also with a knife and tomahawk. To prepare his men for the raid, Lincoln ordered a series of long training marches with time factors. Anyone who failed to complete a march within a prescribed time was excluded.

Though three colonels would be involved, Lincoln specified that Colonel John Brown was to be the senior ranking officer and command the entire group. Colonel Brown also knew the area well. In 1775 and 1776 he had been a key player in planning military operations against British-held Fort Ticonderoga. His expertise would prove invaluable.[3]

Lincoln's plan called for the three separate forces to undertake three specific tasks, though in actuality they would be mutually supportive and work in conjunction to achieve the final mission.

Colonel Brown's mission was to secure Mount Defiance, attack the landing site on the northern shoreline of Lake George where the prisoners were being kept, free them, and destroy whatever boats and supplies he came upon. Lastly, if possible, he was to capture Fort Ticonderoga. Colonel Johnson's primary mission was to create a sizable diversion on Mount Independence to keep Fort Ticonderoga's personnel pinned down. Should Brown conclude that he could assault the fort, Johnson's secondary mission would be to support him.

As for Colonel Woodbridge, his mission was to secure Skenesborough to protect the two attacking forces from any enemy forces suddenly appearing from the south. Scouts' reports revealed that other than some occasional troops in transit, no enemy forces had recently been seen at Skenesborough. Woodbridge was also to destroy any piers, boats, ships, and enemy supply warehouses found in and around the town. He was also to be ready to follow orders to move his force against

Fort Ticonderoga in the event extra manpower was needed for the assault.

At this time, the enemy troop strength at Fort Ticonderoga was estimated at 900 men.[4] Primarily, the 53rd Foot manned the site. However, some naval personnel, Canadians, and a small number of German grenadiers from the Prince Frederick Regiment were also based there.

Arriving in Skenesborough, Colonel Woodbridge and his raiders moved silently and swiftly through the forests from Pawlet to Skenesborough near present day West Pawlet,[5] Granville, Middle Granville, North Granville, and Truthville. To remain undetected, they stayed off the roads and bypassed all villages, hamlets and towns. Though these places were largely deserted, the patriots could not chance running into a sympathizer of the King, as surprise was one of the key elements needed to achieve a successful raid.

As for Brown and Johnson, their raiding groups would initially move together through the wilderness region around Lakes St. Catherine and Bomoseen where the present day towns of Sudbury and Orwell stand. West of Orwell, they would part in two different directions. Brown would head for Lake George, and Johnson for Fort Ticonderoga.

WEDNESDAY, 17 SEPTEMBER
9:00 P.M.

By this hour, all three groups had reached their jumping-off points without incident. Knowing the importance of Mount Defiance, Brown dispatched Captain Ebenezer Allen, a highly aggressive ranger officer, to secure the summit. With his company of frontiersmen, Allen began to stealthily ascend the thickly wooded and brushy slope.

Despite the pitch-black darkness and steep terrain, Allen and his rangers made excellent progress. His men moved swiftly, like cats in the dark. En route, they noted the steep road previously hacked out to haul British cannon to the top. As they neared the summit, they halted. It is not known if the sleeping British soldiers, or their half-asleep sentries, ever heard the chirping sounds of the birds. But those were the signals that indicated the rangers were in position.

Suddenly, the sharp bark of a crow's "Caw! Caw!" was heard. With knives and tomahawks in hand, the rangers stormed the summit. Tomahawks shattered skulls as hands clasped the sentrys' mouths, followed by the swift thrusting of knives to silence the sentries for good.

To prevent any unnecessary noise, the rangers slowly eased the corpses back onto the ground. In the meantime, other rangers rushed those sleeping on the ground. Awakening them, they ordered them to remain quiet or otherwise they too would die. Quickly turning them around, the rangers tied their hands and gagged their mouths. Twenty prisoners were secured.

Allen's rangers moved swiftly, silently, and with skill. Not one ranger was killed or injured in the attack. Knowing that especially at night noise travels, they used extreme caution. For the time being, they would remain on the summit.

Not far from the mountain's base, Colonel Brown was hiding in the woods near a road. He was positioned to rush the Lake George landing. Brown had decided to utilize the road to seize his main objective. He reasoned that the last thing anyone would expect would be someone attacking straight down the road.

From where he stood, Colonel Brown could see the top of the misty summit. Then, he heard the hoot of an "owl." For a full minute the "owl" hooted. To ensure that he would hear the "owl," Colonel Brown had strung out a number of rangers between himself and the base of the summit. The moment the first ranger picked up the hoot of the "owl," he passed it on. Though it appeared as if some hungry or mating "owls" were hooting away, in actuality, the hooting was a signal system used by Colonel Brown's rangers. Swiftly but silently, Brown moved the remainder of his force onto the road and proceeded forward.

Across the lake, Colonel Johnson was slowly moving into position. Hearing the hooting sounds, he knew that his part in the three-pronged action would soon start.

Jogging down the road in the misty semi-darkness, Brown's force was observed by the British sentinels. Believing them to be incoming loyalists, the British did not even challenge them. Then it happened. Within seconds, the sentries were bound and gagged as well. Without even losing one ranger, Brown had succeeded in penetrating a critical British position. Colonel Brown hated war and killing. A graduate of Yale, he had always hoped that the colonists could secede from England through peaceful means. Caught up in the madness of 1777, however, he had no choice but to enlist into the Northern Army.

Now the landing site was just a short way up. Though it was occupied, recent scout reports revealed it to be weakly manned with no fortifications. Quickening their pace, Brown's rangers continued forward.

Nearing the site, they unleashed a massive battle cry. Screaming like madmen and whooping like Indians, it appeared as if thousands were charging in. Quickly, the patriots overran the enemy camp and secured nearly 300 prisoners, most of whom were caught sleeping in tents. Along with the prisoners, 200 bateaux, one sloop, a handful of gunboats, several cannons, hundreds of muskets, and other items of booty were secured as well. But most importantly, over 100 patriot prisoners of war were released.[6]

Unfortunately for Colonel Brown, as he and his rangers charged in, a couple of the British soldiers were outside of their tents in the woods. Hearing the screams and gunshots, they hid out of sight and soon returned to the main fort.

From his position, Colonel Johnson commanded a vigorous fire against Forts Independence and Ticonderoga. Johnson's mission was not to assault the forts. Instead, he was to pin down their defenders with small arms fire. From behind trees, brush, log piles and whatever cover the rangers could find, they directed a rapid staccato of small arms fire against both forts.

When Colonel Brown rushed the landing, he was about four miles away from the main fort. Prior to Colonel Johnson's rangers opening up, Fort Ticonderoga's defenders did not even know that a sizable ranger force was among them. A combination of distance and the roar of the cascading waters of the waterfall concealed the battle noise of Colonel Brown's attack at Lake George for the moment. But when Johnson's rangers opened fire, General Powell was surely awakened. He ordered everyone to arms.

Informed that additional prisoners were being kept at the old French Lines, Brown immediately dispatched some of his rangers to the site. In the meantime, the bulk of Brown's force moved toward Fort Ticonderoga. Scattering the one British company positioned at the French Lines, Brown's men freed more prisoners and secured a handful of British prisoners of their own. Joining those already besieging the fort, following a very short siege, Brown dispatched a messenger under a white flag to the main bastion at Fort Ticonderoga demanding that General Powell surrender. Refusing to do so, Powell's response was both simple and polite.[7]

"The garrison instructed to my charge I shall defend to the last. I am, Sir, your humble servant."

[Signed] H. Watson Powell, Brig. Genl.

THURSDAY, 18 SEPTEMBER–SUNDAY, 21 SEPTEMBER

Bringing up the cannons captured at the landing, Colonel Brown and his force bombarded Fort Ticonderoga and harassed its defenders with small arms fire for the next several days. But no actual assault took place. Concerned about casualties and abiding by General Lincoln's orders not to assault the main works, Colonel Brown issued the order not to attack. In addition to laying siege to the fort, the rangers destroyed all of the docks, bateaux, and sloops along the shoreline of Lake Champlain. All captured horses were secured, but captured cattle were driven deep into the wilderness.

MONDAY, 22 SEPTEMBER

In the morning, Colonel Brown lifted the siege.[8] Though it had been weak, the Patriots' offensive moves had nevertheless caused the British much anxiety. Of historical significance is that the last shots fired on this day were the final ones ever fired against Fort Ticonderoga. Never again would anyone wage battle at this fort.

Colonel Brown, however, was not yet through. He decided to take out the British-held position at Diamond Island located on Lake George. As for Colonel Johnson, he would return to Pawlet with his contingent, the liberated patriots, some of Colonel Brown's rangers, and all of the British prisoners. This time Johnson's force would march along the roads rather than move through the forests. Among the guards now watching over the British prisoners were the newly released patriots. With captured British muskets in their hands, they pushed along and taunted those who, just days before, had been guarding and taunting them.

4:00 P.M.

Returning to the landing on the northern shore of Lake George during the late afternoon., Brown's force with "420 men, officers included," set forth by boat "to attack Diamond Island, which lies within five miles of Fort George."[9] Brown's rangers set forth on "20 sail of (bateaux) boats, three of which were armed, with one small sloop mounting three guns and two British gun boats."[10] Everyone was on a boat. Prior to departing the lake's northern end, nearly 200 piled-up bateaux along with several gunboats and various other captured material were torched. As Brown sailed away, huge bonfires rose upward. His intent was to attack Diamond Island on the morning of the 23rd.

Sailing north on the lake, Brown's fleet captured a man who was rowing a small boat back to Fort Ticonderoga from Diamond Island. He was placed on one of the boats. As Brown's force continued down the lake, very heavy winds suddenly arose, the skies turned dark, and a storm set in. Knowing the danger of remaining on the lake, Brown ordered the entire force to beach. Throughout the remainder of the day and through most of the night, a violent storm pummeled the area. Sometime during this period as his men weathered the storm, their prisoner escaped.

TUESDAY, 23 SEPTEMBER
5:00 P.M.

Early in the morning, the rangers noted their prisoner was missing. It was feared that he had returned to Diamond Island. Or perhaps he had not. Though risky, Brown decided to go for it anyway. But when a heavy wind soon appeared and the waters of the lake became very choppy, Brown was again forced to suspend the attack "until the Morning of the 24th."[11]

Unknown to Brown, their escapee did, in fact, return to his comrades. After escaping, he fled via the shoreline to a point near the island. The man screamed until a sentry spotted him and a boat was dispatched to fetch him back. There, he informed the mixed British-German force[12] commanded by Captain Thomas Aubrey of the 47th Foot Regiment that a sizable enemy force was headed their way. Alerted to the danger and knowing that vital supplies were positioned on the island, Captain Aubrey prepared his defense.

WEDNESDAY, 24 SEPTEMBER
9:00 A.M.[13]

Colonel Brown's intent was to attack the island's northern end using the sloop with its cannon and the two gunboats. "And the other boats, I ordered to swing to the right and left of the island to attempt a landing."[14]

As Brown's flotilla approached, cannon and heavy small arms fire met them. Estimating the island's strength at several hundred defenders, Brown ordered a withdrawal.[15] Shortly afterwards, his force landed a close distance away from the island, somewhere in the vicinity of present day Kattskill Bay and Cleverdale on the lake's eastern shore. After torching all of their boats, Brown's force proceeded through the forests to Skenesborough. Later that day they linked up with Colonel Woodbridge and his rangers, and for the next several days the patriots rested at Skenesborough.

SATURDAY, 27 SEPTEMBER

A combined strength of over 900 patriots headed southeastward through the wilderness back to Pawlet. As they departed, Colonel Brown's rear guard torched all of the remaining boats and docks in Skenesborough. Another major blow had been inflicted upon Burgoyne.[16]

XIX

The First Battle of Saratoga: Freeman's Farm

FRIDAY, 19 SEPTEMBER

Awakening early in the morning, Burgoyne noted the thick white hoarfrost that covered the surrounding landscape. It had been a very cold night. Looking upon the semi-frigid scene, he knew that he could no longer wait before securing winter quarters in Albany. First, however, he had to destroy the nearby Northern Army opposing him.

When General Gates initially fortified Bemis Heights he had focused on the eastern part astride the River Road that would comprise Burgoyne's most desirable line of advance. The western portion was steeper, thus naturally more defensible, and its approaches were more difficult than via the main road near the river. Gates himself did not regard the extreme western sector of Bemis Heights to be of critical importance.[1]

Burgoyne's scouts quickly made note of this. They reported that the western portion of the Heights commanded the remainder of the American line; in fact, from there, one could look down and view Lake Saratoga and even the Hudson River. They also outlined approach routes which, though not as simple as an advance along the River Road, were not overly difficult.

For Burgoyne, this was superb. The British general immediately envisioned a scenario similar to that previously undertaken at Fort Ticonderoga. As one force would advance forward against the main patriot defense system, another, advancing from farther west, would secure the higher ground. Once accomplished, the entire patriot line would be unhinged and a collapse would ensue. At Fort Ticonderoga it was Burgoyne's right, commanded by General Fraser, which had over-

235

come the supposedly impossible terrain and won the day. And so, once again, this tactic would be repeated with Fraser in command.

In all, Burgoyne devised a three-column movement against the patriot positions. His left wing, adjacent to the Hudson River, would consist of a mixed German-English force under von Riedesel, with General Phillips as his second in command. The Germans would be the Brunswick light infantry, commanded by Specht and Rhetz, the Hesse-Hanau artillery with 19 cannons, and 100 jaeger light infantry troops. The left would also contain the entire 47th British Foot Regiment[2] (minus its two companies on Diamond Island). In all, slightly over 1,100 soldiers would comprise this wing.[3]

The center column would consist of over 1,100 soldiers[4] from the 9th, 20th, 21st, and 62nd Foot Regiments, with the 9th serving as a tactical reserve. Six cannons—three 3-pounders and three 6-pounders—would support the center, with Captain Jones commanding the artillery.

The mission of the center was twofold. After reaching the abandoned farm of a loyalist named Freeman, which was selected as a jumping off point, the center's left wing was to assist in pinning the patriots along Bemis Heights while its right was to swing around the patriot left to gain the lightlly defended portion of the Heights. General James Hamilton was to command the center.

The right wing would be composed of troops from the bulk of the 20th, 24th, 29th, 31st, and 34th Foot, and a couple of companies from the 53rd. Major Acland and Major Lindsay, the Earl of Balcarres, two noted soldiers with extensive experience in spearheading attacks, were included. Also included would be von Breymann's corps of about 500 German soldiers. All of the remaining Indians, estimated at about 50,[5] the remaining loyalists, numbering about 150,[6] and Captain Monin and his Canadians were also attached to the right. Four 6-pounder and four 3-pounder cannons were attached to this wing with Lieutenant James Hadden commanding the guns. Excluding the irregulars about 2,000 soldiers were included in the right wing.[7]

Of the three columns, Fraser's right wing was regarded as the most elite and powerful force. But its mission was also the most critical of the three.

First, it was to advance westward through a thickly forested area beyond the Freeman farm. Once accomplished, the right wing would assemble itself into battle lines. Afterwards, along with some of the units from the center, it would advance southward to the base of Bemis

Heights to ascend up and over the undefended western portion. Once over and behind the Heights, Fraser's right wing, along with some of Hamilton's forces, were to quickly reform themselves into battle formations on both sides of Wagon Trek Road. Then the combined forces would advance directly east toward the Hudson River. En route, Fraser would shatter the patriot rear and shove the Northern Army against the banks of the Hudson. Hammered and pressed by the combined forces of Fraser, Hamilton, and Von Riedesel, the patriot army would be unable to escape. Once finished off,[8] the road to Albany would be open. Of his three commanders, Burgoyne regarded General Fraser to be his most aggressive, capable, and mission-focused officer.[9]

On 19 September, Burgoyne's army registered a strength of about 7,700 troops and support personnel, though due to illness and wounds not all were effective.[10] Of his effective strength, some 4,500 would be committed. Another 1,800 would guard the boats, the immediate rear, or stand by as a reserve.[11]

6:00 A.M.

Assembling at Sword's farm, the three wings began to line up in columns. The order of march was von Riedesel, Hamilton, and Fraser. To maintain tactical control, Burgoyne positioned himself in the center directly behind General Hamilton.

8:00 A.M.

With drums beating and flags waving, Burgoyne's army advanced toward the patriots' positions. Excluding von Riedesel's column, which continued to march directly southward, Hamilton's and Fraser's columns soon veered to the southwest to proceed directly toward Freeman's farm.

Burgoyne knew that General Gates possessed more troops. But he also knew that a high percentage of Gates' army was comprised of militiamen—fighters whom Burgoyne did not hold in high esteem. As for the Continentals, Burgoyne was confident that they could be driven back as well. With heavy volleys of fire and cold steel, Burgoyne's more seasoned troops would shatter the patriots. Despite ammunition shortages, Burgoyne ordered each soldier to be issued sixty rounds. Many, however, carried more than that.

To reach the base of Bemis Heights prior to crossing over, Burgoyne's center and right wing would first have to advance through some very rough, thickly wooded, and rolling terrain. Various small streams flowed through this area and some deep gullies existed. Excluding several small farm fields chopped out here and there, the area was wooded. In consideration of the terrain, Burgoyne estimated that his center and right wings would need about two hours to reach and realign themselves in and around Freeman's Farm. Once realigned, another hour or so would be needed to get to the base of Bemis Heights with about another hour to cross over. As for von Riedesel's force, they too would need some time to clear some of the obstacles, repair a section or two of the road, and prepare to cross, on order, the Great Ravine.

As presented, the main jumping off point would be Freeman's farm. It was the ideal site with its approximately fifteen cleared acres. As for the unit commanders who would not be crossing right through the farm, they were ordered to align their units on an imaginary line running directly to the east and west of it. Once aligned, everyone was to advance directly forward and south toward Bemis Heights which stood almost a mile and a half directly to their front.

The moment Burgoyne's army began to assemble, their movement was observed. From concealed positions atop Bemis Heights, from observation posts established in the forests to the north of the heights, and along with patriots perched high up in the trees, word quickly reached General Gates and his headquarters that the British army was assembling.

10:00 A.M.

By now Gates' "eyes and ears" had also reported that two sizable British forces, augmented with Indians, Canadian, and loyalist personnel, were advancing slowly through the woods. General Arnold, who commanded the patriot army's left, was also notified.

Riding out to General Gates' headquarters, Arnold proposed to counter the British thrust by ordering Morgan's and Dearborn's units forward to the vicinity of Freeman's farm. Gates, however, was reluctant. He wanted the British to advance right up to his breastworks, from which he thought they could be repulsed.

But Arnold was adamant. He argued that if the British stormed the defense line and broke through it, the Americans would not have any place to withdraw. Therefore, by advancing forward and fighting in the woods, the British could be held and weakened. In the event the

Americans had to retire back to the breastworks, they would be able to hold these positions more effectively against a weakened British force.

Acknowledging Arnold's logic, Gates gave in. He informed Arnold that he could advance forward with Morgan's rifle brigade and Dearborn's light infantry. But Gates also ordered Arnold to keep a strong reserve within the defense system.

Informed to advance toward Freeman's Farm, Morgan ordered his troops forward. Armed with rifles and tomahawks, adorned in coonskin caps, floppy hats, and deer hide smocks, with moccasins or light boots for footwear, they surged swiftly forward. Quickly reaching Freeman's farm, Morgan's riflemen positioned themselves behind trees, stumps, and the old wooden and rock fence adjacent to the southern edge of the clearing. Some of his fighters also positioned themselves in the old farm cabin and within the barns. As for Dearborn's fighters, they positioned themselves to Morgan's immediate right. A good number of the riflemen also perched themselves in trees.

Cautiously approaching Freeman's Farm from the northeast was a sizable British force led by Major Gordon Forbes. A veteran of the Battle of Hubbardton, Forbes was very knowledgeable about American fighting tactics in wooded terrain. Now serving with General Hamilton, Forbes was ordered to probe forward. Hamilton especially wanted Forbes to check out the buildings located on Freeman's Farm prior to Hamilton bringing up any additional forces. Following closely behind Forbes were units from Hamilton's center. Along with Forbes, they too, were converging upon the farm.

12:30 P.M.

Some of Morgan's troops perched high up in the trees began to observe Forbes and his troops probing forward. Through a combination of birdcalls and hand signals, Morgan's force was warned. From behind cover, they began to take aim and search for targets.

Approaching the Freeman's farm clearing, Forbes and his troops at first just observed. Then, slowly, they began to step onto the field. With muskets pointed to the front as if anticipating trouble, they proceeded very cautiously.

Suddenly the stillness of the forest was shattered as Morgan's concealed riflemen opened fire and dropped many of Forbes' soldiers. Struck in the shoulder, Forbes fell back. Within several minutes, every officer serving under Forbes had been hit. As more and more of his soldiers collapsed to the ground, the surprised and shocked survivors reeled back.

Noting that the British were in retreat, some of Morgan's men began to pursue. Before Morgan could stop them, others also raced forward. Realizing the folly of this, Morgan began to scream for them to halt and return. But it was to no avail. More and more ran forward. Believing that they had the British beat, and intoxicated with victory, they continued to surge forward. Angry at losing command and control, Morgan cursed and yelled for them to return. In desperation, he even began to call out the specific birdcall signifying the order to fall back. It was, however, to no avail.

Morgan's men, however, did not pursue very far. Suddenly, they ran right into a long line of British troops. The first rank was kneeling and the second was standing upright. With bayonet tipped muskets aimed forward, they were awaiting their officer's command.

"Fire!" The shout of this one word rocked the forest as hundreds of muskets thundered in unison. The British did not even wait for all of Forbes' troops to retire through their line. Caught in the middle, as numerous musket balls flew with tremendous force and speed, some of the original survivors of Forbes' force were killed; however, patriots fell as well. Colonel Morgan's troops were the first patriots to fall that day.

Approximately one mile to the rear of Morgan's and Dearborn's units, General Poor heard the gunfire. Concluding that Morgan would need help, he ordered his Continental brigade, with its three New Hampshire regiments, forward.

Standing in the middle of the open field, Morgan spotted his men falling back through the forest. The moment he heard the massive volley, he knew that his men had run into an angry beehive. Some of the returnees had the body of a friend slung over a shoulder as they ran back. Repositioning himself behind a large tree for protection, Morgan began to signal the birdcall signifying a return to original positions. It was three rapid gobble calls. The moment the others heard it, it was repeated. Within minutes, the wilderness in Morgan's area rang out from wild turkey calls.

Repositioning themselves in their original skirmish line around Freeman's farm, with others hiding within the buildings, Morgan's riflemen quickly reloaded and waited for the next round.

The moment Burgoyne heard the volleys of shots being fired, he looked over to General Hamilton. "If we can get into the rebel rear, they'll be finished. Just like at Ticonderoga," he said.

Sensing that Morgan, Dearborn, and Poor's 900-plus Continental troops would need support, General Arnold ordered Lieutenant-Colonel Brooks and Major William Hull's 8th Massachusetts militia unit, with its 300 volunteers, forward to assist in the battle. Simultaneously, as Arnold was feeding more troops into the fight, British General Fraser was doing the same. With reinforcements pouring in for both sides, it would not be long before a massive struggle was underway.

Noting a sizable force of Canadians, Indians, and loyalists emerging from the wood line, Morgan's riflemen took aim and fired. Among the first to die was Captain David Monin. Witnessing Monin's death was his son, who stood no more than ten feet away. Another father and son team fighting for the British on that day were the Freemans, John and his son Thomas. Struck on the side of his chest, Thomas Freeman went down. Within moments, his father was at his side. Because they were ardent loyalists, in late 1775 both father and son had abandoned their farm and fled to Canada. Now they were fighting on the very same field which, years earlier, they had toiled so hard to clear. Encountering heavy fire, the irregulars withdrew.

As the survivors of Forbes' unit dashed back, they encountered the rest of Hamilton's regiments positioned in several straight lines. The 21st Foot stood on the right (and furthest to the west), the 62nd Foot in the center, and the 20th Foot stood on the left. In reserve, the 9th Foot stood behind them all. Standing shoulder to shoulder with fixed bayonets, the British line looked fearsome. Among them, within the 9th Foot, stood Sergeant Lamb. As they awaited the order to advance, directly behind them cannons were rapidly being swung into action. By now, the survivors of Forbes' force were quickly being reformed and pressed into the line. Their day in hell was not yet over. In fact, it was just beginning.

Appearing on the scene, Poor's New Hampshire Continentals were immediately positioned to the left of Morgan's riflemen. As for the 8th Massachusetts, it fell alongside Lieutenant-Colonel Dearborn's light infantry operating on Morgan's right flank. As it turned out, both units had arrived in the nick of time for the British had just commenced their march. Though not yet visible, the beat of their drums could be heard rippling loudly through the trees.

One can only imagine the terrifying sounds emitting from the forest as four crack British infantry regiments marched forward with fixed bayonets. Such a sight alone could psychologically torment an enemy and put them in flight. But Morgan's and Dearborn's troops, along with the New Hampshire and Massachusetts volunteers, were seasoned fighters. Several months of warfare within the terrible wilderness had transformed raw recruits into deadly warriors.

Some of Morgan's riflemen, who had initially perched themselves up in the trees, had remained in place. Their tan-colored deerskin smocks, raccoon caps and brown or black colored floppy hats blended in perfectly with the colors of the tree trunks and the changing colors of the leaves. Virtually invisible, as the regiments marched below them, Morgan's snipers held their fire. The patriots also noted how their opponents' highly polished bayonets glittered in the long sunbeams that filtered through the trees. With each step, the regiments came closer and closer. As they neared, the patriots were taking aim.

"Fire!" Instantly, with the shout of this command, more than a thousand rounds tore through the British ranks. Men toppled into eternal silence. Bullets and musket balls tore through drums and shattered the lives of teenage drummer boys. Officers and sergeants were specifically targeted. A shot went through the heart of Lieutenant Don of the 21st Foot; 16-year-old Lieutenant Hervey of the 62nd Foot—the youngest officer in Burgoyne's army—went down. As someone attempted to drag him back to cover, another round struck Hervey in the head. Opening his eyes for the last time, he uttered to those around him, "Tell my uncle and family I died like a soldier." With sadness Sergeant Lamb would later record in his journal, "Men, and particularly officers, dropped every moment on each side."[12]

Hamilton's soldiers did not only encounter heavy fire from their immediate front. From "the Americans placed in high trees"[13] patriot sharpshooters delivered devastating fire downward from within and behind. Huge gaps were torn in the British line. Bullets whizzed all around Sergeant Lamb. One round struck the side of a tree, just missing his head by a couple of inches. Angered that another one of their fellow soldiers had just been killed from above, approximately thirty soldiers turned around, aimed their weapons up into a pine tree, and fired. Seconds later a sniper, his deerskin smock splattered in blood, came crashing down through the branches. The sharpshooter was dead before he hit the ground. To ensure that he had been killed, one of the grenadiers drove his long bayonet deep into the body.

Despite the heavy firepower, the British thrust could not be stopped. Fallen officers and sergeants were replaced with new leaders. Blowing whistles and shouting orders, they maintained command and control.

With bayonets dripping blood, the British continued to press forward. Quickly, they succeeded in penetrating deep into the cleared field. Attempting to halt their advance as they neared his sector, Lieutenant-Colonel Brooks' men fired two rapid volleys into the oncoming force. Shouting "Charge," with a pistol in one hand and a sword in the other, Brooks surged forward with his militiamen.

Officially, the 8th Massachusetts was the first patriot unit to charge forward that day. Grappling with the British, a vicious no-quarter hand-to-hand and tomahawk-to-bayonet struggle ensued.

At the very moment that a massive battle was being waged on the 350-yard cleared field, heavy fighting was also taking place within the woods around Freeman's Farm. With tremendous sadness and tears in his eyes, Northern Army Chaplain Enos Hitchcock administered the last rites to those dying—whether patriot or enemy. The cabin at Freeman's farm was holed like a sieve from numerous rounds. Breaking down its door, British regulars charged inside. Emerging moments later with bayonets dripping blood, they rejoined their comrades fighting on and near the farm. By now the barn and support buildings were fully ablaze.

Despite the best efforts of the patriots to hold the enemy thrust in and around Freeman's farm, elements of the British army did succeed in penetrating the patriot line. But they lacked the strength to effectively attack Gates' left flank. So, until strengthened with additional units, this small force could only wait. From their position on higher ground they did fire down upon any patriots they saw.

Amid the massive gunfire and thunderous noise of the battle, both Colonel Morgan and General Arnold noted that a sizable gap had developed in the British line. Somehow, during the furious fighting, the 21st Foot had separated itself from the main body. Morgan now reasoned that if he could turn the flank of the 21st Foot, he would be able to destroy it. General Arnold, though supportive, envisioned a bigger plan. He would not only turn the 21st's flank, he would also advance beyond it into Fraser's rear and attack his entire force from behind. If successful, Arnold would not only separate the entire British right wing, but after cutting it off, the patriots could then push Fraser's forces against the base of Bemis Heights to destroy them. Afterwards, the patriots would finish off those who had positioned themselves on the Heights.

To achieve success, General Arnold knew that he had to hit hard and fast with superior force. Against the 21st Foot he committed General Poor's New Hampshire brigade and Colonel Morgan's and Lieutenant-Colonel Dearborn's units. Realizing that he needed more troops to exploit the gap, Arnold also ordered General Learned's brigade along with Lieutenant-Colonel Marshall's 10th Massachusetts Regiment from General John Paterson's brigade, to advance forward. Marching into battle, Agrippa Hull, an African-American male who five months earlier had joined the Northern Army and was serving in Paterson's brigade, wondered if he would survive the day. Like so many others who marched into combat that day, Hull prayed to the Lord for protection.

Shortly afterwards, Sergeant Lamb recorded in his journal, "The Americans advanced a strong column, with a view of turning the British line; here they met the grenadiers and light infantry, who gave them a tremendous fire."[14]

Seeing what was happening and to counter General Arnold's tactic, General Hamilton immediately regrouped the 21st Foot to face westward; simultaneously Fraser, skilled general that he was, observed the situation. Determined to counter the patriot thrust, fill in the gaps, and place more troops upon the Heights, he ordered that more artillery be brought up, and he committed the brunt of the 24th Foot and von Breymann's German force into the battle. The moment they arrived, they encountered Learned's brigade, the 10th Massachusetts, and some of the New Hampshire troops.

Both the patriots and the British-German force refused to budge. The two sides shot it out at point-blank range. Then they lunged at one another. Within the thick smoke and dust, units became intermingled. Tomahawks were wielded and, in skilled hands, these weapons proved to be just as lethal as a bayonet-tipped musket. Perhaps General Glover summed it up best, "Both armies seemed determined to either conquer or die!"[15]

By now the field in front of Freeman's cabin was covered with corpses and writhing wounded. As for the woods ringing the farm, the bodies of the dead and dying lay for hundreds of yards all around. Yet the battle was far from over.

Determined to break through, the British brought up additional cannons. Not only were all of Hamilton's and Fraser's gunners committed, but so too were the gunners from von Riedesel's force. The moment a British or German cannon crew galloped in, its artillerymen quickly unhitched the horses from the cannons and ammunition wagons, loaded either grapeshot or ball into the tubes, and fired away.

4:00 P.M.

By this hour, the battle had been raging for approximately four hours; yet there was no sign of it letting up. Amid its horrendous noise, explosions, massive amounts of thick smoke, and the dead and dying, several small forest fires had broken out. Though uncontrolled, some of the patriot commanders began to carefully monitor them. Morgan knew from previous firsthand experience the lethality of a massive forest fire, especially for wounded caught in its ensuing whirlwind of heat and flame. Lieutenant Digby later noted, "The crash of cannon and musketry never ceased till darkness parted us. The heavy artillery, joining in concert like great peals of thunder, assisted by the echoes of the woods, almost deafened us with the noise."[16]

On two or three occasions, the Americans actually overran sections of British cannon. But without horses they were unable to remove the guns and each time lost them again to British counterattacks.

For those manning the cannons the battle was especially vicious, as American marksmen singled them out in order to stop them from servicing their deadly iron tubes. Of the 48 artillerymen in the center, 36 were struck. Among the dead was Captain Jones. Of the 22 artillerists under Lieutenant Hadden, 19 were killed or wounded. Desperate to obtain more men for his guns, Hadden, whose cap was shot off his head, raced back to General Hamilton requesting additional artillerymen. When informed that none were available, Hadden requested some infantrymen. Hamilton, however, informed the lieutenant to see General Phillips, who had appeared on the scene along with Burgoyne.

Positioning himself in the center behind the 62nd Foot, Burgoyne began to take charge. He also began to suspect that the key to victory now lay with Hamilton's center rather than with Fraser's right wing.

Burgoyne, however, was not the only one sensing that a victory could be achieved in the center. So too, was Arnold. Suspecting that the British center was on the verge of collapse, Arnold reasoned that if he could penetrate just a little deeper, he could isolate both the right and left wings. In order to do this, he first needed Gates' authorization and additional manpower.

Galloping to Gates' headquarters, Arnold briefed him on the situation. He requested that Gates shift some of the Northern Army units positioned in the eastern sector adjacent the Hudson River, moving them to reinforce the center.

Gates, however, refused. He feared that if he shifted troops away from the Germans on the right, von Riedesel would note the movement and attack. With fewer patriots manning that sector, despite the trench, batteries, and numerous obstacles, the enemy could succeed in penetrating the Heights. His fears, however, were unfounded.

Prior to repositioning himself further to the west, Phillips had consulted with von Riedesel. As both commanders stood on the left flank adjacent to the Hudson, they concluded that it would be too costly to attempt to barrel their way through the various obstacles, the deep trench protected by the large U-shaped fortress, the extensive picket fences positioned by the patriots, and their various barricades.

The British concluded that Gates was in no position to attack through this sector as well. The deep trench and extensive obstacles—though great for defense—would likewise hinder his effort to conduct an effective offensive. Confident that they could release some of their forces, General Phillips rode out to see Burgoyne. In the meantime, von Riedesel ordered elements of the Brunswick light infantry regiment to doubletime toward the center where they could take Arnold's foremost units in the flank. He also ordered Captain Pausch, who commanded the artillery, to move as quickly as he could to assist Fraser. Pausch was to take two of the 6-pound cannons.

For the last five or six hours, Tim Murphy had been fighting like a demon. With his specially designed over-and-under two-barreled rifle, Murphy dropped officers and grenadiers from point blank range to distances beyond 300 yards. With his tomahawk, he smashed skulls, broke bones and shattered lives. Murphy took no scalps, simply because there was no time for it.

Rushing forward up a slope, he plopped himself behind the shattered stump of what, until 19 September, had been a tall, healthy tree. Either a heavy cannon ball or a massive blast of grapeshot had knocked it down. Immediately, he began to scan for any cannoneers in the distance. As he searched, he spotted what appeared to be a senior ranking officer. Murphy estimated the shot at about 350 yards. It would be long, but with his eagle eyes and exceptional shooting ability, it could be done.

Noticing the body of a British grenadier lying in front of him,

Murphy decided to crawl toward it. Afterwards, he would position his rifle directly on the body to steady his aim. Crawling forward, he reached the corpse, rested his rifle upon it, and began to take aim.

Catching sight of General Burgoyne, Captain Charles Green, who served as an aide to General Phillips, rode up to deliver a message. From far away, Murphy observed the incoming rider. How immaculate he looked in his uniform. And, unlike the others, Murphy noted the beautiful, hand-woven, richly laced saddlecloth with its yellow fringes. Convinced that the rider was a high-ranking officer of some sort, Murphy reshifted his aim toward the new arrival. To allow for bullet drop, he kept his sights slightly higher. He wanted to fire the bullet right into the officer's chest.

The moment the captain began to converse with Burgoyne, Murphy began to slowly squeeze. Raising his left arm upward to hand Burgoyne the message, Captain Green suddenly lurched back and tumbled from his horse. Within seconds, he stood up again clasping his left arm. Murphy swore. He then knew that his bullet had struck his victim in the arm. Murphy did not like this. Rarely, if ever, did he miss.

He prepared to fire again. But the British line, which had been advancing forward as Murphy had been engaging his faraway targets, was getting closer. Quickly shifting his aim to a grenadier, Murphy fired and killed him. Running half bent over to the rear, he quickly got back behind the stump. Then scrambling down the slope like a wild rabbit pursued by a coyote, Murphy leaped over the dead as he ran. It was time for him to reposition himself further to the rear.

Despite General Gates' order to Arnold that he could not have any of the troops positioned on the Northern Army's right flank facing von Riedesel, Arnold somehow succeeded in gathering up enough militia and Continental troops to hold and repulse the British in the center. Some of these came from the reserve.[17]

By now, various militias, commanded by General Ten Broeck along with militia Colonels Cook and Latimer, and New York militia commanders James Livingston and Van Cortlandt, as well as elements from certain Connecticut militias, were reinforcing and fighting alongside the Continentals from the New Hampshire Brigade, Marshall's Regiment from Paterson's Brigade, and the various Massachusetts line continentals. General Learned's Massachusetts continental brigade, comprising the regiments of Colonels Bailey, Weston, and Jackson, were also redirected to the center. Amid the noise, smoke and chaos, Learned's brigade

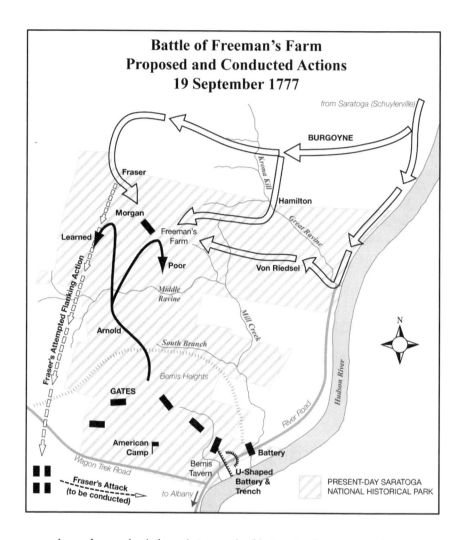

veered too far to the left and, instead of being in the center where it was most needed, became once again engaged with the British right wing.[18]

The 20th, 62nd, and 21st Foot Regiments were also feeling the pressure. The 62nd was especially hard-pressed. Its commander, Lieutenant-Colonel Anstruther, was seriously wounded. His assistant, Major Harnage, assumed command. Harnage, however, did not command for long before he was struck and wounded. Though at first he continued to command, another round killed him. Hardly any of the forward artillery remained operational, most of the cannoneers having fallen. To assist the frontline infantry, soldiers from the 9th Foot were fed piece-meal into each of the regiments as reinforcements. Though helpful, their appearance actually did little to alter the situation. Toward the end of the day, the 9th Foot itself had sustained heavy casualties.

Arriving in the battle area, the German Brunswick light infantry, along with the rest of von Breymann's unit, attempted at first to scale the Heights but the stiff patriot resistance halted the German effort. Unable to advance any further and still smarting from the lessons learned at Bennington, the Germans positioned themselves on Fraser's right and took cover behind the trees, logs and slopes found within the rolling wooded terrain. Although some hand-to-hand combat contin-ued, by and large it turned into a shooting match between the Germans versus the continentals and militiamen.

Von Breymann's unit, however, held firmly in place and resisted effectively. By their actions, the Germans thwarted Arnold's forces from penetrating into Fraser's rear. Their tough resistance also enabled both the 21st and the newly committed 24th Foot Regiment to fight more effectively. According to Lossing, "Colonel von Breymann, with his German riflemen, fighting bravely, averted the blow that might have been fatal to the British army."[19]

6:00 P.M.

Realizing that it was getting late in the day and time was of essence, von Riedesel ordered the remainder of the Brunswick infantry regiment, two companies from the Rhetz Regiment, and two additional cannons to immediately turn around, march a short distance northward, and turn left on a road about one-and-a-half miles in length. Leading west-ward, this road terminated on a knoll from which von Riedesel, who would be accompanying this force, would be able to observe the fight-ing and also be close to Freeman's farm. Once he arrived, the German general would then make a determination as to what exactly should be done. As for the remaining German personnel on the left, they would remain in place, along with the British 47th Foot. With von Reidesel's departure, Colonel Specht assumed command of the left wing.

By now, the patriots were beginning to feel the pressure. No less than six times they had hurled themselves against Hamilton's center while simultaneously battling Fraser's right wing. For no less than six hours, a vicious battle had seesawed back and forth. Many of the patri-ots were dead or wounded. The New Hampshire Continentals incurred exceptional losses. The 8th Massachusetts was virtually decimated. With its commander killed and well over 50 percent of its personnel dead, wounded, or missing, the 8th was on the verge of collapse. Major Hull assumed command. Though suffering a deep bayonet slash across his lower stomach, he continued to lead. Despite its losses, the unit's surviving militiamen continued to resist ferociously. Colonels Adam, Colburn, Brooks and Francis were some of the senior ranking officers killed in action.[20] A cannonball passed so close to General Nixon's head that it impaired the sight and hearing in his left eye and ear for the rest of his life.

In the main patriot hospital located in Albany, Doctor Thacher, who directed thirty other doctors and hundreds of women and male nurses, amongst whom were many kind-hearted Mennonites, knew that it was going to be an exceptionally long day and night. Noting the awful distant rumble, the doctor ordered that everything be prepared. At first the wounded had trickled in a few at a time. But in the last couple of hours, casualties poured in. Wagon after wagon filled with wounded and injured combatants, some of whom were English, German, or loyalist, arrived. Among the wounded lay the dead who had died en route.

Most of the battlefield treatment had been basic at best. Noting the situation, Doctor Thacher immediately put out a call for more civilian assistance. Heeding his call, Albany's residents, bolstered by the numerous refugee men and women residing within the town, came to assist. Many more Mennonites also appeared. Fluent in German, they were also useful as interpreters.

Noting the situation, von Riedesel conducted a forced infantry march to reach the main battle area as quickly as possible. En route, he encountered Captain Pausch and his cannoneers. Angry that Pausch had not yet arrived at the British center, von Riedesel verbally assailed him. So furious was the general that he contemplated dismissing Pausch from his command. "Jawohl, Herr General!" was Pausch's final response as he fell in with von Riedesel's group.

From where von Riedesel had previously stood near the river, he could hear the sounds of the battle and smell its smoke. But as von Riedesel neared the center, the intensity and roar of the battle was at a much, much higher tempo. Von Riedesel had seen a few battles in the past, but what he witnessed in this God-forsaken American wilderness was far worse than anything he had experienced yet.

Burgoyne knew that someone or something would have to give.

This could not go on much longer. It would soon be dark. Burgoyne also knew his troops were exhausted. Units had incurred heavy losses, especially the 21st and 62nd Foot Regiments. The rebels had fought well. Too well. Even their damn militia had acquitted itself bravely.

Arriving at the front, von Riedesel appeared right at a critical moment. The patriots were once again hurtling themselves forward. Ordering his regiment and Rhetz's two companies into a battle line, the German grenadiers resisted effectively; simultaneously, Pausch and his gunners, moving with speed and precision, fired numerous rounds of grapeshot into the patriot forces.

Grapeshot balls tore through trees, brush, and human flesh. Here and there, a body was blown into smithereens. Fired at close range, the shot created vicious gaps in the patriot ranks.

Von Riedesel ordered a charge. With fixed bayonets, the Germans surged forward. To support their thrust, Pausch ordered his gunners to change their load from grapeshot to solid shot. Tilting the barrels upward, the gunners fired rounds over the heads of their compatriots. Flying in an arch, the rounds landed and exploded amid the patriots.

Under such pressure, the patriots fell back. Who, if anyone, ordered the retreat is not known. Seeing the patriot withdrawal and encouraged by the German attack, the survivors of the 9th, 20th, 21st, 24th, and 62nd foot Regiments charged forward as well. From their throats a massive battle cry was heard far and wide. Among those who surged forward was Sergeant Lamb.

The patriots retreated to their fortified positions on Bemis Heights. They were too exhausted to battle the fresh, elite incoming German troops backed by British regulars. As darkness settled, the final shots were fired and the battle ceased.

9:00 P.M.

That evening, the temperature fell. It was cold by midnight. Further to the north on the higher peaks, the first snow flakes of 1777 came down. Though only a dusting, it further dampened the spirits of those at Fort Ticonderoga, Diamond Island, and Fort Edward. Sadly, some of the wounded remained through the entire frigid night lying between the two armies.

When Burgoyne ordered his troops to stand down, he also withdrew that part of Fraser's force which had briefly occupied a sector within the western portion of Bemis Heights. As they retired, they picked up some of the wounded. For both sides, it was a cruel time as doctors and med-ical personnel struggled through the night and into the following day. Outside of Albany a massive trench was dug. After identifying as many bodies as possible, the dead were laid to rest.

The fight of 19 September 1777 became known in history as the Battle of Freeman's Farm or the First Battle of Saratoga.

Tactically, it was an English-German victory. They had remained on the field of battle and had successfully repulsed the patriots' coun-terthrusts. Like Blucher's men at Waterloo decades later, the Germans had come upon the field at just the right time to decide the day. Whereas Bennington had been a disaster for the German contingent of Burgoyne's army, at Freeman's Farm they had redeemed themselves.

But was it really a victory for Burgoyne? According to Luzader, "Considering the opposing commanders' objectives, the Americans had won an important victory. Burgoyne possessed the field, but Gates still blocked the route to Albany."[21]

In consideration that his casualties had been heavy, and that the patriots had not been destroyed and were still in place, such factors can diminish any claims of a British victory. In fact, it may even be argued that the patriots had won. Perhaps, Lieutenant Anburey summed it up best:

> Notwithstanding the glory of the day remains on our side, I am fearful the real advantages resulting from this hard fought bat-tle will rest on that of the Americans, our army being so much weakened by this engagement as not to be of sufficient strength to venture forth and improve the victory, which may, in the end, put a stop to our intended expedition.[22]

Another British officer, Lieutenant Digby, added in his journal, "...they retired to their camp, leaving us masters of the field; but it was a dear bought victory if I can ever give it that name, as we lost many brave men."[23]

English troops were not the only ones who questioned if 19 September was a victory. So too, did many of the Germans. One German soldier wrote how nothing positive had been accomplished, "... than to bring fame to the house of a poor farmer... for it has given to this day's engagement the name of the Battle of Freeman's House."[24]

In the end, 19 September proved to be a monumental day for the Northern Army. But there was a price to pay, as is often the case. Though the patriot casualties were significantly lower than their enemy's, over 300 Continentals and militiamen had been killed or wounded. Many others were reported missing.

XX

Troops Dig In and
Patriot Generals Collide

SATURDAY, 20 SEPTEMBER
During the evening hours of 19 September, Burgoyne commenced preparations to launch another attack the next morning. But General Fraser urged him to postpone the attack until the 21st, arguing that his troops, especially the light infantry, had been up the entire previous night. It had been a very long and hard day, and right now they were burying their dead and taking care of many other matters. Simply put, they were too exhausted to renew the fight within hours. General Hamilton cited that his center had borne the brunt of the fighting and his regiments needed to be reformed, fed, rested, and moved into new positions.

Von Riedesel argued that he did not have enough time to move around the woods in pitch-black darkness to reposition his soldiers, presently occupying positions adjacent to the Hudson River, toward new positions beyond Freeman's farm. And none of the commanders had yet received any specific reports as to what, exactly, had been their losses.

Taking in all of this information, Burgoyne gave in. He agreed that, perhaps, a rest would benefit the troops. But he did inform his commanders to be ready to attack on the 21st.

While fighting on the 19th, the Northern Army had fired off a tremendous amount of ammunition. When informed by his quartermaster that very little powder, musket balls, and bullets remained and that each soldier could currently be issued no more than forty rounds, Gates was shocked. Immediately, he issued an order to find and secure—wherever and however—powder and ammunition. Gates feared that in the event of another British attack, he could lose this time, simply from lack of ammunition.

Upon hearing this, General Schuyler immediately ordered a massive search for the critically needed powder and ammunition. Although he had been superceded as commander, Schuyler was still loyal to the cause and to the Northern Army, which he felt was still his child. Schuyler also knew that it would not be long before America's Continental Congress would see the true picture and fully exonerate him in the end. Already there were those speaking on his behalf. But for now, more pressing matters were at hand.

A massive appeal went out to all armed citizens in and around Albany to bring in as much of their powder and ammunition as possible. Schuyler also dispatched wagon teams to each fort and outpost, no matter how small, with orders that they were to immediately hand over fifty percent of their ammunition. Every artillery battery in and around Albany was also stripped of its ordnance. Express riders galloped off to West Point, western Massachusetts, and Connecticut to inform various commanders and political leaders of the urgency of immediately coming up with more powder and ammunition. By the end of the day, Gates began to receive the first shipments of the needed supplies.

Doctor Thacher was relieved to see that each patient brought in had been taken care of, and in general the care had gone well. Lives had been saved. Because most of the casualties had their wounds immediately cleaned upon their arrival by the orderlies and women, the threat of blood poisoning had subsided tremendously. Most of the wounds to the arms and legs did not result in an amputation. Doctor Thacher was also glad that there was no immediate follow-up battle. With no rumbling in the distance, he did not have to worry about another incoming stream of casualties.[1]

SUNDAY, 21 SEPTEMBER

Early in the morning, just hours before the British army was to renew its attack, a courier slipped through the lines carrying a message for Burgoyne from General Clinton. At this time, Clinton was still sitting in New York City and he wanted to know if Burgoyne needed assistance. Clinton wrote:

> You know my good will and are not ignorant of my poverty. If you think two thousand men can assist you effectively, I will

make a push at [Fort] Montgomery in about ten days, but ever jealous of my flanks. If they [the patriots] make a move in force on either of them, I must return to save this important post [New York City]. I expect reinforcement every day. Let me know what you wish.[2]

Immediately, Burgoyne responded, "Do it, my dear friend, directly."[3] That same day Burgoyne dispatched the messenger back to New York urging Clinton to hurry. He would now await Clinton's arrival.

Burgoyne reasoned that he still had about two weeks of provisions on hand. With some local foraging, although difficult and risky, along with some further rationing, he would be able to extend his supplies a little longer. By then, Clinton should arrive.

Burgoyne knew that if Clinton made a sudden appearance in the patriots' rear, Gates would be forced to counter the British army advancing north from New York City. This would mean splitting the American forces. Perhaps, by then, some additional reinforcements might also come down from Canada. If Gates' army could somehow be caught between the armies of Burgoyne and Clinton, it could be crushed. Until then, Burgoyne would wait.

Of course, there was some risk to standing still. But for the moment, Burgoyne felt he had no choice. Deciding to remain in place he suspended his proposed attack and ordered his troops to dig in.

MONDAY, 22 SEPTEMBER–SUNDAY, 5 OCTOBER

Desertion, always problematic, especially when times are tough, rose significantly. On 23 September, a soldier caught deserting received one thousand lashes; on 26 September, seven Canadian wagon drivers and workers deserted. Sensing defeat and unnerved by the sequence of events, they headed back north.

Angered by the news, Burgoyne dispatched his Indians to capture the wagoneers. Permission was also given to kill and scalp them. After the Indians returned with their scalps, Burgoyne assembled the remaining Canadians and informed them that anyone else caught in the act of deserting would suffer the same fate.

Yet despite Burgoyne's brutal measures to curb the desertions, it was to no avail. Every day one or more soldiers fled. In one particular case approximately twenty armed German soldiers, all from the same company, came marching toward the American line. Flying a huge white flag, they were even accompanied by a drummer boy beating the parley beat of surrender.

Burgoyne, however, was not the only one digging in. Realizing the importance of fortifying the western portion of Bemis Heights, Gates pushed the army's front-line defense positions all the way to the end of the Heights. Fortunately for Gates, the constant flow of incoming volunteers helped. As more and more men appeared, Gates' confidence rose significantly. He now had enough soldiers and militia personnel to man the entire front from the Hudson River to Saratoga Lake. Additionally, Gates also began to position more troops on the eastern side of the Hudson. With enough supplies and ammunition flowing in to support and feed the army, morale remained high. Again, Schuyler was a key player in supporting the Northern Army, selflessly working on behalf of his former command.

MONDAY, 29 SEPTEMBER

General Lincoln and his 2,000 troops stationed east of the Hudson returned to the main army.[4] As for General Stark, though Gates would have been more than happy to incorporate him formally into his command, the stubborn New Hampshire native continued to operate as an independent force. But Gates did carefully monitor Stark's activities and the two generals corresponded on a weekly basis. Gates was pleased that Stark was still guarding Vermont's western border because as long as Burgoyne knew that a sizable patriot force commanded by an exceptionally tough and skilled commander was continuing to hover on his flank, Burgoyne would have to take measures to counter it. And in the event the British conducted a coastal landing in Connecticut in an attempt to reach Burgoyne, Stark would be in their way.

General Gates, however, was not just waging a war with Burgoyne. He was now also warring with General Arnold.

Even prior to the 19 September battle, Gates and Arnold had been quarreling. After Freeman's Farm, their relationship deteriorated to the point where neither could stand the other.

During the battle, Gates had stayed behind the lines at his command post near the center. Not once did he venture forward. Unlike Arnold, who had been constantly in the thick of the fighting, Gates never appeared near the front. Therefore, in the aftermath of the battle, there were those in the army who were crediting Arnold, and not Gates, for achieving the critical victory. In turn, this angered Gates.

Within several days of the battle, Gates submitted to the Continental Congress a detailed report in which he said nothing about Arnold's role. In fact, not once was Arnold's name even mentioned. No praise or credit was extended to the man who commanded the left wing where all the fighting had taken place, and who had done most to lead the patriots in actual combat.

Upon learning of this, General Arnold dispatched a letter to Gates. In it he requested that Gates issue him three passes, one for himself and two for his aides. Arnold wanted to meet with America's Congress. In front of them, he would personally inform the Congress of his performance at Freeman's Farm. As for his aides, they would testify, if necessary, on his behalf. Arnold also requested that Gates establish a meeting time as soon as possible because Arnold wanted to personally speak to Gates about this matter.

Gates, in turn, responded to Arnold with his own letter, declining the request for passes. He did, however, offer to submit another letter directly to John Hancock, the President of the Continental Congress. In this letter, Gates would acknowledge Arnold's performance on the battlefield. As for the meeting Arnold requested, Gates added that there was no need for one for the moment.

Arnold became furious. Deciding to confront Gates at his headquarters, Arnold mounted his horse. He was going to have a face-to-face meeting whether Gates wanted it or not. Prior to his departure Arnold was angry, but his ferocity would only rise upon meeting with his commanding officer.

Almost immediately the generals began to argue. Gates informed Arnold that, "I do not regard you as a major general because some time ago you, Sir, yourself submitted a resignation to the Congress." Gates also said that, to the best of his knowledge, no one had formally appointed Arnold to the Northern Army. As Gates put it, "You just rode in one day."

Arnold's anger had been intensifying. But when Gates added, "As of this moment, General Lincoln will assume command of the Army's left wing," and with those words, for all intents and purposes, removed Arnold from command, Arnold's blood began to boil. Adding insult to injury, Gates added that now he would grant Arnold the previously requested passes.

Arnold, however, now refused to accept this thinly veiled invitation to leave the army. He knew that if he accepted the passes, Gates would be getting rid of him. Possibly, with his departure, Arnold might not even return. Congress might reassign him to another army or theater. And the Northern Army was his home. What especially angered Arnold was the comment, "You just rode in one day." Now, on top of everything, Gates was removing him from command.

In a hostile tone of voice, Arnold reminded Gates, "I have been with the Northern Army virtually since the first day! I was one of its first volunteers!" He demanded both an apology and to be reinstated to command. Gates, however, would not budge.

And neither would Arnold. The argument rose. It became so intense that it was heard far beyond the building. Profanity, along with shouts of "How dare you!" and "How dare you speak to me like that!" filled the air. So furious was Arnold that he even challenged Gates to a duel. Gates declined on the grounds that he had previously banned dueling in the Northern Army.

Following a pause, and realizing that he could do no more, Arnold quietly informed his commander that he would acknowledge Lincoln's authority and relinquish his command. But by way of last word, he added, "As for me, I will not depart the Northern Army!" Storming out of the headquarters, Arnold remounted and rode away.

Another incident which also arose during this time involved the case of a patriot corporal named Samuel Gay, whose real name was Ann (or possibly Nancy) Bailey.[6]

In February 1777, Ann joined the Northern Army. Knowing that she would be rejected for service because of her sex, she cut her hair, dressed like a man, spoke with a heavy voice, and enlisted under the name of Samuel Gay. She was posted to a company commanded by Captain Abraham Hunt within the 1st Massachusetts Continental Regiment serving at Fort Ticonderoga under General St. Clair. As a result of Private "Gay's" loyalty and bravery at Fort Ticonderoga, she was promoted to corporal, a non-commissioned officer's rank.

Somehow, at Saratoga, it became known that Corporal "Gay" was actually a woman dressed in men's clothes,[5] and "Gay" was immediately suspended.

Desperate to retain her rank and status, Bailey appealed the matter directly to General Gates. But Gates enforced the discharge. He did, however, propose that the brave soldier be offered a position in some support role such as the military hospital in Albany. But Bailey refused and demanded to remain in her old unit.

By now, everyone in the army was aware of this affair. It is said that on the day she left many were saddened. Thousands of soldiers cursed Gates for his decision. Among them was General Arnold, who stated that he would have kept her.

XXI

Burgoyne's Strategy Unravels

A major issue was presented to General Gates by the Shakers, just as they had previously raised it to General Schuyler. An offshoot of the Mennonites, this religious group derived its name from the fact that when they prayed they were so fervent they actually shook. Appearing one day at Gates' headquarters, the group of Shakers demanded an immediate end to the war, preached brotherly love, and promoted spiritual reconciliation. Since it was a very short meeting and nothing was recorded, it is not known how Gates reacted to them. Undoubtedly, he was sympathetic. Realistically speaking, however, there was absolutely nothing the Northern Army commander could do about their demands.[1]

Back on the battlefield, both sides continued to entrench during this time. Fighting positions were constructed, and Gates continued to dispatch short- and long-range patrols. Scout teams continued to probe deep behind Burgoyne's lines.

Despite the lull, shots were fired every day. Snipers crawled up as close as they could toward enemy lines. Shots were directed against Burgoyne's army from both close and distant ranges. Not a day or night passed without some incident. As Lieutenant Anburey noted, "We are now become so habituated to the firing that the soldiers seem to be indifferent to it, and eat and sleep when it is very near them."[2]

Brave, hearty individuals approached pickets on guard duty, usually late at night. For them, it was a sport to sneak up on an enemy sentry and kill him with a knife or tomahawk. Among those who participated in this type of action was the eminent rifleman of the Wilderness War of 1777—Timothy Murphy.[3]

261

After issuing the order to dig in, Burgoyne's troops began to construct an elaborate defense system. From the Hudson River to a point slightly west of Freeman's farm, Burgoyne's troops dropped trees, dug various positions, and constructed three sizable redoubts. The trees were felled with their tips and branches facing the patriots. Many abatis—thick branches with sharpened tips pointing toward the patriots at an angle—were also inserted all around, especially in front of major positions.

Burgoyne's army was positioned from the Hudson River westward. All of the British naval personnel were positioned behind the front line adjacent the river. The bateaux, canoes, and other river craft were parked on the Hudson's western bank. The army's commissary and the main supply point along with many of the wagons were positioned to the north of the naval depot. The main hospital was also located here. Nearby was the headquarters of the loyalists under the command of Colonel Peters, who had recovered from his Bennington wound. The naval personnel, supply depot, and Peters' headquarters were positioned between the western bank of the Hudson and the eastern edge of River Road.

Adjacent to River Road was positioned the 47th Foot Regiment in reserve. Its mission was to protect the units and supplies near the river.[4]

To the southwest of the 47th Foot stood a battery from the Hanau Artillery. Positioned on high terrain, this artillery battery also covered the River Road. Next to the Hanau gunners and extending westward stood the Rhetz and Specht units, units of the Royal Artillery, the 20th Foot, 62nd Foot, 21st Foot, and the 9th Foot. Because all of these English-German units were tremendously understrength, they were positioned along with their artillery in a large fortification referred to as the "Great Redoubt."[5]

Continuing westward, various grenadiers, bolstered by more Royal Artillery, held the line. Around Freeman's farm stood another breastwork referred to as the "Balcarres Redoubt." In this long redoubt was the 24th Foot, Balcarres' remaining light infantry, and the remainder of the Royal Artillery.

The distance from the Hudson River to the Balcarres Redoubt was about 4.5 miles. Ahead of this entire line were various outposts and batteries. Approximately a half mile to the northwest of the Balcarres Redoubt was established the von Breymann Redoubt. This was built to face west, though it could defended in either direction.[6] Von Breymann's mission was to protect Burgoyne's rear. In length, the redoubt extended about 1,000 feet from its southern tip to its northern edge. Here was positioned von Breymann's own unit, the Chasseurs, some Hanau artillery and the jaeger soldiers.

Farther north were the remaining American loyalists. Their mission was to intercept any patriot teams or patrols probing into Burgoyne's rear and to provide warning of the approach of any sizeable forces. The loyalists accomplished this by dispatching their own patrols both westward and northward. Between the Balcarre's Redoubt and the von Breymann Redoubt were the Canadians, occupying a couple of fortified cabins.

By now, the British had also constructed a small floating bridge over the Hudson River. Here, close to the river, a small position was established by soldiers from the 47th Foot Regiment, and a few bateaux were also parked here.

General von Riedesel commanded the eastern sector from the Hudson to the Great Redoubt. General Hamilton commanded the western (right) wing, including the two other major redoubts. For tactical efficiency, Burgoyne positioned his headquarters in a cabin home behind the center between the Balcarres Redoubt and the Great Redoubt.[7]

As mentioned, on 21 September Burgoyne had dispatched Clinton's messenger back to New York, though he could never be sure if his couriers could get through. Additional runners were sent on the 22nd, 23rd, 27th, and 28th of September. Burgoyne was desperate for news.[8]

Indeed, his situation worsened daily. The desertion rate rose. On one occasion reinforcements did arrive. From out of the blue a force of approximately sixty Indian warriors appeared. But within a day or two, most departed.[9] Despite threats, more whippings, and another execution, Burgoyne could not curb the desertions. To raise morale and stiffen his army, Burgoyne issued proclamations that "powerful Armies of the King" were en route.[10] No one, however, believed him. Burgoyne probably himself did not believe it.

Tensions and animosities rose. Burgoyne's and von Riedesel's relationship increasingly deteriorated. Von Riedesel wanted to retreat to Fort Edward, which he felt would be a better location to await Clinton's arrival. In the event that Clinton failed to appear, von Riedesel argued that from Fort Edward the army could exit its way quicker out of this godforsaken wilderness to Fort Ticonderoga and from there, north through Lake Champlain to the safety of Canada. Burgoyne disagreed.

He still considered Albany the focal point of the campaign, and he had not given up his hopes for ultimate success. He not only refused to further distance himself from Albany, but also from Clinton's forces advancing northward.

Increasingly, Burgoyne kept to himself. He thought more and more about his wife, who had passed away just a year earlier. Seeking a way to escape his problems, he began to scribble plays. He thought more and more about theater and the arts. He wished that he was in England directing a group of actors for an upcoming show rather than directing troops waiting for an upcoming battle.

The days became shorter, the nights longer and colder. The howl of wolves and coyotes were constant and frightening. Cold rains further dampened spirits.

Half-starved horses began to collapse. Hunger pains gnawed at the troops. The wounded and ill could not be properly cared for. Suicides rose. Gun battles on the perimeter raged day and night. Nothing further was heard from either Clinton or Carleton. From Fort Ticonderoga word reached Burgoyne of the patriot raid that had briefly put the fort under siege. In addition to releasing prisoners, the patriots had captured over 300 men and destroyed much of the flotilla. To add to his misery, on 3 October Burgoyne was forced to cut the food ration by a third.[11] And the already harsh conditions only got worse for his troops.

North of Fort Edward, more trouble loomed. Although Burgoyne was not yet aware of it, another sizable unit from New Hampshire, commanded by Brigadier General Jacob Bayley, had moved eastward. Bayley, an aggressive fighter, appeared with 2,000 militiamen on high terrain to cut the main road and communication line between Fort Edward and Canada. In the event Burgoyne appeared from the south, a strong and well dug-in militia force would be opposing him.

SUNDAY, 5 OCTOBER

Sometime during this day, Burgoyne met with Generals von Riedesel, Phillips, and Fraser. It was agreed among them that another attack should take place.[12] Though it would be limited in scope, if successful it would be immediately exploited. Wanting to attack as soon as possible, Burgoyne stipulated that it would commence sometime in the late morning of 7 October. For the remainder of the day Burgoyne worked on the details as his generals prepared their units.

MONDAY, 6 OCTOBER

Clinton's force had started from New York City, advancing up the Hudson for an eventual link with Burgoyne. Late in the evening hours of 6 October, Forts Clinton and Montgomery fell to the British.[13] General Clinton was poised to strike further northward. For the time being, however, his progress was unknown to Burgoyne.

TUESDAY, 7 OCTOBER

A troop-count submitted on this day to Gates revealed that the Northern Army registered a strength of 10,000 to 11,000 Continentals and militia.[14] This number, however, did not include the many hundreds of women in the rear rendering important support, or General Bayley's command, the Continental strength still manning Fort Stanwix, or the Mohawk Valley militia, or the various units (such as General Stark's) in New Hampshire, Vermont, Connecticut and Massachusetts. It did not count the Continental and militia strength found in the Highlands such as at West Point, or the strength of the 15th Militia Regiment operating in Schoharie Valley. It also did not include the many agents, spies and couriers effectively monitoring British activities from Manhattan to Canada. If one included the strength of all of these other combat, support, and irregular forces, the Northern Army's strength would be significantly higher. Furthermore, whereas Gates' strength was growing on a daily basis, Burgoyne's was steadily declining.

The Second Battle of Saratoga: Bemis Heights

TUESDAY, 7 OCTOBER
7:00 A.M.

Burgoyne confirmed to his generals that the attack he had proposed in the prior days would indeed take place. He was unwilling to retreat, yet unable to sit still in the face of diminishing supplies and growing patriot strength. Patriot General Gates refused to come out of his works on Bemis Heights to challenge Burgoyne's own defenses, thus the British commander's only remaining option was to weaken the Northern Army by initiating a battle and possibly still forcing open the route to Albany. If he could gain that post and be joined by Clinton coming up from the south, British fortunes in the theater could still be reversed.

Unlike the three-pronged attack on 19 September, however, this one would be in the form of a strong reconnaissance-in-force. Burgoyne stated that his intent was again to maneuver around the patriot left flank in order to secure high ground overlooking the western portion of Bemis Heights. The immediate object, however, was to see if the patriots could be forced to give way, or if they had already grown too strong. Burgoyne couldn't afford to commit his entire army to an open-field maneuver, leaving his camp and remaining supplies at the mercy of the patriots in case of defeat. But if the strong initial probe found a soft spot in the patriots' defenses, it could be reinforced by the bulk of the army on the following day, 8 October, to exploit the initial success.

The plan called for Captain Alexander Fraser, with his ranger company and the remaining Indians, loyalists, and Canadians, to screen the attack on the far right. If possible, after advancing through the woods, they were to gain the patriots' rear and tie down units that would otherwise join the battle. Once located and penetrated, a sizable British-German force would be inserted into the same spot to further exploit the initial penetration. Afterwards, a much larger British force, commanded by General Simon Fraser (Alexander's uncle), would push rapidly through in order to secure the upper portion of Bemis Heights. With a group of 500 crack infantrymen, he was to position his force upon the Heights. General Fraser's effort would also be supported by no less than 1,500 to 1,800 soldiers.[1] Adding the irregulars and General Fraser's strength, over 2,200 would be involved.[2] Six 6-pound cannons, two 12-pound cannons, and two 3-pound howitzers, commanded by Major Williams, were to render artillery support.[3] Captain Pausch and his gunners would also be involved. All uncommitted units, such as the 47th Foot and the naval personnel, were to be placed on a standby alert. As for those conducting the attack, though they would all be organized into one wing designated as the right wing, in turn this wing would be divided into three parts.

Major Balcarres' light infantry, along with German troops from von Riedesel's and von Breymann's units and some British grenadiers, comprised the right wing's right end. Immediately behind Balcarres was positioned General Fraser who, with the 24th Foot, was to spearhead the attack onto the heights. As for von Breymann, though he would commit some of his troops to the attack, he would remain in his redoubt with his remaining troops. Generals Phillips and von Riedesel would command the right wing's center while the left portion of the right wing would be comprised of British grenadiers commanded by Major Acland. As for the top commanding officer, Burgoyne designated General Fraser.

If the western portion of the heights could be secured, Burgoyne stated that on the following day he would exploit the initial victory by inserting 4,000 troops over and beyond Bemis Heights. Virtually every soldier that he had remaining would be inserted beyond the heights. Though a much smaller force would conduct a feint against the patriot positions adjacent to the Hudson River to keep the patriots in place, the 4,000 plus soldiers, along with the 2,000 plus previously committed, after quickly assembling themselves on both sides of Wagon Trek Road, would advance eastward to finish off, once and for all, the patriot forces opposing them. True, Burgoyne and his commanders knew that Gates possessed a numerically stronger force. But they reasoned that the British-German elan, combined with cold steel, would overcome them.

After positioning their units into three columns to the north of the

Balcarres Redoubt, the British force advanced southwestward for about three-quarters of a mile where they halted to the west of the Balcarres Redoubt. To the north of them, very near by, lay the von Breymann Redoubt. On a piece of ground overlooking the North Branch of Mill Creek, the three columns reformed themselves into one continuous line about 3,000 feet in length. Both the British right and left flanks were anchored on thick woods. Immediately to their front was a sizable field, part of the Barber farm.[4] Although abandoned, its wheat crop had not been burned. Halting at the edge of the field, foragers were ordered to enter the field and cut down as much of the wheat as possible. The harvested wheat was to be used for baking bread.

In the meantime, as the foragers were rapidly working, the British-German troops rested as they awaited their next orders. As for the irregulars and the British troops accompanying them, they probed further to the south and southwest seeking an opening. In the meantime, General Burgoyne, accompanied by several other officers, positioned himself upon the roof of a deserted cabin owned by a Mr. Munger, who just weeks before had fled with his neighbors, and began to observe the situation.

Unknown to Burgoyne was that General Gates had extended his line westward. In fact, by now, the entire length of Bemis Heights was occupied. As more and more militia appeared, Gates had been able to strengthen the line. Lincoln's 2,000 militia and ranger soldiers, for example, were among some of those recently positioned into the Heights' western portion.

As all of this was occurring, General Gates and Colonel James Wilkinson were conferring with Colonel John Brooks.[5] A tough and aggressive leader, Brooks was briefing the two about a plan he had formulated to launch a raid into Burgoyne's rear.

As Burgoyne was observing and Gates was conferring with Brooks, Captain Fraser, along with his loyalist rangers, Canadians, and Indians, was making contact with the patriots. Shots were fired, tomahawks swung, and the Indians took several scalps; however, by now, the British and German line had also been noticed. A patriot sergeant was immediately dispatched to Gates' headquarters to warn the patriot high command.

Continuing to probe through the thick forest, Captain Fraser swung further around the western (left) flank of the Northern Army in his desperate effort to find the opening so critically needed by the British. Yet wherever he went, he encountered patriots and stiff resistance. From behind trees, brush, and from treetops, accurate rifle and musket fire dropped Britons, Canadians, and the irregulars. Weird animal sounds, effectively utilized for psychological warfare and to communicate, continuously echoed through the woods. Again, the sharp bark of a raven was echoed. Seconds later, two rifles cracked. Another Canadian collapsed to his death. Swinging further to the west, Captain Fraser hoped that perhaps, very soon, somewhere in this wooded jungle, he would finally find the opening he so desperately was seeking.

It was to no avail. The patriots were firmly in place. Wherever Captain Fraser probed, he only encountered more patriots. It was becoming more and more obvious by the minute—the patriots had succeeded in fortifying the entire length of Bemis Heights. Captain Fraser began to fear that his mission might fail.

Hearing shots, Colonel Morgan immediately placed his brigade on alert. A tough woodsman, Morgan sensed that trouble was brewing. Whenever Morgan got a hunch about something, he was usually right.

Arriving at Gates' headquarters, the sergeant reported directly to the Northern Army general. After hearing the sergeant's report, Colonel Wilkinson asked Gates for permission to ride forward to take a quick look. Gates agreed. Accompanied with the sergeant, Wilkinson set forth.

Continuing to observe from the rooftop of the cabin, Burgoyne saw no sign of the enemy. Some activity was noted to the southwest. But other than the wheat cutters busily at work, everything else seemed quiet.

Arriving at the scene, Wilkinson dismounted and proceeded cautiously forward. Squatting down behind some brush, he observed the scene. For almost fifteen minutes his eyes studied the terrain gently rising upward. He noted the wheat cutters, the long line of enemy troops, the enemy officers perched on the cabin's roof observing, and the two forested areas on the enemy's flanks. Wilkinson concluded that this force was planning to reconnoiter the Northern Army's left (western) flank.

Shouldering his custom double-barrel rifle, rifleman Tim Murphy was eager to get back to war.

1:00 P.M.

Returning to General Gates, Wilkinson immediately reported, "they are foraging, and endeavoring to reconnoiter your left. And I think, Sir, they offer you battle."[6]

"What is the nature of the ground? And what is your opinion?" asked Gates.

"Their front is open. Their flanks rest on woods, under cover of which they may be attacked; their right is skirted by a lofty height. I would indulge them."

"Well then," responded General Gates, "order Morgan to begin the game."[7] With these words, the Battle of Bemis Heights, or the Second Battle of Saratoga, formally commenced.

The plan was that Colonel Morgan's elite fighters, along with Lieutenant-Colonel Dearborn's light troops, would first circle around from the west; afterwards they would advance through the thick woods to attack the British right flank held by Lord Balcarres and a part of the 24th Foot. In the meantime, General Poor would circle and approach the British left flank from the east and, after advancing through his sector of thick woods, would attack the left flank held by Major Acland's troops.

Once the flank attacks had materialized, General Learned would attack the British center bolstered with the Germans. It was to be a three-pronged attack. In the event that any of these forces would require any support or reinforcement, General Ten Broeck's entire 3,000 strong Albany County Militia, along with General Paterson's Brigade, were placed on standby.[8]

2:30 P.M.

Advancing up the incline toward the forested area, General Poor's brigade was observed. Poor's brigade, however, was a highly experienced combat unit. Its three New Hampshire regiments were still commanded by Colonels Cilley, Reid, and Scammel. Poor's brigade was also accompanied with two New York regiments commanded by Colonels Van Cortlandt and Henry Livingston. Approaching closer, the patriot forces came under heavy fire but most of the cannon shot and musket rounds flew high over their heads.

"Regiments, Halt! Ready! Aim! Fire!" Over a thousand muskets and rifles roared in unison as the continentals and militiamen fired a volley into the British left. Struck in both legs, Major Acland went down. "Charge!" A massive battle cry was heard far and wide as the patriots surged forward with fixed bayonets and tomahawks in hand.

Initially, Gates had wanted to attack the British on both flanks simultaneously. But, as it often happens in combat, unforeseen and unpredictable things occur.

En route to his new location, Colonel Morgan's riflemen encountered Captain Fraser's irregulars and Britons still seeking an opening. Morgan's riflemen, however, quickly tore them into pieces. Long- and short-range shots dropped many. Tomahawks silenced others. Canadians, loyalists, and Indians, along with British regulars, began to flee into various directions. They could not be controlled. Fraser noted how Colonel Peters, slightly wounded, was himself fleeing like a rabbit. Their performance disgusted Captain Fraser. How ironic this was. When posted several months earlier by his uncle, General Fraser, to serve with the irregulars, Captain Fraser had accepted his new assignment with pride and gratitude. To develop a closer harmony with the irregulars, he frequently dressed as they did and covered his face with war paint. But as the weeks went by, the young captain's view of the irregulars had changed dramatically. Unable to do anymore, Captain Fraser withdrew. He had failed in his mission.

As for the Indians, Canadians, and loyalists who had not been killed or deserted, 7 October may be cited as their day of final doom. After this day, the remaining survivors began to desert in earnest. Fleeing into the wilderness, they simply disappeared. In the following days and weeks, the Indians would resurface in their native villages while the Canadians and loyalists wound up in Canada. They would speak of the defeat of Burgoyne, denounce the British high command for recruiting them, and cite how the British had mistreated and abused them. The loyalists even brought word to Colonel Peters' wife that her husband had been killed on 7 October.[9]

After scattering the irregulars ahead of them, Morgan's sharpshooters approached the British right flank and poured heavy fire into it. Balcarres' troops began to fall. Others sought cover behind trees, logs, and in ground depressions. Once under cover, they began to return the fire. A brisk and heavy firefight ensued.

Not far away, General Benedict Arnold could hear the roar of the battle. He was raring to go. God, how he wanted to get into it. But he had no command, no soldiers to lead, and he was under strict orders to stay put. Cursing "that bastard Gates," Arnold fumed and pouted that he could not go.

Charging into the British left, Colonel Cilley, the commanding offi-

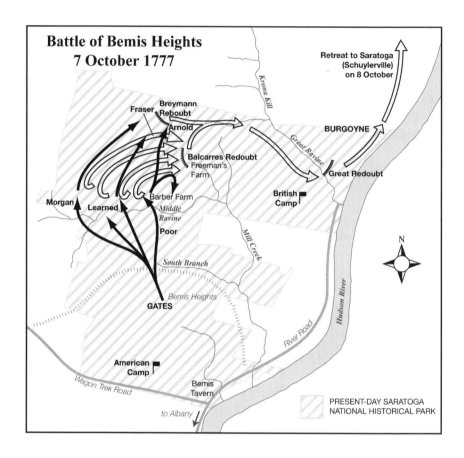

cer of the 1st New Hampshire Regiment, noted the dead and dying all around. Among them lay Major Acland. Immediately, an order was given to remove the major to the rear. Placed upon a stretcher, Acland was taken to a wagon which transported him to the Northern Army's field hospital. His days of serving the Crown in the Wilderness War of 1777 were over. Spotting a cannon, Cilley ordered that it be turned around. Rapidly reloading it, the cannon was effectively utilized against the British who were now reeling back.

Noting that the British were being hammered from both sides and were now falling back, General Learned ordered his entire brigade to advance forward. The 2nd, 7th, 8th, and 9th Massachusetts continentals, along with Colonel Henry Livingston's New York regiment, pressed forward. At the same time, General Ten Broeck's and General

Paterson's brigades moved up closer to the battle area.

Rushing forward, rifleman Tim Murphy plopped to the ground and began to scan the front. Suddenly, amid the bullets and musket balls flying all around, he spotted a target. Taking aim, his rifle held firmly in steady hands, he exhaled half of his breath and slowly squeezed. It would be a long shot, but Murphy excelled at long shots. With tremendous force and speed, Murphy's .58 caliber round tore deep into Burgoyne's aide, Sir Francis Carr Clerke, wounding him seriously.

Ignoring Gates' orders to remain in the rear and mounting his horse, General Arnold galloped toward the battle. Nothing was going to stop him.

Disregarding their casualties, Colonel Poor's troops continued to press forward. Reforming into line, they fired another heavy volley into the enemy. British army Captain David Wright, a company commander, fell dead. Immediately, Lieutenant Digby assumed company command. In actuality, the company no longer existed. Whereas just five months previously in June over fifty proud soldiers had marched off in the campaign, now, only Digby and four others remained. As for the others, excluding the few which lay in a hospital or were in captivity, most were buried in makeshift graves from Fort Ticonderoga to Saratoga.

For the last four months Digby had watched the company shrink in size and strength. True, the company had received a handful of replacements. But they made no difference. Besides, they too soon ended up dying in battle. Standing amid the insanity of 7 October, Digby knew that England would no longer win here. British defeat was inevitable. What especially saddened Digby was how within this godforsaken wilderness, the pride of the British Empire was perishing.

Despite Poor's heavy attack, the British troops quickly rallied. At close range they successfully repulsed Poor twice. But it was to no avail. Heavily outnumbered and operating against superior firepower, the British could no longer hold. By now, most of their artillery gunners had been killed or wounded. Several of the guns were in the hands of the patriots. With their artillery lost and with the capture of Major Acland, no effective leader existed. The British left had been destroyed. Dropping their weapons and raising their hands upward, they began to surrender while others fell back.

Unable to hold, Balcarres' troops retreated behind a rail fence. From here, they continued to fire against Morgan's and Dearborn's incoming troops. Continuing to advance forward, Morgan's and Dearborn's fighters encountered the 24th Foot. Heavy gunfire rocked the area as the patriots and British shot it out.

Within the center also stood the Germans. Pressed from the flanks and front, they began to fall back slowly. Noting a dangerous situation, Captain Pausch pulled his two guns to the rear. Repositioning his gun crews adjacent an abandoned cannon, Pausch continued to fire the guns as rapidly as he could.

What worsened the situation for the Germans was that General Learned was not only pressing hard from the front but also had just been reinforced. From out of nowhere, Colonel Johnson suddenly appeared with his 200 rangers. Just recently Colonel Johnson, as a member of Colonel Brown's force, had been raiding British positions in and around Fort Ticonderoga and Lake George. Now, Johnson's rangers were fighting as regular troops. Armed with rifles, Johnson's rifle shooters possessed far greater and accurate range than the Germans. The rangers not only protected Learned's Continentals but, just as importantly, supported Learned's vigorous attack with accurate rifle fire.

4:00 P.M.

By now, the battle had lasted for over an hour. Hundreds of British soldiers, along with approximately 300 Germans, were continuing to resist ferociously and effectively. Although they were slowly being pushed back, they were still holding their own.

Screaming like a madman, General Arnold rode full-fury into the battle. Seeing Arnold, New Hampshire's and New York's troops began to cheer. A number of the men even raised up their hats and coonskin caps in his honor.

Moments before appearing on the scene, General Arnold had stumbled into Colonel Brooks and his militiamen heading into the battle. As previously mentioned, Colonel Brooks had been conferring with General Gates about conducting a raid when the sergeant had suddenly arrived with news of the British advance. When Lieutenant-Colonel Wilkinson verified the sergeant's report and provided additional information, Gates suspended the raid for the time being. Colonel Brooks then asked Gates for permission to support Learned's brigade. With permission granted, Brooks rode off, gathered up his militiamen, and marched into battle. En route and very near to where the battle was taking place, Colonel Brooks encountered General Arnold. Noting the militia force and knowing how much more impressive he would appear if he rode into the battle at the head of some troops, General Arnold began to issue orders. As for Colonel Brooks, it appears that he didn't care one way or another. After all, General Arnold was General Gates' problem, not his.

Sensing an opportunity to outflank Balcarres' troops and the 24th Foot, Colonel Morgan reshifted a part of his unit, as well as Dearborn's fighters, toward the direction of the Balcarres Redoubt. If he could get behind the 24th Foot, Morgan knew that he would be able to surround the entire British-German force. Confident that he could shatter the enemy force, Morgan began to rush many of his troops through the dense forest to reach a ridge overlooking the British below. Among those who helped to secure the ridge was Tim Murphy. As he ran to the new location, he reloaded one of the barrels on his rifle. From their new position behind and amid the trees, Morgan's troops poured heavy fire down upon the enemy. The 24th Foot began to collapse.

During this entire time, Burgoyne was near the front. Unlike Gates who commanded from the rear and issued orders via dispatches, Burgoyne was very near. In fact, he was so close that several times bullets just barely missed him.

4:30 P.M.

Shouting "Victory or death!" General Arnold was all over the battlefield. Commanding no unit in particular, Arnold rushed from one engagement to another. But his presence did motivate the soldiers. Informed that General Arnold was among the combatants, General Gates immediately ordered Major John Armstrong to seek Arnold out and personally escort him back to the main headquarters. Armstrong was also to inform General Arnold that he was acting under the authority of General Gates. In the event that Arnold should refuse to comply, Major Armstrong was to use "what ever means is necessary" to restrain him.

Some have alleged that Arnold was under the influence of alcohol during this time. Possibly he was. With no specific command he might have been drinking, and certainly wasn't the only one on that field borrowing a bit of courage from a flask. But it does not matter. What matters is that Arnold was motivating troops at a critical moment and he was playing a vital role in repulsing the British attack.[10]

Perched high up in a thick oak tree, Timothy Murphy sighted a high-ranking British officer, dressed in an immaculate uniform astride a white horse. Riding back and forth, he was issuing orders. Undoubtedly, the sight of the beautiful pure white horse was what first caught Murphy's eye. The patriot rifleman also concluded that the man upon this exotic animal was one of high stature. No less than a general.

It would, of course, be a long shot. Well over 300 yards, if not 400. But it could be done. With an eagle eye, Murphy began to sight in. He would wait until the horseman had halted. As long as he reined his horse back and forth, Murphy was in no position to take him down.

Noting the stiffening resistance, Morgan began to fear that, perhaps, he would not be able to get into the British rear. But for the time being, he would continue in his attempt to do so.

By now, Pausch and his gunners were totally exhausted. Most of the British guns were no longer in action. A few of their guns were now in the hands of the patriots and these were being utilized effectively by the patriots. Yet, Pausch continued to fire his remaining cannons. He also noted that the barrels were red-hot. Despite swashing the barrels with cool water, the barrels remained dangerously hot. The danger of an internal explosion killing or injuring its crew was great.

Pausch, however, had no choice. He had to continue to fire. Though two times he had moved his guns further to the rear, it made no difference. He and his men remained under the constant heavy fire of the advancing patriots, and the patriots were edging closer. Bullets and musket balls continuously whizzed past his head. Pausch, however, could no longer pull back. He had to stand fast in order to support the line. Hearing the scream of a horse, Pausch momentarily glanced back. Another one of his horses lay dead on the ground.

Reining his horse around to the front, General Fraser faced the patriots directly. Sitting fully upright behind the 24th Foot, he began to issue orders. Not far behind, General Burgoyne was on his horse observing Fraser. "If anyone can save this situation and turn it around, it will be Fraser."

Or so Burgoyne thought.

As Burgoyne was observing and Fraser was directing the defense, Murphy was slowly squeezing the trigger from hundreds of yards away. Suddenly, Burgoyne witnessed Fraser toppling from his horse. Shortly afterward, Lieutenant Digby noted in his journal how with the general's fall, the patriots were able "to turn the fate of the day."[11]

Immediately, Burgoyne ordered that Fraser's body be recovered. He also ordered General Phillips and von Riedesel to retreat. Burgoyne knew that it was all over.

5:00–8:00 P.M.

Pressed from all sides and receiving no reinforcements, the English and German soldiers began to fall back. Struck in the head, Captain Money fell dead. Loading and firing his two remaining cannons as rapidly as possible, Captain Pausch and his gunners worked amid mobs of disorganized soldiers surging past them. At first, it had just been one or two, and most of these were the walking wounded. Nursing a wound, they fell back to seek treatment. Now, it was entirely different. Despite the valiant efforts of Lieutenant-Colonel Ernst von Speth to hold the line, command and control was steadily being lost. Pausch, however, continued to load and fire.

Until now, the soldiers who had been left behind in the Balcarres and von Breymann Redoubts had not been involved. But, as the battle neared closer and closer to them, they began to sense that it would not be very long before they, too, would need to take action.

With no less than 7,000 Continental and militia troops from Morgan's, Learned's, Poor's, Ten Broeck's, Brooks', Dearborn's, Johnson's, and a part of Paterson's brigade surging in, von Riedesel, Phillips, and von Speth were unable to conduct an organized retreat. As the remnants of the English-German force retired, Arnold, noting an opportunity to capture the western redoubts, shifted Learned's troops toward these targets.

Pausch was shocked! Though he knew that the English-German line had been ordered to retreat, this was no retreat. With Fraser gone and no firm commander in charge, the advance line had totally collapsed. British and German grenadiers were rapidly fleeing north and east. Some were no longer armed. Entire units were intermixed. Some officers were trying to regain control among the carnage but it was to no avail. The front had ceased to exist.

Hearing a huge battle cry to his front, Pausch looked up. Spotting a massive number of patriots charging forward, he knew that in less than one minute they would be upon him and his men. Ordering his gunners to abandon the cannons and hop into the ammunition wagon, Pausch raced the team of horses down the rough trail to safety.

When the retreat was initially ordered, Burgoyne had hoped that the Americans would not pursue or advance any further. In the event they

did, the British-German line, now between the redoubts, would be supported with fire from the redoubts and the various batteries positioned
around and between the redoubts. Caught in a huge engagement area,
the patriots would be decimated.

But this did not occur. There was no line. With no organized resistance, most of the outer batteries fell quickly to the charging patriots. In
some cases, when the grenadiers fell back, the soldiers who had been
manning these batteries simply joined the fleeing mass. Only the formidable Balcarres Redoubt held firm against the surging patriot tide.

Caught in the open and unable to escape, Major Williams quickly
raised his hands upward. Williams was actually one of the lucky ones.
Most of his gunners were dead. Taken into captivity, he was marched
southward.

Pushing on, the units commanded by Learned, Poor, Brooks,
Dearborn, and Ten Broeck now surged toward the von Breymann
Redoubt. As for Ten Broeck's militiamen, they were now avenging
General Herkimer. Amongst Ten Broeck's militiamen were many veterans of the Battle of Oriskany; others had seen action in the Schoharie
Valley fighting McDonell's and Crysler's invaders, while others had
marched to raise the siege of Fort Stanwix. Some had even been previously wounded. After recuperating, a number of the previously wounded soon enlisted into the Albany County Militia Brigade which, in turn,
was incorporated into General Ten Broeck's militia division. Armed
with muskets, rifles, and tomahawks, they surged forward.

Though he had not seen them yet, von Breymann knew that the
patriots were coming his way. He could hear them through the woods,
and the fleeing loyalists, Indians, British, and Germans running past his
redoubt further reinforced his fears.

In itself, the von Breymann Redoubt was a strong position. It was
well constructed. Over 200 yards of brush and trees had been cleared all
around. In the event the patriots were to assault the redoubt, they would
first have to charge through this open terrain.

But von Breymann also knew that every fortification has its weaknesses. Although he was supposedly in a strong position, only about
200 soldiers now manned this position. Continuing to watch, he noted
more and more English and German soldiers fleeing past his redoubt
with no leadership. Noting also the Herculean noise of the attackers as
they neared closer and closer, von Breymann ordered his men to get
ready. The brutal commander that he was, von Breymann also warned

them that he would kill the first man who attempted to either flee or surrender.

Swinging his sword and still raving like a madman, Arnold surged with the others toward the von Breymann Redoubt. To this day no one knows exactly who first ordered the assault against the von Breymann Redoubt. Possibly no one did. After pursuing the British-German force and penetrating toward the enemy's main positions, the patriots first attacked the Balcarres Redoubt. But their impetuous assault was repulsed with heavy loss. But more patriot formations were coming up, and many veered over toward the left, northwestward, toward the von Breymann Redoubt. As for the rest, as often happens in combat, the majority simply followed. Arnold himself raced on horseback between the Balcarres and Breymann Redoubts—in between the opposing lines—and somehow emerged unscathed.

Despite all that had happened, the patriots were still maintaining a strong command and control. Amid his shouts of encouragement, Arnold repeatedly swung his sword around in the air and into the direction of the redoubt. In his excitement, he accidentally struck Captain Robert Ball on the side of his head. For the rest of his life, Ball would have a deep scar on his head and face as a reminder and souvenir of that heroic day.

Suddenly, from out of the wood line, the patriots began to emerge. So many that it appeared to von Breymann and his defenders that an army of ants was heading their way. Ordering his militiamen into a line of two columns, Colonel Brooks proceeded to advance against the redoubt; simultaneously, as Brooks was advancing, more patriot units appeared on the scene. Even Morgan's riflemen were now there. Surrounded from all sides, the von Breymann Redoubt was heavily besieged. Pointing his sword toward the enemy, von Breymann shouted just one word—"Feuer!"

Musket balls flew toward the patriots as the redoubt's two cannon roared in unison. Yet, miraculously, only a few of the patriots were struck. Halting in place no more than 150 feet from the redoubt, the patriots unleashed a massive amount of small arms firepower into the German position. Reloading as rapidly as possible, the patriots continued to pour musket and rifle fire into the redoubt. As thousands of rounds poured in, German grenadiers began to topple. The defenders could not fire back effectively. The moment anyone exposed himself in the least, he was struck. Noting fear, indecision, and panic amongst his troops, von Breymann began to carry out his threat. Determined to hold, he actually struck a couple of those appearing to waver.

"Charge!" With a massive battle cry heard far and wide, the patriots rushed forward from all four sides. One of them was Nicholas Stoner, a famous trapper from the wilderness region of central New York. Suddenly, a German cannon thundered again. Its cannon ball demolished the head of a volunteer named Tyrrell. As bits and pieces of Tyrrell's skull few into various directions, some of the bone fragments struck Stoner's face. Blinded and knocked unconscious, Stoner collapsed to the ground. He lay there until Colonel Livingston ordered a search for him, Tyrrell, and a few of the others.[12]

From where he now stood, slightly over one mile further to the east, Burgoyne knew that the rebels were attacking the von Breymann Redoubt.

Riding amidst a small group of patriots, General Arnold got behind the redoubt on its left as its German defenders began to collapse. Noting the patriot general on a horse, a wounded German grenadier took aim and fired. He struck the horse. Collapsing onto its side, the horse not only pinned the patriot general to the ground but also crushed Arnold's leg. Amidst the inferno of the battle, General Arnold attempted to extract himself from underneath the horse.

Suddenly, Private John Redman rushed up. He wanted to assist General Arnold. Noting that the German grenadier who had just fired at Arnold was lying only yards away, Redman leaped forward to either shoot or bayonet the grenadier.

Shouting "Don't shoot! Don't hurt him! He is a fine fellow and only did his duty!"[13] General Arnold demanded that he not be harmed. The wounded grenadier was taken alive.

As he struggled to free himself, General Arnold looked up and saw that Colonel Brooks and his militiamen were now coming over the top. More patriot units appeared from the edge of the wood line and immediately joined the battle. Arnold now knew that the redoubt was theirs. Charging in, the patriots observed German grenadiers standing with their hands high in the air shouting "Bitte!" ("Please!") as others lay all around. Colonel von Breymann was among the dead.[14] To the patriots, it appeared as if the German commander had been shot by one his own men.

Suddenly it was over. Positioning themselves on and around the two redoubts, the patriots noted an eerie silence. By now it was dark and both sides had ceased to fight. Other than a rare shot, all was quiet. The Battle of Bemis Heights, or the Second Battle of Saratoga, was over. Of historical significance is that this would be the very last battle to be fought by the Northern Army in the northern theater.[15] From the dark forest an express rider emerged with a message from General Gates. The patriots were to hold both redoubts. Not one of the Germans who previously had been surrounded in the von Breymann Redoubt had escaped. All were killed or captured.

9:00–11:00 P.M.

While the patriots removed their wounded, the last of the prisoners were gathered up and, along with those captured during the assault on the von Breymann Redoubt, were escorted to the main camp of the Northern Army. In the late evening hours, Major Armstrong finally returned with General Arnold. Placed upon a stretcher, the general was carried by a team of soldiers headed by Sergeant Samuel Woodruff.[16]

On the British side stragglers were picked up, reorganized, and either reincorporated into their own units or placed into other units for the time being. Fearing a rebel night attack, Burgoyne began to make preparations. On his side, doctors and their orderlies were very busy. Another exceptionally long night awaited them.

11:00 P.M.

As he was reorganizing the shattered German units, Lieutenant-Colonel Ernst von Speth learned that the von Breymann Redoubt had been overrun. While the British had held at the Balcarres Redoubt, it had been the German barrier that had fallen, thereby making the entire army's situation untenable. Immediately, von Speth decided to retake the position. He concluded that the last thing the patriots would expect would be a night attack. Perhaps, the patriots had even abandoned the redoubt to return to their original positions.

En route to the redoubt, the Germans became disorientated. It was exceptionally dark amid the trees in the very late night hours. Visibility was almost zero. Suddenly, they encountered an armed man who claimed to be a "loyalist." He would guide the German force to the redoubt through a forest, "provided, of course, you let me partake in taking the position." Von Speth agreed to it.

The "loyalist" led the Germans into a thick forest. Somewhere, deep inside the woods, he ditched the Germans. Lost, and unable to reorient themselves in the dark, von Speth and his troops just blundered aimlessly in the woods through the remainder of the night, finally surrendering to patriot skirmishers. They never reached the redoubt they planned to retake.

XXIII

The British Begin to Collapse

WEDNESDAY, 8 OCTOBER

Despite the heavy fighting, a troop accountability revealed that the patriot forces had incurred only 150 casualties. This included both the dead and wounded.[1] Although any loss is tragic and demoralizing, in consideration of the size and scope of the battle the patriot casualties were in fact relatively light. A number of reasons may be cited as to why this was so: the patriot's quick reaction to Burgoyne's moves, a solid command and control which enabled patriot commanders to maintain effective usage of their troops, and the incorporation of large number of troops with a massive amount of firepower against the enemy. Combining these factors along with initiative and, of course, sheer guts and bravery as exhibited by those such as General Arnold, enabled the patriots to first hold and then win. Unlike previously on 19 September where hand-to-hand combat was the norm, on 7 October, it was very limited. The hand-to-hand combat that was waged was largely by the irregulars and when the patriots assaulted the redoubts.

For Burgoyne, 7 October was another major disaster. Again, he had been decisively defeated. No less than 600 British and German soldiers had been killed, wounded, or captured.[2] Of these, approximately 250 went into captivity.[3] The figure of 600, however, did not include the losses incurred by the Indians, Canadians, and loyalists.

A huge amount of weaponry and equipment was also lost. Six cannons within the line, two apiece in each of the redoubts, and some other cannons in the smaller batteries were lost as well. The consumption of ammunition and gunpowder had also been heavy. But the most damaging loss was with in leadership—General Fraser, Colonel von Breymann,

Major Acland, Major Williams, Captain Money... these were but just some of the key leaders lost by Burgoyne.

8:00 A.M.

After a painful night, General Fraser succumbed to his mortal wound. Talkative throughout the night, he requested to be buried at the Great Redoubt. He wanted to be with his fellow soldiers. British Army Chaplain Reverend Edward Brudenell officiated.[4]

The day was characterized by intermittent gunfire, the burying of the dead, and Burgoyne commenced his first preparations for a retreat. Approaching a forward position, General Lincoln received a severe upper leg wound. Though the ball was skillfully removed, his bone was shattered. For him, as for Major General Arnold, the Wilderness War of 1777 was finally over.[5]

The battle fought on 7 October placed Burgoyne in a very precarious situation. Strong patriot forces were now positioned to his front (south), right (west), and directly across the river to his left (east). In fear of becoming totally surrounded, Burgoyne dispatched Lieutenant-Colonel Nicholas Sutherland to reconnoiter the road north to Saratoga and occupy a safe assembly area somewhere in its vicinity. Accompanied with members from various units, Sutherland immediately set forth.

On this day, Burgoyne also slightly reformed his army. Because both the 9th and 47th Foot Regiments were tremendously under strength, the survivors of the 9th Foot were merged into the 47th Foot and from these two under strength regiments, a stronger 47th Foot was created. As for the 9th, it ceased to exist. Among the survivors of the 9th Foot who were merged into the 47th Foot was Sergeant Roger Lamb. Also on this day, Burgoyne was personally briefed by Colonel Peters that the loyalists were no longer an effective force and they were deserting.[6]

Burgoyne was not the only one dispatching troops that day northward to Saratoga. In an attempt to trap the British army, General Gates ordered General John Fellows and his brigade of 1,300, armed with two cannons, to proceed north. Fellows' mission was to march to where the Batten Kill flows into the Hudson River. There, across from Saratoga, his force was to dig in. In the event that Burgoyne attempted to cross the Hudson there, Fellows' militia would bar the way. Besides digging in, Fellows was also to establish contact with the 2,000 militiamen positioned near Fort Edward. He was also to be ready to re-cross the Hudson to engage Burgoyne directly from the north if the need should arise.

To reach their new location, Fellows' militiamen first crossed the Hudson to its eastern bank. Once across, they marched up the road. Because a small part of Burgoyne's army was still positioned across the river and was occupying a part of the road, Fellows and his men simply bypassed them. After returning to the main road, they proceeded to the Batten Kill River.

As the patriot force proceeded up the river, Fellows deliberately spread his militiamen out to portray a huge strength. En route up the river, they sang songs and displayed feelings of confidence. Fellows and his militiamen exerted upon Burgoyne another feeling of defeat. Noting the sizable patriot force moving north, Burgoyne hastened his preparations to retreat.

But General Fellows and British Lieutenant-Colonel Sutherland were not the only ones marching that day.

Following his victory at Bennington, General Stark had returned to his native state of New Hampshire. His unit was disbanded.

Stark, however, was not yet through with soldiering. Despite his continuing ill feeling towards the Continental Congress, Stark was still devoted to the cause. And, of course, Molly was still exerting her influence on him. Within a month, Stark had reorganized his brigade, accepted new volunteers, and marched off with over 2,000 fighters. His role in the Wilderness War of 1777 was not yet over. Among those who marched off with Stark was a veteran of the Battle of Bennington—John Hakes.

9:00 P.M.

With Captain Fraser and the irregulars in the lead, Burgoyne's army began to retire northward. Captain Samuel MacKay, who commanded what remained of the Loyal Volunteers Company, was also inserted into Fraser's group. The loyalist strength was now very low and Fraser knew that by morning, a few more would be gone. For him this entire campaign had been nothing but one huge disaster. He had lost his uncle, his irregulars had been shattered, and he had been defeated the previous day. Now, he was tasked to lead what remained of Burgoyne's army back north.

Excluding Lieutenant-Colonel Sutherland's small force which was further up north in the vicinity of the Fish Kill Creek, Burgoyne's army was organized into three groups. Up front and not far behind Fraser were the Germans, commanded by Von Riedesel. In the center fell the brunt of the British foot regiments. These were commanded by Burgoyne, who also positioned himself in the center. A rear guard, commanded by General Phillips, was also organizedv Because Burgoyne insisted on taking each and every cannon, a total of 27 cannons were pulled along.[7] The bateaux and naval personnel were to simultaneously row up the river alongside the marching troops. In itself, this was no easy task because it was fall, the first heavy rains had come down, and the Hudson River's current was considerably stronger. The British troops, positioned on the eastern edge of the Hudson River, were withdrawn back across to the western side of the Hudson. Once across, their floating bridge was demolished.

Another problem facing Burgoyne was what to do with the sick and wounded. Always problematic for a military force but especially troublesome for a retreating army, it was decided to leave the wounded behind. Approximately 400 incapacitated personnel were left. Doctor John MacNamara Hayes, Chaplain Brudenell, and a handful of medical orderlies remained behind to assist them.

Determined to learn the fate of her husband, Lady Harriet Acland approached Burgoyne and demanded that she be left behind as well. Knowing that he would be unable to change her mind, General Burgoyne decided to use her in delivering an important letter to General Gates. In his letter, Burgoyne requested that General Gates kindly assist Lady Acland in finding her husband, and Burgoyne also requested that Gates treat the wounded with respect and decency. Accompanied by her maid, a slightly wounded male servant, and Reverend Brudenell, the four journeyed downriver toward a patriot position[8] in a small rowboat under a huge white flag.

To reach their new location behind the Fish Kill Creek, Burgoyne's army would have to march nearly ten miles north. Though not a long distance, it quickly proved to be a very difficult ordeal.

Thursday, 9 October
12:00 P.M.

Indeed, it became an exceptionally difficult march. Before the army had commenced its retreat, a heavy rain had begun and it poured all night. Parts of the dirt road turned into a quagmire of mud. Half-starved horses, sometimes whipped viciously by angry drivers, pulled with difficulty. Thoroughly soaked soldiers pushed the wagons as cursing drivers struck the horses in their attempts to free stuck wagons. Here and there, a horse collapsed. Some of the carts toppled over. Some of the wounded, not wanting to be left behind, came along. They either hobbled on crutches or were carried on stretchers by relatives or close friends.

The night was exceptionally harsh for General Phillips and his rear guard. In addition to marching and ensuring that no patriot force came near, they were also tasked to tear down the bridges, destroy random sections of the road, and lay obstacles. Felling trees in pitch-black darkness amid a massive cold rain proved to be both difficult and dangerous. By now, it was obvious to everyone—Burgoyne's army was rapidly dying.

En route to their new location, Burgoyne ordered that the homes and farms of known patriots be burned. At Coveville, Colonel Van Vechten's home and stately barn was torched.[9] Just several months before in August, the colonel had lost his son, Lieutenant Tobias, in a battle near Fort Edward. Upon his return with his family in late October, they encountered only ruins. Homeless, they returned to Albany and survived the winter with the assistance of the Northern Army's relief bureau.

Van Vechen's home, however, was not the only one to be torched. Despite Burgoyne's orders, virtually every building was torched. It made no difference whose place it was. By the time Phillips' rear guard passed through Coveville, the entire settlement was fully ablaze. Even with the heavy rain, the fires burned uncontrollably.

12:00 A.M.

Informed that Burgoyne had retreated, Gates decided for the time being to remain in place. Besides, the cold rain was still pouring outside. Gates also knew that Burgoyne would not be able to escape easily. The tremendous distance along with the inclement weather would hamper any retreat. And General Jacob Bayley, who was positioned just to the north of Fort Edward, was blocking the route. It was also reported to General Gates that a Major Charles Cochrane, with 200 militia troops, was now occupying the ruins of Fort Edward. With General Fellows flanking Burgoyne's army and Stark nearby, there was no need to rush. For the time being, Gates would let time, nature, and the weather do its job in further weakening Burgoyne's army.

4:00 P.M.

Unlike Burgoyne's army, General Fellows' militia troops had marched rapidly. By the end of the day on the 9th, they had reached the Batten Kill. Positioning themselves there, they prepared to defend the area. En route to this location, General Fellows' scouts encountered some of General Stark's scouts probing westward. By the end of the day, runners from Fellows' force had informed Gates that Fellows' unit was in place and contact had also been made with Stark, who with over 2,000 fighters was planning to conduct further operations against Burgoyne.

In the evening hours of 9 October, Burgoyne's troops began to ford Fish Kill Creek. But as with the march, it would not be an easy crossing. Unlike in September when the water was not very high, now it would be difficult. The water averaged three to four feet in depth with a strong current. The creek banks, though not steep, were very muddy. The water was also cold. A few of the carts and wagons flipped over in their attempt to cross over. Spirits were further dampened by the cold night temperature. A handful of soldiers and drivers actually perished in the creeks murky and fast flowing waters.

As his army was crossing the creek, General Burgoyne again moved into General Schuyler's House. Schuyler's house stood to the immediate south of Fish Kill Creek and almost adjacent to the road leading to and beyond the creek. In fact, from Schuyler's house, one could see Fish Kill Creek. At Fish Kill Burgoyne also reestablished contact with Captain Fraser and Lieutenant-Colonel Sutherland.

After conferring with them, Burgoyne dispatched the two commanders on another mission. Both officers were to proceed all the way up to Fort Edward. Their mission was to check out the road leading to the Hudson River, find a suitable crossing site, and once across the Hudson inspect the road leading to Fort Edward and beyond. As for Sutherland, he and his soldiers were also to repair any section of the road needing it and to construct a bridge across the Hudson River at a site selected by Fraser. Once across, Sutherland was also to march to Fort Edward. Along the way he was to continue to repair any roads and bridges. Here and there, Sutherland was also to position small groups of soldiers to protect each bridge and serve as guides to the main body and rear guard of Burgoyne's army as it proceeded north. Burgoyne also posted additional soldiers into Sutherland's group to ensure success.

FRIDAY, 10 OCTOBER

Assembling his key commanders in Schuyler's home, Burgoyne briefed them on what was to occur. From where Burgoyne and the others stood inside Schuyler's living room, they could see the remains of their army crossing Fish Kill Creek. As their soldiers crossed the creek in waist- and chest-high water, Burgoyne informed his commanders that unless he heard something very soon and positive from Clinton, he would retreat to Canada on the 12th. In the meantime, Lieutenant-Colonel Sutherland was to immediately commence the construction of a sufficiently strong bridge and repair any sections of the road needing improvement in the event of a retreat.

Burgoyne was not the only one moving his forces, however. From the north, south, east, and west, patriot forces were rapidly converging upon Burgoyne.

Stark's and Fellows' scouts were probing all around Fort Edward. Major Cochrane, who was occupying Fort Edward, established observation posts along the northern edge of the Hudson River. General Bayley, who was still positioned just to the north of Fort Edward, was dispatching patrols southward. General Gates was also moving and his scouts and Indians were circling around Burgoyne's western flank. And General Stark decided to reposition his force further to the northwest. When conferring with General Fellows, Stark correctly concluded that Burgoyne would be utilizing the roads leading into and out of Fort Edward, repositioned his force further to the northwest. Stark's scouts had also been informing him that the British were moving northward. Therefore, by repositioning his force to the north of the Hudson River, Stark would not only cut off the road but, most importantly, he would help trap Burgoyne's army. Between Bayley, Cochrane, Fellows, and Stark, no less than 6,000 patriots were operating against Burgoyne from the north, northeast, and east.

In the early morning of 10 October, Gates issued two orders: the brigades of Learned, Nixon, Glover, and Morgan, accompanied by Dearborn's light infantry, were to march immediately to the Fish Kill. Their mission was to locate and attack Burgoyne's army in the vicinity of Saratoga. In the meantime, Gates would prepare to move the main body of the Northern Army. Within a day or two, Gates hoped to have his army repositioned in Saratoga. Not wanting to waste any time, and hoping to catch Burgoyne on the march, the patriot units which received the order to march, moved within several hours. As for the remainder of the army, every individual was busily involved in undertaking preparations for their march. Gates, however, would not be the one to finally trap Burgoyne in place.

Approaching the Hudson River's southern bank, Captain Fraser and his irregulars cautiously studied the river at a site they had identified as being the ideal place to construct a bridge. It seemed as if no one was on the other side. Once across the river, the road to Fort Edward and beyond should be open. Or so Fraser hoped.

Crossing over on a handful of boats found in the area, Fraser and his men proceeded to probe further ahead. Then it happened. A tomahawk, hurtled with tremendous force and speed, buried itself deep into the back of a loyalist. Shots dropped several more. Weird shouts, screams, and chants were heralded from amid the trees. Who exactly Fraser encountered is not known. Maybe they were some of Cochrane's militiamen. Or perhaps they were Stark's scouts. They could have been the Indians serving loyally in the Northern Army. Or it could have been the devil-fighters who had been harassing Burgoyne's army since the moment he entered this wilderness. History does not recall who they were. It does not matter. What matters is that Fraser, taking casualties and fearful of a major attack, ordered his men to run back to the boats and retire back across the river to its southern bank. As they fell back, the tempo of the insane screaming and shooting rose to a higher pitch.

Lieutenant-Colonel Sutherland, while inspecting a section of road with several others, heard the shots. Though he was only about a mile or so behind Fraser, Sutherland knew that the road to Fort Edward and beyond would have to be contested. He just knew it. Experiencing a sick feeling, he feared that the army was now possibly surrounded. Mounting his horse, Sutherland galloped north to see for himself what was going on.

These shots, however, were not the only ones to be fired. Throughout the day, as Morgan's and Dearborn's troops along with various other patriot units began to catch up with Burgoyne's retreating force still moving at a snail's pace, shots were continuously exchanged. Skirmishing occurred with Phillips' rear guard and even with Burgoyne's main body. Supported by over one hundred Indians, Morgan continued to flank Burgoyne's retreating army.

Approaching the Hudson River, Lieutenant-Colonel Sutherland encountered Captain Fraser. Taking full control, Sutherland informed

Fraser that he should have never pulled back and should have stayed on the other side no matter how many casualties he was taking. The army, insisted Sutherland, must have a crossing site. Otherwise, it would perish. After dispatching a message to Burgoyne, Sutherland ordered Fraser to fall in with the others and prepare to re-cross the Hudson.

Inside Schuyler's mansion, which was turned into a temporary headquarters, Burgoyne heard shots. As Phillip's rear guard neared Fish Kill, it was fighting off the spearheads of several patriot units. Simultaneously, Burgoyne also heard shots directly to the west of him. It was now obvious—enemy forces were attacking his army.

Yet, before he could even analyze the situation, Sutherland's dispatch rider rode in. Informed that Sutherland and Fraser were battling patriots to the north beyond the Hudson River, Burgoyne realized that his hopes for a quick dash to Fort Edward and beyond were slim. Even worse, Burgoyne had to immediately make several quick command decisions on what to do.

Unfortunately for his army, at this urgent time, Burgoyne became very indecisive. It appears as if he no longer knew what to do. But he did make some decisions. He ordered Phillips's rear guard to quickly cross over Fish Kill Creek. He also dispatched a quick note to Sutherland ordering him to cease, for the moment, any renewed attempts to again cross the Hudson River. Ordering his staff to fall in with the rear guard, Burgoyne proceeded to reposition himself further up north just slightly beyond Fish Kill Creek. Stepping outside of Schuyler's majestic villa, Burgoyne then issued another order—torch the house along with all of the barns, stables, and support buildings.

1:00–2:00 P.M.

That afternoon, as his army hastened its preparations to march north, General Gates wrote a letter to General Burgoyne. General Gates was responding to the letter previously addressed to him by Burgoyne and delivered by Lady Acland.

In his letter, General Gates assured Burgoyne that both Lady Acland and the wounded were being well treated; however, Gates emphasized that he was tremendously distressed by the numerous acts of arson. Gates wrote:[10]

> Sir, I have the honor to receive your Excellency's letter by Lady Acland. The respect due to her ladyship's rank, and the tender-

ness due to her person and sex, were alone sufficient securities to entitle her to my protection, if you consider my preceding conduct with respect to those of your army whom the fortune of war had placed in my hands. I am surprised that your Excellency should think that I could consider the greatest attention to Lady Acland in the light of an obligation. The cruelties which make the retreat of your army, in burning gentlemen's and farmers' houses as they [British army units] pass along, is almost, among civilized nations, without a precedent. They should not endeavor to ruin those they could not conquer. This conduct betrays more of the vindictive malice of a bigot, than the generosity of a soldier. Your friend, Sir Francis Clerke, by the information of the director-general of my hospital, languishes under a dangerous wound. Every sort of tenderness and attention is paid to all of the wounded who have fallen into my hands, and the hospital, which you were obliged to leave to my mercy.

Receiving Burgoyne's dispatch that he is not to cross the Hudson, Lieutenant-Colonel Sutherland immediately dispatched the messenger back to Burgoyne. Sutherland was requesting a confirmation. "Surely," thought Sutherland, "this must be a mistake." Sutherland, however, would not cross over without the confirmation.

Staring directly northward across the Hudson, Sutherland saw only the trees. A peaceful mist rose gently over the waters of the river. But as he continued to stare, a sudden chill overcame him. He knew that on the other side thousands of patriots were lying in wait. Sutherland also sensed that it would be a long time before he would once again see either Canada or his native England.[11]

Unknown to Burgoyne, after capturing various forts in the Highlands from 6–8 October, General Clinton began to withdraw back to New York City on 10 October. Other than leaving a token force in the Highlands for the time being, Clinton did no more. He did, however, dispatch a messenger to Burgoyne.

SATURDAY, 11 OCTOBER–SUNDAY, 12 OCTOBER

Within just a day of his arrival in New York City, General Clinton decided to again assist Burgoyne. He ordered General John Vaughan to probe further up the Hudson River Valley. With 2,000 soldiers and a small naval force augmented with civilian river pilots, Vaughan was to see how close he could get to Burgoyne.

From Scheider's Mills near the Hudson River, Simeon Alexander and a couple of patriot officers were observing a red house. It was out of range of small arms fire. "Who knows," someone said, "but maybe Burgoyne is in that house. We will try it and see," said an officer.

Bringing up a cannon, the patriots aimed it at the house. Firing, they heard the crash of the round striking its frame. Quickly reloading and firing again, the gunners noted a number or redcoats, who appeared to be officers, fleeing from the house.

Throughout the day, artillery and small arms fire raked the British. "Numerous parties of American militia swarmed around the little adverse army like birds of prey,"[12] wrote Sergeant Lamb in his diary. As for von Riedesel, all day he pleaded, argued, and insisted to conduct a hasty retreat across the Hudson River via Fort Edward and Lake Champlain. In order to save the army, argued von Riedesel, it had to abandon everything other than just small arms and provisions. Even von Riedesel's wife was supportive of a retreat. As she later noted,[13] "The whole army clamored for a retreat, and my husband promised to make it possible, provided only that no time was lost. But General Burgoyne, to whom an order had been promised if he brought about a junction with the army of General Howe, could not determine upon this course, and lost everything by his loitering."

Dejected, disgusted, disillusioned, and realizing that nothing more could be accomplished by further resistance, sizable numbers of British and German soldiers began to surrender. For the first time in this battle, officers even began to call it quits. Such was the case on 12 October when several British army officers deserted to the patriots. After surrendering, they were interrogated. One of them cited how just the day before he had been inside a house which had suddenly been struck by two cannonballs penetrating through the walls.[14] In another case, a sizable group of about fifty German soldiers, accompanied by an officer, walked over. To save face, von Riedesel informed Burgoyne that this group, positioned on the edge of a perimeter, had been overrun.

Late that evening, General Gates wrote a letter to John Hancock, the President of the American Continental Congress. In his letter, the Northern Army general informed Hancock as to what had been happening and that much success had been achieved. Gates also praised his Indian contingent when he wrote, "The Six Nation Indians, having taken up the hatchet in our favor, had been of great service and I hope the enemy will not be able to retreat from them."[15]

Not far from where Gates was writing his letter, von Riedesel was meeting with Burgoyne. The German general wanted to know why Burgoyne was not preparing to move out. Previously, Burgoyne had assured his commanders that if nothing was heard from Clinton by the 12th, he would order a full retreat. Yet, nothing was being done in preparation for it. Von Riedesel was informed that he would have wait a little longer for the retreat, and he began to fear for the worst.

MONDAY, 13 OCTOBER

From the base of the Fish Kill northward to the vicinity of where the Hudson River bends to the northwest, Burgoyne's army lay near the western edge of the river. It occupied an area slightly over one and a half miles in length and over a half mile in width. Inside this pocket, the Germans held the northern perimeter; the center was held by the 20th Foot Regiment along with some German grenadiers and a handful of the remaining Canadians, and the southern perimeter was held mostly by the British from other various regiments. The few remaining loyalists and Indians were positioned throughout the locations. The cannons were dug in on the highest points around the perimeter. Within Burgoyne's perimeter stood the ruins of the old Fort Hardy overlooking the Hudson, but it was not occupied. Burgoyne's headquarters was located in the center.

By now, Burgoyne's army was entirely surrounded by a steel ring of patriot forces. The 7th Massachusetts Continentals, along with Glover's, Paterson's, and Nixon's brigades, were positioned against Burgoyne's army from the south and southwest. Learned's and Morgan's brigades and Dearborn's light troops were in place to the west. General Bayley's unit, though still across the Hudson, moved slightly southward and positioned itself in an area from the northwest to the northeast. A part of this sector was now also covered by General Stark's force which had approached during the last several days. Among those who moved with Stark into the new position was John Hakes. As Hakes moved in, he kept wondering what would happen next. Behind these two commanders stood Major Cochrane's unit which was still occupying Fort Edward. Directly east across the Hudson River was positioned General Fellows. By the hour, the patriot strength continued to rise as more and more individuals and small units appeared.[16]

In terms of strength, Burgoyne's army stood at slightly over 6,000 personnel.[17] As for the patriots opposing them, their strength was much greater. Various authors cite different figures, but all agree that no less than 14,000 to as many as "20,000 well-fed" fighters ringed Burgoyne.[18] There was also a considerable amount of artillery.[19]

Finally deciding to retreat, Burgoyne ordered Lieutenant-Colonel Sutherland to cross over the Hudson River. Burgoyne still believed that he could escape. Despite Sutherland's and Fraser's best efforts, nothing positive was achieved. They simply could not cross over the Hudson. That evening, Sutherland personally briefed Burgoyne that superior patriot forces, estimated at many hundreds if not thousands, were positioned to the north of them immediately across the river. Until, somehow, a strong force could be inserted across the Hudson to defeat the patriots in that particular location, a bridge could not be built. Sutherland also warned Burgoyne that the patriots would strongly contest any attempt to cross the river.[20]

One of the golden rules of warfare is "don't get yourself surrounded." In the event a unit or army should find itself in that unfortunate position, the best option is to either remain in place until relieved or conduct an immediate breakout from encirclement. Needless to say, a decision must be made quickly. Since it was not known if Clinton (or anyone else) was en route, Burgoyne was faced with only one of three options: defend in place, break out, or surrender.

With supplies, time, and ammunition running out, and with no prospect of being relieved, Burgoyne's army could not stay in place. If it did, starvation would be the end of them. And a cold winter was just around the corner. Therefore, the first option was impossible.

The second option was to break out. A breakout is strictly an offensive operation undertaken by those surrounded in order to escape. A force is considered encircled when its supply, reinforcement, and ground routes are completely severed by an advancing enemy. The purpose of conducting a breakout is to allow the encircled force to reestablish contact with its respective army, to avoid further destruction or capture, and to survive for future operations. In order for Burgoyne to conduct a breakout, there were many things he first had to do. He had to deceive the patriots in regard to his army's composition, strength, and intents; he had to conduct successful reconnaissance; he then had to organize the breakout, support, flank and rear guard forces; he had to organize a security force which could be rushed to any critical sector; and lastly, he had to concentrate sufficient combat firepower at the breakout points.

Unfortunately for Burgoyne, though he was in a position to reorganize his army for a breakout, he would still have to cross the Hudson River. Even if he did succeed in fighting over the river, very little, if any, support would be forthcoming from Canada. And a retreat to Canada involved many other obstacles. There was a tremendous distance to go. Numerous streams, now deepened and widened with the fall rains, posed serious hazards. Major rivers and lakes also needed to be crossed or traveled upon. With most of the army's bateaux, boats, sloops, and ships destroyed by patriot raiders, watercraft would have to be secured or built and there was no time for this. Bridges and roads would also have to be built and repaired. Even if everything was discarded and the cannons, baggage, carts, wagons, and weakened animals were left behind, Burgoyne's army would still be hampered with the wounded and numerous civilians attached to it. Von Riedesel, for example, still had his wife and three children. Yet speed was of the essence. The distance, the lack of boats, the natural dangers of the wilderness, and a weakened army burdened with families precluded, for the moment, any chance of a speedy exit back to Canada.

Meeting with von Riedesel, Phillips, and Hamilton, Burgoyne proposed five possible courses of action: 1. Stay in place and wait for either the patriots to attack or Clinton's arrival; 2. Attack Gates; 3. Attempt to retreat with all of the artillery and baggage; 4. Retreat, but only at night and with only what the soldiers could carry; or, 5. Attack the enemy with the intent to drive for Albany. Perhaps, they would link up with Clinton in Albany yet.

Following a lengthy discussion amid nearby exploding cannon balls, it was decided to break out and retreat northward. Once again, Lieutenant-Colonel Sutherland was tasked to lead the way.

Throughout the day, a young soldier serving in Fellows' brigade had been watching the horses grazing across the Hudson River on a small pasture adjacent to an old fort. He also noted that at this particular location, the bank was not very steep or high. He decided to conduct a one-man midnight raid onto the other side.

At approximately midnight he stripped to his shorts and swam over to the enemy side. At first, the daredevil raider just lay amid some bushes and waited. Concluding it was safe to move, he ran slumped over to where the horses were grazing. Mounting a young animal, he rode the horse bareback to where the bank was not very steep and prodded the horse into the river. This was noticed by several British soldiers, and he was fired upon, but he was too far out in the water. Both the horse and soldier made it over to the patriot side.

XXIV

Burgoyne Surrenders

TUESDAY, 14 OCTOBER–WEDNESDAY, 15 OCTOBER

Hearing about the one-man raid, the company commander demanded that the soldier who had swum across the river be immediately brought in. Upon reporting and saluting his commander, the young horse raider stated, "It is not proper that a private should ride, whilst you are on your foot. So, sir, if you have no objections, I will go and catch another for you. And the next winter when we are home, we will have our own fun in driving a pair of Burgoyne's horses."[1] Permission was granted for another raid.

Meanwhile, nearby, as he was removing the scalp from a loyalist, rifleman Tim Murphy looked up and saw five Indians running toward him. With the scalp in his hand, Murphy turned and began to run. Unable to outrun his opponents, Murphy stopped, turned around and knelt, took aim and fired, killing one of the five. Believing they had Murphy, the other four continued to run forward. Reshifting his aim, Murphy fired again and killed another one. Both shots had been fired in a matter of seconds. Noting the two shots and fearing that he possessed some type of demon gun, the others immediately turned and fled. Murphy escaped.

8:00 A.M.

Informed by his scouts that the road and the area to the north of the Hudson was thick with well dug-in patriot forces, Burgoyne summoned his officer corps, including the captains and lieutenants, for a general council in the morning hours of 14 October. It was unanimously agreed to open negotiations with General Gates for an honorable surrender.

That morning 15-year-old George Williams, a drummer boy and nephew of Major Griffith Williams, was observed crossing the Fish Kill Creek. Once inside the patriot lines, he was immediately escorted to General Gates. Williams carried a message which stated, "General Burgoyne was desirous of sending a field officer to him [General Gates] upon a matter of great moment to both armies."[3]

"Ten o'clock, at the advanced post of the army of the United States,"[4] was the response.

Over the following days, the two army commanders negotiated. On the British side, Major Robert Kingston was a key player; on the American side was Lieutenant-Colonel James Wilkinson.

General Gates, however, was not only corresponding with General Burgoyne. He was also corresponding with Governor Clinton. Much of this correspondence was done via Matthew Visscher, a civilian state representative who was posted to the Northern Army. On 14 October, Visscher dispatched a letter to Governor Clinton about the situation. Visscher was responding to a letter dated 13 October from Governor Clinton warning Gates that British forces from New York City and the Highlands were renewing an attack up the Hudson River. Visscher added, "Deserters and prisoners are bro't into our camp every hour. Burgoyne must fight his way thro' or surrender, and from the situation of affairs the latter is most likely."

General Gates was fully aware that his Northern Army had not been totally successful in the Highlands and that the patriots had been defeated there. But Gates also knew that for the British, it had not been a true victory either. In the aftermath of capturing Forts Clinton and Montgomery, General Clinton had immediately withdrawn to New York City. Though within days another force had been dispatched to return north, Gates was confident that the advancing British force would soon be repulsed. Daily, fresh militia and continental forces were appearing on the scene and Gates was gearing up to battle the British in the Highlands.

General Gates fully understood the significance of ejecting the British out of the Highlands. Even if Burgoyne surrendered, the victory would not be so meaningful if a sizable part of the recently created New York State would still remain in the hands of the British. With the British occupying nearly half of the Hudson Valley, a large portion of New England would be cut off; likewise, the British would remain as a threat to both that region and the rest of New York State. Their occu-

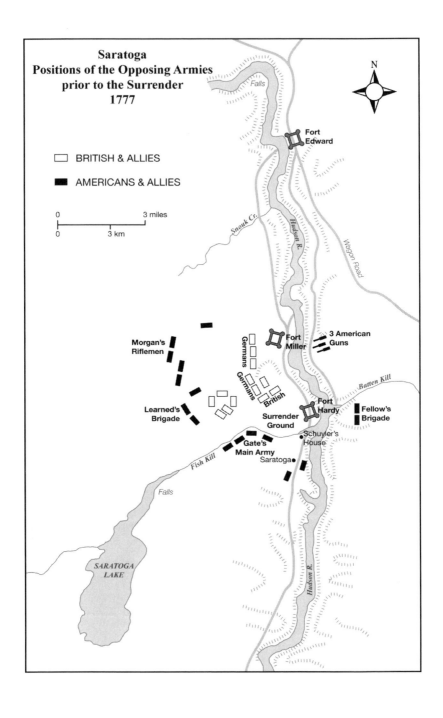

Saratoga
Positions of the Opposing Armies
prior to the Surrender
1777

□ BRITISH & ALLIES

■ AMERICANS & ALLIES

0   3 miles

0   3 km

pation of West Point would also deny the patriots a critical military site along with a vital communication and transportation route. And the Highlands could be utilized as a springboard for future operations. Therefore, to push the British out of the Highlands entirely, Gates began to take action.

Besides dispatching advisors, he began to shift army and support personnel to Governor Clinton. Gates also ordered the 3rd Continental Regiment, now commanded by Colonel Van Schaick, to return to the Highlands. A crack regiment, the 3rd Continental had previously served in the Highlands. Prior to its deployment to Fort Stanwix, it had served and fought in the Highlands. Elements of the 9th Massachusetts Continentals, another very good outfit, were also ordered into the Highlands along with Major William Hull's battle-hardened 8th Massachusetts militia battalion rebuilt with the numerous volunteers. Realizing the importance of harvesting a good crop, Gates also began to rotate more and more of the militia back home. In the meantime, newly arriving militiamen replaced them. Such a rotation ensured a good harvest and raised morale.[5]

In a letter dated 15 October 1777,[6] General Gates provided Governor Clinton some very good news:

Dear Sir, I have just received your letter of the 13th Inst. It is certainly right, to collect your whole Force, and push up the East Side of the River, after the Enemy.... Yesterday General Burgoyne proposed to surrender upon the inclosed Terms, the Capitulation will, I believe, be settled today, when I shall have Nothing but [British] General [Sir Henry] Clinton to think of. But if you keep Pace, with him on one Side, the Governor on the other and I in his Front, I cannot see how he is to get home again.

General Gates also submitted copies, to include any changes, on the letters going on between him and Burgoyne. This way, the governor would know how the surrender process was being handled.[7]

One of the thorny issues that needed to be resolved dealt with the use of a specific word. Burgoyne did not want to use the terms "Surrender" and "Capitulation"; rather, he requested that "Convention" be used instead.

To his surprise, Gates accepted. For Burgoyne, "Convention" had its advantages. It allowed his soldiers to march out with full honors. After grounding their weapons, free passage to England and Germany would be granted. Provisions were also to be provided to those returning to these two nations. The British and German soldiers would be escorted back to Boston, also agreed upon, by their own officers. The officers would retain their sidearms and swords. All of the soldiers would keep their personal belongings. None of their baggage was to be searched. All sailors, bateau personnel, drivers, workers, wagoneers, axmen, Canadian personnel, Indians, and followers of the army "who come under no particular description," would return immediately and by the shortest route to their homes in Canada or in the colonies. As for Burgoyne and his senior ranking officers, they would be allowed to return to England and Germany under parole, as stipulated by one of the agreements of the Convention. As one historian summed it up best, "No defeated general could have hoped for more than that."[8]

By the evening hours of 15 October, both sides had agreed to the Convention. The signing was to take place on the 16th.

THURSDAY, 16 OCTOBER
2:00 A.M.

The daredevil soldier who had secured for himself a horse the night before by swimming across the river now repeated his feat. Proudly, he presented to his commander a horse. By now, everyone in the Northern Army was aware of his feats, including Gates.

Yet, virtually at the same time that the young swimmer was slipping his way out of the British camp, Captain Alexander Campbell, an officer from the 62nd Foot, was slipping his way through the tight patriot lines into the British zone. Dressed in civilian attire, Captain Campbell succeeded in reaching Burgoyne's trapped army. Immediately, he was brought to Burgoyne to report in.

Campbell brought news of the fall of West Point and that General Vaughan, escorted by Commodore Wallace's fleet, had reached Kingston. According to Campbell, Sir Henry Clinton was making a strong effort to reach Burgoyne's army.

Prior to Campbell's arrival, Burgoyne did note that Gates was not argumentative or particularly tough in the negotiations. The patriot general even seemed to be in a rush to conclude the talks. "Does Gates know something I don't? Is Clinton coming up behind him? Does Gates want me to surrender so that he can turn full fury upon Clinton?"

Such questions undoubtedly went through Burgoyne's mind.

Assembling his officers, Burgoyne asked them if he could break the agreement with Gates. Burgoyne's officers insisted that it was a matter of honor to stay with the terms of the agreement. Exhausted, hungry, and fearful of what could happen if the struggle should continue, they urged Burgoyne to accept as agreed upon earlier.

Despite their opinions, Burgoyne decided to stall. He felt that perhaps, Clinton was en route and would soon arrive. Burgoyne was also confident that his remaining British-German troops, now solid veterans, could be counted upon for one more battle.

After stalling for several more hours, Burgoyne dispatched a message to General Gates. Demanding an accountability of his Northern Army, he accused Gates of sending many of the Northern Army's soldiers south to Albany or beyond. Burgoyne cited that this was a violation of the negotiations of the Convention because had he (Burgoyne) known that Gates was not in command of a superior force he would have never negotiated in the first place. Burgoyne also requested to send some of his officers into the camps of the Northern Army to confirm its true troop strength.

Angered with Burgoyne's message, Gates immediately warned Burgoyne that if he failed to yield, the patriots would attack. Gates informed Burgoyne that no one would be inspecting the Northern Army or counting its troop strength. To prove that he meant business, Gates brought up units closer to the British lines. Finally heeding Gates' warnings and the advice of his officers to accept, Burgoyne gave in, signed the agreement, and dispatched it to General Gates. Burgoyne's messenger also informed Gates that Burgoyne's army would surrender on the morning of 17 October.

Late that night the remaining loyalists and Indians fled. Reporting to General Phillips, the Canadian militia leader, Colonel Peters, requested orders. Phillips was surprised that Peters was still around. Peters demanded that General Phillips issue him either a discharge or a formal leave of absence. Upon his return to Canada, Peters did not want anyone to accuse him of desertion or cowardice. For all it was worth, Phillips quickly wrote something out for Peters, who then immediately disappeared into the darkness. Accompanied by Skene and a handful of other loyalists, Peters started north for Canada that night, and upon his return he would proceed to assemble a new loyalist force. But he would never again play an influential role.[9]

FRIDAY, 17 OCTOBER

Early that morning, Burgoyne assembled his remaining officers. He thanked them for their efforts and their honorable service. Then, Burgoyne issued his final order. He ordered his officers to return to their units and assemble their soldiers and workmen. The officers were to inform their men on what would be taking place and each officer was also to thank his men for their efforts and devotion. Of historical significance is that in the annals of the Wilderness War of 1777, this would be Burgoyne's very last order to his command. In fact, it would be the last order Burgoyne would ever issue on the North American continent.

11:00 A.M.

Burgoyne's troops began to march out. Upon a field now known as the "Field of Grounded Arms" near the ruins of the old Fort Hardy, just across from Fish Kill Creek, Burgoyne's soldiers began to lay down their weapons. Some, in protest that they had to lay down their arms, instead smashed their weapons directly in front of their officers. From a short distance away, Burgoyne himself supervised this activity. Other than Lieutenant-Colonel Wilkinson and one or two other patriot officers, no other Americans were present at this site.

Once the arms were piled, Burgoyne stated to Lieutenant-Colonel Wilkinson that he would now like to be introduced to General Gates. Crossing Fish Kill Creek, the mounted officers rode to where Gates waited. Burgoyne was also accompanied by his adjutant general, Major Kingston, and his two aides, Captain Lord Petersham and Lieutenant Wilford. Generals Phillips, von Riedesel and Hamilton followed with several other officers.

The moment Burgoyne and Gates met, they saluted one another and shook hands. Raising his hat upward, Burgoyne remarked, "The fortune of war, General Gates, has made me your prisoner."[10] In response, Gates said, "I shall always be ready to bear testimony that it has not been through any fault of your excellency."[11] Burgoyne and his commanders and staff were then invited to sit down to a simple but wholesome meal.

After laying down their arms, the English and German soldiers were marched into captivity by Major Morgan Lewis, who had turned 23 years of age just the day before. Morgan was the son of Francis Lewis, one of the signers of the Declaration of Independence. Young Lewis escorted Burgoyne's surrendered army through the long lines of

American soldiers. As the captured personnel marched, they were tremendously awed by the appearance of the Continental and militia troops. True, there was a lack of uniformity. Even most of the officers, including colonels, did not possess a standard uniform. Yet such was noted:

> ... they stood like soldiers, erect, with a military bearing which was subject to little criticism. All their guns were provided with bayonets. The riflemen had rifles. The people stood so still that we were greatly amazed. Nature had formed all the fellows who stood in rank and file, so slender, so handsome, and so sinewy. It was a pleasure to look at them... Such a finely built people... The officers wore very few uniforms and those they did were of their own invention.... There was not a man among them who showed the slightest sign of mockery, malicious delight, hate, or any other insult. It seemed rather as if they wished to do us honor. [12]

According to Lossing, on that day 5,791 prisoners marched out.[13] Ward cites 2 lieutenant-generals, 2 major generals, 3 brigadiers, 299 other officers in the rank of ensigns to colonel, 389 non-commissioned officers, 197 musicians, and 4,836 privates.[14] Scheer and Rankin cite 7 generals, over 300 other officers, and over 5,000 others of various ranks.[15] According to Carlton Hayes, "British General Burgoyne with some six thousand men surrendered at Saratoga, on 17 October 1777, after an unsuccessful invasion of northern New York.[16]

The figure of 17 October, however, did not include the approximately 600 captured at Bennington, the 500 captured during the Saratoga battles, the over 300 captured at Fort Ticonderoga and Lake George, and the nearly 400 wounded left behind just days before with doctors, a chaplain, and medical orderlies. Also not included were the many who either deserted to the patriots—sometimes in groups up to as large as 50—or were captured. These figures also do not include the captured loyalist, Canadians, and Indians. If the irregulars were to be figured in, in a period of approximately four months, around 8,000 British and German soldiers and irregulars from Burgoyne's army went into captivity. For the patriots, Saratoga was indeed a massive victory.

That evening, General Gates submitted a troop strength return of "the army of the United States under the command of H. Gates, Major

General, 17 October 1777." A total strength of 22,348 was cited.[17] This troop strength figure, however, did not include the entire strength of the Northern Army. In addition to the approximately 20,000 facing Burgoyne, other Continentals and militiamen were still stationed in Fort Stanwix and in the Mohawk and Schoharie Valleys.

As for the patriot forces shattered days before in the Highland region, they were now regrouping near that region and in the Hudson Valley. This figure also did not encompass the militia strengths found throughout the New England states; or the various militia units coming into the Highlands to support the Northern Army in its defense of the Highlands. Gates' figure of 17 October also did not include the hundreds of men and women providing direct support in the rear area of Albany. Also not included were the numerous agents, spies, and couriers. If one included all of the fighters and supporters found in the Northern Army from the period of January to October 1777, then nearly 40,000 to 45,000 personnel served in some capacity within its ranks.[18] Never, in faraway England, would anyone have imagined in 1776 and early 1777 that such a large troop strength could have been amassed.

SATURDAY, 18 OCTOBER–FRIDAY, 7 NOVEMBER

News of Burgoyne's surrender spread far and wide. Throughout the North American continent, many found it difficult to believe that a powerful and undefeated army could succumb to a recently organized force.

Immediately following Burgoyne's surrender, some of the militiamen began to return home; others, attaching themselves to various Continental units, began to proceed southward. There was still the British threat to their rear. But the veterans of Saratoga would see no further action in the concluding weeks of 1777. Upon hearing of Burgoyne's surrender, General Vaughan proceeded no further. His force retired all the way back down to New York City. Had he attempted to continue, it would have made no difference. He was still miles away from Saratoga, his boat pilots and river men, composed mostly of civilian personnel, were refusing to venture any further upriver, and patriot forces were massing in strength.[19]

From the loyalists, Canadians, Indians, and the surviving British and German troops drifting back into Canada, Governor General

Carleton learned of Burgoyne's surrender. Carleton, however, was not surprised in the least. For weeks, he had known that the campaign was drifting aimlessly. In response, Carleton issued the order that all units still remaining to the south of Canada's border were to immediately withdraw back into Canada. Little did Carleton realize that soon, he too would be a victim of the Wilderness War of 1777.[20]

SATURDAY, 8 NOVEMBER

General Powell ordered the evacuation of Fort Ticonderoga, including Diamond Island. Prior to their departure, the British destroyed everything.

Further to the east, Captain Ebenezer Allen, who played an instrumental role in the patriot victory of 1777, commenced a long-range patrol to probe deep into the area of Lake Champlain. From Fort Ticonderoga to the Canadian border, Allen's scouts were to seek out and identify any positions still manned by the British. Allen, a native of Vermont, was also undertaking this mission on request of Vermont's legislative body who were deeply concerned as to what was occurring within the wilderness region west of Vermont's western border.

Packing his rucksack, rifleman Tim Murphy began to wonder what new adventures would lie ahead. Murphy's brigade, along with Glover's, Poor's, and Nixon's brigades, were recalled by Washington back to the main Continental Army. [21] Along with these units, Generals Benedict Arnold and Benjamin Lincoln and various other leaders also previously dispatched by Washington, were ordered to return as well.[22]

SUNDAY, 9 NOVEMBER

After checking out Skenesborough, Captain Allen neared the ruins of Fort Ticonderoga. Immediately, he and his men noted that the blackened limestone rock, shrouded with mist and overcast with dark clouds, exhibited the look of something very terrible. As the captain stood upon the western bank where the bridge connecting over to Mount Independence had recently stood, he could not fail to note the eerie silence. It was, indeed, a very ugly place.

Captain Allen, however, did not stay long. After checking out the fort, he and his rangers began to probe northward. Soon, they encountered signs of a retreating force. Wanting to know what lay ahead, they began to pursue.

WEDNESDAY, 12 NOVEMBER

In the vicinity of present day Willsboro on the Bouquet River, Captain Allen and his scouts spotted a small group of British soldiers on the shoreline. They had pulled over with their boats to rest.

Under normal circumstances, it would have been best to observe and follow them from a safe distance since they were fleeing to Canada. They posed no visible threat. And they were unaware that Captain Allen and his party were trailing them. Yet there was something very strange about this group, and a black woman with a baby among them stood out. Possibly she was a tag-along, but perhaps she was not.

It was common knowledge throughout the wilderness that when people of African descent, whether slave or free, were captured by British units, especially by the mercenaries operating for the British, they usually ended up being resold into slavery or were kept by a high-ranking British official for personal use. Deciding to do something about this suspicious situation, Allen and his scouts surrounded the group. Ordering his men to hold their fire, Allen stepped forward to speak with their leader.

The woman was identified as Mrs. Dinah Mattis. The baby, only two months old, was her child Nancy. Mrs. Mattis had previously been a domestic slave on a sizable farm prior to British raiders attacking it. But the British did not liberate her. Instead, she was regarded as nothing but another trophy of war to be resold in Canada.

A humane person, Captain Allen informed his British captives that the woman and her child would be taken to Vermont. The others would be released if they promised to never again participate in any action either against the newly born American nation or the newly established "nation" of Vermont. Upon their return to Canada, the soldiers were to remain there or return to Great Britain. Not wanting to battle the patriots, the British commander agreed to the terms.

Of historical significance is that this action taken on 12 November 1777 was not only the last action of the Wilderness War of 1777, but it was an action based solely on a humane issue. What started eleven months earlier over 200 miles to the south on the edge of New York City in mid-January 1777, when Generals William Heath and John Scott engaged the British on a cold winter day, was now, at long last, ending. Taken to an army headquarters in Pawlet, Vermont, the woman was provided food, housing, and employment.

FRIDAY, 28 NOVEMBER

Mrs. Mattis was provided paperwork declaring that she and her child were free citizens. Their freedom was also recorded as a public document.[23] The Wilderness War of 1777 finally came to its conclusion on its northern front with this action. Mrs. Mattis' situation was one example of the change that came about as a result of the war. Along with countless others, she achieved both freedom and a new way of life in an entirely new nation as a result of the Wilderness War of 1777.

Acknowledgments

In order to accomplish any kind of mission, one needs the advice and assistance of others. This is especially true when undertaking a project like this one.

In Oswego, New York, is found Fort Ontario State Park. The origins of Fort Ontario date back many decades before the eruption of the Revolutionary War and the events of 1777. It is one of several forts which stood, at one time or another, in and around Oswego. Presently, it is the only remaining fort there. It was also in Oswego where my project was initially greeted with great enthusiasm and encouragement.

Fort Ontario's director, Paul Lear, directs this site, which also has a library. Though not formally open to the public, it may be utilized for research. This library holds many old and recent books, journals, and manuscripts pertaining to not only the Revolutionary War but also to many other historical events associated with Oswego. Mr. Lear not only kindly permitted me to utilize this library but he also answered my questions as best as he could.

Another key player in Fort Ontario is Richard LaCrosse, Jr. The author of a fabulous book "*The Frontier Rifleman: His Arms, Clothing and Equipment During the Era of the American Revolution, 1760– 1800.*" Mr Lacrosse is an expert both on riflemen and their weapons, tactics, equipment and uniforms. He has written numerous articles pertaining to the historical events of that era and he frequently gives lectures to the public.

I would like to express my appreciation to Gail Goebricher, who not only assisted me immensely with my first book, but also with this one. Ms. Goebricher carefully typed and edited on her computer some of the major chapters. Her input and ideas enabled me to produce stronger work. Without her, my mission would have been much more difficult.

Gail, once again, thank you so very much.

In Fort Stanwix at Rome, New York, curators and historians William Sawyer and Craig Davis tremendously assisted me with the events which occurred during the siege of Fort Stanwix during the monumental month of August 1777. One of the thorny issues that plague historians to this day is whether the American flag was actually first flown in combat in Fort Stanwix in 1777 and what was the fort's troop and overall personnel strength at the time of its encirclement. Via our discussions and various source materials suggested by them, I was able to reach this conclusion: clearly, the American flag was actually first flown in combat during the Wilderness War of 1777. Whether it was flown on a battlefield at an intersection adjacent to the settlement of Hubbardton in Vermont, or on a wilderness hilltop position in the vicinity of Fort Anne to the southeast of Lake George is, and always will be, disputed. But, without a doubt, when it comes to the question as to in what fort was the nation's flag first flown during combat, then I am convinced that it was in Fort Stanwix. As for the troop and support strength found in Fort Stanwix during its siege, after several discussions with Mr. Sawyer and studying the various references and source materials he suggested, I have concluded that a strength of close to or about 850 would be correct. To these fine gentlemen and Ft. Stanwix's staff, I extend my thanks.

Fort Ticonderoga's chief historian, Christopher Fox, was also of tremendous help. Through several phone conversations, we discussed the events of 1777. Just as importantly, Mr. Fox explained to me how the terrain features found around Fort Ticonderoga helped collapse the British campaign of 1777. Because of our discussions, I was able to better piece together the entire campaign in the vicinity of Fort Ticonderoga, Lake Champlain, the La Chute River, and Lake George. Fort Ticonderoga was a vital site and position in the early years of America's history. Thank you, Sir, for your help.

In central/western Vermont is located the Hubbardton battle site. Here, in 1777, a very short but bloody battle was fought. Carl Fuller is the site interpreter. Via our discussions, I obtained additional information on the history of the region and the origins of the state of Vermont, as well as the role its key leadership undertook to establish Vermont as a separate nation which, in due time, would become a state within the American nation. Thanks, Sir, I appreciate everything.

In the Wilderness War of 1777, people of African descent played a vital role in not only helping the Northern Army achieve a victory in that year but, just as importantly, in establishing the new American nation. It is vital for a reader to have some understanding of how and why black people initially arrived in the wilderness regions, and how they lived, worked, and struggled to achieve for themselves a life with others in this new land. Throughout my book I made numerous references to those of African heritage. Yet, their contribution was so great that in the end I ended up writing an entire chapter on African-Americans. Needing a strong authority to ensure that what I was presenting was factual, I consulted with William Watkins, a leading expert on the history of slavery in New York State. Prior to retiring from the New York State Parks and Recreation Service, Mr. Watkins managed several historical sites in eastern New York State. As acknowledged by Mr. Watkins, the issue of slavery, which finally collapsed in New York State in the early part of the 19th century, was a difficult and trying period for the state which started well over a century before New York State was officially born in 1777.

Mr. Watkins also kindly sent me a work he had published pertaining to African people. Titled "Slavery in Herkimer County. African-Americans Were Here from the Beginning," this journal is filled with fascinating information. After writing my chapter, I submitted it to Mr. Watkins for his review. He read it, offered additional input, and steered me toward other quality sources. Because of his efforts, I was able to present to my readers a stronger work pertaining to the role black people of African descent played in the turbulent year of 1777.

Once again, down in New York City, William "Bill" Nasi proved to be an asset. A first rate historian and very informed on what life in New York City was like during the British occupation, Mr. Nasi gave me the facts. And it was no picnic! In fact, he was so informative that I sometimes think that Mr. Nasi actually lived in the city in 1777. To him, I say again, "Thanks, Bill, very much."

In Washington, DC is located the Charles Summer School Museum. An African-American Institute, its floors are filled with numerous artifacts, articles, documents, photographs, and letters relating to African-American history. Harriet Lesser is the curator and director of this exhibit. Amongst the items on display is a huge map depicting where men and women of African heritage served and fought on the North American continent. Battles, along with dates, are cited. Of importance is that in virtually every battle of the Revolutionary War, men and women of African heritage participated. Here, in this museum, I was able to obtain additional names and deeds of brave African-American volunteers who served in the Northern Army in 1776-77. I extend my thanks and appreciation to Ms. Lesser and her staff.

In the village libraries of Fair Haven and Hannibal, New York, some old books, especially those which cite the early histories of Cayuga and Oswego Counties written in the early 1800's, reveal a good amount of information on the Revolutionary War period. The old books dealing with the land grants are especially interesting to study because they not only reveal the names of the individuals who inherited land but, to an extent, their activities during the American Revolutionary War. Various other books, which I also needed, were found and ordered by the staff of the Fair Haven library. To these individuals, I owe my gratitude as well.

The various New York State Historic Site Tour Guide Pamphlets, published by the New York State Office of Parks, Recreation and Historic Preservation, were of immense help. The information and simple maps in them proved very valuable, especially in depicting battle events. To the publishers of these pamphlets, I express my thanks.

To H. David Wright, a renowned painter of the early American frontier, I express my gratitude. Mr. Wright and I first met at the old Fort Ontario in Oswego, New York, where, one weekend, he was selling his paintings and limited edition prints. A U.S. Army veteran of the Vietnam conflict, Mr. Wright shared both his art and discussed his time spent in a combat zone. Kindly, he has allowed me to use a handful of his works for my book. Exhibited in the following pages, these works truly magnify the importance of the Wilderness riflemen during the monumental year of 1777. His art can be viewed on his website www.davidwrightart.com.

And to Don Troioni, another renowned painter of early American history. Adorning the cover of my book is his painting depicting American patriots charging an enemy position with the frontier weapons I so vividly describe. To these fine artists, I express my deepest appreciation."

George Sheldon, my dear friend in Fair Haven, New York, is an avid sportsman who hunts and shoots with a muzzle-loading rifle. During my writing, on more then one occasion, I needed to know something about this weapon. With the patience of a first-rate instructor, George always explained to me what I needed to know. Realizing that I needed to fully grasp the lethality of this rifle, George even took me out to a range on a couple of occasions where we fired his rifle. George is so proficient with it that he can actually reload while on the run. Whether he shoots from a standing, prone, sitting, or kneeling position, he can easily drill a bullet into any target at 250 to 300 yards. Imagine having two hundred soldiers such as George in a unit in 1777. Environmentally minded, he is currently employed with O'Brien & Gere, a major company which undertakes the clean up of various pollution sites. One such project recently completed by them was in the vicinity of Fort Edward where much of the fighting took place in 1777. George, thank you and keep up the good work! Future generations will benefit from your efforts.

To Ralph Kindig, whose computer skills enabled me to undertake and complete this project. Determined that I complete this book, he was always there with any advice and assistance, Ralph, thank you very much. And to my editor through Casemate Publishers, Jay Franco, whose time and expertise added immeasurably to this project.

Also to Michael G. Trent, CW5, U.S. Army, with whom I had the pleasure to serve during Operation "Iraqi Freedom." A teacher for many years, Mr. Trent carefully reviewed and edited my original work. His efforts and advice led to stronger work. Sir, thanks so much.

To the memory of my father, Taras, who loved to live in nature and taught us to do so. And to my uncle, Walter Logush who in November 2002 passed away suddenly. My uncle especially loved and respected the environment and the wilderness. Decades ago, in the early 1950s, he was one of the first who advocated the importance of maintaining open spaces adjacent to cities and large towns. He tried to educate others about the dangers of air and water pollution. He also argued that wilderness and forested regions are vital for humanity, and they offer much for proper physical and mental health development. He was saying this well before most were speaking about it or taking any kind of action. At least, in the last years of his life, my uncle had the satisfaction to witness and know that, at long last, people were actually doing something about it.

Last, but not least, this book is dedicated to all those who have served in our nation's armed forces—both in peace and war, and to those serving even as I write.

C'est la Guerre!

Notes

Chapter 1: Setting the Stage in the Northern Theater

[1]Henry F. Graff, *America: The Glorious Republic* (Boston: Houghton Mifflin Co., 1990), p. 143.

[2]Rupert Furneaux, *The Battle of Saratoga* (NY: Stein and Day, 1971), p. 20; Lieutenant-Colonel Joseph B. Mitchell and Sir Edward Creasy, *Twenty Decisive Battles of the World* (NY: The MacMillan Company, 1964), 2nd ed., p. 202. See also maps pp. 201 and 205. (Hereafter cited as *Twenty Decisive Battles*). For an extensive study of this, see John Luzader, *Decision on the Hudson: The Saratoga Campaign of 1777* (Washington, DC: National Park Service Publications, 1975).

According to T. Harry Williams, *The History of American Wars. From Colonial Times to World War I* (NY: Alfred A. Knopf, Inc., 1981), p. 25, "The British objective was to suppress the rebellion and persuade the Americans to return to their allegiance to the empire." (Hereafter cited as *History of American Wars*).

[3]Samuel Eliot Morison and Henry Steele Commager, *The Growth of the American Republic* (NY: Oxford University Press, 1952, 3rd Printing), p. 213. Of interest is that as early as 1767, Governor General Guy Carleton proposed: a "place of arms" in New York City, a citadel in Quebec, and a chain of forts through the Lake Champlain-Hudson River line. The entire defense system would stem from Quebec to New York City and would be utilized in suppressing any internal revolts. See also Furneaux, *The Battle of Saratoga*, p. 20.

[4]From hence forward through the entire book the term patriot—rather than rebel—will be used when referring to the Americans opposing England.

[5]John Luzader, *The Saratoga Campaign of 1777*, pp. 8–9; Furneaux, *The Battle of Saratoga*, p. 26; and George F. Scheer and Hugh F. Rankin, *Rebels and Redcoats* (NY: The New American Library, Inc., 1957), p. 285.

[6]Lord Germain's position in itself helped to complicate the command situation. Prior to and during the Revolutionary War, the British command system

was nothing but a highly complicated agency with numerous military and civilian departments. The American command system was much more simple and followed such a pattern—the Congressional Congress with its War Department, General George Washington, and the top ranking commanders of the Continental Armies.

[7]Hereafter simply referred to as "Thoughts…"

[8]Luzader, *The Saratoga Campaign of 1777,* p. 9.

[9]The Canada Army was the British Army based in Canada.

[10]Luzader, *The Saratoga Campaign,* p. 9.

[11]Ibid. According to Furneaux, neither Burgoyne nor Howe ever properly explain the word "junction." See *The Battle of Saratoga,* p. 27.

[12]Luzader, p. 9. In his "Reflections Upon War in America," which in 1775 was first presented to the British government, Burgoyne reasoned that the key to victory lay with the capture of New York City, soon followed by a coordinated junction between two British armies somewhere to the north of that city. The British Canada Army, advancing southward, was to perform a junction somewhere in the Hudson River Valley area with another British army advancing northward. Of interest is that Governor Carleton, though supportive of an offensive action in 1777, advocated that the main thrust should commence not from Canada (as he previously had advocated) but from Oswego located on Lake Ontario to strike through the Mohawk Valley towards Albany and the Hudson. See Piers Mackesy, *The War for America, 1775-1783* (Nebraska: University of Nebraska, 1993), p. 114.

[13]Furneaux, p. 23.

In 1767, General Carleton recommended to "establish a place of arms" in New York City along with a chain of forts northward from New York City straight up to Quebec along the Champlain-Hudson River line. Carleton's recommendation was based on the fact that British authorities, in both America and Canada, had begun to sense that a possible revolt was in the making. Fearing even the possibility of such a revolt, it was advocated that such a defense system would crush a rebeelion if indeed it should ever arise. In 1775, Carleton again advocated this defense plan and that same year it was endorsed by Lord Dartmouth, also a Colonial Secretary.

[14]According to some sources, the British adopted the strategy to divide the American colonies along the line of the Hudson River in 1776. To accomplish this, New York City would first be seized and used as a base of operations. See Joseph Plumb Martin, *Private Yankee Doodle. Being a Narrative of Some of the Adventures, Dangers and Sufferings of a Revolutionary Soldier* (Boston: Little, Brown and Company, 1962), p. 18.

Joseph P. Martin was a Revolutionary War soldier who, on 6 July 1776 enlisted in Connecticut. At the time of his enlistment, Martin was just 15 years old. At this time, Connecticut was tasked by the Continental Congress to reinforce the Continental Army in New York City. In response, Connecticut organized seven battalions. (Ibid., p. 15). Each recruit was to serve until 25 December 1776.

Martin soldiered in Captain Samuel Peck's 3rd Company. This company was a part of Major William Douglas's 5th Battalion which, in turn, fell under General James Wadsworth, Jr.'s' brigade.

Shortly after participating in the fighting in New York City, Martin returned home. He did not serve in the winter battles. But on 12 April 1777, Martin re-enlisted. He entered Colonel John Chandler's 8th Connecticut Continental Regiment. Martin remained in service for the duration of the war and, in 1777, saw much action in the Wilderness War of 1777.

[15]Luzader, p. 11. Both letters reached Lord Germain on 30 December 1776 in London, England.

According to R.E. Dupuy and T.N. Dupuy, "the entire affair—[campaign of 1777] originally conceived by Burgoyne—was bungled by Lord Germain who, as secretary of state for the colonies in Lord North's cabinet, was in control of operations in America. There was no coordination. Burgoyne had been ordered to meet Howe, but Howe's operations were left to his own discretion. The results were disastrous to England." See "1777. British Plans. Northern Campaign, 1777" in *The Encyclopedia of Military History from 3500 B.C. to the Present* (NY: Harper and Row Publishers, 1977). (Revised Ed.)., p. 713.

According to George Bancroft, "The conduct of the war on the side of Canada was left entirely to Lord George Germain; the chief command and the planning of the next campaign within the United States remained with Howe, who was strong in the support of Lord North and the King." See "England Prepares For the Campaign of 1777" in *The American Revolution* (Boston: Little, Brown, and Company, 1875), Vol. III, 5th Edition, p. 312.

[16]Luzader, p. 11.

[17]Philadelphia was the capital of the newly established American nation. Undoubtedly it was in late 1776 (and even before Washington's attack on Trenton and Princeton), that Howe was starting to first hold the view that Philadelphia needed to be taken. See "Howe's Plans of Campaign" in Piers Mackesy, *The War for America, 1775–1783*, pp. 109–112; 116–118; 121–124; and 157.

[18]Luzader, *The Saratoga Campaign*, p. 11.

[19]Howe also proposed to attack Virginia at this same time. Luzader, p. 11. See also Furneaux, *The Battle of Saratoga*, pp. 23–24.

Clearly, General Howe was now looking more and more at Philadelphia. Initially the British plan for 1777 was for General Burgoyne to move with an army southward to Albany to link up with General Howe moving simultaneously northward to Albany. But now, Howe was eyeing Pennsylvania more and more and decided to attack there first. (See also Robert Leckie, *The Wars of America* (NY: Harper Collins Publishers, 1992, Updated Edition), pp. 163–164. Howe might have even possibly believed that by moving into Pennsylvania, it would make it easier for Burgoyne to operate in the Northern theater.

[20]Luzader, p. 11; Furneaux, p. 23, cite Howe requested a reinforcement of up to 36,000 soldiers.

[21]Luzader, p. 11.

[22]Ibid. According to Furneaux, p. 24, "Howe allocated 10,000 troops for the purpose of taking Albany by an advance from New York." At this time, Howe also "implied that the junction of the northern and southern armies would precede the attack on Philadelphia." (Ibid.). However, as was soon evident, Howe changed his mind.

[23]This was never done. Of interest is that some Poles (both from the area of Poland controlled by the Austro-Hungarian Empire as well as the area controlled by Russia) did serve in Washington's army. Two of Washington's key officers, Colonel Thaddeus Kosciuszko and General Casimir Pulaski, were born in Poland. (Actually, Kosciuszko was born near Vilnius, a Baltic city within the Grand Duchy of Lithuania in 1746. Administered at the time by Russia, Kosciuszko's father, a Pole employed in the Russian government, married a Lithuanian woman. And to this union was born America's most famous military combat engineer).

[24]Luzader, p. 11; Furneaux, pp. 25-26.

[25]Martha Byrd, *Saratoga: Turning Point In the American Revolution* (England: Auerbach Publishers, Inc., 1973), p. 33. (Hereafter cited as *Saratoga: Turning Point*).

According to Furneaux, p. 25, "Howe's radical change of plan was based on the inability of the [British] government to fulfill his demands for reinforcements, which would restrict his operations." Howe was "also influenced by his desire to capture the rebel capital, a stronghold of loyalism and could be taken easily." (Ibid.). As for any offensive toward Albany, it would be undertaken solely by an army operating from Canada. A minor movement could be undertaken in the lower Hudson area to support the major thrust, but Howe no longer favored a junction in Albany. (See page 25.)

According to Luzader, pp. 11–12, Howe began to increasingly favor an offensive into Pennsylvania. This in itself was a "major plan in strategy." (Ibid., p. 12.)

Howe was, in fact, now thinking like a typical European general. European tactics frequently called for the capture of an opponent's capital. Simply put, to capture a nation's capital—in this case Philadelphia—was to win the war. Concluding that Washington would defend Philadelphia, Howe also reasoned that somewhere in its vicinity he would defeat the patriot army and afterwards capture the city. A series of mopping up operations here and there throughout the colonies would then suppress any remaining resistance.

[26]Luzader, p. 12.

[27]Ibid.

[28]Ibid. This was more in the form of a quick letter or dispatch.

[29]Ibid.

[30]Such as the dispatch of 29 December 1776.

[31]Luzader, pp. 12-13.

In March, 1777, both King George III and Lord George Germain approved a three-pronged campaign. But, as acknowledged by Oscar Theodore Barck, Jr., "Unfortunately, the third phase was not adequately planned, possibly because Burgoyne was so confident of his own overwhelming success in the venture that Howe's role would be insignificant and possibly unnecessary. And Germain, instead of sending specific orders to move toward Albany, approved of Howe's campaign against Philadelphia, probably assuming that its swift conquest would leave Howe ample time to join Burgoyne at Albany." See Barck, "The Three-Cornered Campaign" in *Colonial America* (NY: The Macmillan Company, 1958), p. 623. A copy of this letter was also forwarded to Carleton.

[32]Indeed, since the conclusion of the French and Indian War, there were many of those in England's military and ministry who sincerely believed that if ever a moment of opportunity arose for France to once again install its rule on the North American continent, it would do so.

[33]Luzader, p. 13.

[34]Ibid.

[35]Jeremy Black, *War for America: The Fight for Independence, 1775– 1783* (Great Britain: Sutton Publishing Company, 1998), p. 119, also cites 2 April 1777 as the date of Howe's letter and that in it, "Howe complained to Germain about a lack of reinforcements." (Ibid). (Hereafter cited as *War for America*).

[36]According to various sources, the British government knew and supported the three-pronged offensive to be commanded by Lieutenant-General Burgoyne, Barry St. Leger, and General William Howe. The government also believed that "the three armies are to form a junction at Albany." See Richard Wheeler, *Voices of 1776* (NY: Thomas Y. Crowell, Co., 1972), pp. 190–191.

Though this plan had been conceived in England, Sir William Howe's role in the overall plan was not clearly defined and Howe was also provided much leeway as to what he could do or not do. Germain, Lord North, Governor General Carleton, and even the King believed that Howe would advance up the Hudson River toward Albany. (See also Wheeler, p. 191). Yet, despite various discussions, as verified by Wheeler, "He [Howe] had no explicit orders to do so." (Ibid.). Of interest is that in 1777, England's public opinion generally supported their government's policy regarding the colonies. See George Bancroft, *The American Revolution*, Volume III, 5th Edition, p. 324.

[37]Richard M. Ketchum, *Saratoga: Turning Point of America's Revolutionary War* (NY: Henry Holt and Company, 1997), p. 87. (Hereafter cited as *Saratoga: Turning Point*).

In all true sense, the moment Burgoyne walked up the gangplank and placed his feet upon the deck of the *Apollo*, his campaign of 1777 was in motion. See Lieutenant-Colonel Dave Palmer, *The River and the Rock: The*

History of Fortress West Point, 1775–1783 (NY: Greenwood Publishing Co., 1969), p. 82. (Hereafter referred to as *History of West Point, 1775–1783).* (Palmer retired in the rank of General).

[38]Bruce Lancaster and J. H. Plumb, *The American Heritage Book of the Revolution* (NY: Dell Publishing Co., Inc., 1981), pp. 213–214. See also Ketchum, *Saratoga: Turning Point,* p. 79.

For Charles James Fox's famous comment to Burgoyne, see Robert Leckie, *The Wars of America,* p. 179.

[39]Luzader, pp. 13–15; Black, *War for America,* pp. p. 120.

Chapter 2: Lord Germain's Proposals

[1]Lord North, also the Earl of Guilford, headed the cabinet which directed the colonies. Lord Germain was subordinate to Lord North.

[2]Luzader, p. 16.

[3]Ibid. See also Barck, *Colonial America,* p. 623; and "Burgoyne Invades From Canada" in Richard Wheeler, *Voices of 1776,* p. 189. According to George Bancroft, *The American Revolution,* p. 322, it was the King who selected St. Leger to capture Fort Stanwix and the Mohawk Valley.

[4]Vicinity of present day Binghamton, a city located in southern New York State near Pennsylvania's border.

[5]Letter of Germain to Howe, 3 March 1777. Howe's letter of 20 December 1775 provided Germain two golden opportunities. If successful, they would have both control of the Hudson and the capture of Philadelphia, the patriot capital.

According to Harry Williams, *History of American Wars,* p. 63, "The British strategic plan for 1777 was so bad as to be almost unbelievable. The product of several minds, it emphasized unrealistic objectives, divided command, and separated armies. The blame for it must rest collectively on its architects, Lord Germain in England, General Howe in America, and a new figure in the British command structure in America, General Sir John Burgoyne."

In fact, Sir William Howe's part was never clearly defined. "He was indeed expected to ascend the Hudson [northward to Albany], but had no explicit orders to do so." See "Burgoyne Invades From Canada" in Wheeler, *Voices of 1776,* p. 191.

Of course, the possibility also exists that Germain "may have thought Howe could capture Philadelphia in time to return and aid Burgoyne." (T. Harry Williams, *The History of American Wars*), p. 64. "But he [Germain] never explained to Howe the mission of the northern [British Canada] army, which was to force its way to Albany, where it would come under Howe's command." (Ibid.). And, "not understanding what was expected of him, and perhaps not wanting to understand, Howe felt free to pursue his move on Philadelphia." (Ibid.)

[6]According to various sources, Lord Germain himself was in no rush to respond to Howe.

In 1782, William Knox, England's Under Secretary for the Colonial Department (also known as the Under Secretary of State for the Colonies), revealed how Germain's Deputy Secretary, a Mr. O'Dyly, had informed Lord Germain that General Howe had not yet been properly informed that he was to conduct an operation in time to assist Burgoyne. But Germain, in a rush to either meet with his mistress or late for a drinking and socializing meeting, stated, "So, my poor horses must stand in the street all the time, and I Shan't be to my time anywhere." (Reginald Hargreaves, *The Bloodybacks: The British Serviceman in North America and the Caribbean, 1655–1783* (NY: Walker and Company, 1968), p. 287. In response to Germain's remarks, O'Dyly informed Germain that he had better go and that he (O'Dyly) would write the letter to Howe instead. O'Dyly also added that he would include, along with the letter, copies of the instructions recently provided to Burgoyne. (Ibid.) This way, Howe would have a much better understanding of what Burgoyne's mission truly was and what was going on.

Satisfied with O'Dyly's offer, Germain left. This was on 18 May 1777. Whether O'Dyly responded that same day or waited for a while is not known. Regardless of what exactly happened it is known that incompetency, along with a lack of urgency to accomplish critical matters, did exist in the upper circles of Germain's bureau.

Furneaux, *The Battle of Saratoga*, pp. 31–32, acknowledges this event. But Furneaux added that the letter written by O'Dyly was placed into a pigeon-holed desk where it was found long after the campaign of 1777. Never presented to Germain by O'Dyly, the letter remained unsigned and forgotten.

According to David Saville Muzzey, "Burgoyne's Surrender at Saratoga," in *An American History* (Boston: Ginn and Company, 1911), p. 117, "Lord George Germain was anxious to get off to the country to shoot pheasants." Therefore, "Howe's instructions to move up the [Hudson] river were tucked into a pigeonhole by the war minister, Lord Germain, and left there to gather dust of years." See Point 135, "Burgoyne's Surrender at Saratoga," p. 117.

And Colonel (Ret.) Stanley M. Ulanoff, ed., *American Wars and Heroes: Revolutionary Through Vietnam* (NY: Arco Publishing Inc., 1985), p. 32, cites, "Gemain approved two separate and uncoordinated plans, and Howe and Burgoyne went their separate ways, doing nothing to remedy the situation." This was done despite "Burgoyne's plan calling for an advance southward to 'a junction with Howe'" as also submitted previously to Germain. (Ibid.)

O'Dyly's name has also been spelled as D'Oyley.

[7] Luzader, p. 16.

[8] "The Old Fox" was a term coined by General Cornwallis for General George Washington in December, 1776.

[9] According to Jeremy Black, *War for America*, p. 120, Germain was not the only one at fault. Howe and Burgoyne were also at fault. "Germain for failing to reconcile the plans of the two generals; Howe for neglecting the [British]

northern army; and Burgoyne for failing to appreciate the strength of the opposition." (Ibid.)

So, in the end, the question still remains: What, exactly, did Burgoyne advocate in "Thoughts...." Did he advocate a junction with Howe in Albany? And if so, once done, would the rendezvousing armies just sit there awaiting General Washington's arrival? Would both armies later strike into Connecticut? Did Burgoyne plan on reaching Albany by himself? Indeed, what exactly Burgoyne was proposing and thinking has, to this day, left historians in the dark. Factually speaking, "Thoughts...." (as written by Burgoyne) does not reveal any clear military objectives or intents.

Of interest to note is that in 1940, General Phillipe, a staff operations officer within the 5th U.S. Army Reserve which covered the northeast, prepared from his headquarters in Ward Island in New York City a detailed report about such a possible scenario: if Nazi Germany ever secured eastern Canada and decided to invade the United States from the north, a Nazi force would advance down the Lake Champlain route to first capture Albany. In the meantime, a sizable diversionary force sub-divided into two attack groups would advance eastwards from Oswego through the Mohawk Valley in conjunction with another force (also from Oswego) attacking southeastwards first toward Binghamton and then into and through central Pennsylvania toward Washington, DC. From Albany, the invaders would continue to advance southward to cut off the New England states, bypass New York City, and strike southwestward toward Washington, DC.

Chapter 3: General Burgoyne's Plan to Get to Albany

[1]In the spring of 1777, Captain Pausch, a German artillery officer serving in Canada who later would be captured at Saratoga, noted in his journal on 15 May:

"For three weeks we have been under orders to be prepared to march. St. Jean [St. John's] is the weapons and assembly point and the principal magazine for munitions as well as provisions. Our fleet also lies there, all the large and small vessels at anchor. Everything there is to be transported to Isle aux Noix in bateaux when the army moves out of winter quarters. At that time we will occupy our post at Crown Point, which was captured last year, and from there undertake our expedition against Carillon, or Ticonderoga. The enemy fleet reportedly is still in a poor condition there. On the other hand the fort and its surrounding area is rather well-fortified and equipped with cannons."

Indeed, a simple review of Captain Pausch's account reveals that this low-ranking officer knew not only the approximate dates of movement but, as well, the areas to be traversed while en route to the objective Fort Ticonderoga. And by the usage of the word "we," Captain Pausch indicated that just about everyone—from senior ranking leaders to the lowest ranking soldiers—knew of the upcoming operation. See Bruce E. Burgoyne, *Enemy Views: The American*

Revolutionary War as Recorded by the Hessian Participants (Maryland: Heritage Books, Inc., 1996), p. 186.

[2]A prime example is the poor performance of the wagon drivers in General Edward Braddock's army during the French and Indian War. En route to Fort Duquesne in 1775, Braddock's force fell into an ambush. The first who began to panic and flee were the wagon drivers. Among them was a 20-year-old who later would become a famous American: Daniel Boone.

The problem with transport was finally rectified by the British government in 1799, when an independent army transportation corps was established. From then on, civilians no longer directed the British army's transportation. Soldiers were selected and trained to perform transport duties and they were guided by military transport officers and sergeants.

[3]Furneaux, p. 34. Yet, according to Furneaux, p. 35, at one point no more than 637 horses were available. Luzader, *Decision on the Hudson*, p. 17, does not cite a figure; however, the implication that a serious shortage of animal transport plagued Burgoyne is noted when Luzader acknowledged that "a sufficient supply of draught horses [existed]." (Ibid.)

[4]Furneaux, p. 34.

[5]Ibid. According to Byrd, *Saratoga. Turning Point*, p. 37, "Neither was Carleton able to help Burgoyne obtain all the horses and wagons that would be needed for the campaign."

[6]British army lieutenant William Digby, who survived the campaign of 1777, kept a fascinating journal. In his work, Lieutenant Digby acknowledged problems with transport, drivers and the lack of animal power. For references to it see Digby, *The British Invasion From the North: Digby's Journal of the Campaigns of Generals Carleton and Burgoyne From Canada, 1776– 1777* (Albany, 1887). Edited by James Phinney Baxter.

[7]According to Major General William Phillips, Burgoyne's second-in-command, 400 horses were needed to pull the cannons alone, and another 1,000 to pull the various carts and wagons. See Furneaux, p. 34. Luzader, *The Saratoga Campaign*, p. 17, does not cite a figure; however, the implication that a serious shortage with animal transport plagued Burgoyne is noted when Luzader wrote: "… problems in collecting adequate carts and a sufficient number of draught horses [arose]…"

In fact, the problem was very severe. As late as 20 August 1777, Burgoyne reported that only one-third of his horses had arrived. Furthermore, from the outset, there was a lack of drivers. Amongst those hired, many proved to be unreliable. Some began to desert as the campaign wore on. See "Problem of Transport" in Edward E. Curtis, *The Organization of the British Army in the American Revolution* (NY: Ams Press, 1969) (Reprinted from the 1926 edition), p. 145. (Hereafter referred to as *The Organization of the British Army*.)

[8]For additional information on the bateaux and canoes widely used on the river and lake systems of Colonial America, see Robert E. Hager, *Mohawk*

River Boats and Navigation Before 1820 (Syracuse, NY: Canal Society of New York State, 1987).

[9]During the winter of 1776–1777, the bulk of the force that followed Burgoyne was based in the town of Chambly. General Carleton was very supportive of Burgoyne and gave him much assistance. So the relationship between the two was excellent. (See George M. Wrong, *Canada and the American Revolution: The Disruption of the First British Empire* (NY: Cooper Square Publishers, Inc., 1968), p. 323. (However, in actuality, almost right from the beginning Carleton was unable to assist Burgoyne with all of his needs.) According to Wrong, "It was intended that Howe, in possession of New York [City], should send an army northward towards Albany to meet Burgoyne advancing southward and that the united forces should hold the line from Canada to New York." (Ibid.) (Hereafter cited as *Canada and the American Revolution*.)

[10]Burgoyne was also to link up with a smaller force directed by loyalist leaders McDonell (MacDonald) and Crysler. This force, originating in the vicinity of the present-day city of Binghamton, was to proceed northeastward through the Schoharie Valley. En route, they were to recruit additional loyalists, destroy patriot facilities, farms and estates, and spread pro-British propaganda. Somewhere, to the west of Albany, they were to link up with the forces of British general Barry St. Leger marching in from Oswego. Placing themselves under his command, once united, the combined forces were soon to link up with Burgoyne arriving from the north.

Chapter 4: The British Army in Canada

[1]At the beginning of the Revolutionary War in 1775, Great Britain's army comprised a strength of about 48,000 soldiers. (See Edward E. Curtis, "The Recruiting of the Army" in *The Organization of the British Army*, p. 511). This strength, however, did not include the personnel of the Royal Navy, the approximately 2,000 Royal Marines, nor the personnel strength of England's indigenous forces serving throughout the world in its numerous militia units such as those which existed on the North American continent.

Of the strength of 48,000, in 1775 approximately 11,500–12,000 were stationed in North America, including Canada. (See Alan Kemp, *The British Army In the American Revolution* (Great Britain: Almark Publications, 1973), p. 3. But war demands on the North American continent along with the need to maintain military strengths throughout the entire British empire, forced a major expansion. By 1781, 110,000 men had been enrolled. (Curtis, p. 51). Of this strength, approximately 56,000 were based in America or the West Indies. (Ibid.)

Because England's Army was a volunteer army, England secured manpower by such ways: voluntary (often times with promises of bounty), and recruiting the so-called jailbirds or those headed for a period of incarceration. Another method employed to keep soldiers in service was the so-called "pardon" system. Simply put, if a soldier was accused of some type of crime—within or outside of his unit—(such as, for example, desertion, theft, repeatedly being drunk), the accused would be informed that all charges would be dropped if he would agree to extend his service time. Remembering that at that time the British army's discipline system was very harsh (in fact, on occasion, it was brutal), most of those accused of some infraction or crime, if offered the option to redeem themselves by reenlisting or extending, chose to stay within the ranks.

[2]Among the so-called "English" were many Irish, Scots, and Welsh. One of the most famous soldiers serving within Burgoyne's army was the Irishman Roger Lamb, who served with the rank of sergeant.

[3]The Germans were recruited from Germany's various provinces. Because many were recruited from Hesse, the term "Hessian" was often applied to any German serving in the British army. As for the German "volunteers," many were actually coerced into service by regional German rulers. (See Bancroft, *The American Revolution*, p. 320). According to Jeremy Black, *War for America*, pp. 28–29, "German auxiliaries provided 33 percent of the British strength in America in 1778–1779, a percentage that rose to 37 in 1781." In all, 29,867 German soldiers (this figure does not include the German doctors and army workers who accompanied the soldiers) served in the colonies during the Revolutionary War. (See "The Germans Are Coming!" in Thomas Fleming, *Liberty!*, pp. 192–193). Fleming, however, acknowledges that many of these Germans were "virtually kidnapped." (Ibid., p. 192.) In addition to those who hailed from the province of Hesse-Cassel, others came from the provinces of Hesse-Hanau, Anspach-Bayreuth, Anhalt-Zerbst and Waldeck; however, some were recruited from as far away as Prussia and the Baltic region. In addition to those who were forcefully recruited or pressed into service while incarcerated in a jail, others joined only to find free passage to America where, already, tens of thousands of Germans were residing. In due course, they would desert over to the patriot side.

[4]Regarding the recruitment of Canadians, problems immediately arose. Burgoyne was initially promised a strength of 1,500–2,000 Canadians. Bancroft, *The American Revolution,* p. 320, cites "two thousand French Canadians were called for and expected." In actuality, far fewer Canadians appeared. According to Reginald Hargreaves, *The Bloodybacks: The British Servicemen in North America and the Caribbean, 1655–1783,* p. 289, of the 1,500 promised, at best 148 appeared. According to Christopher Ward, *The War of the Revolution* (NY: The Macmillan Co., 1952), Vol. I, p. 403, the irregular [Canadian] auxiliaries were also included in Germain's plans and a figure of around 2,000 was desired. However, in actuality, only 150 were recruited. According to Ward, the majority of Canadians were of French ancestry and England's war with the Americans meant nothing to them. (Ibid.) Furneaux, p. 35, cites that 2,000 workmen or "hatchet men" were sought, but in actuality,

Burgoyne possessed fewer then 300. (Ibid.)

Martha Byrd, *Saratoga: Turning Point*, p. 37, cites that Burgoyne and Germain did count on the Canadian support (along with American loyalists and Indians) "to supplement the regular troops, but although some such troops were raised, they were fewer than desired. The Canadians just wanted to be left alone." (Ibid.) Byrd does not provide a figure; however, she makes it clear that the British effort to recruit Canadians was, overall, a dismal failure.

As for the Canadians to be recruited, they were to fall into two categories: the fighters and the workers. It was hoped that at least 500 Canadian combatants and at least 1,500 axmen, drivers, wagon personnel, boatmen, etc., would be recruited.

What, exactly, was the true size of the Canadian contingent accompanying Burgoyne is not known. Regarding its combat personnel, it may be surmised that at the outset, about 150 Canadians were recruited. Though more would appear in the following weeks, in the end the figure was never impressive.

In all, at the outset of the campaign, about 300 Canadians were recruited for labor. Another 150 to about 200 were recruited as mercenary fighters. Though a few more would appear here and there along the way, at the outset of Burgoyne's campaign about 450 to 500 Canadians (from both groups) were found. This is, indeed, far less than what Burgoyne had expected and needed.

[5]Regarding how many Indians were actually recruited, figures vary but it is known that approximately 400 were initially gathered up. Hargreaves, p. 289, cites that it was proposed to recruit "some five hundred Indians." Ward, *The War of the Revolution*, Vol. I, p. 402, cites 400 Indians were recruited out of the 1,000 initially desired. John Luzader, p. 17, cites also about 400 Indians started off with Burgoyne. Martha Byrd, *Saratoga. Turning Point*, p. 38, cites about 400 Indians; and Furneaux, p. 36, cites "only 400 Indians assembled." These figures do not include an additional 400 to about 700, in small and larger groups, appearing later on. In the end, however, the Indian role, as with the Canadians and loyalists, proved to be unproductive.

[6]Loyalists, also known as Tories. (In itself, "toraidhe" or, simply, tory, is an old Irish Gaelic word depicting a thief, someone who cannot be trusted, a swindler, or a "pursued [wanted] man" like, for instance, an outlaw.)

Loyalists (or tories) were those who resided in the colonies but professed loyalty to England and the Crown. They strongly opposed the patriots and the newly established American nation. Because loyalists themselves hated the word tory, they referred to themselves as loyalist.

(Hereafter the term loyalist or loyalists will solely be utilized).

By 1777, many of the loyalists who had been residing in the British Colony of New York had fled either to Canada or New York City. There, they began to render support to British authorities planning a major invasion of the northeast. Along with the Canadians and Indians, Burgoyne had expected a sizable number of loyalists to appear. But again, this proved to be a disappointment. In the end, few appeared. Ward, Vol. I, p. 402, cites about 100 enlisted. Luzader, p. 17 and Byrd, p. 38, both cite 250 Canadians and loyalists. For a detailed study of their role and units see, Philip Katcher, *The American Provincial Corps, 1775–1784* (NY: Osprey Publishing Ltd., 1973); Wallace Brown, *Tories In the Revolution* (Oswego, NY: Fort Ontario Archives); Robert McCluer Calhoon, *The Loyalists in Revolutionary America, 1760–1781* (NY: Harcourt Brace Jovanovich, Inc., 1973); Donald Barr Chidsey, *The Loyalists. The Story of Those Americans Who Fought Against Independence* (NY: Crown Publishers, Inc., 1973); and "The Problem of the Loyalist" in Richard B. Morris and James Woodress, ed's, *Voices From America's Past. 1 The Colonies and the New Nation* (NY: E.P. Dutton and Co., Inc., 1961), pp. 100–104; H.C. Burleigh, *Captain MacKay and the Loyal Volunteers* (Canada: Bayside Publishing Co., 1977); and Stephen G. Strach, *Some Sources for the Study of the Loyalist and Canadian Participation in the Military Campaign of Lieutenant-General John Burgoyne 1777* (Eastern National Park and Monument Association, 1983).

[7]The 9th Regiment of Foot was formed in 1685. It received its numerical designation in 1751. Prior to that, the regiment was titled with the names of its various commanders. Its home base was East Norfolk; hence, its title as the Royal Norfolk Regiment. In the late spring of 1776, the 9th deployed to Canada where it arrived to Quebec in May 1776. As a part of Burgoyne's army, the 9th Foot surrendered at Saratoga in October 1777. Until 1781, it was interned in the vicinity of Saratoga, and then its survivors were returned to the British Isles. Lieutenant-Colonel John Hill was listed as the commanding officer of the 9th Foot from 1775–1782. From 1783 (now in the British Isles), Major General Thomas Lord Saye and Sele commanded the 9th Foot Regiment. Reconstituted into the British army, in the modern British army the 9th Foot became the 1st Battalion of the Royal Anglian Regiment.

[8]Known throughout the British army as the regiment where "a good band of eight musicians existed," the 20th Regiment of Foot was formed in 1688. Its home base was Lancashire. It was also a fusilier unit. Deployed to Canada, the 20th Foot arrived to Quebec in May 1776, and it was virtually annihilated in the Wilderness War of 1777. In 1781, its few survivors were returned to the British Isles. Lieutenant-Colonel John Lind commanded the 20th Foot from 1776–1782.

[9]The 21st Foot Regiment was formed in 1679 and initially was titled Colonel the Earl of Mar's Regiment of Foot. Re-designated in 1707 as the Scots Fusilier Regiment of Foot, it was soon re-designated in 1712 as the North British Fusiliers Regiment. In 1751, it received its numerical designation. Arriving to Quebec in May 1776, the 21st Foot was a part of Burgoyne's army. Initially, it served on and around Lake Champlain but was shifted further

southward. Surrendering at Saratoga, the 21st Foot returned to the British Isles in 1781. Reconstituted into the British army, the 21st Foot became known as the Royal Highland Fusiliers.

[10]Formed in 1689, until 1751 the 24th Foot Regiment served under various Colonels. In 1751, it was numerically designated the 24th Foot. Based in South Wales and known as the "South Wales Borderers," the 24th Foot was an elite infantry regiment. Arriving to Quebec in May 1776, it participated in Burgoyne's campaign. At Saratoga, the 24th Foot suffered heavy losses and its commander, General Simon Fraser, was killed. Interned at Saratoga, its survivors did not return to England until the end of the war.

[11]The 29th Foot Regiment was formed in 1694. The regiment served under various Colonels until 1751. That year, it was numerically designated the 29th. Worcestershire, England, was its home station. Deployed to Halifax, Canada, in September 1768 it moved to Boston, Massachusetts. In March 1770, personnel of the 29th fired on an angry crowd and created what became known to history as the "Boston Massacre." In May 1776, the 29th was redeployed to Quebec. Throughout the Revolutionary War, the 29th's light "centre" companies remained in Canada. However, the 29th's two flank companies—the light and grenadier companies—were posted to Burgoyne's force. In the ensuing campaign, both companies were destroyed, their survivors surrendering at Saratoga.

[12]Organized in 1713, the 31st Foot Regiment was first known under various colonels. In 1751, it received its numerical designation. Huntingdonshire was its home base. Deployed first to the West Indies, in May 1776, it was redeployed to Quebec. Throughout the Revolutionary War, it was stationed in Canada; however, its light and grenadier flank companies partici-pated in Burgoyne's expedition and were captured in Saratoga.

[13]Formed in 1741, the 47th Foot Regiment received its numerical designation in 1751. It was based in Lancashire. Deployed to New Jersey in 1773, in the following year, it was re-directed to Boston. In 1775, the 47th Foot marched to relieve the battered personnel sent to Lexington and Concord. Later, the 47th Foot fought at Bunker Hill, where it suffered heavy casualties. Reinforced with replacements, the 47th Foot was deployed in March 1776, from Boston to Quebec to assist in repulsing the American winter campaign against Quebec and Montreal. Participating in Burgoyne's campaign, the 47th Foot surrendered at Saratoga. Regarded as an elite regiment, it was utilized largely as Burgoyne's chief reserve. The 47th's released soldiers returned to England in 1781.

[14]Initially formed in 1755 as the 55th Regiment of Foot, the 55th Foot was renumbered the 53rd Foot in 1757. Its home base was Shropshire. In May 1776, the 53rd Foot was deployed to Quebec. Participating in Burgoyne's campaign, the 53rd took heavy casualties and its survivors surrendered at Saratoga; however, some units of the 53rd, involved in guarding Burgoyne's rear, succeeded in withdrawing to Canada following Burgoyne's encirclement. Those

who were captured returned to England in 1781; the others remained in Canada. Its survivors were utilized as a base and cadre for the creation of a new 53rd Foot Regiment. Freshly arriving reinforcements enabled the 53rd Foot to be fully rebuilt in 1778–1779. The regiment returned to England in 1783–1784.

[15]In 1756, the 4th Regiment of Foot was raised. In 1758, the 4th Regiment's 2nd Battalion was utilized as a nucleus for the creation of the 62nd Regiment of Foot. Deployed to Canada in 1776, the 62nd Foot arrived at Quebec in May 1776. Participating in Burgoyne's campaign, the 62nd Foot was decimated. Its survivors surrendered at Saratoga and were returned to the British Isles in 1781.

[16]Raised in Brunswick, Germany, Regiment Von Rhetz was deployed to Canada and arrived at Quebec in September 1776. That year, it participated in operations on Lake Champlain. Participating in Burgoyne's 1777 campaign, the regiment surrendered and was interned at Saratoga.

Its field commanders were Lieutenant-Colonel Johann G. von Ehrenkrook and Major B.B. von Lucke. Von Ehrenkrook, however, succeeded in escaping to Canada where an entire new regiment, composed of German survivors of Burgoyne's ill-fated campaign, along with fresh German troops from Europe, was raised around von Ehrenkrook. Until its return to Germany in 1783, the second von Ehrenkrook regiment served in the Trois Rivieres area of Canada. In 1777, the regiment registered a strength of 27 officers and 653 enlisted men. As for the regiment von Rhetz, it was never rebuilt.

[17]The Musketeer Regiment Von Specht was also organized in Brunswick. The regiment arrived in Quebec in September 1776. Participating in Burgoyne's campaign, it surrendered and was interned at Saratoga. Survivors fled to Canada and were incorporated into both the new von Ehrenkrrok Regiment and the Regiment von Barner, a regiment also posted to Burgoyne's army and destroyed. In 1778, orders were issued to rebuild both regiments.

[18]Raised in Brunswick, the Musketeer Regiment von Riedesel deployed to Canada and arrived in Quebec in June 1776. In the field, it was commanded by Lieutenant-Colonel E.L. Walther von Speth. The von Riedesel Regiment participated in Burgoyne's campaign and surrendered at Saratoga. Some survivors, however, did succeed in fleeing north to Canada. The von Riedesel Regiment was never rebuilt. Its 1777 survivors were merged into the von Ehrenkrook Regiment.

[19]Regiment Prinz Frederick was raised in Brunswick, and in June 1776 it arrived in Quebec. Participating in Burgoyne's campaign with a strength of 27 officers and 653 enlisted, the bulk of this regiment, approximately 450 soldiers, were left behind to guard Fort Ticonderoga and Burgoyne's rear. A small detachment continued on with Burgoyne, and following their surrender at Saratoga was interned at that location. Those provided the task of guarding Fort Ticonderoga retreated back to Canada.

[20]Raised in the German province of Hesse-Hanau, the Hesse-Hanau

Regiment deployed to Canada and arrived in Quebec with a strength of 668. Participating in Burgoyne's campaign, the regiment surrendered and was interned at Saratoga.

[21]Philip R. Katcher, *The Encyclopedia of British, Provincial, and German Army Units, 1775–1783* (Pennsylvania: Stackpole Books, 1973), p. 13; Anthony D. Darling, *Red Coat and Brown Bess* (Canada: Museum Restoration Service, 1970), p. 6.

[22]Katcher, p. 13.

[23]Darling, *Red Coat and Brown Bess*, p. 6.

[24]Ibid.

[25]Ibid., p. 8.

[26]In that era, it was not uncommon for companies to be understrength. Desertions, discharges from service, transfers, accidents, and difficulties in recruiting enough manpower kept many companies from being at full strength. Darling, *Red Coat and Brown Bess*, p. 8, cites a strength of about 56 men per company.

Prior to the commencement of a campaign or major offensive sort, efforts were always made to ensure that a company, battalion, or regiment was in full or near full strength. As for Burgoyne's force, the units under his command were all in full or near full strength.

[27]Alan Kemp, *The British Army In the American Revolution*, p. 9, cites about 450 soldiers. But possibly, Kemp's figure takes into consideration that it was not uncommon for a company to possess 5–15 soldiers less than what was authorized.

In actuality, a typical British infantry foot regiment averaged a strength of approximately 650 soldiers. However, the figure of 650 did not include the 20 or so repair personnel, doctors, surgeons mates, drummer boys, clergyman, or advisors from some other unit or any local guides (such as loyalists), posted into the regiments.

[28]Katcher, *Encyclopedia of British, Provincial, and German Army Units, 1775–1783*, p. 13.

[29]Ibid. Usually, a lieutenant colonel commanded a foot regiment. If a lieutenant colonel was not in charge, a major commanded. On occasion, a full colonel or even a general commanded, but this was rare.

[30]There was also the "India" model. For extensive details on these weapons see Darling, pp. 14–54.

[31]Ward, *The War of the Revolution*, Vol. 1, p. 403.

[32]Ibid.

[33]Ibid.

[34]Ketchum, *Saratoga*, p. 137, cites 3,981 English personnel and 3,116 Brunswick and Hesse-Hanau soldiers. Including the artillery, over 7,000 soldiers. (Ibid.) This figure, however, did not include the irregulars.

[35]James Kirby Martin, *Benedict Arnold, Revolutionary Hero: An American*

Reconsidered (NY: New York University Press, 1997), p. 346. (Hereafter cited as *Benedict Arnold, Revolutionary Hero*). Again, this figure does not include the irregular Canadian, Indian, and loyalist fighters. Nor did it include the civilian workers being utilized in support of Burgoyne's army.

[36]Martin, *Benedict Arnold, Revolutionary Hero*, p. 346.

[37]Martin, p. 346.

[38]Reginald Hargreaves, *The Bloodybacks*, p. 289. Carrington, *Battles of the American Revolution*, p. 304, cites that Burgoyne commanded 7,173 English and German troops. According to Mackesy, *The War for America, 1775–1783*, p. 115, "8,000 regulars, 1,000 or more Indians, and 2,000 Canadians" were to accompany Burgoyne.

[39]Luzader, *The Saratoga Campaign of 1777*, p. 17.

[40]Furneaux, *The Battles of Saratoga*, p. 40.

[41]Ibid.

[42]Ibid. It is not known how many women accompanied Burgoyne's expedition. Figures range anywhere from about 400 to as many as 2,000. It appears, however, that the figure of 2,000 is greatly overestimated. Wrong, *Canada and The American Revolution*, pp. 324–325, cites that "There were many women in the army." Many of the officers brought wives and even entire families. In England, the gossip ran that "in all there were two thousand women with Burgoyne's army; no doubt this is a gross exaggeration but the scandal had some basis." (Ibid., p. 325). Especially in consideration that "Burgoyne himself was not without female consolation." (Ibid.)

[43]The term "camp follower" was a loose generic term which usually designated any women following an army. (The term, however, was also applied to males). It could include the wives, mistresses, or girlfriends of the officers or enlisted personnel; it included the women who accompanied an army to serve as cooks and bakers, laundry women, sewing women, nurses, and sometimes included women doctors or singing entertainers who were usually paid for their services. And of course it included the prostitutes who tagged along the rear of any army of that era. The majority of the "camp followers," however, were women of honesty and integrity.

[44]Though initially both regiments were to participate in their entirety, all eight of the 29th and 31st Foot Regiments' "centre" companies remained behind in Canada and did not participate in Burgoyne's campaign. Worried about another patriot attack into Canada, Governor-General Carleton decided at the last minute to withhold the bulk of the soldiers from these regiments.

Carleton's worries, of course, were totally unfounded. With Burgoyne marching southward, there was no way that a sizable patriot force could have threatened Canada. Needless to say, Burgoyne himself was very disappointed by Carleton's decision. Besides depriving Burgoyne of valuable manpower, Carleton's decision was also in clear violation of Germain's order to Carleton that he was to support Burgoyne in every possible way.

[45]James Phinney Baxter, *The British Invasion From the North: The Campaigns of Generals Carleton and Burgoyne From Canada, 1776–1777, With the Journal of Lieute. William Digby, Of the 53rd, Or Shropshire Regiment of Foot.* (Albany, NY: Joel Munsell's Sons, 1887), pp. 194–198. (Hereafter cited as *The British Invasion From the North. Digby's Journal*). In his journal, Lieutenant Digby cites a "33rd regiment with other regiments under the command of Lieutenant Nutt are, for the present, to serve on board the fleet" (p. 194–195). Regarding the "33rd [Foot] Regiment," either Digby erred or, possibly, a numerical error was made during the publishing of Digby's journal because no "33rd Regiment" ever existed in Burgoyne's army. During this time the 33rd did exist, but the regiment was far away in Pennsylvania serving with General Howe. See Katcher, *Encyclopedia of British, Provincial and German Army Units, 1775–1783*, p. 47.

[46]Byrd, *Saratoga, Turning Point*, p. 38, cites "perhaps 400 [Indians]." Byrd, however, acknowledged that no precise figure could ever be established on them because "… the Indians, came and went and hence were hard to count." (Ibid.)

[47]In actuality, many of the Canadians were very sympathetic to the rebellion occurring in the colonies. And they had no desire to involve themselves in a campaign perceived by many as being of no concern to them.

[48]Approximately half were workers and the others served as combat personnel. But workers and axmen could, on occasion, be utilized as fighters.

[49]Stephen G. Strach, *Some Sources For the Study of the Loyalist and Canadian Participation In the Military Campaign of Lieutenant-General John Burgoyne 1777*, p. 6. Along with these two Canadian companies, four loyalist units and a handful of individuals from a fifth loyalist unit ended up accompanying Burgoyne's army. Such units were committed: Queen's Loyal Rangers, commanded by Lieutenant-Colonel John Peters; King's Loyal Americans (also known as Jessup's Corps), commanded by Lieutenant-Colonel Ebenezer Jessup; Loyal Volunteer's, commanded by Captain Samuel MacKay; and one unnamed company commanded by Colonel Francis Pfister though Captain Daniel MacAlpine assumed command after 16 August 1777. (See p. 6.) Another interesting work is titled *Captain MacKay and the Loyal Volunteers* by H.C. Burleigh (Ontario, Canada: Bayside Publishing Company), 1977. According to Burleigh "when he [Lieutenant-Colonel Francis Pfister] died the 17th of August, 1777, as a result of a wound received at the Battle of Benington, the command fell to Captain Samuel MacKay, who had been serving under Burgoyne as a volunteer." (See p. 3.) A roster of those participating in Captain MacKay's Loyal Volunteer's Company in 1777 is found on p. 4. Altogether, 33 volunteers are shown. Of these, 1 is a captain (MacKay), 3 are lieutenants, 2 are ensigns, 6 are sergeants, 4 are corporals, and 17 are privates.

As for the fifth unit, designated "The Royal Highland Emigrants," by-and-large this company remained in Canada with the mission to provide rear logistical support to Burgoyne's army. (Strach, p. 14.) However, six of its personnel did accompany Burgoyne's army into the wilderness primarily as "Engineer-Artificers." (Ibid.)

Chapter 5: The British Campaign Commences

[1]At this time, the Richelieu River was also known as the Sorel River. The name derived from a Marcel de Sorel, who built Fort Sorel. Prior to being renamed the Richelieu River, Champlain referred to it as "The River of the Iroquois." As for Richelieu, the name derived from the eminent French Cardinal Richelieu.

[2]The fleet was commanded by Captain Thomas Pringle, a Scot by birth. In all, the fleet consisted of twenty-nine vessels armed with eighty-nine guns, not counting the mortars. (See James Baxter, *The British Invasion From the North, Digby's Journal*, pp. 151–152). 670 well-trained navy men manned the vessels. (Ibid.) In addition to the nine named ships, twenty of the vessels were gunboats. (Ibid., p. 152.) The figure of 29 vessels did not include the numerous bateaux, canoes, and other water craft found in the fleet.

[3]Carrington, *Battles of the American Revolution*, p. 304, cites that Canada's Governor General Carleton maintained 3,770 soldiers in Canada. For an exact breakdown of what forces remained in Canada see p. 304.

[4]A number of these carts and wagons had just been constructed. Unfortunately for Burgoyne, soft and unseasoned wood was mostly utilized since the well-seasoned hard wood had disappeared. (Undoubtedly, it had been stolen.) As a result, en route to St. John's, wagon wheels collapsed, wood planks shattered underneath the heavy loads, and some supplies, placed alongside the roads to be recovered later, simply disappeared.

[5]The mean water level is 95 feet above the sea level. The lake is also very deep. Some parts are more than 300 feet deep. (For more information on this lake see William T. Couch, ed., *Collier's Encyclopedia* (NY: P.F. Collier and Son Corp., 1955), Vol. 5, p. 13.

[6]Lake George, in elevation, lies above Lake Champlain. The waters of Lake George tumble down a high and steep waterfall. From the base of this waterfall a small river, known as the La Chute River, flows almost 4 miles northeastward and right past Fort Ticonderoga into Lake Champlain.

[7]Now known as Whitehall. In the aftermath of the Revolutionary War Skenesborough (named after the tory Philip Skene), was renamed Whitehall.

[8]Basically, the so-called "French Lines" were piles of dirt, stones and rocks thrown against sizable logs placed on the ground. For extra protection, the lines were protected by numerous poles constructed of tree branches with sharpened ends inserted into the ground at an angle protruding outward.

[9]Meaning Lake George and Lake Champlain.

[10]Isle la Noix means Island of Nuts or Nut Island. So named by Samuel Champlain because of the many nut trees found there. Just to the south of

Plattsburg flows the Saranac River which empties into Lake Champlain.

[11]According to Colonel Vincent J. Esposito, ed., *The West Point Atlas of the Civil War [Adapted From the West Point Atlas of American Wars]* (NY: Praeger Publishers, 1962), Vol. I, Map #6a, Burgoyne completed the concentration of his army at a point just above the Saranac River by 18 June. That day he resumed his advance. (Ibid.)

[12]This bird is now extinct.

[13]Ketchum, *Saratoga*, p. 139. Though critical of certain places and fearful of snakes, Doctor Julius Friedrich Wasmus was fascinated by the rich animal and plant life. In his journal (captured from the doctor at the Battle of Bennington but returned to him within a day or two), Doctor Wasmus wrote extensively on what he witnessed and endured. For the doctor's observations and, in general, his experiences on the North American continent but especially in 1777 see Mary C. Lynn, ed., *The Specht Journal: A Military Journal of the Burgoyne Campaign* (Contributions in Military Studies, Number 158, 1995), p. 85. (The Specht Journal, originally written in German by a soldier named Wilhelm Specht who participated in the 1777 British campaign, was translated into English by Helga Doblin). (Hereafter cited as *The Specht Journal*.)

[14]According to certain authors, Burgoyne had a reputation of being a womanizer. See also Ketchum, p. 73.

[15]Benson J. Lossing, *The Empire State. New York: Settlement Through 1875* (Conn.: American Publishing Co., 1888), p. 256. As for Cumberland and Gloucester Counties, in time they would become a part of the State of Vermont.

[16]According to Harry F. Landon, *History of the North Country: A History of Embracing Jefferson, St. Lawrence, Oswego, Lewis and Franklin Counties* (Indiana: Historical Publishing Co., 1932), p. 77, "not until 1777 did the war touch Northern New York."

[17]Today a town known as Schuylerville exists in this location.

[18]General Philip Schuyler would be the Northern Army's first commanding officer. According to James A. Huston, Logistics of the Saratoga Campaign" in *The Sinews of War: Army Logistics, 1775–1953* (Washington, DC: U.S. Government Printing Office, 1966), "Maj. Gen. Phillip Schuyler of New York assumed command of the Northern Army in mid-1775, he had to start virtually from scratch to organize an effective military force and the logistical facilities to maintain it at a considerable distance from his bases of supply. The Northern Army was also concentrated at [Fort] Ticonderoga." (Hereafter cited as *The Sinews of War*). Of interest is that in 1775–1776, the Northern Army was also referred to as the "Separate Army." This designation, however, would no longer be utilized after 1776.

[19]Pronounced as "Sin-clair."

[20]Baldwin's brother, Issac, was killed at Bunker Hill.

[21]To construct this bridge, American ingenuity at its best was utilized. Over twenty huge log crates, each measuring 24 square feet and 30 feet in height,

were constructed. After being placed on the thick ice about 50 feet apart and filled about halfway up with rocks, holes were cut around the towers to enable them to slowly sink and position themselves in place. Once in place, the water spaces between the towers were "filled with separate floats, each about 50 feet in length and about 12 feet in width, strongly fastened with iron chains and rivets." (Words cited by Fort Ticonderoga's Chief Doctor and Surgeon, Doctor James Thacher.) See Ketchum, *Saratoga*, p. 122.

[22]Also known as Sugar Hill.

[23]These ranges were estimated by Lieutenant William Twiss, an English engineer officer attached to Burgoyne's advance force. It was Lieutenant Twiss who, in early July 1777, climbed up with a Captain James Craig to secure the key terrain.

[24]Mark M. Boatner III, *Landmarks of the American Revolution: People and Places Vital to the Quest for Independence* (Harrisburg, PA: Stackpole Books, 1992), p. 321.

[25]For Trumball's interesting arguments see Ketchum, *Saratoga*, pp. 116–117. See also William Stone's, *The Campaign of Lieut. Gen. John Burgoyne and the Expedition of Lieut. Col. Barry St. Leger*, pp. 14–17.

[26]For this, General Schuyler can be faulted.

[27]Excerpts from a letter written to General Gates, Assistant Commander of the Northern Department, Albany, May 1777. (Cited also from Ketchum, *Saratoga*, p. 132). Kosciuszko, a strong admirer of the famed Carthagian General Hannibal, even argued how in the beginning of the Second Punic War of 219–202 B.C., Hannibal crossed the Alps in October, already heavy with snows, with tens of thousands of soldiers, elephants, horses, and wagons.

[28]The Bouquet River flows just to the south of Willsboro Point. This point is a piece of ground which protrudes straight northward like a spear point. Almost adjacent the southern portion of this point, the Bouquet River flows into Lake Champlain's western edge. This river also flows through the town of Willsboro just before it empties into the lake. Undoubtedly, many of Burgoyne's troops camped out on this point.

[29]Both prisoners were captured in the vicinity of modern day Colchester within several miles of Lake Champlain's Mallets Bay. (In 1777, the name of this bay did not exist). As for Colchester, it lies in western Vermont and Mallets Bay is located on the eastern bank of central Lake Champlain directly north of the current city of Burlington also located in northwestern Vermont.

[30]See also Ketchum, *Saratoga*, pp. 124-126.

Chapter 6: British Moves and Patriot Uncertainty

[1]Currently, the town of Willsboro, on the Bouquet River and almost adjacent to Lake Champlain, is located there. Willsboro Point, a promenade jutting northward into Lake Champlain, is located immediately to the north of both the Bouquet River and the town of Willsboro. Some of Burgoyne's troops

established their camps at this site as well.

[2]Named after Henri Bouquet, a Swiss mercenary who, while serving in the English Army during the French and Indian War of 1754-1763, regarded the American Indian as a professional fighter from whom certain tactics could be developed. Organizing light infantry battalions, Bouquet combined Indian and European tactics into the terrain of the North American continent and successfully developed light infantry fighters which could perform successful military missions in heavily forested areas.

[3]Baxter, *Lieutenant Digby's Journal*, p. 201. According to William L. Stone, *The Campaign of Lieut. Gen. John Burgoyne and the Expedition of Lieut. Col. Barry St. Leger* (NY: Da Capo Press, 1970), p. 11, Burgoyne sailed up Lake Champlain and, on 17 June, camped on the western shore of that lake at the falls of the Bouquet River, now known as Willsboro. (On p. 11 Stone spelled Willsboro as Willsborough. Possibly, this was the spelling of the town in the 19th century). (Hereafter cited as *The Campaign*). According to Martha Byrd, *Saratoga. Turning Point*, p. 38, Burgoyne's expedition totaled some 7,800 soldiers. To this figure Byrd cites another 1,000 noncombatants—musicians, cooks, sutlers, and women camp followers who also accompanied Burgoyne's force. As for the camp followers, many were the wives of the soldiers. (Ibid.). Byrd's figure, however, does not include the strength of the Indians, loyalists, or Canadian mercenaries. Hubbard Cobb, "Burgoyne's Saratoga Campaign, July 5–October 17, 1777" in *American Battle-fields. A Complete Guide to the Historic Conflicts in Words, Maps, and Photos* (NY: Simon and Schuster, Co., 1995), p. 46, cites General Burgoyne commanded an impressive force composed of 3,000 British; 3,000 German mercenaries from the Dutchy of Brunswick; 250 Canadian and loyalist militia; and about 400 Indians. (Hereafter cited as *American Battlefields*). In *The War of the Revolution*, Vol. 1, p. 403, Christopher Ward cites such a strength: British, 3,724; German, 3,016; 478 artillerymen of which 245 were regular British artillerymen, 150 were drawn from the infantry; and 78 composed the Hesse Hanau company. "In all the army numbered 7,213 rank and file." (Ibid.). Ward also cites the Canadians and loyalists mission was to cover the British right wing commanded by General Phillips whereas the Indian mission was to cover the German left wing commanded by Von Riedesel. Regarding this, it must be stated that in actuality, the Canadians, loyalists, and Indians were found all around Burgoyne's army and fought wherever the British and Germans were committed into action. According to James A. Huston, *The Sinews of War*, pp. 51-52, problems were immediately encountered with recruitment. "The British commander [Burgoyne] had hoped to have 2,000 Canadian militiamen with his army of something over 8,000 regulars (including over 3,000 German mercenaries) to serve as escorts and pioneers to clear roads and built bridges, but the total number of Canadians dwindled to about 150, and he had about half the 1,000 Indians he had anticipated." However, Huston acknowledges that

"despite difficulties with procuring transportation and with local recruiting, Burgoyne set out from Canada in the middle of June with a respectable force of about 9,500 men." (Ibid., p. 52).

[4]Byrd, *Saratoga. Turning Point*, p. 37; Leckie, *The Wars of America*, p. 169; and Colonel (Ret'd) Stanley Ulanoff, p. 36, cites 138 as well. Hubbard Cobb, *American Battlefields*, cites 138 pieces of artillery and siege cannon with about 400 men to handle the cannons. Ward, *The War of the Revolution*, p. 402, cites 138 guns ranging from 4.4 inch mortars and light 3-pounders to heavy 24-pounders. Furneaux, *The Battle of Saratoga*, p. 44, cites 138 guns. Amongst these guns were also found such weapons: 16 twenty-four pounders; 2 light twenty-four pounders; 10 heavy twelve pounders; 8 medium twelve pounders; 1 light twelve pounder; 26 light six pounders; 6 eight-inch howitzers; and 46 mortars of various calibers. Ward also cites 250 were regular artillerymen, 150 were drawn from the infantry and 100 were German gunners. (Ibid.).

[5]Byrd, *Saratoga. Turning Point* p. 40, cites 21 June 1777. Ketchum, *Saratoga*, p. 141, cites the army was camped on both banks of the Bouquet River on 20 June.

[6]According to Stone, *The Campaign of Lieut. Gen. John Burgoyne*, p. 11, Burgoyne's army encamped on the River Bouquet. Though Stone is correct in his observation, the final assembly of Burgoyne's army did not occur until 21 June 1777.

[7]Benson J. Lossing, *The Empire State: A Compendious History of the Commonwealth of New York* (Hartford, Conn.: American Publishing Co., 1888), p. 263. (Hereafter cited as *The Empire State*). Luzader, *The Saratoga Campaign of 1777*, p. 20.

[8]Lossing, *The Empire State*, p. 265, cites "not more than thirty-five hundred men." Luzader, *The Saratoga Campaign of 1777*, cites 2,500 Continentals (regular army soldiers) and militiamen; Leckie, *The Wars of America*, p. 169, cites "only about 2,500 Americans." Byrd, p. 53, "less than 3,000 men fit for action;" and Hubbard Cobb, *American Battlefields*, p. 46, cites "Major General Arthur St. Clair had about 2,500 men." Reginald Hargreaves, *The Bloodybacks*, p. 291, cites "some 3,000 American troops." According to Stone, *The Campaign*, p. 13, Ticonderoga's garrison was estimated from 4,000 to 5,000 men. Stone's estimation, however, appears to be somewhat high and possibly encompassed the strength of the entire Northern Army from Albany to Forts Edward, Ticonderoga and the other sites.

[9]Stone, *The Campaign*, p. 13.

[10]John Patterson was a continental army commander.

[11]Enoch Poor was a continental army commander.

[12]A Frenchmen who held a high rank in the Northern Army, de Rochefermoy would soon be dismissed from command. He was, in fact, highly incompetent and alcoholism was one of his problems.

[13]Furneaux, *The Battle of Saratoga*, pp. 51-52.

[14]Supposedly, these words were yelled out by Colonel Ethan Allen to Captain Delaplace when Delaplace, the British commander of Fort Ticonderoga, asked Allen "on whose authority am I to surrender?" Historians actually dispute to this day if Allen did indeed say those words.

[15]Furneaux, *The Battle of Saratoga*, pp. 56-57. Undoubtedly, this reference was made in regards to General Abercrombie's fatal attack in 1758 against the French manning Fort Ticonderoga. This attack cost Abercrombie approximately 2,000 casualties in just one day. Wayne also added: "Ft. Ticonderoga is the ancient Golgotha—the Place of Skulls. Skulls are so plentiful here that our people, for want of other vessels, drink out of them, whilst the soldiers make tent pins of the shin and thigh bones of Abercrombie's men."

As for the casualties, they were mostly suffered to the west of Fort Ticonderoga when Abercrombie, in an effort to outflank Ft. Ticonderoga, repeatedly hurled his troops against a defensive system referred to as the "French Lines." In 1777, this position was still known and referred to as the "French Lines."

[16]For a verification of ample food supplies, see Ketchum, *Saratoga*, pp. 153-154; and Stone, *The Campaign*, p. 18. General Schuyler also established a policy in the Northern Army that each company was to designate two or three men to serve as cooks; furthermore, an officer from each company was required to consume at least one or two meals per day. This was deliberately done to ensure that proper meals were cooked and consumed; therefore, in the annals of the American army, the Northern Army appears to be the first U.S. Army to designate certain personnel to serve as cooks. According to James A. Huston, "Logistics of the Saratoga Campaign" in *The Sinews of War: Army Logistics, 1775–1953* (Washington, D.C.: U.S. Government Printing Office, 1966), Chapter IV, pp. 48-49, "Attentive to the health of his troops, Schuyler ordered the post commanders at Ticonderoga to insist on personal cleanliness of their men and the cleanliness of their quarters, and to supervise the preparation and cooking of food. He asked that an officer oversee the cooking in every company every day. He [General Schuyler] thought it best to have the food for a whole company cooked together, and ordered twenty large kettles for that purpose." Schuyler also "ordered the construction of a general hospital large enough for 600 patients at Mount Independence." (Ibid., p. 49). General Schuyler also disliked using soldiers for service chores. (Ibid., p. 50).

[17]One of the missions of the scouts was to ensure that the garrison was well supplied with wild game. Until the fall of Fort Ticonderoga, the scouts did bring in much game.

[18]Much of this flour was gathered up and delivered to the fort by women sympathetic to the patriot cause. Among whom was Abigail Adams, the wife of John Adams.

[19]Schuyler addressed this letter directly to its president, John Hancock. In a previous letter, Congress' New England's representatives were angered by

Schuyler's criticism of the troops sent to him. "Old men, Boys, and Negroes. Unfit for garrison duty and their Armes very bad and but one bayonet to ten men." See also Ketchum, *Saratoga,* p. 253.

[20]George F, Scheer and Hugh F. Rankin, *Rebels and Redcoats* (NY: The New American Library, 1957), p. 289.

[21]Ibid.

Chapter 7: Burgoyne Advances and Fort Ticonderoga Falls

[1]Furneaux, *The Battle of Saratoga,* p. 47. This strength did not include the watermen, or the labor personnel, or the camp followers many of whom were also employed in some capacity.

[2]Baxter, *Lt. Digby's Journal,* p. 356. This date was cited by Lieutenant Digby, who also witnessed Burgoyne's speech to the Indians. Byrd, *Saratoga, Turning Point,* pp. 40-41, also cites 21 June as the day Burgoyne's Indian contingent was addressed by Burgoyne.

[3]Baxter, p. 357.

[4]Ibid., p. 359.

[5]Ibid., pp. 360-361. Burgoyne's words were carefully recorded. Lieutenant Digby, an officer in the 53rd Foot Regiment, signed as a witness. See also pp. 360-361.

[6]Ibid., p. 189. Unlike the previous speech of 21 June which was addressed to the Indians, Burgoyne's speech on 22 June was addressed to the colonists. James Kirby Martin, *Benedict Arnold, Revolutionary Hero. An American Warrior Reconsidered* (NY: New York University Press, 1997), p. 347, cites Burgoyne issued this proclamation on 22 June 1777. (Hereafter cited as *Benedict Arnold*). But Ketchum, *Saratoga,* cites 20 June 1777 as the date. Regardless of the exact date, it is known that Burgoyne, on or about 22 June, did issue his proclamation from the Bouquet River. Stone, Ketchum, Furneaux, and Byrd also cite the proclamation was issued on the Bouquet River. But Lossing, *The Empire State,* p. 265, cites Burgoyne issued his pompous proclamation at Crown Point. Regarding Lossing's observation, he slightly erred. Burgoyne's proclamation to the colonists was actually issued on the Bouquet River.

[7]Martin, *Benedict Arnold,* p. 347.

[8]Possibly, this was an acknowledgment by Burgoyne that he would be unable to control them.

[9]For the entire proclamation, see Stone, *Lieutenant Digby's Journal,* pp. 189-192.

[10]Ketchum, *Saratoga,* p. 160.

[11]Ibid.

[12]In a personal discussion with Richard LaCrosse, Chief Historian at Fort Ontario in Oswego, New York, Mr. LaCrosse stated that there are documented cases of individuals being scalped and surviving the ordeal. During the

process, they endured tremendous pain and, in its aftermath, were never able to regrow their hair.

[13]Furneaux, *The Battle of Saratoga*, p. 49.

[14]Undoubdetly, the officer MacIntosh was referring to was Colonel Kosciusko.

[15]Fort No. 4 is the present day city of Charleston, New Hampshire.

[16]Castleton is presently spelled as Castletown and is located in western Vermont right across the New York State border.

[17]Skenesborough, presently known as Whitehall, is located at the head of Lake Champlain.

[18]During the French-Indian War, the settlement and fort were totally destroyed. Only the ramparts and stone chimneys remained standing. Byrd, *Saratoga. Turning* Point, p. 41, cites "The Americans made no attempt to hold Crown Point, and by June 30 the British army was encamped there." Ketchum, *Saratoga*, p. 163, cites Crown Point is located 11 miles to the north of Fort Ticonderoga. According to Esmond Wright, ed., *The Fire of Liberty: The American War of Independence seen through the eyes of the men and women, the statesmen and soldiers who fought it* (NY: St. Martin's Press), 1983, p. 93, Burgoyne arrived to Crown Point on 27 June. (Actually, reconnaissance personnel had reached the site on or about 27 June, despite the heavy storm). According to Wright, "Burgoyne hoped to supplement his 7213 men (three brigades of British regulars and three of Hessians) with Canadian Loyalists, and 'one thousand or more savages.' However, only about 250 Tories and 400 Indians joined the expedition. A massive artillery train of 138 guns was to be manhandled along forest trails, succeeded by large numbers of women and children, who followed their men to war in the wilderness." (Ibid.). Wright also cites that Burgoyne "issued his orders for the attack on Ticonderoga" from Crown Point. (Hereafter cited as *The Fire of Liberty!*)

[19]Stone, *The Campaign*, p. 12; Byrd, *Saratoga. Turning Point*, p. 41; and Ketchum, *Saratoga*, p. 163

[20]Stone, *The Campaign*, p. 12. (Stone, however, deluded a few of Burgoyne's sentences). Ketchum, p. 163; Luzader, p. 17; Hargreaves, *The Bloodybacks*, p. 290; Byrd, *Saratoga: Turning Point*, p. 41; and Furneaux, *The Battle of Saratoga*, p. 41; Wright, *The Fire of Liberty!*, p. 94. See also Scheer and Rankin, *Rebels and Redcoats*, p. 286.

[21]Furneaux, *The Battle of Saratoga*, pp. 50 and 62. On 1 July 1777, General Burgoyne's personnel muster cited such a strength: British regulars, 3,724; Germans, 3,016; Artillery regulars, 473 for a total of 7,213. Canadians and Provincials, approximately 250; and Indians, approximately 400. Total, approximately 8,863 personnel. Source: Carrington, *Battles of the American Revolution*, p. 307. (This figure, however, does not include the naval men, axmen, wagoneers, doctors, chaplains, other support personnel and camp followers). Wright, *The Fire of Liberty!*, p. 93, also cites a strength of 7,213 not

counting the loyalist and Indian strength.

[22]Scheer and Rankin, *Rebels and Redcoats*, p. 286.

[23]Stone, *The Campaign*, p. 13. According to Ketchum, *Saratoga*, p. 143, MacIntosh estimated about 4,000 were defending Fort Ticonderoga.

[24]Furneaux, p. 49.

[25]Ibid.

[26]Ibid.

[27]Ward, *The War of the Revolution*, Vol. 1, p. 407. However, as acknowledged by Ward, none of the regiments were in full strength. Regimental strengths ranged from 45 to, at best, 265. The average strength of a regiment stood at 160. (Ibid.).

[28]Previously, Mount Independence was known as Rattlesnake Hill.

[29]From here, in the back of the hill, was a road. This road led southward and eastward to various settlements and towns.

[30]Regarding the time, different authors cite various times. Stone, *The Campaign*, p. 14, cites it was at noon. (1200 hrs). But perhaps Stone refers to the time when the brunt of Fraser's force advanced. Undoubtedly, elements of Fraser's force began to advance forward much sooner. Ketchum, p. 165, cites Fraser advanced shortly before 9 a.m.

[31]To this day, this particular piece of ground is known as Mount Hope.

[32]According to Furneaux, *The Battle of Saratoga*, p. 64, it was St. Clair who issued such an order: "Send out a corporal and a file of men, and let the poor fellow be brought in and buried." The "deceased man" was eventually identified as being a member of the 47th Foot Regiment and, possibly, was attached to the 24th Foot attacking the French Lines. (Or, possibly, he just simply revealed false information). Of interest to note is that although not one American was hit by the fusillade, the captured soldier exclaimed to the patriots "By Jasus [Jesus], I killed the man at the Sallyport. [Referring to a position in the French Lines]. A fair shot!" (Ibid.).

[33]Ketchum, *Saratoga*, p. 169.

[34]Ibid.

[35]Stone, *The Campaign*, p. 16. See also Ward, *The War of the Revolution*, Vol. 1, p. 410.

[36]Recently known as Sugar Loaf Hill.

[37]Ward, Vol. 1, p. 410; Hargreaves, *The Bloodybacks*, p. 291. Upon hearing of the find, General Burgoyne himself approved the operation to secure Sugar Loaf Hill or Mt. Defiance. And General Phillips, who personally and expeditiously delivered the two cannons to the base of the summit, moved so fast that in his anxiousness, he broke no less than fifteen canes in beating the racing horses pulling the cannons. (See Stone, The Campaign, fn. 1, p. 17).

[38]Ketchum, *Saratoga*, p. 171, cites, "a detail of four hundred men to clear the road and construct a battery."

[39]Ketchum, pp. 170-171.

[40]William B. Willcox, *Portrait of a General. Sir Henry Clinton in the War of Independence* (NY: Alfred A. Knopf, 1962), p. 153. As acknowledged by Willcox, "Howe's eyes were on Pennsylvania." (Ibid.). For the various discussions amongst Howe and Clinton see especially pp. 148-160. (Hereafter cited as *Portrait of a General*).

[41]According to Mark Boatner, *Landmarks of the American Revolution. People and Places. Vital to the Quest for Independence* (Pa.: Stackpole Books, 1992), p. 319.

"The significance of the enemy guns on Mount Defiance was not that they could pound the fort into submission; the range was too great for precision fire, but, even more important, not enough ammunition could be supplied over the improvised road for a proper bombardment. But these guns could wreck the floating bridge and boats brought up to evacuate the garrison."

Though Boatner is correct that the guns could have destroyed the bridge and boats, he is incorrect when he cites that Fort Ticonderoga could not have been pounded into submission. The guns on Mount Defiance could have, in due time, pounded the fort into submission. And the 12-pound guns, along with the placement of some additional heavy naval guns, did actually possess an effective range. As for the comment that "not enough ammunition could be supplied..." this is also incorrect. One way of bringing up the ammunition would have been done by simply establishing a "human chain." The ammunition would have been passed from hand to hand. (Hereafter Boatner's work will be cited as *Landmarks of the American Revolution*).

[42]Ketchum, *Saratoga*, p. 172.

[43]Ibid.

[44]Now known as Whitehall.

[45]According to Doctor Thatcher, a total of 5 armed galley's and 200 hundred bateaux's, all heavily laden, sailed from Fort Ticonderoga to Skenesborough. See Richard Wheeler, *Voices of 1776* (NY: Thomas Y. Crowell Co., 1972), p. 194.

[46]Stone, *The Campaign*, p. 17. Stone also cites 5 armed ship galleys and 200 bateaux boats. Stone also cites "600 hundred men" but cites that these 600 "set out with the sick and wounded for Skenesborough."

[47]Ketchum, *Saratoga*, p. 174.

[48]In modern military terminology, a retreat is referred to as a retrograde operation.

[49]Ketchum, p. 176.

[50]According to Boatner, *Landmarks of the American Revolution*, p. 319, the fire was started at about 3 a.m. by General Fermoy when he prepared to depart. The fire illuminated the entire scene, revealed what the patriots were up to, and prompted a vigorous reaction from the enemy.

Chapter 8: Cries of Retreat and Forest Battles

[1]To help protect the New England region, in the summer of 1776 Washington ordered the construction of Fort Lee right across the Hudson River in New Jersey and Fort Washington in upper Manhattan. But in November 1776, Washington watched helplessly from the New Jersey side as about 3,000 of his troops along with about 150 cannons, were overrun by English and German forces. (Boatner, *Landmarks of the American Revolution*, p. 272, cites that these soldiers were some of Washington's best troops). (As for Fort Lee, it currently is a town in New Jersey. The moment a motorist drives across the Washington Bridge and enters New Jersey, the driver is in Fort Lee. As for Fort Washington, it stood where currently West 183rd St. is adjacent the Washington Bridge in Manhattan). In response to the loss of these forts, it was decided to fortify the Highlands to the north of New York City at a sight recently designated as West Point. By controlling the Hudson River and the roads adjacent the heights, it would bar any British attacks northward from New York City to either cut off or seize New England. So a series of forts, Forts Montgomery, Clinton, Independence, and Constitution, began to appear in 1776 and 1777. As Washington told General Schuyler in early 1777, "If I can keep Howe below the Highlands, I think their schemes will be entirely baffled."

[2]Richard B. LaCrosse, Jr., *Daniel Morgan's Riflemen on America's Northern Frontier, 1778-1783* (Unpublished text submitted to author by Mr. LaCrosse), p. 4. (Hereafter cited as *Daniel Morgan's Riflemen*).

[3]Ibid., p. 3.

[4]Ibid.

[5]Ibid. To better understand a patriot rifle unit (such as the elite rifle corps commanded by Colonel Daniel Morgan or the unit commanded by Colonel Seth Warner), one has to take into consideration certain factors. First, the temperament of its men was influenced by the North American wilderness along with its native animal life. Second, from early youth these men (and many women) grew up with guns. In Europe, such as in England, excluding the nobility, no one had guns. Private gun ownership was forbidden; likewise, Europe was old. The rich animal life found on the North American continent did not exist in Europe. Growing up with guns, frontiersmen frequently hunted. With rifles in their hands they knew the importance of the "one shot—one kill!" theory. Whether the game was a wild goose or squirrel, or a black bear or moose, the game was usually eliminated with head, neck, and heart and lung shots. This explains why during the Wilderness War of 1777 (as throughout the entire Revolutionary War), a patriot soldier or militiamen, whether armed with a musket or rifle, always aimed instinctively at a target whereas his European opponent (most who never held a gun in their hand until they entered the army), were trained to fire volleys with little regard for aiming. Amid the trees and wooded terrain as well as against the patriot earth-works, volleys were not

effective. When General Frederick Von Steuben, an officer from Prussia, Germany, arrived to train Washington's army, though Von Steuben did incorporate European (especially German army methods and tactics), he did create changes and altered tactics to not only suit the temperament of the individual American warrior but, most importantly, to exploit the accuracy and shooting ability of the American frontiersmen.

It must also be mentioned that in general, the physical health of a frontier warrior was considerably better than that of the European. On the average the wilderness resident was taller, stronger, could move vast distances much faster, was not so immune to natural and weather hardships, and always kept his eyes and ears open for any kind of danger. After all, pursuing wild big game for miles and getting caught up in a rain storm or heavy snowfall while gutting the killed animal and afterwards carrying 50 or 60 pounds or more of wild meat on his back while, simultaneously, dragging additional meat and hide on a makeshift stretcher created a more physically and mentally hardier individual. In Europe, the male lived on his small plot of land or in a row house. If it rained, he went inside. Rarely, did he ever venture more than 5 or 10 miles from his domain. The market place, church, or workplace was very nearby. Few ever chopped down a tree. They never had to communicate with animal sounds. And so it went. For a view and comparison on how ordinary life in itself created the European and American combatant see Robert B. Asprey, *War In the Shadows. The Guerrilla in History* (NY: Doubleday and Company, Inc., 1975), Vol. I, pp. 97-99. See also "Rifleman" in C. Keith Wilbur, *The Revolutionary Soldier 1775-1783* (Conn.: The Globe Pequot Press, 1969), p. 30. According to Wilbur, "From the western reaches of the southern colonies and the Pennsylvanian frontier came a new breed of man. The primitive life molded them into stout and hardy individuals, frequently more than six feet in height." (Ibid.).

[6]Both barrels were equal in length but one barrel was laid underneath the other. Two separate flintlocks were also utilized.

[7]Eugenia Campbell Lester and Allegra Branson, *Frontiers Aflame! Jane Cannon Campbell. Revolutionary War Heroine When America Had Only Heroes* (NY: Heart of the Lakes Publishing, 1987), p. 20.

[8]Ketchum, *Saratoga*, p. 286.

[9]Regarding this incident, Sergeant Lamb wrote, "After the enemy retreated we marched down to the works, and were obliged to halt at the bridge of communication which had been broken down. In passing the bridge and possessing ourselves of the works we found four men lying intoxicated with drinking, who had been left to fire the guns of a large battery on our approach. Had the men obeyed the commands they received, we must have suffered great injury; but they were allured by the opportunity of a cask of Madeira to forget their instructions and drown their cares in wine. It appeared evident they were left for the purpose alluded to, as matches were found lighted, the ground was strewed with powder, and the heads of some powder-casks were knocked off in

order, no doubt, to injure our men on their gaining the works. An Indian had like to do some mischief from his curiosity - holding a lighted match near one of the guns, it exploded, but being elevated, it discharged without harm." Stone, *The Campaign,* pp. 18-19. As for the four, they joined the others who had stayed behind because either they had not received the word to withdraw or, remained to loot and were captured by the incoming British and Germans.

[10]Stone, *The Campaign,* p. 18.

[11]Ibid.

[12]Ibid.

[13]According to Lieutenant Digby's journal, the Americans had made an attempt to burn the bridge which spanned the water between Mount Defiance and Mount Independence. But perhaps, Lieutenant Digby erred in his observation because in itself the bridge could serve as a water obstacle. Furthermore, fire from the bridge could have ignited the poles and water rafts which held up the so-called chain boom. (See p. 208). Digby also acknowledges, "had [the American defenders] placed one gun, so as the grape shot take the range of the bridge—and which surprised us they did not, as two men could have fired it, and then made off—they would, in all probability, have destroyed all or most of us on the Boom." (Ibid., pp. 208-209). By his comments, it appears that Digby was not on the bridge when it was initially overrun and he had no knowledge of the four intoxicated men left behind with a loaded cannon aimed straight down the bridge. It also appears that Digby never spoke with Sergeant Lamb as to what he had encountered when assaulting the bridge.

[14]Unknown to Colonel Long, the British force commanded by Commodore Ludwidge was rapidly closing in. As for Long, he can be faulted for being negligent since he failed to leave behind a token force to halt - and warn - the patriots that an enemy force was approaching. Prior to reaching Skenesborough, the southern portion of Lake Champlain tremendously narrows. Had just a few trees been dropped and a small force left behind, the British thrust could have been halted and Long's main body would have been warned as well.

[15]Stone, *The Campaign,* p. 23. Stone cites that three British foot regiments were landed but Stone does not provide their numerical designation. Ketchum, *Saratoga,* p. 225 identifies the three as the 9th, 20th, and 21st. (However, the entire 20th Foot was also not committed).

[16]Willcox, *Portrait of a General,* p. 160.

[17]Ibid.

[18]Ibid.

[19]Ibid. Willcox also cites Howe was in agreement with Clinton that he could resign. But for the time being, Clinton had to stay in command during Howe's absence.

[20]Ketchum, *Saratoga,* p. 225.

[21]Ibid.

[22]Furneaux, *The Battle of Saratoga,* p. 70, cites 190. Furneaux also cites

Hill's rank as being "Colonel" rather than Lieutenant-Colonel. Sergeant Lamb's journal also cites a strength of 190.

[23]Skene's wife was reburied in a garden.

[24]And once again, Clinton would be unsuccessful.

[25]According to Sergeant Lamb who witnessed this "deserter" and the incident, the date was 8 July. (See Ketchum, *Saratoga*, p. 227). Stone, *The Campaign*, p. 25, cites, "early July 8th, Long suddenly issued from the fort and attacked the English."

[26]Furneaux, p. 70; and Ketchum, p. 227, cite "about 1,000 men."

[27]In the aftermath of the campaign, Captain Money (who also served as a Deputy-Quartermaster for Burgoyne), cited "the Americans' fire was heavier at Fort Anne than on any other occasion during the campaign, except in the action of the 19th September [Battle of Saratoga]." See Stone, *The Campaign*, fn. 1, p. 26.

[28]Stone, *The Campaign*, p. 25. See also Ketchum, *Saratoga*, p. 229. Sergeant Lamb's observation was more then correct because sometime between the hours of 10 and 11 a.m., Colonel Van Rensselaer and his militiamen appeared on the scene. Reinforced with news from the "deserter" who, in actuality, was a spy operating for Colonel Long, the patriots not only learned the true British strength but that a Lieutenant-Colonel Hill was in command. Acting on this information, Colonel Long dispatched Van Rensselaer and his fighters to assist Captain Gray. Colonel Long reasoned that Van Ransselaer's fighters would not only reinforce Gray's men but, likewise, this action would give Van Ransselaer's militiamen some combat experience. And in the event the British were overcome and captured, this would tremendously raise the morale of the patriots and slow (if not totally halt for the moment), the thrust of the British attacking from the west.

[29]Figures range between 12-14 privates, 1 army captain, and 1 doctor surgeon as being captured.

[30]See Chapter 6, pp. 120-124, "Philadelphia and Saratoga. 1. Howe and Burgoyne" in Piers Macksey, *The War for America 1775-1783*.

[31]According to Luzader, *The Saratoga Campaign of 1777*, p. 16, "Germain's March 3 letter to Howe approved the plan to attack Philadelphia. Ten days later, Germain wrote that the King, confident of Howe's judgment, approved of any alteration Howe made in his plans, "... trusting, however, that whatever you may meditate, it will be executed in time for you to cooperate with the army ordered to proceed from Canada and put itself under your command.'" See also Macksey, 3. "Howe's Plans of Campaign" in *The War for America, 1775-1783*, pp. 109-112.

[32]Sergeant Lamb was not among the prisoners. According to Stone, *The Campaign*, p. 26, it was "General Phillips, who with the 20th regiment consisting of five hundred and twenty men and two pieces of artillery, was pressing forward to the assistance of Hill...and General Phillips, learning upon his arrival, that the enemy had retired, immediately marched back to

Skenesborough, leaving a sergeant [Sergeant Lamb] and a small guard to take care of the wounded."

[33]Stone, *The Campaign*, p. 27, also cites one woman. (See fn. 2, pp. 26-27). The woman was never identified in name. It is known, however, that she had been following her husband who, though wounded in action but not captured, was assisted both by her and Sergeant Lamb.

[34]Ibid., p. 27

Chapter 9: The Battle of Hubbardton

[1]The battle was actually fought in a town now known as East Hubbardton which lies just to the east of Lake Bomoseen. As for Hubbardton, it lies on the northern edge of Lake Bomoseen.

[2]Furneaux, *The Battle of Saratoga*, p. 77.

[3]Ibid.

[4]Ibid. Hubbard Cobb, "Battle of Hubbardton—July 7, 1777" in *American Battlefields*, p. 47, cites Colonel Seth Warner had 150 Vermont men.

[5]Furneaux, p. 77.

[6]Though described by many as being a sound patriot, Ethan Allen was also a suspect in several previous bank robberies. As for his "patriotism," it may be questioned. Possibly, the main reason why Ethan Allen struck Fort Ticonderoga on 10 May 1775 was to secure the British garrison's pay chest with its money. Captured near Montreal in September, 1775 he was held in confinement until exchanged in 1778. Released that year, Ethan returned to Vermont and along with his brother, Ira, he largely dealt with the issue of Vermont's territorial disputes and its claims for recognition as an independent nation. He also negotiated secretly with the Governor of Canada to have Vermont established as a Canadian province. When this became known to the public, Ethan Allen's reputation fell tremendously. (Some have even speculated that while in British captivity both in Canada and England, he might have developed a pro-British sentiment). Regardless, his negotiations forced the Continental Congress to conduct some favorable actions pertaining to the issue of Vermont. In the aftermath of his release he served briefly as a lieutenant-colonel in a Vermont continental unit and, after the Revolutionary War, was a major general of Vermont's militia. But he never again saw any combat activities following his release. Born in 1738, Ethan Allen died in Vermont in 1789.

[7]Cobb, *American Battlefields*, pp. 47-48, cites a distance of "some one thousand yards, anchored on the left on the side of a hill, now called 'Zion Hill.'"

[8]Ketchum, Saratoga, p. 200. Cobb, p. 47, implies a strength of close to 1,200 when he cites 150 Vermont men and "about 1,000 men in all" from Francis's Massachusetts and Hale's New Hampshire regiments.

[9]Also spelled as Jessop. Ebenezer also had a loyalist brother named Edward who served on and off in the Jessup Corps.

[10]Zion Hill was on the patriot left and the saddle ridge was on their right.
[11]The rest of the 20th Foot Regiment was operating at this very moment further to the west in the vicinity of Fort Anne.
[12]Cobb, p. 47.
[13]It was not a serious wound and within several days, Major Lindsay wrote to his sister Margaret to inform her that "it was not my day to die!" Later, the major counted ten holes through his clothes and noted that his personal weapon had been hit two times.
[14]Ketchum, p. 199.
[15]Stone, *The Campaign*, p. 20.
[16]The British and Germans who engaged the American force estimated they were up against a strength of about 2,000 or so rebels. (See Ketchum, *Saratoga*, p. 200). Balcarres estimated 3,000 (Ibid.). In actuality, the Americans had, at Hubbardton, about 1,200, not all of them combatants.
[17]Ketchum, p. 202.
[18]As for Colonel Hale, he and the other prisoners were transported back to Fort Ticonderoga where rebel prisoners, prior to being transported north to Canada, were kept. Here, Lieutenant-Colonel Christian Pratorius interrogated Hale. Pratorius did not draw a very high opinion of Colonel Hale. "A simple sutter. Far from a professional military men."

While in captivity, stories soon began to surface that Colonel Hale was not only an incompetent commander and coward but, as a prisoner, maintained such a close relationship with Burgoyne that it could be regarded as outright treason to the patriot cause. In short time, these stories reached Hale himself.

On 20 July 1777, Colonel Hale was released on parole so that he could defend himself. Upon reaching the Northern Department's Albany headquarters, Hale learned that the American high command had never regarded him to be an incompetent commander. And no one had ever charged him of treason. Although Colonel Hale requested a formal inquiry, his request was denied because no charges had ever been placed upon him and the Northern Army was, overall, satisfied with the events at Hubbardton.

Unfortunately for Colonel Hale, right at that very moment there was no British colonel in captivity to be exchanged for him. Because Hale had given his word that he would return to captivity if no exchange could be arranged, Hale did return to the British despite being in poor health. On 23 September 1780, as a prisoner of war in Long Island, New York, Colonel Hale died. He was 37-years-old.

In the aftermath of Burgoyne's surrender, General Burgoyne himself provided such a hand written statement: "Colonel Hale, never communicated to me any improper information, and further, that no conversation even, had passed between us except the ordinary dinner table courtesies between gentlemen." (Stone, *The Campaign*, p. 22).

At Hubbardton, Colonel Hale, though in poor health and in command of a weak regiment, did the best that he could. From what is known of Hale's performance and General Burgoyne's statement, it is known that Colonel Hale was a very brave and dedicated officer, an honorable man, and a true patriot.

[19]So wrote Digby in his journal of the gallant Colonel Francis. See also Ketchum, *Saratoga*, p. 205.

[20]In the aftermath of the British surrender at Saratoga, Lieutenant Digby was one of those who became a prisoner. In 1778, Digby was held captive in Cambridge, Massachusetts. And it was here that he had a most unusual—but very moving—experience.

Along with several other captive officers, Lieutenant Digby stopped by a house to request some food. At this time, Digby noted an elderly woman closely observing the group of captive officers. As the group began to depart, the woman suddenly approached them and asked the captive British officers if they knew her son, a Colonel Ebenezer Francis, who had been killed in Hubbardton the year before.

The British officers politely informed the woman that they actually did see him, but only after his death. Colonel Francis' mother then inquired if they knew anything of the papers found on him since they also dealth with matters related to his estate. And she also inquired if they, by any chance, knew anything about a watch he had.

At this point, Captain Ferguson informed the woman that regarding any papers, they were either lost or destroyed. Feeling sorry for her, he pulled out a watch from a pocket and stated to her, "there, good woman. If that can make you happy, take it and God bless You." According to Lieutenant Digby, Captain Ferguson had purchased the watch from a drummer boy who was a participant at the Battle of Hubbardton and, on that day, was given the watch.

Upon receiving the watch, the woman began to sob. It was her son's. Kissing it several times, she grasped Captain Ferguson's hands for his kindness. For Lieutenant Digby and his fellow officers the scene was very emotional. Indeed, so emotional that the officers even promised to see if they could somehow recover his papers. (See also Furneaux, *The Battle of Saratoga*, p. 86).

[21]Colonel Dupuy, *Encyclopedia of Military History*, p. 714. According to Leckie, *The Wars of America*, pp. 169-170, "The British were momentarily delayed at Hubbardton, where the Americans fought a stubborn delaying action." Yet, others hold a different view. According to Lieutenant-Colonel James Wilkinson, who served as a Deputy Adjutant to the Northern Army, Wilkinson wrote, "Colonel Warner was a hardy, valiant soldier, but uneducated and a stranger to military discipline; his insubordination at Hubbardton, exemplifies the danger and misfortunes which attend the disobedience of military commands; for, if he had obeyed the orders he received, our corps would have been united, and as the discipline of the enemy could have availed them little in a mountainous country covered with wood, we should infallibly have

dismembered, and probably captured, the flower of the British army." (See Stone, *The Campaign,* fn. 1, p. 20, and Furneaux, The Battle of Saratoga, pp. 85-86).

[22]British fears were not imagined. The patriots were starting to react effectively to the events at Hubbardton.

[23]Furneaux, p. 86.

[24]Cobb, p. 48.

[25]Ibid.

[26]Ibid.

[27]Indeed, these are very heavy losses. In comparison, if a modern day divisional commander is commanding a heavy division of 18,000 soldiers and he incurs about 325 casualties in 45 minutes, then within 90 minutes (or an hour-and-a-half), he would take about 650 casualties. In three hours, a loss of 1,300; twelve hours, 5,200; in twenty-four hours well over 10,000 casualties. (Although, in actuality, under the continuing heavy strain of combat, the casualties would be higher). But even if one cited 10,000 by the end of a twenty-four hour period, the divisional commander would no longer be commanding an effective division.

[28]Furneaux, p. 84.

[29]Ibid.

[30]Ibid.

[31]Ibid.

[32]Ibid. Some humanity was shown to the captives. Ebenezer Fletcher, a continental soldier, was shot in the back. Lying on the ground, he pretended that he was dead. But soon some local civilians appeared on the scene and began to loot. Approaching Fletcher, they began to steal from him when, suddenly, a British officer noted the looters and ordered his men to shoot all looters on sight. Approaching Fletcher, the officer noted that he was still alive. Carrying him to a cabin converted into a makeshift medical center, an English doctor removed the ball and dressed the wound. Two days later, Fletcher was placed on a stretcher and American captives carried him back to Skenesborough. Shortly afterwards, he and a sizable group of prisoners were placed into a prisoner column to be marched northward to Fort Ticonderoga. Somewhere along the road, Fletcher bolted into the wilderness. On July 23, after spending a number of days in the forests, he appeared at his home. Shortly afterwards he rejoined the Northern Army in Albany and saw action at the Battle of Saratoga. On the 50th anniversary of the Battle of Hubbardton, Fletcher decided to write his story.

[33]Ketchum, p. 214.

[34]According to various sources, it was a very heavy rain. "The long day ended in drenching rain." (See Furneaux, p. 86; and Ketchum, p. 212).

[35]And so it was. The wounded were recovered within several days.

Chapter 10: Fighting Off Marauders and Raiders

[1]Lossing, *The Pictorial Field-Book of the American Revolution*, p. 40.

[2]Ketchum, *Saratoga*, p. 277.

[3]Ibid.

[4]Despite his very strong "pro-British sentiment," Rivington was actually one of General George Washington's personal spies.

[5]In fact, all of these men were slavers or supported slavery.

[6]The Sir Johnson's were not only slavers but they had a fiery hatred of the patriots.

[7]Lossing, *Pictorial History of the American Revolution*, Vol. I, p. 266.

[8]Michael Pearson, *Those Damned Rebels. The American Revolution As Seen Through British Eyes* (NY: G.P. Putnam's Sons, 1972), p. 294. (Hereafter cited as *The Revolution Seen Through British Eyes*). According to George Bancroft, *The American Revolution*, Vol. III, 5th Ed., p. 365, Edmund Burke, in England, was a strong critic of employing irregulars such as the Indians. In the House of Commons Burke, "pronounced that they were not fit allies for the king in a war with his people; that Englishmen should never confirm their evil habits by fleshing them in the slaughter of British colonists." (Ibid.). (Of importance to note is that Edmund Burke supported England's supremacy over the colonies and he insisted that London must remain in the seat of power over both the colonies and Ireland; however, Burke was known to be critical of any repressive policies undertaken by the Ministry as well as the practice of using Indians to further England's needs. See Wrong, *Canada and the American Revolution*, pp. 123-124). In the House of Commons, Burke argued that keeping Indians under control after releasing them to raid is like releasing captive zoo animals within a city and expecting these animals not to endanger anyone. "My gentle lions, my humane bears, my tender-hearted hyenas, I exhort you as you are Christians… to take care not to hurt man, woman or child." (Wrong, pp. 330-331). And Charles Fox, a strong critic of the war and admirer of George Washington, likewise In the House of Commons blamed and reprimanded King George III for allowing, "brutality, murder, and destruction were ever inseparable from Indian warriors." (Bancroft, p. 365. See also Wrong, p. 124). And Lord Chatham himself spoke out against the brutalities being inflicted upon the colonists and the usage of Indians for warfare. (Ibid.).

[9]Lossing, *Pictorial Field-Book of the American Revolution*, Vol. 1, p. 266. "Scalping parties continued to infest the Schoharie [Valley] and neighboring settlements until quite late in September." (Ibid., p. 267).

[10]Clinton Rossiter, *The Federalist Papers* (NY: The New American Library, Inc., 1961), No. 46, p. 299.

[11]Later, these scalps were sold. Another case of barbarity occurred in the vicinity of Fort Miller. German soldiers recovered the body of a patriot officer who had not only been scalped but the soles of his feet had been sliced off with

a knife. After examining the dead man, Doctor Wasmus concluded that he had been physically abused prior to dying or being finished off. By now, the German doctor was well aware that such excesses were fairly widespread. Directly, Doctor Wasmus lodged a strong protest about the torture killing of this officer to both General Von Riedesel and General Burgoyne.

[12]To cite an example: because of the Wilderness War of 1777, New York City would suffer immense food shortages during the winter of 1776–77 leading to outright starvation for many.

Chapter 11: Chaplain and Early Intelligence Gatherer

[1]Shortly afterwards, the Continental Congress allocated Chaplain Kirkland another 444 dollars for his work as an American missionary among the Indians. See Walter Pilkington, *The Journal of Samuel Kirkland, 18th-century Missionary to the Iroquois, Govern-ment Agent, Father of Hamilton College* (Clinton, New York: Hamilton College Publishing, 1980), p. 120.

[2]As a result of this, Kirkland not only became prominent on the North American continent for being an Indian expert prior to 1777 but, likewise, was also well-known in Canada, England and Scotland.

[3]Donald A. Grinde, Jr., *The Iroquois and the Founding of the American Nation* (New York: Indian Historian Press, 1977), pp. 99 and 113. The exact dates of this Great Council were 16-19 January 1777. This council was held in the present day Onondaga County adjacent the current city of Syracuse, New York.

[4]However, sizable numbers of individual Indian warriors from the Cayugas, Senecas, Mohawks, and Onondagas did side with the patriots. Such was evidenced during the Battle of Oriskany, during the siege of Fort Stanwix and, in September, 1777, when 150 warriors from the Iroquois Confederacy joined the Northern Army at Saratoga. Needless to say these were not the only warriors serving in the vicinity of Saratoga in 1777. Others had already been serving for a while. For an in-depth study of the Native American Indian's military role in 1777 as well as their lives, activities and hardships during the Revolutionary War see also Barbara Graymont, *The Iroquois in the American Revolution* (Syracuse, New York: Syracuse University Press, 1972).

Chapter 12: Burgoyne's Tactical Plan to Reach Fort Edward

[1]Ward, *The War of the Revolution*, Vol. 1, p. 418. As for Castleton, it is now spelled Castletown and is located in Vermont to the southeast of Lake Bomoseen and south of present day East Hubbardton. With this placement, Burgoyne's army was actually spread throughout a sizable area. Surely, Vermont's inhabitants must have been in tremendous fear knowing that elements of a sizable and strong army corps were positioned in Vermont proper.

[2]The 62nd Foot Regiment was almost annihilated at Saratoga. Bobrick, *Angel In the Whirlwind*, p. 254, cites Burgoyne hoped to get Carleton to garri-

son Fort Ticonderoga with 1,000 men. According to Bancroft, *The American Revolution*, Vol. III, p. 370, "Burgoyne asked Carleton to hold Ticonderoga with a part of the 3,000 troops left in Canada but Carleton refused."

[3]For the strong criticism of St. Clair see Furneaux, Battle of Saratoga, p. 88; and Ketchum, *Saratoga*, pp. 217-219. For the comment of how "silver balls" were fired into the fort to be shared by both Generals St. Clair and Schuyler see Scheer and Rankin, *Rebels and Redcoats*, p. 292. At this time, some claimed that "Gates would have saved [Fort] Ticonderoga." (Furneaux, pp. 88-89). And Reverend Chaplain Thomas Allen, who fled to his home town in Vermont, was also tremendously critical of St. Clair. (For the Reverend's comments see Ketchum, p. 219). Reverend Allen, however, would soon join General John Stark's brigade and witness combat at the Battle of Bennington.

[4]Burke Davis, *George Washington and the American Revolution* (NY: Random House, 1975), p. 207; Bobrick, *Angel in the Whirlwind*, p. 253.

[5]Furneaux, p. 88.

[6]These letters were written mostly from Dorset.

[7]There were, however, many who quickly came to the defense of General St. Clair such as Colonel Alexander Scammell who served at Fort Ticonderoga. Describing the fort as "a perfect Mouse Trap!" Scammell insisted that Fort Ticonderoga "was evacuated for want of men, the untenableness of the post." Scammell argued how General St. Clair never received any sizable reinforcement and that the entire defense system could have been easily surrounded by Burgoyne's approaching army leaving the patriots "totally blockaded and [with] communications cut off, Burgoyne would have had it in his Election [choice] to either kill, starve, or take us prisoners." Scammell added that Burgoyne would then have reached Albany since no troops would have been around to defend the route to Albany. "By retreating, the troops were available for another time."

So insisted Colonel Scammell. (For his remarks see Ketchum, *Saratoga*, p. 220).

In actuality, after reaching Fort Ticonderoga, Burgoyne did not have to assault it. By simply positioning some of his naval ships and gunboats just a short distance away, Burgoyne afterwards could have also utilized members of their crews in a ground role. Reinforced with a small number of British or German troops, they could have ringed cannons all around Fort Ticonderoga and bombarded the place. In the meantime, with the bulk of his army encountering no solid resistance, the chance of Burgoyne marching to Albany and, even beyond, would have been possible.

Perhaps, Doctor Thatcher summed it up best when he predicted that the fall of Fort Ticonderoga would result, in the end, in a British defeat. "Though so calamitous [disastrous], will ultimately prove advantageous by drawing the British army into the heart of the country and thereby place them more immediately within our power." See Bobrick, *Angel in the Whirlwind*, p. 255.

[8]In the end, this would be acknowledged by many to include the initial critics.

[9]Presently, Fort Edward no longer exists. However, various markers do exist to indicate where various parts of the fort once stood.

[10]A combination of natural and man-made changes in this area of the Hudson River has somewhat altered the view of the area. See "Fort Edward" in Boatner's, *Landmarks of the American Revolution*, pp. 238-240. For an entire history see pp. 238-242.

[11]In actuality the "Old Fort House" was never a fort. It was a sizable two story building which contained an inn, courtroom, rooms for rent, and was a meeting place. The house was also utilized in 1777 by various generals and dignitaries as a headquarters, command post, and residence. Patriot Generals Schuyler, Arnold, Stark, and Gates; British Generals Burgoyne and Fraser; and German General Von Riedesel, are just some of the more prominent men to have utilized and stayed in this home.

[12]Currently, this settlement is the Village of Fort Edward and is located on Routes 4 and 197. Hargreaves, *The Bloodybacks,* p. 299, cites "Fort Edward is less than forty-five miles from Albany."

[13]Furneaux, *Saratoga,* p. 92. Various authors cite distances of 23-26 miles. Wheeler, *Voices of 1776,* p. 198, cites "about twenty-five miles." Ketchum, p. 249, cites the distance between Fort Anne and Fort Edward is 18 miles. Scheer and Rankin, *Rebels and Redcoats,* p. 294, cite a distance of "Twenty-three miles from the heart of Mr. Skene's great wilderness empire to Fort Edward on the upper Hudson."

[14]This straight line distance was determined by the author utilizing a Rand Atlas map.

[15]As already presented, Lake George in elevation lies higher than Lake Champlain. According to certain accounts, Burgoyne should have turned back from Skenesborough and moved to the Hudson River by way of Lake George and the old road. Instead, Burgoyne decided to take a "short cut" through a wilderness bristling with woods, numerous creeks and treacherous terrain with morasses. More than 40 bridges along with a "log-work" road spanning through a swampy morass 2 miles in length had to be constructed along with the removal of layers of fallen timber trees. The heavy work, heat conditions, insects... such appalling conditions dispirited his troops. See Bancroft, Vol. III, pp. 370-371.

[16]Ketchum, *Saratoga,* p. 241. In actuality, some held the view that Burgoyne should have taken the Lake Champlain-Lake George-Fort George-Fort Edward route to the Hudson River. Among them was Lieutenant Digby who would note such in his journal, "Many here were of opinion the general had not the least business in bringing the Army to Skenesborough." Digby also felt that, "the victories of Fort Anne and Hubbardton served no visible advantages except proving the goodness of our troops at the expense of some brave

men." Lieutenant Digby felt that General Burgoyne should have returned to Fort Ticonderoga and from there, proceeded through Lake George. (See also Byrd, *Saratoga*, p. 54).

Yet, Lieutenant Digby erred. Though it was easy for Digby to write this, in actuality this was not the case.

According to Furneaux, p. 94, "there were insufficient [numbers of] horses and oxen both to drag the cannon overland and to pull the carts, and also to transport the boats across the portage at Ticonderoga and overland from Fort George to the Hudson. Ten to fifteen animals were required to drag each boat." According to Mr. Christopher Fox, Fort Ticonderoga's historian, the region's terrain in itself was very harsh. In 1777 (as presently), the so-called La Chute "River" between Lake George and Lake Champlain was no river. It was only a very narrow rock filled creek with an average water depth of, at best, one to three feet and, in many places, it was not even that deep. The trail traversing this creek would have to be widened and the trail going uphill to reach Lake George (over 200 feet in elevation over the La Chute River and Lake Champlain) was also very steep and would have to be widened. And the entire region was very thickly forested. (Personal discussion with Mr. Fox).

And Ward, *The War of the Revolution*, Vol. 1, p. 418, cites that "He [Burgoyne] did, however, decide to send his gunboats, his artillery, and his heavy stores in boats by way of Lake George to its head. That lake being more than 200 feet higher than Champlain, its waters descended through the narrow gorge that connected the two [lakes] in a series of falls and rapids in which boats could hardly be propelled. It was necessary to carry his bateaux and barges around by land about three miles, a very difficult and slow operation."

[17]Furneaux, *The Battle of Saratoga*, p. 94.

[18]Ketchum, *Saratoga. Turning Point*, p. 241. In the aftermath of the Revolutionary War, Skene submitted to the British ministry what he had lost as due compensation. Amongst his losses he cited 56,350 acres of land. See Donald Barr Chidsey, *The Loyalists*, p. 167.

[19]Furneaux, p. 94, cites "Colonel Skene persuaded Burgoyne, for his own ends, to rebuild the road, which would enhance the value of his property." But Furneaux also acknowledges "Burgoyne could not have chosen other than he did." (Ibid.). According to Cumming and Rankin, *The Fate of a Nation*, p. 145, "At Skenesborough, Burgoyne allowed himself to be persuaded by the loyalist Philip Skene, eager to improve his property, to hack a road through the wilderness to Fort Edward on the Hudson." Byrd, *Saratoga*, p. 54, cites that Skene "[Burgoyne's] loyalist advisor and host owned the lands along Wood Creek." Al-though a path or track did exist, "a good road would improve the value of his [Skene's] land." Byrd contends that "[Skene] may have influenced Burgoyne's decision in favor of the Wood Creek route" but "exactly how much he swayed Burgoyne is uncertain." Bancroft, *The American Revolution*, Vol. III,

p. 371, cites "Burgoyne should have turned back from Whitehall (Skenesborough), and moved to the Hudson River by way of Lake George and the old road." However, Stone, in *The Campaign*, p. 28, fn. 1, totally discredits the view "that Burgoyne chose the route to Fort Anne in order to oblige his friend Major Skene." Rather, Stone cites "Burgoyne was an honorable man. He probably simply erred in judgment." (Ibid.).

[20]So in the end, Burgoyne was forced to construct two separate roads. As acknowledged by Furneaux, "Burgoyne used both routes." (Ibid., p. 94).

Chapter 13: Bolstering Forces on Both Sides

[1]Bobrick, *Angel In the Whirlwind*, p. 259. Washington was born with the ability to sense a situation. He also possessed a strong strategic and tactical vision. In 1777, Washington was confident that even if the patriots suffered additional reversals in Pennsylvania and Philadelphia fell to the British, all of these reversals would be nothing compared with a patriot victory in the northern theater. And in his letters to Schuyler, Washington offered much strategic advice. Such as evidenced in the letter, "You mention their having a great number of horses, but they must nevertheless require a considerable number of wagons, as there are many things which cannot be transported on horses. They can never think of advancing without securing their rear, and the force with which they can act against you will be greatly reduced by detachments necessary for that purpose. And as they have to cut their passage and to remove the impediments you have thrown in their way before they can proceed, this circumstance, with the encumbrance they must feel in their baggage, stores, etc., will inevitably retard their march and give you good leisure and opportunity to prepare a good reception for them." (Ibid.).

[2]Bobrick, p. 254. General Washington was also very familiar with both the terrain and the combat conditions of the northern wilderness. Washington informed Schuyler that Burgoyne will be forced to drop off some personnel here and there along the way and he will be forced to garrison some forts. This, in turn, will weaken them and in due time, "Burgoyne's forces could not much soon exceed 5,000 [fighting] men." Likewise, their progress will be delayed by their baggage and artillery. "New roads need to be cut and clear the old roads." Washington also advised the Northern Army's high command that General Arnold should be deployed westward to Fort Stanwix and that a, "party [a military force of some sort] should be stationed in Vermont to keep them [the British] in continual anxiety in their rear." (Both of these measures were done). Washington also concluded that the entire British offensive in the north was being sub-divided into detachments. "One vigorous fall upon some one of these detachments might prove fatal to the whole expedition." Washington expressed to the New York Council that Burgoyne's success is temporary. "The worst effect of the loss of [Fort] Ticonderoga was the panic which it produced." Washington also wrote to various Generals in Massachusetts and Connecticut

urging them to dispatch about one-third of their militia for the Northern Army. (For Washington's predictions and assurances see Bancroft, *The American Revolution*, Vol. III, pp. 374-376).

[3]Scheer and Rankin, p. 292; Ketchum, *Saratoga*, pp. 279-280.

[4]Ketchum, *Saratoga,* pp. 246 and 248; Scheer and Rankin, *Rebels and Redcoats*, p. 292. Nixon's unit, which was located in the Highland's at Peekskill, arrived on 12 July. (Ketchum, p. 248).

[5]Scheer and Rankin, pp. 292 and 298; Ketchum, pp. 279-280.

[6]Ward, *The War of the American Revolution*, Vol. I, p. 424, cites 1,492 men. Scheer and Rankin, p. 298, cite 1,500; Lockie, *The Wars of America*, p. 172, cite "nearly 1,500 men."

[7]Scheer and Rankin, p. 298;Ward, *The War of the Revolution*, Vol. I, p. 424.

[8]Bobrick, p. 255; Ketchum, p. 297. Simultaneously, an "Alarm list" mobilizing all eligible men between 50 to 65 to stand-by was created. (Ibid.).

[9]Willcox, *Portrait of a General*, pp. 156-157. For the various views Howe presented see especially pp. 150-168. Howe even stated that in the event Washington moved northward and engaged Burgoyne, "I shall soon be after him to relieve you." Howe made this remark to Clinton in New York City to assure Clinton that he would return in time to assist Clinton. Needless to say, Clinton was not assured by Howe's words. See Willcox, *Portrait of a General*, fn. 9, pp. 166-167. See also pp. 158-160.

[10]Willcox, p. 155. Furthermore, according to Willcox, p. 158, "Clinton saw the situation, the British on Manhattan [New York City] had to achieve two things: prevent the rebels from detaching to the northward in enough force to stop Burgoyne short of Albany; and clear the Highlands."

[11]Bobrick, *Angel In the Whirlwind*, p. 255. Shortly afterwards, John Adams submitted another letter to his wife citing how "In the northern department they begin to fight."
See Scheer and Rankin, *Rebels and Redcoats*, pp. 293-294.

[12]Mostly they were Ottawa (or Ouatoais), Fox, Mississauga, and Chippewa.

[13]See Baxter, *The British Invasion From the North*, p. 68. As late as 26 May 1778, members of the English Parliament "accused Burgoyne of employing savages and sanc-tioning their barbarities... and maliciously destroying property on his march toward Albany." (Ibid.). According to Stone, *The Campaign*, pp. 357-358, "The march and counter march of this hostile army with its barbarous allies, had completely desolated the whole region hereabouts." According to Lossing, *Pictorial Field-Book of the American Revolution*, Vol. I, p. 73, "the English burned the houses they had occupied, and many other things which they could not carry away with them. They also wantonly set fire to several buildings on the way, by order of Burgoyne himself; ... [such as] the mansion of General Schuyler, his mills and other property,

amounting in value to twenty thousand dollars, were destroyed by them."

[14]In response to these attacks, many fled. Others, however, formed self-defense teams and organizations. As verified by an old account: "The inhabitants throughout this part of the country, having been much harassed by the Indians and tories, and in constant danger of their lives, were consequently under the necessity, for their own safety, of building, at different stations, what they termed block houses." (See Stone, *The Campaign,* p. 261. For a view and description of a block house, see pp. 261-262).

Chapter 14: Burgoyne Hacks His Way South

[1]Even for a modern day army with its bulldozers, heavy cranes, trucks, and power tools such as chain-saws, to construct a road through such difficult terrain would be no easy task. In fact, it would require a good number of days to complete.

[2]August Schlozer, a German officer serving with Burgoyne noted such within the American forces, "No regiment is to be seen in which there are not Negroes in abundance. And among them are able bodied, strong and brave fellows." See Briefwechsel (Gottingen: Vandenhoek, 1780-82), Vol. IV, p. 365. See also Edgar J. McManus, *A History of Negro Slavery in New York* (NY: Syracuse University Press, 1966), p. 157.

[3]In fact, the term may have even been coined in the Wilderness War of 1777.

[4]Scheer and Rankin, *Rebels and Redcoats*, p. 295; Bancroft, Vol. III, pp. 370-371.

[5]Bobrick, p. 258, cites that, "by the time Burgoyne had reached Fort Edward, his supply line extended over 185 miles." This is, indeed, a lengthy supply line.

[6]See also Bobrick, p. 256.

[7]Many authors have acknowledged that during this period Burgoyne did attempt to curb excesses. But he was unable to do so. Despite his orders forbidding all unnecessary killing and pillaging, in actuality many of the raids and attacks ended quite brutally. See Bobrick, *Angel in the Whirlwind*, p. 258; John Preston, *A Short History of the American Revolution,* pp. 234-235; Byrd, *Saratoga. Turning Point,* p. 56, cites "Burgoyne's Indian's had promised obedience to his rules, but violations had occurred." See also Scheer and Rankin, pp. 296-297. Lt. Colonel Mitchell and Sir Edward Creasy, *Twenty Decisive Battles,* pp. 203-204, cites "though Burgoyne labored hard to check the atrocities which they were accustomed to commit, he could not prevent the occurrence of many barbarous outrages, repugnant both to the feelings of humanity and to the laws of civilized warfare." Stone, p. 361, acknowledged Burgoyne became disgusted and, "laid restraints upon their dispositions to commit other enormities." According to Burgoyne, "these children of the wilderness did not render all the assistance that was expected of them." (Ibid. Numerous other pages cite the

various difficulties experienced by Burgoyne regarding atrocities). See also Ketchum, *Saratoga Turning Point,* pp. 269-271. According to Bancroft, Vol. III, p. 371, in early July 1777, Burgoyne confided to Germain in a message, "were the Indians left to themselves, enormities too horrid to think of would ensue; guilty and innocent, women and infants, would be a common prey."

[8]Ketchum, p. 279-280. In the meantime, as Burgoyne's army was clearing and hacking its way forward to reach Fort Edward and the Hudson River, the Indian-loyalist raids not only continued but, on occasion, rose in severity. Near Fort Edward, a strength of no less than 400 Indians, augmented with loyalists and English advisors, tangled with the 7th Massachusetts Continental Regiment. A brief but vicious battle ensued with casualties noted on both sides. In another incident, Major Daniel Whiting and his entire detachment became surrounded. Resisting furiously, they succeeded in holding out. To assist Whiting, Brigadier General Ebenezer Learned rushed in with 500 continental troops. A heavy downpour, however, put an end to that entire affair. Regardless, in those days, commanders such as General Learned and their troops skirmished frequently with raiders. From these engagements vital combat experiences were gained, lessons were learned, and the troops were toughened.

Unfortunately, military personnel were not just targeted. So too, were many civilians. Perhaps, a patriot paymaster summed it up best, "It is believed the Tories have sculp'd [scalped] many of their countrymen, as there is a premium from Burgoyne for sculps [scalps]. One hundred Indians in the woods do as much harm than a thousand British troops. They have been the death of many brave fellows."

[9]Ketchum, *Saratoga,* p. 251.

[10]Such as in Stark's unit.

[11]Willcox, p. 166. See also fn. 9.

[12]When Burgoyne received Howe's letter of 17 July 1777, Howe was no longer in New York City. Needless to say, after reading Howe's letter, Burgoyne was very distressed by it.

[13]Willcox, pp. 164-165.

[14]By mid-1777, the city's spy system was in full swing.

[15]Willcox, *Portrait of a General,* p. 157.

Chapter 15: The Tragic Case of Jane McCrea

[1]The Connecticut River originates in the Canadian Province of Quebec. It flows southward and divides New Hampshire from Vermont and flows through Massachusetts and Connecticut. One of the oldest and most historic towns which existed in 1777 on this river was Charlestown, New Hampshire.

[2]John Hakes would not be the only Hakes to serve. Six other Hakes: Solomon, Jonathan, Jr., George, Caleb, Richard, and James Hakes would serve with the patriots. Though the Hakes family hailed from Connecticut and large-

ly resided in the area of Stonington, they served in various New Hampshire, Connecticut, New York, and Rhode Island continental and militia units. Of interest is that James, who served in the Main Continental Army and fought at Trenton and Princeton in late 1777/early 1778, was a personal friend of General George Washington. Indeed, so close were the two men that Washington, when informed that James' wife was soon to give birth, requested that in the event a boy was born, that he be named after him. And so it was. James' son was named George Washington Hakes. (Letter of Major Gerry Messmer, U.S. Army, on 1 April 2003 to author). As for Major Messmer, he is a direct descendant of Solomon Hakes.

[3]For a lengthy version of what allegedly occurred see Stone, *The Campaign*, Appendix IV, pp. 302-313; and Elizabeth Ellet, *The Women of the American Revolution*, Vol. I, pp. 221-226; and Lossing, *The Pictorial Field-Book of the Revolution*, pp. 96-102.

According to Lieutenant Anburey, her death occurred during a dispute between two Indians escorting her back. "Suddenly one of them, fearful of losing the reward for bringing her safe into camp, most inhumanely struck his tomahawk into her skull and she instantly expired." (See Anburey, Travels Through the Interior Parts of America," Vol. I, pp. 219-220. See also Esmond Wright, *The Fire of Liberty!*, p. 100. For the famous picture of the painting depicting her being tomahawked see Fleming's, *Liberty!*, p. 252).

[4]Some allege that David Jones held the rank of Captain. See "Jane McCrea" in Ellet's, *The Women of the American Revolution*, Vol. I, pp. 223 and 226. In actuality, David was a lieutenant. It was his brother, Jonathan, who was a captain and Jonathan was also serving in Jessup's Corps at this time. See also Lossing, pp. 98-98.

[5]Jane's family actually sided with the patriots and, possibly, Jane herself was pro-patriot. Her oldest brother, John McCrea, was at the very moment serving as a colonel in the Northern Army. But since Jane was in love with David Jones, she opted to remain behind to soon join him.

[6]Some sources cite Standish's first name was Miles. See Furneaux, *The Battle of Saratoga*, p. 97.

[7]Others say she was tomahawked. See Scheer and Rankin, *Rebels and Redcoats*, p. 296.

[8]Wyandot Panther was a Huron whose real name was Le Loup.

[9]As for Jane McCrea, she is currently buried in Union Cemetery, not far from the town of Fort Edward. She was exhumed and reburied two times until a third, and final, formal burial of her remains finally took place in 1852. For more details on Jane McCrea see, "Fort Edward" in Boatner's, *Landmarks of the American Revolution*, p. 240.

[10]Lossing, *Pictorial Field-Book of the American Revolution*, p. 100, cites, "Lieutenant Jones, chilled in horror and broken in spirit by the event, tendered a resignation of his commission, but it was refused. He purchased the scalp of

his Jenny, and with this cherished memento deserted, with his brother, before the army reached Saratoga, and retired to Canada." (Ibid.). David Jones never married and lived his entire life in sadness and was "melancholy and taciturn." (Ibid., p. 101).

[11]Ward, Vol. I, p. 420; Williams, *The History of American Wars*, pp. 67-68; and Byrd, *Saratoga. Turning Point*, p. 56. According to Leckie, *The Wars of America*, p. 170, cites, "On 29 July, three weeks from the day he had landed at Skenesborough, Burgoyne reached Fort Edward. It had taken him three weeks to advance 23 miles, seven of which had been over uncontested water." Bobrick, *Angel In the Whirlwind*, p. 256, cites, "Burgoyne finally reached and took Fort Edward 30 July." (The actual date was, however, 29 July 1777).

As early as 1758-59, a European military observer named Kalm criticized both Forts Ticonderoga and Edward. "The fact is Fort Edward was not a strong position. They [Forts Edward and Ticonderoga] were the result of jobs badly located and badly built, with the design to put money into some favorite's pockets." Kalm's observations were also seconded by Major General Marquis de Chastellux, a French general. De Chastellux wrote: "Such is Fort Edward. So much spoken of in Europe. Although it could in no time have been able to resist 500 men, with four pieces of cannon." See Stone, *The Campaign*, Appendix, p. 343.

[12]*The Military Journals of Two Private Soldiers, 1758–1775, with Numerous Illustrative Notes* (Poughkeepsie: 1845), pp. 14-15. Although the Journal deals mostly with the French and Indian War strong references, usually in footnotes, are made to the Revolutionary War of 1775–1783.

[13]William Duer was a patriot, a close personal friend of General Schuyler, and a delegate representing New York State to the Continental Congress. With the approach of Burgoyne's army, his family fled southward to Albany. Prior to Burgoyne settling in, General Simon stayed in Duer's home as well. The house was also located near Fort Edward.

[14]At this time, Schuyler's strength in the vicinity of Fort Edward and at the Moses Kill stood at about 4,000. (Furneaux, *The Battle of Saratoga*, p. 89). Schuyler's strength also rose slightly with the incorporation of General St. Clair's continentals and militiamen retreating from Fort Ticonderoga. Of Schuyler's strength, about 3,000 were continentals. (Ibid.). Byrd, *Saratoga. Turning Point*, p. 57, does not cite a strength but acknowledges "Schuyler's army, badly disorganized, was still small."

[15]the *Military Journals of Two Private Soldiers, 1758–1775*, p. 15.

[16]Presently, the area is known as Schuylerville.

[17]Not to be confused with Manchester, New Hampshire.

[18]Scheer and Rankin, p. 297. According to these authors, it was Washington who dispatched Lincoln to take command of the New England militia. (Ibid.).

[19]The name derived from a little Dutch village which stood just a short dis-

tance from the bridge.

[20]The highest terrain which is found in Massachusetts lies in the northwestern region of that state. Vermont's famous "Green Mountains" also lie in the southern/southwestern portion of the state and from here, numerous brooks and streams feed the rivers such as the Hoosic which also flows through southwestern Vermont.

[21]Little White Creek was also known as White Creek. In 1777, a small settlement stood here. Currently, it is the Village of White Creek.

[22]By 1815, it was known as the Van Schaick Bridge. See Stone, *The Campaign,* Appendix, p. 298. Also named after a small Dutch settlement on the edge of the Hoosic River.

According to an account written in New York City at 12 Clinton Place on 25 July 1877 by a Mr. J. W. Richards to Mr. William Stone, the Walloomsac River on occasion was also known as the Bennington River. "The three streams—White creek, Walloomsac and Hoosick—unite near this bridge. The road passing over this bridge, was the great market road, leading to the North [Hudson] river, Albany, Halfmoon [Half-Moon], etc. A branch road left off in a northwesterly direction to Cambridge, Batten kil [Kill], Fort Edward, etc. At the point where the bridge spans the creek, there is a deep, narrow ravine, extending for a considerable distance above and below the bridge. Hence the bridge was important; indeed it was indispensable to Baum's marching army. It was a wooden bridge, covered with loose plank, not very long but very high." (Ibid., pp. 298-299). (For the battle which took place for this bridge and Eleazur Edgerton's role in it, see pp. 299-300).

[23]Stone, *The Campaign,* p. 258. Schroon Lake is to the west of lake Champlain and Fort Ticonderoga. A village named Schroon Lake lies on its northern shore.

[24]In the aftermath of the Wilderness War of 1777, when the loyalists faced banishment from the new nation, Colonel Cochran testified on behalf of the woman. Unfortunately, her name became lost. But her deeds are noted. And though her husband and his brothers fled to Canada, she stayed behind and ended up owning the farm.

As for Colonel Cochran, he prospered in business. One day, he accidentally came across the woman who, years earlier, had assisted him. Informed that she had fallen on hard times, Colonel Cochran rewarded her with a handsome sum of money. As for Colonel Cochran, he died in 1822, near Sandy Hill, Washington County. Because his family had a plot in the town now known as Fort Edward, he was buried there. Of interest is that his one-man spy mission originated from Fort Edward.

Chapter 16: The Battle of Bennington

[1]Furneaux, *The Battle of Saratoga,* p. 119; Scheer and Rankin, *Rebels and Redcoats,* p. 299, cite Baum commenced his operation on 11 August from a

camp he had established at Fort Miller. This date was also cited by General Von Riedesel in the aftermath of the Revolutionary War. Philip Lord, Jr., *War Over Walloomscoick. Land Use and Settlement Pattern on the Bennington Battlefield - 1777* (Albany, NY: State University of New York, 1989), p. 6, cites "By August 10th, Baum had reached fort Miller on the Hudson, south of Fort Edward, and turned eastward, leaving the Hudson Valley for the highlands of New England." Though Lord, Jr., is not explicit on the exact date, he does imply 11 August as the date of Baum's departure from Fort Miller. (Hereafter cited as *War Over Walloomscoick*).

[2]Boatner, p. 228; Fleming, *Liberty!* p. 247 cites 374 Germans, 300 loyalists and Canadians; and a sprinkling of Indians. Ketchum, *Saratoga*, p. 292, cites that when Baum set off from Fort Miller, he had around 650 troops. Furneaux, p. 120, cites a strength of "about 800 men." Of these 175 were dismounted dragoons; less than 200 German infantry; a squad of Hesse-Hanau artillerymen with two 3-pounders; 50 English marksmen; 300 tories (loyalists) and Canadians; and a small number of Indians. Musicians were also found (Ibid.). Lord, Jr., cites "a number of British marksmen, 150 Tories from Peter's Provincial Corps, some 56 Provincial and Canadian Volunteers, and over 100 Caughnawaga Mohawk Indians aligned with the British cause." See *War Over Walloomscoick*, p. 6. Lord, Jr., also acknowledged that "Baum hoped to augment [his force] from local Loyalist supporters en route." (Ibid.).

[3]Fleming, *Liberty!*, p. 247. Lord, Jr., p. 6, cites, "over 200 Brunswick Dragoons, originally a German mounted unit which was forced to march on foot for lack of the horses they were being sent to procure."

[4]Ketchum, p. 292.

[5]Ibid.

[6]Furneaux, pp. 118-119. Lord, Jr., *War Over Walloomscoick*, p. 6, cites, "As guide and advisor, Philip Skene of Skenesborough (now Whitehall), a prominent Loyalist of the region, was dispatched to assist Baum, who spoke no English."

[7]For a fairly detailed command structure see Ketchum, p. 292. Another loyalist officer serving Baum's force was Captain Francis Pfister. Of interest is that Pfister's nationality was German and he was born in Germany. At a young age, he joined the British Army and retired from that service on the North American continent. Always loyal to the King, Pfister quickly sided with the patriots. Pfister's rank has also been cited as being "colonel" but he never was in that rank.

[8]In "Thoughts..." Burgoyne even advocated reaching the Connecticut Valley and occupying it to await a thrust from Rhode Island. "Should the junction between the Canada and Rhode Island armies be affected upon the Connecticut, it is not too sanguine an expectation that all the New England provinces will be reduced by their operations." (See Mackesy, *The War for America, 1775-1783*, p. 114. See also pp. 115 and 132. See also Willcox,

Portrait of a General, Sir Henry Clinton, p. 150; and Luzader, p. 9.

[9]Mackesy. P. 114; and Luzader, p. 9.

[10]These would include the loyalists, Canadians, German and English light troops.

[11]These distances are straight line distances. By themselves, they are long distances.

[12]For the entire "Instructions to Lieutenant-Colonel Baum on a Secret Expedition to the Connecticut River" see Stone, *The Campaign*, Appendix, pp. 277-285. Burgoyne's instructions were lengthy with much detail.

[13]Ketchum, p. 292, cites their strength at "about 150 men."

[14]Pfister actually entered the colonies and the wilderness region with Burgoyne. But several days before the battle of Bennington, he departed Burgoyne's army to gather up additional loyalists.

[15]Covel hailed from Cambridge.

[16]Dupuy, *Encyclopedia of Military History*, cites, "700 Brunswickers under Colonel Friedrich Baum." Along with the English, loyalists, Canadians and Indians, Baum clearly possessed a fighting strength of well over 800 if not close to 950. However, Ketchum, p. 292, cites, "along the way to his destination Baum picked up what may have amounted to 500 or more Tories, giving him a strength of nearly 1,200 men."

[17]Stone, *The Campaign*, Appendix, p. 281. Needless to say, Baum would not be able to enforce this rule. Both the loyalists and Indians committed atrocities. On 14 August 1777, Baum wrote to Burgoyne "they could not be controlled." Bancroft, *The American Revolution*, Vol. III, p. 281. Of interest is that prior to Baum's dispatch, Burgoyne had already written to both Germain and Howe voicing a strong criticism of the Native warriors. See "Burgoyne to Germain," 11 July 1777 and "Burgoyne to Howe," 6 August 1777. (See Bancroft, pp. 381-382).

[18]Ketchum, p. 296. By now, much of the civilian population was fleeing in the wake of the enemy advance. Some people even buried their valuable items prior to fleeing. "The cattle and livestock of all descriptions were driven off into Vermont." The famous German army physician, Doctor Wasmus, himself witnessed this flight. In the vicinity of Walloomscoick, Dr. Wasmus recorded what he saw, "The inhabitants had two wagons loaded with furniture, each with six oxen harnessed to them, about to be carted away and take flight in the Wilderness." (Dr. Wasmus' entry was made on 14 August 1777 in his personal journal). For the hardships experienced and the efforts made to flee and save personal belongings and livestock see Lord, Jr., *War Over Walloomscoick*, pp. 119-122. Page 122 also depicts a clear 19th century painting of "battlefield refugees" fleeing in a wagon pulled by six oxen.

[19]Ketchum, pp. 296-297. Lord, Jr., *War Over Walloomscoick*, pp. 6-9 cites various instances of skirmishing between Baum's force and the patriots.

[20]Ketchum. 297.

[21]Furneaux, p. 115, cites 8 a.m. As for Sancoick, it has also been spelled as San Coick. Currently, it is known as North Hoosick. In 1777, Sancoick was located in Rensselaer County which bordered on Washington County to its north and Bennington County to its east. The entire Battle of Bennington was actually fought in Rensselaer County; however, a portion of Colonel Nichols' encircling movement was undertaken through the southern portion of Washington County. Presently, Rensselaer and Washington Counties are in New York State (as they were in 1777) and Bennington County is in Vermont State which, in 1777, existed not as a state but as a separate nation.

[22]Ward, *The War of the Revolution*, Vol. I, p. 425, cites that prior to entering Sancoick, Baum had "several light skirmishes with small parties of the local militia." (Ibid.).

[23]Stone, *The Campaign*, p. 300. By now, Baum was battling Colonel Gregg's 200 militiamen. See also Lord, Jr., p. 120.

[24]Ward, Vol. I, p. 425, cites, "They [the Americans] broke down a bridge." Furneaux, p. 121, cites, "a volunteer from Bennington, Eleazer Edgerton, delayed Baum's advance for an hour by staying behind with two companies to break down the bridge. This they accomplished under heavy fire."

[25]Scheer and Rankin, p. 300. This letter was written on the head of a barrel used as a desk. Lord, Jr., *War Over Walloomscoick*, p. 7, cites the letter was written on "Aug. 14, 1777, 9 o'clock." Baum wrote, "They [the patriots] broke down the bridge, which has retarded our march about an hour." Baum, however, soon succeeded in capturing the nearby mill and reported to Burgoyne, "They left in the mill about seventy-eight barrels of very fine flour, one thousand bushels of wheat, twenty barrels of salt, and about one thousand pounds' worth of pearl and potatoes." (Ibid.) (Though captured, none of these supplies ever reached Burgoyne's army). Baum also cited a strength of "fifteen to eighteen hundred men are in Bennington." (Ibid. For Baum's entire letter, see p. 7).

[26]Scheer and Rankin, p. 300; Lord, Jr., p. 7.

[27]Luzader, p. 28. Luzader also cites, "the two forces met... where a small bridge crossed the alloomsac." (Ibid.). Luzader, however, incorrectly cites the date was 15 August when, in actuality, it was 14 August. Furneaux, p. 122, cites, "Baum continued his pursuit of Greg's men, reaching to within four miles of Bennington before nightfall."

[28]Ketchum, p. 301; Boatner, p. 229, cites "about 150 of his [Baum's] men, most of the Tories, constructed a hasty fortification that became known as the "Tory" redoubt." Furneaux, p. 124, also cites a strength of 150.

[29]Hence its name because it was a tory (loyalist) redoubt position.

[30]Ward, Vol. I, p. 426, cites, "more than a half-a-mile." See also map on p. 427. Including the outposts and where the Indians were positioned, Baum's entire area would have covered a distance of at least three quarters of a mile.

[31]Ketchum, pp. 300-301.

[32]Ibid., p. 300.

[33]Furneaux, p. 124.

[34]Ibid.

[35]Ward, Vol. I, p. 429, cites "642 men and two fieldpieces." Ward also cites Von Breymann departed at 8 o'clock. Furneaux, p. 123, cites Von Breymann possessed a strength of 550 and two 6-pound cannons. Cobb, *American Battlefields*, p. 51, cites a strength of 642. Boatner, p. 230, cites "about 650 slow-moving German grenadiers, chasseurs, riflemen, and two cannons." Byrd, *Saratoga. Turning Point*, p. 64, cites 550; and Scheer and Rankin, p. 302, also cite 550. The authors also cite that Von Breymann was in the rank of Lieutenant-Colonel. Fleming, *Liberty!*, p. 249, also cites Von Breymann was a Lieutenant-Colonel in rank with a strength of "800 men, most of them Germans." Morris, *Encyclopedia of American History*, p. 97, cites 650 troops; and Dupuy, *Encyclopedia of Military History*, p. 714, cites, "Reinforcements for 650 Brunswickers under Colonel Heinrich von Breymann, arriving later that day..."

[36]According to Byrd, p. 65, "Warner's regiment got within six miles of Stark before halting for the night."

[37]Furneaux, p. 123. Ward, Vol. I, p. 429, cites, "The heavily uniformed and equipped Germans were notoriously slow in movement. They had twenty-five miles to go. In rigid, regular formation, halting frequently to re-dress their ranks, they progressed at the rate of half a mile an hour, making only eight miles that day."

[38]Furneaux, p. 125. For Stark's plan of attack, see also p. 125; Ward, Vol. I, p. 426; Byrd, p. 65; and Ketchum, p. 307. For a specific breakdown of Stark's and his commanders' movements with arrows and graphics see Lord, Jr., pp. 10-12. For an entire detailed portrayal of Colonel Gregg's reconnaissance and Baum's movements see p. 8. Stark's men also moved around Baum's entire force very cautiously. To cite an example: those selected to attack the Dragoon redoubt, "marched across the [Walloomsac] river by a circuitous route of five or six miles, mostly through the woods, with all possible silence and brought them up in a piece of woods at the enemy's rear." (See Lord, Jr., *War Over Walloomscoick*, p. 65). Colonel Herrick's column moved through such dense woods that they actually could barely see one another. (See p. 66).

[39]Throughout the battle, Stark fought solely on foot. Paintings and drawn illustrations of Stark sitting on a horse in a continental army uniform and holding up a sword toward the enemy are incorrect. In fact, on that day, Stark did not possess a sword. He was armed with a rifle (not a musket), a short hunting knife, and a tomahawk. His head was adorned with a black floppy hat with a brown star depicting a general's rank exhibited on its front. For clothing he wore buckskin type pants and a buckskin smock. A wide leather belt with a metal buckle tightened his smock and the tomahawk was inserted into it in the front. Heavy woolen socks with moccasin type ankle boots characterized his footwear. (As for the star, it was a gift from his wife Molly who always

knew that soon, he would make general).

[40]Stark personally reported this to the commander of the Northern Army, General Gates, in October, 1777. Undoubtedly the massive battlefield noise unnerved the Canadians and Indians to the point of fleeing rapidly out of the area. According to Cobb, *American Battlefields*, p. 51, "Baum's Canadian and Indian auxiliaries proved worthless as they fled at the first sound of enemy musket fire." Lord, Jr., p. 65, cited this to the fact that "the Indians were thrown into confusion... they made but a faint resistance, and then fled with precipitancy."

[41]Ketchum, p. 319. As acknowledged by Ketchum, Colonel Warner continued to serve.

[42]Furneaux, p. 129. Ketchum, p. 314, cites, "an advance guard of sixty grenadiers and chasseurs plus a score of jagers." With this, Ketchum implies a strength of over 60.

[43]Furneaux, p. 129, cites 4 p.m.; Luzader, p. 30, cites "Breymann's column reached Van Schaick's Mill at 4:30 p.m." It is known that somewhere around 4:30 p.m. Von Breymann's spearhead finally reached Sancoick. Shortly afterwards, Von Breymann himself appeared with the main body and pushed on.

[44]Ketchum, p. 315.

[45]Surely, Stark must have been in a high state of anxiety. See also Luzader, p. 31; and Ward, Vol. I, p. 429.

[46]Fleming, p. 249, cites "Seth Warner's continentals were backed by some 200 Green Mountain Boys." Ward, Vol. I, p. 430, cites, "the rest of Warner's regiment, 130 men led by Lieutenant-Colonel Safford, and 200 rangers, had made a long day's march until midnight." (As for Safford, at this time he was in the rank of major). Byrd, p. 66, cites, "Warner's 350-man regiment, having made an unhurried march to the scene, arrived at a crucial moment." Of interest is her comment "unhurried march." In actuality, Warner's men did push hard to get to the scene.

[47]Morris, *Encyclopedia of American History*, p. 97; Fleming, *Liberty!*, p. 249.

[48]See also Robert Furneaux, *The Pictorial History of the American Revolution* (Chicago: J.G. Ferguson Publishing Co., 1973), p. 161; and Furneaux, *Battle of Saratoga,* p. 131; Cobb, *American Battlefield*, p. 52; Ward, Vol. I, p. 431; Scheer and Rankin, p. 303; and Bobrick, *Angel in the Whirlwind*, p. 260. Long after the battle, German dead were still being found. As recalled by eyewitness Peter Clark, "... we do not know how many we have killed, our scouts daily find them in the woods." (See Lord, Jr., p. 70). This was, indeed, for Burgoyne a very heavy loss.

[49]Ward, Vol. I, p. 431; Cobb, p. 521; Lossing, *The Empire State*, p. 269 cites, "about seven hundred of them became prisoners."

[50]Ward, Vol. I, p. 431.

[51]Furneaux, p. 131; Leckie, *The Wars of America*, p. 173; and Boatner, p. 230.

[52]Scheer and Rankin, pp. 303-304.

[53]Ibid. Nor did it include the Indian loss. In late 1778, Corne St. Luc acknowledged in Canada that at Bennington, of the 150 committed Indians, "a large number of savages had perished on the battlefield with their redoubtable chief." (See Stone, *The Campaign*, Appendix, pp. 366-377). And the Canadians took some losses as well. How many Canadians perished is not known but it is known that they, too, took some casualties. According to Corne St. Luc, "of sixty-one Canadians [committed to Bennington], forty-five only escaped death." (Ibid., p. 367).

In 1778 Burgoyne, now back in England, was known to be very critical of the Indian performance. Such was evidenced on 26 May 1778 in the House of Commons in front of the English Parliament. Upon hearing of Burgoyne's criticism back in Canada, St. Luc responded with, "a very vigorous letter, dated at Quebec, October 23, 1778, which appeared in French, in the London papers." (Stone, Appendix, p. 365). In his letter, St. Luc charged that, "Burgoyne destroyed [meaning Burgoyne himself destroyed] one of the finest armies that had come into the country." (Ibid., p. 366). As for the criticism of the Indians, St. Luc cited, "Burgoyne refused them [the Indians] provisions, shoes, and the services of an interpreter," and "that if the Indians had little by little deserted the English army, it was because Burgoyne had not given them enough attention, nor taken sufficient care of them. In the affair at Bennington, August 16, 1777, when several hundred of the English were killed or taken prisoners, among whom were a good number of savages, the Indians were astonished to see, for instance, that Burgoyne sent no detachment to rally the stragglers of the vanquished body, or to succor the wounded, of which many died." (Ibid. pp. 366-367). As for Burgoyne's allegations that St. Luc also deserted (in the aftermath of Bennington St. Luc did return to Canada with some Indians without Burgoyne's knowledge or consent), St. Luc claims that Burgoyne actually, "asked me to return to Canada, bearing dispatches to General Carleton praying to his Excellency to treat the Indians with kindness, and to send them back to you." St. Luc also added that he wanted to rejoin the army, "had not the communications been interrupted [between him and Burgoyne]." (Ibid., p. 367). Though acknowledging to be "sixty-seven years" of age, St. Luc cited he is still willing to, "cross the ocean to justify myself before the king, my master, and before my country, from the ill-founded accusation that you [Burgoyne] have brought against me, although I do not care at all what you personally think of me." (Ibid., pp. 367-368). For much of what St. Luc wrote, see pp. 366-368.

Burgoyne's criticism of the Canadians was also very severe. (See Stone, Appendix, pp. 363-364). In response, a former Canadian participant named Garneau said, "This general [Burgoyne], wished to throw the blame upon the Canadians; but in his army of eight thousand men, there were but one hundred and fifty [Canadian] combatants from our province." (Ibid., p. 364).

⁵⁴Luzader, p. 31. Fleming, p. 249, cites, "Bennington cost Burgoyne more than 1,000 men."

⁵⁵Bobrick, p. 260. Preston, *A Short History of the American Revolution*, p. 196, cites, "400 Hessian dead or wounded." In the following days and weeks, more German bodies would be found throughout the entire region.

⁵⁶In the aftermath of Lieutenant-Colonel Pfister's death and the decimation of his unit, the few who survived were reorganized again. The unit was now commanded by Captain Samuel MacKay, also a participant of the Bennington battle. See *Captain MacKay and the Loyal Volunteers*, p. 3. But Stephen G. Strach, *Some Sources for the Study of the Loyalist and Canadian Participation in the Military Campaign of Lieutenant-General John Burgoyne 1777*," p. 6, cites a Captain Daniel MacAlpine took command following "Colonel" Pfister's death. Possibly, MacAlpine did. But soon, MacAlpine and the survivors of Pfister's so-called "Unnamed Company" were incorporated into MacKay's Loyal Volunteers who, at Bennington, also took heavy losses. As for Lieutenant-Colonel Peters (soon promoted to Colonel and probably only so as a desperate measure by Burgoyne to keep him in place), Peters was lightly wounded. (In Canada, some loyalist deserters actually informed his wife that Peters had been killed at Bennington). Regardless, all four loyalist units: "The Queen's;" "The King's;" "The Loyal Volunteers;" and the "Unnamed Company" referred frequently to as "Pfister's Unit," took very heavy losses at Bennington.

⁵⁷Captain F. Montague, who took part in Burgoyne's 1777 campaign, declared to the House of Commons on 1 June 1779, "that many savages quitted the army at different times after the defeat at Bennington." (See Stone, *The Campaign*, Appendix, p. 367, fn. 1).

⁵⁸See also Stone, *The Campaign*, p. 361. For an interesting view of Burgoyne's sentiment towards his Indians see Lieutenant Anburey's account in Stone, Appendix, pp. 361-363.

⁵⁹Furneaux, *The Pictorial History of the American Revolution*, p. 173.

⁶⁰Leckie, p. 173; Cobb, *American Battlefields*, p. 51.

⁶¹Within several days, Stark posted a twenty dollar reward either for the recovery of his horse and/or the arrest of the horse thief. Though the word was put out far and wide and several newspapers even ran advertisements, the horse and saddle were never recovered.

⁶²Shortly afterwards, he passed away. Doctor Wasmus learned of his death on 13 September 1777.

⁶³Ketchum, p. 326. Although Colonel Seth Warner's actions were noble, it was not reflective of the overall character of the American behavior. On 3 October 1782, Lieutenant Michael Bach, who was one of the artillerymen captured at Bennington, wrote a letter to his Prince in Germany citing that he had not only been robbed, but "completely plundered" in Bennington, and until his final release in 1782, he experienced hardships in Massachusetts, Pennsylvania,

and New Jersey. Lieutenant Bach was frequently fed poor food (he referred to it as "Negro food") and was moved around through various provinces with poor quarters and other necessities. Although via a truce the prisoners were provided some money on and off, the Americans had a habit of overcharging them for anything which they attempted to purchase. The lieutenant was also critical of Sir Henry who, in October 1778, fell through with his efforts in having them exchanged. For Lieutenant Bach this was, indeed, a hard time. (See Bruce Burgoyne, *Enemy Views. The American Revolutionary War As recorded by the Hessian Participants*, pp. 193-194).

[64]Philip Katcher, *The American Provincial Corps, 1775-1784*, p. 11. Later on, the state government ordered the loyalists to be utilized in clearing the deep snow off the roads. Despite the fact that most were clad in summer clothing, had thin footwear and, in some cases, were even barefoot, no concern was shown for this. Under such conditions, loyalists sickened and died.

[65]Pearson, *Those Damned Rebels. The American Revolution As Seen Through British Eyes*, p. 265.

[66]Ketchum, p. 325.

[67]On 19 August, the German-English prisoners began their march to Boston. En-route, they were provided provisions. Reaching Boston, Dr. Wasmus resided and even practiced medicine there until his departure back to Canada in late, 1781. Two years later, in 1783, he finally returned to his native land of Germany.

As for the Battle of Bennington, the famed British military historian John Fortescue cited that it was a mortal blow against the British. "A stronger man [than Burgoyne] might indeed have retreated, whatever his instructions, after the reverse at Bennington." It was also reported that, "when Washington heard of Bennington, he regarded it as deciding the fate of Burgoyne and dismissed from his mind all further anxiety about this invasion [from Canada]." See Lord, Jr., p. 5.

[68]Rear Admiral Furlong and Commodore McCandless, *So Proudly We Hail: The History of the United States Flag*, p. 105. See "The Battle of Bennington" in pp. 105-107.

[69]Ward, Vol. I, p. 431; Ketchum, p. 327. On the following day, 5 October, President John Hancock wrote directly to Stark informing and congratulating him on his promotion. Ward cites that this was a unanimous decision.

Chapter 17: Schuyler Relieved of Command

[1]Eckert, *The Wilderness War*, p. 149; Bancroft, Vol. III, p. 376, cites, "by 14 August Schuyler moved his Army to the first island in the mouth of the Mohawk River.

[2]Furlong and McCandless, *So Proudly We Hail*, p. 107. According to Colonel (Ret'd) Downey, *Indian Wars of the U.S. Army*, p. 9, "militia rallied to the support of the Continental regiments of the Northern Army, demoralized

by retreat and defeat since Ticonderoga."

[3]Numerous historians have acknowledged this fact. See "North America: New World Warriors" in David E. Jones, *Women Warriors. A History* (Virginia: Brassey's, 2000), pp. 220-229. According to Jones, p. 224, "North American women were routinely involved with [Revolutionary Continental] armies in the field. Indeed, with the constant manpower shortages, sustaining Washington's armies in the field or in garrison would have been impossible without them." One can even take the example of the Battle of Bennington. At the very moment when Nathaniel Lawrence, a local resident, was serving and fighting with Stark's unit, his wife Mrs. Lawrence was involved in a massive relief operation. Such women assisted and fed the hundreds of refugees who had fled in Baum's advance, baked much bread, drove supply wagons and, in the aftermath of the battle, took care of the wounded and injured. Their efforts made it easier for Stark to conduct his military operations; it reduced panic, raised the morale of both the military and civilian populace, helped to maintain a somewhat normal environment within an invaded region and saved lives. The women even gathered up all of the little children who somehow had become separated from their families and until they were reunited with their families, were housed and cared for.

[4]In a sense, the Northern Army was the Congressional Congress' "private army."

[5]Harrison, *Battles of the Republic*, p. 69; Luzader, p. 36; Admiral Furlong and Commodore McCandless, *So Proudly We Hail*, p. 107; Furneaux, p. 146; and Scheer and Rankin, p. 311.

[6]Philip John Schuyler, however, returned in a number of days and began to assist the Northern Army in whatever way he could. (Though relieved of command, he still maintained his rank of General). As acknowledged by James A. Huston, *The Sinews of War: Army Logistics*, p. 56, "Though naturally disappointed at being relieved of command, Schuyler was not one to sulk in his tent and he offered to give what service he could in any capacity. Back in Albany, he collected lead from the windows and roofs of the city to make the musket balls Gates' army so badly needed. At his own expense, he also sent lumber to built a pontoon bridge for retreat to the east side of the Hudson should that become necessary." In the aftermath of the Wilderness War of 1777, Schuyler demanded a Congressional review of his performance and, he was acquitted of the charges. By now, most agreed that Fort Ticonderoga could not have been effectively defended in consideration of various factors and, under very difficult conditions, Schuyler had actually performed superbly. Many individuals also testified positively on his behalf. On 19 April 1779, General Schuyler resigned his commission though he remained as one of Washington's best friends and advisors. A true admirer of Native Americans, he served the new nation as the Commissioner for Indian Affairs.

Of interest to note is that when Schuyler used to hunt with Native

Americans in the wilderness, though he was a reservist in the British army, it was they who first inspired Schuyler that British rule must end on the North American continent. See *The Papers of Sir William Johnson,* Vol. II, pp. 699 and 702. In a report dated from "Oneida April 7th. 1757" and submitted by Thomas Butler who was a strong advocate of the King and during the Revolutionary War was a strong loyalist along with his relative Colonel John Butler, Thomas Butler warned Sir Johnson that it was brought to his attention that an Indian is instigating Philip Schuyler against English rule. As Butler wrote to Sir Johnson, "To acquaint you what passed between Lieut. Schuyler and a young Onondaga Indian as they were out Shooting [hunting] Together. The Indian knowing him to be of Dutch Extrackt [extraction or nationality] began to Speak words reflecting on the Engilish and told Schuyler it wou'd be Good that the Albany people or Dutch with the Indjans Shou'd joyn & drive the Engilish out of the Country. Schuyler Says he was Surpris'd To hear the fellow talk in that manner & turning To him Said we are all people and under one King." Regardless, though at that time Schuyler held a loyalty to the English Crown, in the near future it would diminish; undoubtedly, the Indians continued to exert their influence upon Schuyler. And, of course, Schuyler was always grateful for their service in his Northern Army especially during the critical year of 1777.

In the aftermath of 1781, Schuyler returned to his estate, rebuilt the burned down buildings and until his death in 1804, remained active in business and regional politics, even serving two terms as a United States Senator. For more on Schuyler and how, "throughout his public career he was conspicuous for his great abilities, his staunch patriotism, and his unselfish devotion to duty," see Joseph Laffan Morse, *Funk and Wagnalls Standard Reference Encyclopedia* (NY: Standard Reference Works Publishing Co., Inc., 1958) (Reprinted), Vol. 21, p. 7860.

[7]This view was expressed by General Nathaniel Greene. See Ketchum, *Saratoga,* p. 337.

According to Colonel William A. Ganoe, "Just when Schuyler had successfully built up optimism from depression and was gaining adequate numbers, Congress decided on the brilliant scheme of sending the subtle Gates to take over the northern command." See *The History of the United States Army,* p. 46. See also pp. 46-47.

[8]Baxter, pp. 24-25.

[9]Ibid.

[10]For an interesting account of the ordeals of German soldiers, including how they were recruited, see "The Germans Are Coming!" in Fleming's, *Liberty!,* pp. 192-193.

[11]Fleming, pp. 192-193.

[12]In the aftermath of the British surrender at Saratoga in October, 1777, Von Riedesel would be a strong critic of Burgoyne. As for his wife, Frederika

Charlotte Louise von Massow-Riedesel, she would be a strong defender of the American cause. And when she gave birth to another daughter, she named her "Amerika" (America).

[13]Ketchum, p. 346.

[14]Ibid.

[15]Ibid., p. 337.

[16]As anticipated by Gates, Burgoyne would make a last ditch-effort to cross the Hudson River.

[17]This bridge spanned the Hudson River about 2 miles above the present day town of Schuylerville just below the Saratoga Falls and about 4 miles south of Fort Miller . (See Stone, *The Campaign*, p. 37, fn. 1). The bridge stood between present day Thomson and Clark Mills and Northumberland. Northumberland is located on the western bank of the Hudson River; Thomson and Clark Mills are located on the eastern bank of the Hudson River. At this time the British also constructed some fortification, "entrenchments three hundred feet in length and from four to six feet high" to protect the army in its crossing of the river. Many decades later, these positions were still visible. (Ibid.).

[18]Eventually, however, many of the captured soon ended up on the infamous prison ships only to languish till death. And many of the survivors developed lifetime health problems as a result of their incarceration.

[19]Such a case was also reported to Burgoyne: a loyalists wife, after being informed that her husband had been killed-in-action, was repeatedly violated sexually by a crowd of patriot men in front of her child. On the following day, she died from the physical abuse.

[20]General Gates also abhorred scalping and, along with dueling, forbade it in the Northern Army.

[21]Dale Van Every, *A Company of Heroes: The American Frontier, 1775-1783* (NY: William Morris and Company, 1962), p. 123. General Washington also received a copy of Pickering's letter.

[22]Stone, *The Campaign*, p. 37; Byrd, Saratoga. *Turning Point*, p. 82; Ward, Vol. II, p. 13; and Ketchum, p. 342.

[23]Stone, *The Campaign*, p. 41; and Byrd, 82.

[24]Now known as Coveville, a small village.

[25]Ketchum, p. 354. This sizable position was established adjacent the trench between the River Road and the Hudson River. Almost 2 miles to its north was Mill Creek where, some breastworks and a battery were also established overlooking the creek. In the event the patriots would have to retire from Mill Creek and retreat back down the road, they would fall into the U-shaped position. As mentioned, it was a three-sided position. Cannoneers would be able to fire into three directions: westward toward the eastern slope of Bemis Heights as well as onto the slope itself, northward, and eastward into the Hudson River as well as onto its eastern shoreline and road across the river. In

the event this position should be encircled from behind, some cannons would be turned around to fire southward toward the intersection and the Bemis Tavern. One of the missions of this U-shaped position was also to protect the open ground from the base of the eastern slope of Bemis Heights to the cliffs overlooking the Hudson River. (For its position, see Ketchum, p. 361).

[26]In the aftermath of the Hubbardton Battle, the remnants of this brigade were temporarily commanded by Colonel George Reid, also a New Hampshire commander and regimental commander. Soon, General Enoch Poor, likewise a native of New Hampshire and veteran of Fort Ticonderoga, assumed command. When this happened, Reid returned to command his original regiment but remained in the brigade.

[27]For the rank structure and various positions held Scheer and Rankin, pp. 313-315; Ward, Vol. II, p. 506; and Ketchum, pp. 395-397; and Lossing, *Pictorial Field-Book of the Revolution*, pp. 49-50. Lattimer is also cited as being a militia commander. Stone also cites an Oliver Wolcott, a militia commander, as being in the army.

[28]Scheer and Rankin, p. 320. See also Preston, p. 238.

[29]Scheer and Rankin, p. 320.

[30]From the period of 15 September until Burgoyne's surrender, desertions were noted every day. English and German personnel were also among those deserting.

[31]Lossing, *The Pictorial History of the American Revolution,* p. 59, cites the Indians, "joined the republican [Northern] army within three days after the battle of the 19th." Among these Indians were a number who just recently had served in the western theater of the Wilderness War. The famed warrior Honyery, who fought so bravely at the Battle of Oriskany, was one of those.

[32]In 1776, Issac Franks joined Colonel John Lasher's New York Volunteer Regiment. He fought at Long Island, retreated into New York City but there, was captured. Some months later, he managed to escape. Locating a leaking boat, at night he crossed the Hudson River to New Jersey. Heading north, he avoided British patrols and in the Highlands, joined the Northern Army. Posted to the quartermaster department, he served and fought in the vicinity of West Point throughout 1777 and following the Wilderness War, he remained there for four more years. He ended the war as an ensign in the 7th Continental Massachusetts Regiment. For more on Frank's see also Jacob Radus Marcus, *United States Jewry, 1776-1985* (Michigan: Wayne University Press, 1989), Vol. I, pp. 67 and 98.

[33]Gathering up his family, the Torah Scrolls, certain holy objects, prayer books and candle sticks, Rabbi Seixas fled as General Washington retreated from the city. Fleeing to Stratford, Connecticut, the rabbi continued his spiritual work and rendered support to the Northern Army. Deborah Pessin, *History of the Jews in America* (NY: The United Synagogue Press of America, 1957), pp. 91-92.

[34]For an interesting account of Solomon's exploits see "Dollars For Freedom" in Lowell Thomas and Berton Bradley, *Stand Fast for Freedom* (Philadelphia, Pa.: The John C. Winston Company, 1940), Chapter XIII, pp. 124-133; Pessin, *History of the Jews in America*, pp. 92-93; and Marcus, *United States Jewry*, pp. 67-68.

[35]In fact, as acknowledged by various historians, soldiers of numerous ethnicities and nationalities served in the various continental armies and navy during the Revolutionary War. See also Willard S. Randall, *George Washington*, pp. 341-344.

[36]Lossing, *The Pictorial Field-Book of the American Revolution*, p. 50.

[37]For Burgoyne's chief officers see Lossing, *Pictorial Field-Book of the American Revolution*, p. 50. According to Lossing, "they were men of tried courage, and ardently attached to their general and the service." (Ibid.).

Chapter 18: The Patriots Raid Fort Ticonderoga

[1]Pawlet, Vermont, is about 15 miles to the northwest of Manchester, Vermont.

[2]Ketchum, p. 376.

[3]In early 1777, Colonel Brown confided to some of his close associates that although General Arnold was a very capable commander, Arnold is always in need of a large sum of money. "Money is this man's God, and to get enough of it he would sacrifice his country," Brown said. Needless to say, Brown's prophecy soon proved to be correct. See also Ketchum, p. 377.

[4]Ward, Vol. II, p. 523.

[5]Presently, a West Pawlet exists and it is within Vermont almost on the New York-Vermont border. The patriot raiders also went through this area.

[6]Ward, Vol. II, p. 523. According to Ketchum, p. 378, 118 American's were released. From among the enemy prisoners 12 were British officers, 143 were sergeants, corporals, and privates and 119 were Canadian personnel for a total of 274. The greater percentage of the British prisoners was from the 53rd Foot Regiment; however, Ketchum also acknowledges that, "they [the raiders] seized a group of naval officers and men." (Ibid.). It appears that these naval personnel were not in the count of 274 because in all, 325 prisoners were taken back to Vermont.

[7]Ketchum, p. 379.

[8]22 September is the date Colonel Brown cited in a report he wrote from, "Skeensboro Friday, 11 o'clock, a.m. Sept 26th 1777." For his entire report see Stone, *The Campaign*, Appendix, pp. 351-352. As for his date, it was correct. However, it was not a "Sabbath Day" [Sunday] as stated by Brown but rather, 22 September was a Monday.

[9]Ibid., 351. As for Diamond Island, it was named after the numerous fake but beautiful crystal diamonds found all over the island.

[10]Ibid., p. 351.

[11]Ibid.

[12]Ibid., p. 346; *The Military Journals of Two Private Soldiers*, pp. 24-25; as well as Colonel Brown's personal report in Stone, Appendix, pp. 351-352, verify the island's defenders were a mixed German-British force and that the raiders attacked Diamond Island on 24 September. Two British companies from the 47th Foot were positioned upon this island.

[13]This time was cited by Brown as being the "Time I advanced." (Ibid., p. 351). Shortly after, he reached Diamond Island.

[14]Ibid., p. 351.

[15]Stone, *The Campaign*, pp. 352-352. Soon after, in his letter to General Lincoln, Brown cited, "The attack on the Island continued with interruption 2 Hours" (Ibid., p. 352) and Brown acknowledged that, "I had two men killed, two mortally wounded and several others wounded." (Ibid., pp. 351-352).

[16]Of interest to note is that for some unknown reason, General Lincoln and the Northern Army high command did not regard the ranger operation as a huge success. Afraid that it could even backfire on the patriots and bolster British morale, they ordered that the operation be kept a secret. No word was to leak out to the public.

But the 1,500 brave rangers who participated in the operation talked and bragged about their exploits. And when some of the British and Canadian prisoners were released and returned home to Canada, they also talked. Within weeks, the entire region of New England was aware of it. Lincoln's plan, and Colonel Brown's execution of it, raised tremendously the morale of the patriots, induced more fear and uncertainty into the loyalists and drove neutrals into the ranks of the patriots. Even Burgoyne himself soon felt the impact of this raid.

According to Lossing, *The Empire State*, p. 275, Colonel Brown's mission was a tremendous success. Fort George and the landing site of Lake George had been captured, Mount Defiance had been secured, Forts Ticonderoga and Independence had been bombarded with cannon fire, and a British military outpost on Lake George was attacked. 200 vessels, including gun boats and an armed sloop, had been burned at the outlet of Lake George; large quantities of stores had been secured; 100 American prisoners had been released, and almost 300 prisoners had been captured.

Chapter 19: The First Battle of Saratoga

[1]This is odd because at Fort Ticonderoga, Gates was one of those who had warned that Mount Defiance, with its domineering terrain, was a key position.

[2]By and large, throughout this campaign, the 47th Foot had been utilized as a reinforcement and replacement regiment.

[3]Luzader, pp. 43-44, cites, "slightly more than 3,000 men." There is, however, a discrepancy regarding the strength of the left wing. Ward, Vol. II, p. 505, cites a strength of "about 1,100 rank and file." Perhaps, Ward excluded the

strength of the 47th Foot, as well as some of the other personnel. Byrd, p. 84, cites, "Von Riedesel, with eight cannon and 1,100 men started down the river road." Lieutenant-Colonel Joseph B. Mitchell and Sir Edward Creasy, *Twenty Decisive Battles*, p. 207, cite, "the left column, on the east, nearest the river, also contained 1,100 men." But Furneaux, p. 166, cites a strength of "a little more than 2,000 soldiers."

[4]Furneaux, p. 166, cites a strength of "1,100 rank and file." Furneaux also acknowledges that there were six cannons but cites all six were 6-pounders. Lt. Col. Mitchell and Sir Creasy, p. 206, cite 1,100 men in the center. Ward, Vol. II, p. 505, also cites 1,100; but Luzader cites a strength of 1,600.

[5]By now, the Indian strength was very low. Ward, Vol. II, p. 505, cites about 50.

[6]Ibid. In addition to the loyalists, about 70–80 Canadians were found as well. (Ibid.).

[7]Furneaux, p. 164, cites, "The right wing was composed of the elite of the British troops." Furneaux cites 900 English troops, 500 Germans, 800 Canadians and loyalists, and "some of the remaining Indians." As for the figure of 800 Canadians and loyalists, this figure (possibly printed incorrectly) is totally incorrect. At best, counting the entire strength of the Canadian, loyalist, and Indian irregulars, it would amount to no more than 300.

Ward, Vol. II, p. 505, cites "about 2,000 men in this wing." Luzader, p. 41, cites twelve guns (cannons) and 2,547 men. Byrd, p. 84, cites a strength "with eight cannons and about 2,000 men." Lt. Col. Mitchell and Sir Creasy, p. 206, cite a strength of "some 2,000 men." Cobb, *American Battlefields*, p. 55, cite General Fraser's strength was 2,200 men.

[8]Lt. Col. Mitchell and Sir Creasy, p. 206, cite "his [General Fraser's] mission was to seize the unoccupied high ground west of the American position, then turn east and drive toward the river." Lossing, *The Pictorial Field-Book of the American Revolution*, p. 51, cites, "The Canadians and Indians in front were to attack the central outposts of the Americans, while Burgoyne and Fraser, with the grenadiers and infantry, in separate bodies, and strongly flanked by Indians, were to make a circuitous route through the woods and [in] back of the hills, form a junction, and fall upon the rear of the American camp."

Lossing also cites, "it was arranged that three minute-guns should be fired when Burgoyne and Fraser should join their forces, as a signal for the artillery to make an attack upon the American front and right, force their way through the lines, and scatter them in confusion." (Ibid.). Clearly, along with Fraser and Burgoyne pressing in from the west toward the Hudson River, Hamilton's and Von Riedesel's forces would also pressure the Northern Army from the north.

[9]Burgoyne's opinion of General Hamilton but, especially of General Von Riedesel, had begun to diminish more and more well before 19 September. By now Burgoyne also regarded Von Riedesel as a defeatist because Von Riedesel

confided to Burgoyne that a retreat all the way back to Canada might have to be considered.

[10]Lt. Col. Mitchell and Sir Creasy, p. 206; Ward, Vol. II, p. 505. Furneaux, pp. 156-157, cites, "Burgoyne now commanded about 4,600 effective regular soldiers, 2,500 of them British, and 1,800 Germans, together with the 300 recruits who had recently joined." Furneaux also cites about 800 Canadians and loyalists, 80 Indians, 300 sailors, bateaux-men, artificers, artillerymen, and Canadian drivers." Furneaux's figures are, once again, correct except for the "800 Canadians and loyalists." Furneaux, p. 157, cites "the total strength to 5,000 men." (Furneaux's figure of 5,000 undoubtedly cites only the strength of the soldiers and the does not include the loyalists, Canadians, Indians, the drivers, military naval personnel, bateauxmen and other support personnel). Ketchum, *Saratoga*, p. 357, cites "in all the army included about 7,700 men." Ketchum cites that both the right and left wings had "about 3,000 each, and some 1,700 under Hamilton in the center." (Ibid.). According to James A. Huston, *The Sinews of War: Army Logistics*, p. 56, "When Burgoyne reached Freeman's Farm on 19 September, Burgoyne had about 6,800 regulars and 870 auxiliaries." And A. J. Langguth, *Patriots. The Men Who Started the American Revolution*, p. 443, cites "By now, Burgoyne's army had been reduced to less than six thousand." Of these, "2,500 were British, 1,800 Germans, 1,100 Canadians and loyalists, 80 Indians, and 300 drivers, sailors and artillerymen." (Ibid.). These strength figures, however, only encompassed those on the Saratoga front and did not include those further to the north in locations such as at Fort Ticonderoga, Diamond Island, along the Richelieu River and various other positions in the wilderness. Counting these military and civilian personnel, Burgoyne's strength could have reached about 8,000.

[11]These, however, were told to be ready to move on a minutes notice. Yet Ward, Vol. II, pp. 506-507, implies that this could have been a problem when he cites, "Burgoyne's army, divided into three widely spaced parts, its communications so difficult because of the broken terrain, was really in a precarious condition."

[12]Furneaux, p. 178; and Cyril Falls, ed., "Saratoga 1777" in *Great Military Battles*, p. 101. Sergeant Lamb also credits General Phillips when citing "Major-General Phillips, upon hearing the firing made its way through a difficult part of the wood to the scene of action, and led up the 20th Regiment at the most personal hazard." (Ibid.).

[13]Furneaux, p. 178. However, the Americans also paid a price. According to Lossing, *Pictorial Field-Book of the American Revolution*, "... so furious was Morgan's [unauthorized] charge that his men became scattered in the woods, and a reenforcement of loyalists under Major Forbes soon drove the Americans back. [In the process] Captain Van Swearingen and Lieutenant Morris, with twenty privates, fell into the hands of the British. For a moment, on finding himself almost alone, Morgan felt that his corps was ruined; but his

loud signal-whistling soon gathered his brave followers around him."

[14]Furneaux, p. 178.

[15]Ibid., p. 182; and Scheer and Rankin, p. 315.

[16]Furneaux, pp. 178-179.

[17]From the American side, it was noted how, "Reinforcements successively arrived and strengthened the American line." Furneaux, p. 178. From the British side, as British Army historian Sir John Fortescue wrote, "Never were troops more hardly tried, nor met their trial more grandly than these three battalions [regiments], with the forty-eight artillery-men who worked their guns by their sides… Again and again the three battalions charged with the bayonet, but Arnold could always bring forward fresh troops to replace those who had fallen." (See Falls, *Great Military Battles*, p. 101).

[18]Furneaux, pp. 182-183. And by this, as cited by Furneaux, p. 183, "where it became engaged with the British right wing to no useful purpose."

[19]Ibid., pp. 184-186. As Von Riedesel soon cited, "A few American brigades had endeavoured to surround the right wing, but Lieutenant Colonel [Von] Breymann, being on his guard, received them with a vigorous fire, and compelled them to retreat after a few discharges." (Ibid., p. 186).

[20]Lieutenant-Colonel Andrew Colburn was Colonel Alexander Scammel's second-in-command. As for General Nixon, the heat and residue flying from the cannonball was so intense that it actually melted his left eye leaving only mucus upon his cheek. The ball also ruptured his left ear leaving him deaf for life on that side and a sizable red colored burn area likewise remained on his upper left cheek and forehead for life. Recovering from his wounds, General Nixon lived into his mid 90s.

[21]Luzader, p. 45.

[22]Furneaux, pp. 186-187.

[23]Scheer and Rankin, p. 316.

[24]Ibid. Lossing, *Pictorial Field-Book of the American Revolution*, p. 51, cites this battle is also known as the "Battle of the Bemis's Heights," "The First Battle of Stillwater," and "The Battle of Saratoga."

Chapter 20: Troops Dig In and Patriot Generals Collide

[1]Edward K. Eckert, "Hospitals and Prisons" in *In War and Peace. An American Military History* (Ca.: Wadsworth Publishing Co., 1990), pp. 61-62. According to "Hospitals" and written on "October 24th, 1777" by Dr. James Thacher, the doctor cited, "This hospital is now crowded with officers and soldiers from the field of battle; those belonging to the British and Hessian troops are accommodated in the same hospital with out own men, and receive equal care and attention." Dr. thatcher cited, "not less than one thousand wounded and sick are now in this city [Albany]; the Dutch church and several private houses are occupied as hospitals. We have about thirty surgeons and mates; and all are constantly employed." Dr. Thacher also acknowledged, "I have been pre-

sent at some of their capital operations, and remarked that the English surgeons perform with skill and dexterity, but the Germans, with few exceptions, do no credit to their profession; some of them are the most uncouth and clumsy operations I ever witnessed." (Ibid., p. 62). For Dr. Thacher, the days were indeed long as, "I am obliged to devote the whole of my time, from eight o'clock in the morning to a late hour in the evening, to the care of our patients." (Ibid., p. 62). (For much more on Doctor Thatcher's experiences, see pages 62-63. "Hospitals" was one of the chapters published under the title of "*A Military Journal During the American Revolutionary War, from 1775-1783.*" It was first published in 1827 in Boston by Cottons & Barnard Publishers).

[2]William B. Willcox, *Portrait of a General*, p. 177. By the word "poverty," Clinton referred to the low troop strength based in and around New York City.

[3]Ibid., pp. 179-180. Burgoyne also added "It will draw away great part of their force, and I will follow them close. Do it, my dear friend, directly." See also Pearson, *Those Damned Rebels*, p. 276.

[4]According to Lossing, *Pictorial Field-Book of the American Revolution*, p. 58, "General Lincoln, with two-thousand New England troops, joined the main army on the 29th."

[5]According to Colonel William A. Ganoe, *The History of the United States Army*, p. 46, Gates, in his report to the American Continental Congress, "... made no mention of Arnold and his heroic deeds."

[6]Linda DePauw, *Four Traditions. Women of New York During the American Revolution*, pp. 24-25.

Chapter 21: Things Begin to Collapse for Burgoyne

[1]General Gates assured the Shakers that he would do all that he could to prevent unnecessary excesses.

[2]Pearson, *Those Damned Rebels*, p. 278. According to Lossing, *The Pictorial Field-Book of the American Revolution*, pp. 58-59, between the period of 20 September to 7 October, "there were constant skirmishes between small detachments, sometimes foraging parties, and at others a few pickets; and not a night passed without the performance of some daring exploit, either for the sake of adventure, or to annoy each other."

[3]Of the over 40 British and allied personnel which riflemen Timothy Murphy killed, the greater number were eliminated with either a knife or tomahawk.

[4]The 47th Foot was by now, at best, in half strength.

[5]This Great Redoubt was positioned half-a-mile to the west of the Hudson River and the River Road. Facing southward, it was created about 1.5 miles to the north of the Great Ravine. About 2.5 miles to the south of this redoubt (and across the other side of the Great Ravine), was established the so-called "Burgoyne Line."

[6]According to Boatner, *Landmarks in American History*, p. 299, "[Von]

Breymann's Redoubt was positioned about 200 yards to the north [of the Balcarres redoubt]." But an examination of a map titled "The British and American positions near Freeman's Farm and Bemis Heights September 19 thru October 8, 1777" reveals a considerably larger distance than what Boatner cites. Canadian personnel were also centered between the two redoubts. (Boatner acknowledges that Canadian personnel were inserted between the two redoubts. Ibid.). However, the distance was much more than just "about 200 yards." In actuality, from the Balcarres Redoubt slightly to the northwest to where the Von Breymann Redoubt stood, the distance was almost 1 mile. In all, the straight line distance from the Hudson River to Von Breymann's Redoubt was slightly over 5 miles.

Stone, *The Campaign*, p. 52, cites Von Breymann's force was a reserve force. Stone also cites, "the reserve corps of [Von] Breymann were posted on an eminence on the western side of the ravine for the protection of the right flank."

[7]The distance of this so-called "Burgoyne Line" was just a little over 2 miles. (This is, of course, measured in straight line distance). In itself, the line was not totally straight. Soldiers, along with some cannons, were positioned along this line.

As for Burgoyne's headquarters, it was neither in the Taylor or Smith House as mistakenly cited by some. (See Stone, *The Campaign*, p. 53). Burgoyne's headquarters stood on a piece of land which, in the near future, would be a part of the Wilbur Farm. Apparently, much drinking must have taken place here because when in the aftermath of 1777 Mr. Wilbur plowed up that particular site he used to "find great quantities of old gin and wine bottles." Always "puzzled to know how on earth those bottles came there" he was, one day, informed that Burgoyne had his headquarters on that site and probably even resided right next to it. (See Stone, p. 53, fn 1).

[8]According to Stone, *The Campaign*, pp. 54-55, "The action on the 19th [of September] had essentially diminished his strength, and his situation began to grow critical. His dispatches were intercepted, and his communication with Canada cut off by the seizure of the posts at the head of Lake George." Most of the runners dispatched by Burgoyne at this point did not make it in. And after 19 September, Burgoyne's supply and communication line with Canada was cut totally.

The runners dispatched on the 21st and 22nd of September disappeared. The runner dispatched on the 23rd reached General Clinton on the 5th of October in the Highlands. The runner dispatched on the 27th was Captain Thomas Scott of the 53rd Foot Regiment. He reached Clinton at Fort Montgomery on the 9th of October. The runner dispatched on the 28th of September was Captain Alexander Campbell from the 62nd Foot Regiment. He also rendezvoused with Clinton in the Highlands on the 5th of October. (See Baxter, *The Campaigns of Carleton and Burgoyne*, pp. 33-36). All of the runners were to rendezvous with Clinton in New York City but several encountered the British commander in the first week of October when Clinton attacked the Highlands.

[9]According to Lossing, *Pictorial Field-Book of the American Revolution*, p. 59, "it was their hunting season, too, and this was another strong inducement for them to return to their wives and children, to keep starvation from their wigwams." But Lossing also acknowledges that "the Canadians and loyalists were not more faithful." (Ibid.).

[10]Ketchum, *Saratoga*, p. 382.

[11]Boatner, p. 299. According to A.J. Langguth, *The Patriots*, p. 447, by early October, Burgoyne's "men [were] already on half rations."

[12]Though it was finally agreed to attack once more, according to Jeremy Black, *War for America*, p. 132, "at a Council of War on the 5th [of October] his officers pressed Burgoyne to retreat while there remained a chance." At this time, Burgoyne possessed a fighting strength of 6,617. (Ibid.).

[13]Two days later, on 8 October, Forts Independence and Constitution would also fall.

[14]Bancroft, *The American Revolution*, Vol. III, p. 416. According to Jeremy Black, p. 132, cites Gates possessed on 5 October a strength of "11,469 effectives."

Chapter 22: The Second Battle of Saratoga

[1]Boatner, p. 299, cites 1,500 regulars and 600 auxiliaries. Bancroff, Vol. III, p. 415, cites Fraser's command had a strength of 700; Von Breymann had 300; and Von Riedesel had 500 specially "picked out for service." Cobb, *American Battlefields*, p. 57, cites "1,500 men with artillery." Ward, Vol. II, p. 525, cites "1,500 regulars" and on p. 526 "Captain Fraser with his rangers and 600 Canadian and Indian auxiliaries." Wards figure of 600 Canadians and Indians is incorrect unless if Ward included the British strength posted to the irregulars.

[2]Almost all of the committed British and German troops came from Balcarres' and Von Breymann's' Redoubts. According to Anthony D. Darling, *Red Coat and Brown Bess*, p. 61, on 7 October, such forces were utilized by the British army at what Darling cited was the Battle of Bemis Heights: Reconnoitering Party; Left, Acland's Grenadiers; Center, 24th Foot Regiment along with Detachments of Brunswicker's and Jaeger's; and Right, Balcarres' Light Infantry.

[3]Byrd, *Saratoga. Turning Point*, p. 99; and Ketchum, *Saratoga*, p. 392; Ward, Vol. II, p. 526. Furneaux, *The Battle of Saratoga*, p. 223, cites the artillery was commanded by Major Griffith Williams but Captain Pausch was positioned in the center with two 6-pounders and two-12 pounders. Bancroft, p. Vol. III, 415, cites "eight brass pieces and two howitzers."

[4]Barbers Farm was located to the west of Freeman's Farm. During the first Battle of Saratoga on 19 September, both sides circled through and around it but, there was only a minimal amount of fighting at this farm.

⁵Colonel John Brooks is not to be confused with the Lieutenant-Colonel Brooks killed on 19 September.

⁶Furneaux, p. 224.

⁷Ibid.

⁸General Abraham Ten Broeck was the top ranking militia commander.

⁹England's Parliament was also critical of how the Indians were utilized. See Barbara Graymont, *The Iroquois In the American Revolution*, pp. 152, 155, 157-160; Donald A. Grinde, Jr., *The Iroquois and the Founding of the American Nation*, p. 88; William Stone, *The Siege of Fort Stanwix and the Battle of Oriskany*, pp. 243-244; and *The Campaign*, p. 99. (Numerous other pages in both of Stone's works detail the problems experienced by the Indians under both Generals Burgoyne and St. Leger).

¹⁰General Arnold was characterized as, "A bloody fellow he was. He'd ride right in. It was 'Come on, boys!' Wasn't 'Go boys!' He was kind to his soldiers." See Colonel William A. Ganoe, *The History of the United States Army*, pp. 47-48.

¹¹Ketchum, *Saratoga*, p. 400. Who, however, exactly shot General Fraser remains unknown. Although Timothy Murphy is credited with the shot, other versions do exist.

One version, provided to William L. Stone in the 1830's, cites how, "an elderly man, with a long [barreled] hunting gun" appeared on the scene and, according to Lieutenant Ebenezer Mattoon (a former patriot continental officer who in future years would make general), "the old man, at that instant, discharged his gun, and the general officer [Fraser] pitched forward on the neck of his horse, and instantly they all wheeled about, the old man observing 'I have killed that officer, let him be who he will.'" In turn, Lieutenant Mattoon responded, "you have, and it is a general officer and by his dress I believe it is Fraser." (For Mattoon's observation see Stone, *The Campaign*, Appendix, pp. 373-374).

For much on what the lieutenant wrote pertaining to the Saratoga battles see "Letter of General Ebenezer Mattoon, a Participant in the Battle, with Notes by the Author," pp. 368-380).

Other versions also exist but the legend persists to this day that it was indeed Murphy who pulled the trigger. In conclusion, it must also be presented that when the mortally wounded Fraser was brought to the rear he did state that just moments before being hit, he observed a puff of smoke and "a rifleman, and up in a tree." (See Funeaux, p. 236). According to Furneaux, Colonel Morgan personally ordered rifleman Murphy to shoot Fraser. (Ibid., p. 235). Under normal circumstances, the shot should have been an immediate deathblow because it did strike and tear through vital organs and Fraser's spine as well.

¹²Always concerned for his troops, Colonel Livingston began an accountability of his personnel almost immediately after the Von Breymann Redoubt

had fallen. Knowing that an Irish lad by the name of Sweeny had been serving alongside Stoner, Colonel Livingston inquired directly from Sweeny if he knew the fate of Stoner. After responding in the positive, "a Lieutenant William Wallace then proceeded to the spot indicated by the Irishman, and found our hero with his head reclining upon Tyrrell's thigh." Picking Stoner up, the lieutenant carried him back. Stoner recovered and survived the war. See Stone, *The Campaign*, pp. 66-67, fn. 2.

[13]Stone, *The Campaign*, pp. 66-67. Nicholas Stoner, shortly before being knocked out, himself witnessed this incident. According to Stoner, pp. 66-67, fn. 2, "The Germans always continued to fight after they were down, because they had been assured by their employers that the Americans would give no quarter."

[14]Von Breymann was soon buried at the site and an honor delegation from the patriots fired a volley of shots in his honor. Burgoyne was also notified of this.

[15]From now on, the rest of the conflict would be characterized by retreats, pursuits, skirmishes, and surrender.

[16]As Sergeant Samuel Woodruff later wrote to Colonel William L. Stone, "He [General Arnold] behaved more like a madman than a cool and discreet officer. But if it were madness, there was 'method in it.' He attacked, with the ferocity of a tiger." (See *The Campaign*, p. 63. For the entire and lengthy letter see Appendix, No. V, pp. 314-327. The letter is Titled "A Visit to the Battle-Ground in 1827.").

As for Major Armstrong, initially dispatched by General Gates, he later informed General Gates that he finally established contact with Arnold late in the evening. Armstrong did, however, accompany Arnold back with the stretcher bearing team.

The possibility exists that Major Armstrong's version was not true. He probably did observe, on and off, Arnold throughout the day from a distance. It must be remembered that throughout the battle, Arnold was right up front; therefore, it would have been virtually suicidal for Armstrong to just ride up and, amidst flying shot, cannon balls, and bullets, attempt to restrain Arnold. Noting the ferocity of the battle, Major Armstrong probably just dismounted from his horse, got behind some huge tree, and stayed there until it was safe to come out.

It is known that when Major Armstrong finally rode up to General Arnold with "an order from Gates to return to camp" (and shortly after Arnold extricated himself from underneath his horse), Major Armstrong was now fully aware that it was somewhat safe to venture forth since the battle was more or less over. Later on, Major Armstrong would testify, along with Sergeant Woodruff, that Arnold's actions did not stem from intoxication. ((See Stone, *The Campaign*, pp. 66-67). Ibid., p. 68).

Chapter 23 The British Begin to Collapse

[1]Byrd, *Saratoga. Turning Point*, p. 105; Furneaux, *The Battle of Saratoga*, p. 240; Lieutenant-Colonel Mitchell and Sir Creasy, *Twenty Decisive Battles*, p. 209; and Lossing, *Pictorial Field-Book of the American Revolution*, p. 64.

[2]Byrd, p. 105, cites, "Gates' total casualties had been only some 150 men, Burgoyne had lost four times that many [600], 250 in prisoners alone. Burgoyne now had no choice; he must retreat." (Ibid.). See also Mitchell and Creasy, p. 209. According to Lossing, p. 64, "The British army suffered severely, and their loss in killed, wounded, and prisoners was about seven hundred."

[3]Furneaux, p. 241, cites, "six captured cannons and 240 prisoners of war." Regarding the cannons, Furneaux's figure does not include the cannons captured at the redoubts.

[4]From a distance, the patriots noted the activity. Aiming a couple of cannons into its direction, the patriots fired at those assembled for the funeral. As Chaplain Brudenell officiated, pieces of ground and debris rained down upon him. Although no one was struck and the funeral was concluded with no interference or casualties, it was a very rushed affair because everyone in attendance was very nervous. In the aftermath of Burgoyne's surrender, when General Gates learned that it nothing more than a funeral, Gates personally apologized to Burgoyne for the patriot action.

[5]General Arnold would be hospitalized for the next four months in the Northern Army's main hospital in Albany. He would be joined by General Lincoln who had been shot in the leg and whose bone was also broken.

[6]Ward, *The War of the Revolution*, Vol. II, p. 532. 7 October may be cited as being the date when the loyalist support for Burgoyne had virtually ceased to exist.

[7]Byrd, p. 107.

[8]Lady Acland was soon united with her husband. She also became an admirer and defender of the American revolutionary cause. Returning to England in 1778 with her husband who was still recovering from his wounds, she was widowed that same year as a result of her husband dying in a duel.

[9]Colonel Van Vechten was a very humane person. When Burgoyne's army marched southward Albany's Committee of Safety ordered him, "to remove every loyalist and disaffected person" to Connecticut. Realizing what hardships these individuals would undergo if forcefully removed, Colonel Van Vechten first traveled to Albany and there, he convinced the Committee of Safety members to rescind the order. Afterwards, Colonel Van Vechten appealed to the loyalists and he actually succeeded in winning a number of them over to the patriot side.

[10]Furneaux, pp. 252-253. Gates was, indeed, very angered and distraught by the mass burnings. As for Schuyler's residence, Burgoyne ordered that it be

burned on 10 October 1777. According to Madame Riedesel, "On the 10th, at seven o'clock in the morning, I drank some tea by way of refreshment; and we now hoped that at last we would again get under way. General Burgoyne, in order to cover our retreat, caused the beautiful houses and mills at Saratoga, belonging to General Schuyler, to be burned..." See Wheeler, *Voices of 1776*, p. 243.

In a personal discussion with Ms. Patricia Dolton, the Curator of the Schuyler Mansion in Albany, New York, Ms. Dolton stated that General Schuyler's home was burned on 10 October. At this time, General Schuyler possessed two homes. One, his main mansion, was located in Albany; the second was located in present day Schuylerville. (In 1777, Schuylerville formally did not exist though a small settlement and some people did reside in its vicinity. But it was destroyed in the events of 1777). Schuylerville was finally incorporated as a town in about 1831).

Upon learning that his property had been torched, General Schuyler wrote to his friend, Colonel Varick, shortly after Burgoyne's surrender on 17 October, "The event [the victory over Burgoyne] that has taken place makes the heavy loss I have sustained sit quite easy upon me. Britain will probably see how fruitless her attempts to enslave us will be." Cited from Lossing, *The Empire State*, p. 281.

[11]And so it would be. Sutherland finally returned to England in 1783.

[12]So wrote Sergeant Lamb. See Ward, Vol. II, p. 535.

[13]Furneaux, p. 255. For her entire account during this very difficult period, see pp. 255-256.

[14]Within days of this story being recalled, Burgoyne surrendered the remnants of his army. (This story was recalled to Simeon Alexander by one of his officers who participated in the bombardment).

[15]Graymont, *The Iroquois in the American Revolution*, p. 155.

[16]To cite an example: when Major Charles Cochrane appeared to Fort Edward and began to operate in and around it his strength consisted of 200 militiamen, some who possessed combat experience. See Lossing, *The Pictorial Field-Book of the American Revolution*, p. 74. According to Lossing, p. 81, after Burgoyne surrendered, General Gates reported to Burgoyne that the Northern Army's patriot force strength was registered at 13,222. Of this strength "9,093 were Continentals, or regular soldiers, and 4,129 were militia." This strength figure, however, did not include General Stark's 2,000 plus fighters, nor General Bayley's 2,000 fighters, nor Major Cochrane's 200 militiamen and so forth.

[17]Cobb, *American Battlefields*, p. 57, cites "He [Burgoyne] found his force of only 6,000 surrounded by gates with an army of 20,000."

[18]Preston, *A Short history of the American Revolution*, p. 241; cites "almost 20,000." Furneaux, p. 257, cites "16,000 Americans"; and Bobrick, p. 279, cites "The American army, which was growing daily, now numbered

16,000." Of interest is that despite the combat activity now occurring further to the south in the Highlands, when General Gates requested from General Putnam help in replenishing his food stores, General Putnam immediately helped out. Some of these final shipments actually occurred right at the moment Sir Henry Clinton was attacking into the Highlands. "Nevertheless, he saw to it that 300 barrels of hard bread were rowed up the Hudson from Fishkill Landing, 300 more from Kingston, and another 300 barrels sent from Sharon, Connecticut. Shortly thereafter, he sent up 1,250 barrels of flour, which he swore would be the last, but a few days later he sent another 300 barrels of bread from Fishkill." (See Huston, *The Sinews of War*, p. 56). It was good that this was done because with the fall of the Highlands and the capture of Fishkill and Kingston the flour, bread, and other food items would have been captured. As for a troop strength, Huston cites "Gates's Northern Army totaled more than 23,000 men—about half Continentals and half militia." (See p. 56).

[19]Ward, Vol. II, p. 535, cites "[Burgoyne] was facing 14,000 rebels [patriots] equipped with 'considerable artillery.'"

[20]Daily, this strength rose as more and more armed citizens also appeared. Mostly, these individuals reinforced the existing militia units.

Chapter 24: Burgoyne Surrenders

[1]Stone, *The Campaign*, pp. 255-256. Unfortunately, neither the daredevil's name, or his company commander's name, was ever recorded.

[2]According to Stone, *The Campaign*, pp. 249-250, Timothy Murphy was an extraordinary individual. "He took delight in perilous adventures. He seemed to love danger for danger's sake." After Burgoyne's surrender, "he boasted he had slain forty of the enemy. More than half of whom he scalped." Ibid., p. 249.

[3]Lossing, *The Pictorial Field-Book of the American Revolution*, p. 78.

[4]Ibid.

[5]Likewise, it not only raised the morale on the home front but, also, obtained additional vital food stuffs for the continental armies.

[6]Erroneously, and probably in a rush, Gates accidentally wrote "Septr." (September) rather than October.

[7]For the various letters and documents to include the entire "Article of Convention Agreed Upon between Him [General Burgoyne] and Major General Gates" see The Public *Papers of George Clinton* , Vol. II, pp. 428-456. For "Major General Gates' Proposals, together with Lieutenant General Burgoyne's Answers" and the "Articles of Convention Between Lieutenant General Burgoyne and Major General Gates" finally agreed upon, see Stone, *The Campaign*, pp. 102-112.

[8]Furneaux, p. 267.

[9]In the aftermath of the Revolutionary War, Peters lived with his family in Nova Scotia, Canada, in near poverty. Desperate to gain help for at least his family, he traveled to England seeking some kind of monetary compensation.

But a new King was in power, new Parliamentarians were in and, simply put, no one felt obliged to assist Peters. One day, Peters suddenly dropped dead on a London street. Totally broke, on the day that he died, he was begging for money on the streets.

[10]Lossing, p. 80.

[11]Ibid., pp. 80-81. See also Furneaux, p. 267; and Scheer and Rankin, p. 327.

[12]Ward, Vol. II, pp. 538-539.

[13]Lossing, p. 81.

[14]Ward, Vol. II, p. 539.

[15]Scheer and Rankin, p. 328; Black, *War for America*, p. 133, cites "5,895 men surrendered."

[16]Carlton J. H. Hayes, *A Political and Social History of Modern Europe* (NY: MacMillan Company, 1916), Vol. I, p. 333. According to Wrong, *Canada and the American Revolution*, pp. 324-325, "Burgoyne knew little of the kind of warfare in which he was to be involved and of the people opposing him." And General Charles Lee, one of General Washington's generals, was more than correct when he stated, "He [Burgoyne] is as ignorant of the dispositions of the people of America as he is of the moon." Burgoyne honestly believed (as did Howe and St. Leger) that mass numbers of people would welcome him. Burgoyne also believed that America's leaders were so corrupt that they could easily be simply paid off and "bought" over to the British side. (Ibid., p. 324). But perhaps, it was not totally Burgoyne's fault because prior to the commencement of the 1777 campaign, "Burgoyne was so mislead as to count on the armed support of the population of New York." (Ibid.).

[17]*The Public Papers of George Clinton*, Vol. II, p. 448. This strength includes the strength of "3,875 on command at Fort Edward." Since it is known that General Bayley never possessed such a strength, undoubtedly, the figure of 3,875 encompassed General Stark's 2,000 plus and Major Cochrane's 200 personnel. Of interest is that a "Return of the [Northern] Army of the United States" cites a total strength of 18,624 personnel. (Ibid., p. 456). This strength cites the troop strength of each brigade and here, General Stark's strength is included as well. Regardless, it may be stated that in the concluding days of the Wilderness War of 1777, just alone in the vicinity of Saratoga a strength of no less than 20,000 fighters were opposing Burgoyne.

[18]The figure of approximately 20,000 cites only those who were serving in the Northern Army in and around the Saratoga front in mid-October. This figure did not include those who, at the moment, were serving in the various other units found within and outside of New York State. (Such as in the Highlands, the Schoharie Valley, and the New England States). Furthermore, the mid-October figure does not encompass those who had served during the period of January to early October but, either because of a wound or injury, illness, or simply being rotated back home, were not included in the Northern Army's

mid-October personnel strength figure. Likewise, a sizable number of men perished in 1777. Additionally, some were captured, others were missing and though desertion was never a serious problem, some did desert. The Northern Army also had thousands who supported its efforts by serving as spies, couriers, propagandists; nurses, transporters, work personnel, cooks, bakers, and so forth. Although some soldiers also performed—or supervised—these vital tasks, by and large they were undertaken by the civilian support personnel attached to this army. And the urban guerrilla fighters who fought in and around New York City (they, too, regarded themselves as members fighting for the cause of the Northern Army), these men and women must also be remembered and included. Therefore, if one added to the mid-October strength figure of 20,000 those serving in the other regions, the killed-in-action, the wounded, ill, missing, deserted, along with those who were relieved of duty for whatever reason as well as the underground and urban fighters who directly or indirectly assisted the Northern Army in 1777—then, surely, an overall strength figure of nearly 50,000 to possibly over 60,000 can easily be attained. This was, indeed, an impressive figure and not the King, Burgoyne, Howe, St. Leger, Carleton, Skene, Peters, the English Parliament or anyone else would have imagined that such an impressive fighting strength could have been amassed from within and around the depths of the northeastern wilderness.

[19]According to Black, p. 133, "... the [river] pilots, intimidated by the American soldiers on both banks, refused to take the transports on towards Albany." (See the Wilderness War of 1777 in the Southern Theater chapter).

[20]Factually speaking, Governor-General Guy Carleton played a major role in Burgoyne's defeat. Despite the fact that Howe was no longer marching northward and this, of course, was soon known to Carleton, Carleton could, and should have, done much more. By trimming Burgoyne's force from the outset, lacking aggressiveness in ensuring that adequate supplies reached him, rarely communicating with Burgoyne, rarely dispatching any reinforcement and maintaining a very lay-back attitude in regards to the entire campaign, such factors helped to undermine the entire British campaign of 1777. This explains why soon after October, 1777, the British ministry relieved Carleton.

[21]The shifting of army units, along with certain commanders and personnel from Washington's Main Continental Army to the Northern Army and afterwards back to Washington's Main Army proved, in the long run, to be of tremendous advantage for the patriot cause. And unlike the British, the American's were able to coordinate their military activities on a much better and higher level. For this viewpoint see Black, *War for America*, p. 117.

[22]Colonel Morgan's rifle corps was one of the units to move. See Richard LaCrosse, Jr., *Daniel Morgan's Riflemen on America's Northern Frontier, 1777-1783*, p. 5. "Initially, Morgan's rifle unit arrived into the Northern theater via a march to Peekskill and from there; boats carried the rifle unit to Albany, reaching the American camp towards the end of August." (Ibid., p. 4). Prior to

their departure from Washington's army, General Washington wrote to Morgan, "I know of no Corps so likely to check the enemy's progress in proportion to their number, as the one you com command. I have great dependence on you, your officers, and Men." (Ibid., p. 4).

[23]See also Ketchum, *Saratoga*, p. 448. In conclusion, the painting by Colonel John Trumbull pertaining to the 'The Surrender of General John "Gentleman Johnnie" Burgoyne at Saratoga is an interesting work depicting the conclusion of the Wilderness War of 1777. (The painting may also be seen in Roy Meredith's, *The American Wars: A Pictorial His-tory from Quebec to Korea 1755-1953* (NY: The World Publishing Co., 1955), p. 60).

But perhaps, Meredith summarized it best when he wrote, "Burgoyne slogged his way through the forest to Saratoga, his army in poor shape to fight after the grueling march." (Ibid., p. 60). The wilderness itself exhausted Burgoyne's army more than he ever could have imagined it would.

Bibliography

A Military Journal During the American Revolutionary War from 1775–1783 (Boston: Cottons and Barnard Publishers, 1827).

John Adams, *Papers of John Adams* (Cambridge, MA: Harvard University Press, 1983). Edited by Robert J. Taylor.

John R. Alden, *A History of the American Revolution* (New York: Alfred A. Knopf, Inc., 1969).

Robert B. Asprey, *War in the Shadows* (New York: Doubleday & Company, Inc., 1975), Volume I.

Thomas A. Bailey, *The American Pageant. A History of the Republic* (Massachusetts: D.C. Heath and Company, 1975), 5th Edition, Volume I.

John Bakeless, *Turncoats, Traitors and Heroes* (New York: J.B. Lippincott Company, 1959).

George Bancroft, *History of the United States, From the Discovery of the American Continent* (Boston: Little, Brown and Company, 1875). (Volume IX, 5th edition).

_____, *The American Revolution*, Volumes I–V (Boston: Little, Brown, and Company, 1875).

Oscar Theodore Barck, Jr., *Colonial America* (New York: The MacMillan Company, 1958).

_____, *New York City During the War For Independence* (New York: Columbia University Press, 1931). (Reprinted: New York: Ira J. Friedman, Inc., 1966).

James Phinney Baxter, *The British Invasion From the North. The Campaigns of Generals Carleton and Burgoyne From Canada, 1776–1777, With the Journal of Lieut. William Digby of the 53d, or Shropshire Regiment of Foot* (Albany: Joel Munsell's Sons, 1887).

Charles A. Beard and Mary R. Beard, *A Basic History of the United States* (New York: Doubleday, Doran & Company, 1944).

Fred Anderson Berg, *Encyclopedia of Continental Army Units. Battalions, Regiments and Independent Corps* (Harrisburg, PA: Stackpole Books, 1972).

Major Tharratt Gilbert Best, *A Soldier of Oriskany* (Boonville, NY: The Willard Press, 1935).

"Biography of Colonel Peter Schuyler." (From: Documents Relative To the Colonial History of the State of New York). (Oswego, NY: Fort Ontario archives).

Jeremy Black, *War for America: The Fight for Independence, 1775–1783* (Great Britain: Sutton Publishing Company, 1998).

Paul E. Blackwood, *The How and Why Wonder Book of North American Indians* (New York: Wonder Books, 1965). (5th Printing).

Bruce Bliven, *New York: A Bicentennial History* (New York: W.W. Norton and Company, Inc., 1981).

Mark M. Boatner, *Landmarks of the American Revolution. People and Places Vital to the Quest for Independence* (Harrisburg, PA: Stackpole Books, 1992).

Benson Bobrick, *Angel In the Whirlwind. The Triumph of the American Revolution* (New York: Simon & Schuster, 1997).

Nikolai N. Bolkhovitinov, *The Beginnings of Russian-American Relation, 1775–1815* (Massachusetts: Harvard University Press, 1975).

Captain Edward C. Boynton, *History of West Point, and Its Military Importance During the American Revolution; and the Origin and Progress of the United States Military Academy* (Freeport, NY: Book for Libraries Press, 1863). (Reprinted 1970).

John Brick, *The King's Rangers* (New York: Doubleday & Company, Inc., 1954).

Peter Brock, *Pacifism In the United States: From the Colonial Era to the First World War* (N.J.: Princeton University Press, 1968).

Richard Brookhiser, *Alexander Hamilton—American* (New York: The Free Press, 1999).

Wallace Brown, *Tories In the Revolution* (Oswego, NY: Fort Ontario Archives).

James W. Burbank, *Cushetunk, 1754–1784. The First White Settlement in the Upper Delaware River Valley* (New York: Sullivan County Democrat, 1975) (3rd Printing).

Bruce Burgoyne, ed., *Enemy Views, (1777). The American Revolutionary War as Recorded by the Hessian Participants* (Maryland: Heritage Books, Inc., 1996).

General John Burgoyne, *Thoughts for Conducting the War From the Side of Canada* (New York: Oswego Fort Ontario Archives).

_____, *A State of the Expedition from Canada as Laid Before the House of Commons* (New York: New York Times & Arno Press, 1969). (Reprinted).

H.C. Burleigh, *Captain MacKay and the Loyal Volunteers* (Ontario, Canada: Bayside Publishing Company, 1977).

Martha Byrd, *Saratoga: Turning Point In the American Revolution* (England: Auerbach Publishers, Inc., 1973).

A.L. Byron-Curtiss, *The Life and Adventures of Nat Foster, Trapper and Hunter of the Adirondacks* (Utica, NY: Thomas J. Griffiths Press, 1897) (Reprinted 1976 by Harbor Hill Books, Harrison, NY).

Robert M. Calhoon, The *Loyalists in Revolutionary America, 1760–1781* (New York: Harcourt Brace Jovanovich, Inc., 1973).

North Callahan, *Flight From the Republic. The Tories of the American Revolution* (New York: Boobs-Merrill Co., Inc., 1967).

Colin G. Calloway, *The American Revolution in Indian Country. Crisis and Diversity in Native American Communities* (New York: Press Syndicate, 1995).

Eugenia Campbell Lester and Allegra Branson, *Frontiers Aflame! Jane Cannon Campbell, Revolutionary War Heroine when America Only Had Heroes*

William W. Campbell and William L. Stone, *Siege Fort Stanwix [Schuyler] & Battle of Oriskany* (New York: Bropard Company, Inc., 1977) (Reprinted).

Jill Canon, *Heroines of the American Revolution* (Santa Barbara, Ca.: Bellerophon Books, 1998).

Henry B. Carrington, *Battles of the American Revolution, 1775–1781. Historical and Military Criticism, with Topographical Illustration* (New York: S. Barnes and Company, 1877).

Adrian G. Ten Cate, *Pictorial History of the Thousand Islands of the St. Lawrence River* (Canada: Besancourt Publishers, 1982).

Donald Barr Chidsey, *The Loyalists. The Story of Those Americans Who Fought Against Independence* (New York: Crown Publishers, Inc., 1973).

George Clinton, *The Public Papers of George Clinton* (Albany, 1904. Published by New York State, Volumes 1–10).

Patricia Edwards Clyne, *Patriots In Petticoats* (New York: Dodd, Mead and company, 1976).

William Colbrath, *Days of Siege. A Journal of the Siege of Fort Stanwix in 1777* (New York: Publishing Center for Cultural Resources, 1983).

Hubbard Cobb, *American Battlefields. A Complete Guide to the Historic Conflicts in Words, Maps, and Photos* (New York: Simon & Schuster Macmillan Company, 1995).

William Colbrath, *Days of Siege. A Journal of the Siege of Fort Stanwix in 1777* (New York: Publishing Center for Cultural Resources, 1983).

William T. Couch, ed., *Collier's Encyclopedia* (New York: P.F. Collier and Son Corporation, 1955).

William P. Cumming and Hugh Rankin, *The Fate of a Nation. The American Revolution Through Contemporary Eyes* (London, England: Phaidon Press, Limited, 1975).

Edward E. Curtis, *The Organization of the British Army in the American Revolution* (New York: Ams Press, 1969). (Reprinted from 1926 edition).

Anthony D. Darling, *Red Coat and Brown Bess* (Canada: Museum Restoration Service, 1970).

Jay David and Elaine Crane, *The Black Soldier: From the American Revolution to Vietnam* (New York: William Morrow and Co., Inc., 1971).

Philip Davies, *The History Atlas of North America. From First Footfall To New World Order* (Simon & Schuster Macmillan Company, 1998).

Burke Davis, *George Washington and the American Revolution* (New York: Random House, 1975).

Linda Grant DePauw, *Four Traditions: Women of New York During the American Revolution* (Albany, NY: New York State American Revolution Bicentennial Commission, 1974).

"Description of the Country Between Oswego and Albany—1757. (Paris Doc. XIII)." (Oswego, NY: Fort Ontario Archives).

Lieutenant William Digby, *The British Invasion From the North: Digby's Journal of the Campaigns of Generals Carleton and Burgoyne From Canada, 1776–1777* (Albany, 1887). (Edited by James Phinney Baxter).

Richard M. Dorison, ed., *Patriots of the American Revolution. True Accounts of Great Americans from Ethan Allen to George Rogers Clark* (New York: Gramercy Books, 1998).

Lieutenant-Colonel Fairfax Downey, *Indian Wars of the U.S. Army, 1776–1865* (New York: Doubleday and Company, 1962).

R. Ernest Dupuy and Colonel Trevor N. Dupuy, *The Encyclopedia of Military History From 3500 B.C. to the Present* (New York: Harper and Row, Publishers, 1977) (Revised Edition).

Trevor N. Dupuy, Curt Johnson, and David L. Bongard, *The Harper*

Encyclopedia of Military Biography. An Invaluable Compilation and Assessment of the 3,000 Most Important Worldwide Military Figures From Earliest Times to the Present (New York: Castle Books, 1995).

Allan W. Eckert, *The Frontiersmen: A Narrative* (Boston: Little, Brown and Company, 1967.

_____, *The Wilderness Empire* (Boston: Little, Brown and Company, 1969).

_____, *The Wilderness War: A Narrative* (Boston: Little, Brown and Company, 1978).

Edward K. Eckert, *in War and Peace. An American Military History Anthology* (CA: Wadsworth Publishing, Co., 1990).

Elizabeth F. Ellet, *The Women of the American Revolution* (New York: Baker and Scribner, 1849). (Reprinted Massachusetts: Corner House Publishers, 1980), Volumes I–II.

David M. Ellis, *New York State, Gateway to America. New York State, Revolutionary Cockpit, 1763–1789* (New York: Windsor Publications, 1988).

Paul Engle, *Women in the American Revolution* (Illinois: Follett Publishing Company, 1976).

Dale Van Every, *A Company of Heroes: The American Frontier, 1775–1783* (New York: William Morris and Company, 1962).

Colonel Vincent J. Esposito, ed., *The West Point Atlas of the Civil War [Adapted From the West Point Atlas of American Wars]* (New York: Praeger Publishers, 1962).

Excelsior Studies in American History (New York: William H. Sadlier, 1921).

Cyril Falls, ed., *Great Military Battles* (London, England: The Hamlyn Publishing Group Limited, 1969).

John C. Fitzpatrick, *The Writings of George Washington, from the Original Manuscript Sources, 1754–1799* (Washington, D.C.: U.S. Government Printing Office, 1931–34) (39 Volumes).

Thomas Fleming, *Liberty! The American Revolution* (New York: Viking Publishers, 1997).

Sylvia R. Frey, "Between Slavry and Freedom: Virginia Blacks in the American Revolution" in *Journal of Southern History* (History Journal 49, 1983).

Rear Admiral William Rea Furlong and Commodore Byron McCandles, Harold D. Langley, *So Proudly We Hail. The History of the United States Flag* (Washington, D.C.: Smithsonian Institution Press, 1981).

Robert Furneaux, *The Battle of Saratoga* (New York: Stein and Day, 1971).

_____, The Pictorial History of the American Revolution (Chicago: J.G. Ferguson Publishing Co., 1973).

Colonel William A. Ganoe, The History of the United States Army (NY and London: D. Appleton and Co., 1932).

Charles Gehring, Agriculture and the Revolution in the Mohawk Valley (New York: Fort Klock).

Don R. Gerlach, Philip Schuyler and the American Revolution in New York, 1733–1777 (Nebraska: University of Nebraska Press, 1964).

Major Tharratt Gilbert, A Soldier of Oriskany (Boonville, NY: The Willard Press, 1935).

Bob Gingrich, Founding Fathers vs History Revisionists: In Their Own Words, Founding Fathers Set the Record Straight (IN.: The Author House, 2007).

Henry F. Graff, America: The Glorious Republic (Boston: Houghton Mifflin, Co., 1990).

Barbara Graymont, The Iroquois in the American Revolution (Syracuse, NY: Syracuse University Press, 1972).

Donald A. Grinde, Jr., The Iroquois and the Founding of the American Nation (New York: Indian Historian Press, 1977).

Edward A. Hagan, War In Schohary, 1773–1783 (The Middleburgh News Press, 1980).

Robert E. Hager, Mohawk River Boats and Navigation Before 1820 (Syracuse, NY: Canal Society of New York State, 1987).

Reginald Hargreaves, The Bloodybacks. The British Serviceman in North America and the Caribbean, 1655–1783 (New York: Walker and Company, 1968).

David J. Harkness, Northeastern Heroines of the American Revolution (Tennessee: University of Tennessee, 1977).

Henry Harrison, Battles of the Republic, By Sea and Land (Philadelphia, Pa.: Porter and Coates, 1858).

Hugh Hastings and J.A. Holden, ed's., The Public Papers of George Clinton, First Governor of New York, 1777–1795, 1801–1804 (New York: AMS Press) (Volumes I–10).

Carlton J.H. Hayes, A Political and Social History of Modern Europe (New York: Macmillan Company, 1916), Volume I.

"Herkimer Home" in State Historic Site, Little Falls, New York, Central Region (NY: Office of Parks, Recreation and Historic Preservation).

History of Civil Affairs (Ft. Bragg, NC: U.S. Army John F. Kennedy Special Warfare Center and School, October, 1992).

Ronald Hoffman and Peter J. Albert, ed's., Women In the Age of the American Revolution (Virginia: University Press of Virginia, 1989).

James A. Huston, *The Sinews of War: Army Logistics, 1775–1953* (Washington, DC: U.S. Government Printing Office, 1966).

Islands. A Description. (Oswego, NY: Fort Ontario Archives).

Mary Jemison, *The Life of Mary Jemison* (New York: James D. Bemis, Publishers, 1823).

Crisfield Johnson, *History of Oswego County, New York, 1739–1877* (New York: 1878).

Lieutenant-Colonel James M. Johnson, "Staff Rides and the Flawed Works of Fort Constitution" in *Engineer. The Professional Bulletin for Army Engineers* (October, 1990).

David E. Jones, *Women Warriors. A History* (Washington, DC: Brassey's, 2000).

Thomas Jones, *History of New York During the Revolutionary War* (New York: 1879), Volumes I–II.

Philip R. Katcher, *The American Provincial Corps, 1775–1784* (New York: Osprey Publishing, Ltd., 1973).

_____, *The Encyclopedia of British, Provincial, and German Army Units, 1775–1783* (Pennsylvania: Stackpole Books, 1973).

John Keegan, *Warpaths. Fields of Battle in Canada and America* (Canada: Vintage Books, 1996).

Alan Kemp, *The British Army In the American Revolution* (Great Britain: Almark Publishing Co., Ltd., 1973).

Richard M. Ketchum, *Saratoga. Turning Point of America's Revolutionary War* (New York: Henry Holt and Company, 1997).

_____, *The Winter Soldiers. The Battles For Trenton and Princeton* (New York: Henry Holt and Company, 1973).

Irving S. Kull, Nell M. Kull, Stanley H. Friedelbaum, *A Chronological Encyclopedia of American History* (New York: Popular Library Press, 1952).

Mark V. Kwasny, *Washington's Partisan War, 1775–1783* (Ohio: Kent State University Press, 1996).

Richard B. LaCrosse, Jr., *The Frontier Rifleman. His Arms, Clothing and Equipment During the Era of the American Revolution, 1760–1800* (Union City, Tennessee: Pioneer Press, 1989).

_____, *Revolutionary Rangers. Daniel Morgan's Riflemen and Their Role on the Northern Frontier, 1778–1783* (Bowie, Maryland: Heritage Books, Inc., 2002).

_____, *Daniel Morgan's Riflemen on America's Northern Frontier, 1778–1783* (Unpublished text. Oswego, NY, Fort Ontario Archives).

Roger Lamb, *An Original and Authentic Journal of Occurrences During the ate American War* (New York: New York Times & Arno Press, 1968).

Bruce Lancaster and J.H. Plumb, *The American Heritage Book of the Revolution* (New York: Dell Publishing Co., Inc., 1981).

Harry F. Landon, *History of the North Country. A History of Embracing Jefferson, St. Lawrence, Oswego, Lewis and Franklin Counties* (Indiana: Historical Publishing Company, 1932), Volumes I–III.

A.J. Langguth, *Patriots. The Men Who Started the American Revolution* (New York: Simon and Schuster, Inc., 1989).

Harold D. Langley, *so proudly We Hail. The History of the United States Flag* (Washington, DC: Smithsonian Institution Press, 1981).

Robert Leckie, *The Wars of America (Updated Edition)* (New York: HarperCollins Publishers, 1992).

Eugenia Campbell Lester and Allegra Branson, *Frontiers Aflame! Jane Cannon Campbell. Revolutionary War Heroine When America Had Only Heroes* (New York: Heart of the Lakes Publishing, 1987).

Phillip Lord, Jr., *War Over Walloomscoick. Land Use and Settlement Pattern on the Bennington Battlefield—1777* (Albany, NY: State University of New York, 1989).

Benson J. Lossing, *The Empire State: A Compendious History of the Commonwealth of New York* (Hartford, CT: American Publishing Co., 1888).

_____, *The Empire State. New York: Settlement Through 1875* (Conn.: American Publishing Co., 1888).

_____, *The Pictorial Field-Book of the [American] Revolution* (New York: Harper & Brothers, Publishers, 1860), Volumes I–II.

Christine Lunardini, *What Every American Should Know About Women's History. 200 Events that Shaped Our Destiny* (Massachusetts: Bob Adams, Inc., 1994).

John Luzader, *The Saratoga Campaign of 1777* (Washington, D.C.: National Park Service Publications, 1975).

John Luzader, Louis Torres, Orville W. Carroll, *Fort Stanwix: Construction and Military History, Historic Furnishing Study, Historic Structure Report* (Washington, D.C.: U.S. Government Printing Office, 1976).

Mary C. Lynn, ed., *The Sprecht Journal. A Military Journal of the Burgoyne Campaign* (Contributions in Military Studies, Number 158, 1995).

Piers Mackesy, *The War for America, 1775–1783* (Nebraska: University of Nebraska, 1993).

John K. Mahon and Romana Danysh, *Army Lineage Series: Infantry Part*

I: Regular Army (Washington, DC: 1972).

Jacob Radus Marcus, *United States Jewry, 1776–1985* (Michigan: Wayne University Press, 1989).

James Kirby Martin, *Benedict Arnold, Revolutionary Hero. An American Reconsidered* (New York: New York University Press, 1997).

Joseph Plumb Martin, *Private Yankee Doodle. Being a Narrative of Some of the Adventures, Dangers and Sufferings of a Revolutionary Soldier* (Boston: Little, Brown and Company, 1962).

David McCullough, *John Adams* (New York: Simon & Schuster, 2001).

Ann McGovern, *The Secret Soldier: The Story of Deborah Sampson* (New York: Scholastic Press, Inc., 1975).

Edgar J. McManus, *A History of Negro Slavery in New York* (New York: Syracuse University Press, 1966).

Mary McNeer, *The Hudson, River of History* (Illinois: Garrard Publishing Co., 1962).

Roy Meredith, *The American Wars: A Pictorial History from Quebec to Korea 1755–1953* (New York: The World Publishing Co., p. 1955).

Charles E. Miller, Jr., Donald V. Lockey, Joseph Visconti, Jr., *Highland Fortress: The Fortification of West Point During the American Revolution, 1775–1783* (West Point: Unpublished text at the United States Military Academy (USMA) Library).

Lieutenant-Colonel Joseph B. Mitchell and Sir Edward Creasy, *Twenty Decisive Battles of the World* (New York: The MacMillan Company, 1964).

Lynn Montross, *The Reluctant Rebels. The Story of the Continental Congress, 174–1789* (New York: Harper & Brothers Publishers, 1950).

Frank Moore, *The Diary of the American Revolution* (New York: Washington Square Press, Inc., 1968).

Samuel Eliot Morison and Henry Steele Commager, *The Growth of the American Republic* (New York: Oxford University Press, 1952). (3rd Printing).

Richard B. Morris, ed., *Encyclopedia of American History* (New York: Collins Publishers, 1996).

Richard B. Morris and James Woodress, ed's., *Voices From America's Past. 1—The Colonies and the New Nation* (New York: E.P. Dutton and Company, Inc., 1961).

Joseph Laffan Morse, *Funk and Wagnalls Standard Reference Encyclopedia* (New York: 1958).

Jim Murphy, *A Young Patriot. The American Revolution as Experienced by One Boy* (New York: Clarion Books, 1996).

David Saville Muzzey, *An American History* (Boston: Ginn and Company, 1911).

Lee N. Newcomer, *The Embattled Farmer: A Massachusetts Countryside in the American Revolution* (New York: 1953).

New York State Preservationist (Fall/Winter), Volume 2/Number 2, 1998.

James F. O'Neil, *Their Bearing is Noble and Proud. A Collection of narratives regarding the appearance of Native Americans from 1740–1815* (Dayton, Ohio: J.T.G.S. Publishing, 1995).

Oswego Palladium Times, Tuesday, November 20, 1945.

LTC William L. Otten, Jr., *Colonel J.F. Hamtramck. His Life and Times Volume One (1756–1783) Captain of the Revolution* (Port Aransas, TX, 1997).

————, *Colonel J.F. Hamtramck, His Life and Times Volume Two (1783–1791) Frontier Major* (Port Aransas, TX, 2003).

General Dave Palmer, *The River and the Rock. The History of Fortress West Point, 1775–1783* (New York: Greenwood Publishing Co., 1969).

Rod Paschall, "George Washington, the Father of U.S. Intelligence" in *Spies and Secret Missions. A History of American Espionage* (Newtown, Pa.: 2002).

Michael Pearson, *Those Damned Rebels. The American Revolution As Seen Through British Eyes* (New York: G.P. Putnam's Sons, 1972).

Lucille Recht Penner, *The Liberty Tree: The Beginning of the American Nation* (New York: Random House, 1998).

Deborah Pessin, *History of the Jews in America* (New York: The United Synagogue Press of America, 1957).

Walter Pilkington, *The Journal of Samuel Kirkland, 18th-century Missionary to the Iroquois, Government Agent, Father of Hamilton College* (Clinton, New York: Hamilton College Publishing, 1980).

Joseph Plumb Martin, *Private Yankee Doodle. Being a Narrative of Some of the Adventures, Dangers and Sufferings of a Revolutionary Soldier* (Boston: Little, Brown and Company, 1962).

John A. Pope, Jr., ed., *Strange Stories, Amazing Facts of America's Past* (Pleasantville, New York: Reader's Digest Press, Inc., 1989).

Arthur Pound, *Lake Ontario. The American Lakes Series* (New York: The Bobbs-Merrill Company Publishers, 1945).

John Hyde Preston, *A Short History of the American Revolution* (New York: Pocket Books, Cardinal edition, 1952).

Benjamin Quarles, *The Negro in the American Revolution* (N.C.: University of North Carolina Press, 1961).

Emily Raabe, *Ethan Allen. The Green Mountain Boys and Vermont's*

Path to Statehood (New York: Rosen publishing Group, Inc., 2002).

Willard Sterne Randall, *George Washington: A Life* (New York: Henry Holt and Company, 1997).

Hugh F. Rankin, *The Fate of a Nation. The American Revolution Through Contemporary Eyes* (London, England: Phaidon Press limited, 1975).

George Reed, *Fort Ontario* (Unpublished Text).

"Revolutionary Vet's Grave Found in Montezuma" in The Post-Standard (Syracuse, NY: June 24, 1998).

Revolutionary War Dates Relating To Oswego (Unpublished text) (Oswego, NY: Fort Ontario Archives).

Revolutionary War Diaries Relating to Oswego (Unpublished text) (Oswego: NY: Fort Ontario Archives).

George W. Roach, *Colonial Highways in the Upper Hudson Valley* (NY: New York State Historical Association, April, 1959).

Lemuel Roberts, *Memoirs of Captain Lemuel Roberts* (New York: New York Tmes & Arno Press, 1969). (Reprinted).

Clinton Rossiter, *The Federalist Papers* (New York: The New American Library, Inc., 1961).

Barnet Schecter, *The Battle for New York. The City at the Heart of the Revolution* (New York: Walker Publishing Company, Inc., 2002).

George F. Scheer and Hugh F. Rankin, *Rebels and Redcoats* (New York: The New American Library, Inc., 1957).

Elizabeth Eggleston Seelye, *Hudson, Mohawk, Schoharie. History From America's Most Famous Valleys and the Border Wars* (New York: Dodd, Mead and Company, Publishers, 1879).

William Seymour, "Turning Point at Saratoga" in *Military History* (December 1999).

Victoria Sherrow, *The Iroquois Indians* (New York: Chelsea House Publishers, Inc., 1992).

Jeanne Meader Schwarz and Minerva J. Goldberg, *New York State in Story* (New York: Frank E. Richards, 1962), Books I–II.

Jeptha R. Simms, *History of Schoharie County and Border Wars of New York* (Albany: Musell and Tanner, 1845).

_____, *The Frontiersmen of New York* (Albany, NY: George C. Riggs, 1882).

Ted Smart, *Colonial Virginia. A Picture Book To Remember Her* (New York: Crescent Books, 1979).

Linda Spizzirri, ed., *Northeast Indians* (South Dakota: Spizzirri Publishing, Inc., 1982).

"St. Leger's Attack on Ft. Stanwix in 1777 Proved Fiasco" *(Oswego*

Palladium-Times, Tuesday, November 20, 1945).

Stephen G. Strach, *Some Sources For the Study of the Loyalist and Canadian Participation In the Military Campaign of Lieutenant-General John Burgoyne 1777* (Eastern National Park and Monument Association, 1983).

William Leete Stone, *Life of Joseph Brant-Thayendanegea: Including the Border Wars of the American Revolution, and Sketches of the Indian Campaigns of Generals Armar, St. Clair, and Wayne* (New York: George Dearborn and Co., 1838), Volume I.

_____, *Life of Joseph Brant-Thayendanegea Including the Indian Wars of the American Revolution* (New York: H.&E. Phinney, 1845).

_____, *The Campaign of Lieut.Gen. John Burgoyne and the Expedition of Lieut.Col. Barry St. Leger* (New York: Da Capo Press, 1970) (Reprinted).

James Sullivan, *The Papers of Sir William Johnson* (Albany, NY: University of New York State, 1922).

Hallie DeMass Sweeting, *Pioneers of Sterling, NY (Cayuga County).* (Red Creek: Wayuga Press, 1998).

Howard Swiggert, *War Out of Niagara* (Port Washington, NY: Friedman Publishers, 1963). *Syracuse Herald-American,* Sunday, July 2, 2000.

"The Battle of Oriskany" in *The Herald-American, Sunday, July 4, 1999. The Campaign of 1777* (Oswego, NY: Fort Ontario Archives).

The Encyclopedia Americana. International Edition (Danbury, Conn.: Grolier Inc., Publishers, 1982).

The Encyclopedia Americana. International Edition. U.S. Constitution Bicentennial Commemorative Edition (Connecticut: Grolier Incorporated, 1988), Volume 21.

The Forts of Oswego (Unpublished text) (Oswego, NY: Fort Ontario Archives).

_____, (Updated Text) (Oswego, NY: Fort Ontario Archives).

The Loyalist Papers (New York: New York Public Library). (Oswego, NY: Fort Ontario Archives).

The Papers of Sir William Johnson (NY: Albany University, 1922).

The Military Journals of Two Private Soldiers, 1758–1775, with Numerous Illustrative Notes (NY: Poughkeepsie: 1845).

Adrian G. Ten Cate, *Pictorial History of the Thousand Islands* (Canada: Besancourt Publishers, 1982).

Lowell Thomas and Berton Bradley, *Stand Fast for Freedom* (Philadelphia, Pa.: The John C. Winston Company, 1940).

Barbara W. Tuchman, *The First Salute* (London, England: Penguin Group Publishers, 1989).

Colonel Stanley M. Ulanoff, ed., *American Wars and Heroes. Revolutionary Through Vietnam* (New York: Arco Publishing, Inc., 1985).

Highland Commanders (Unpublished text at West Point Archives).

Carl Van Doren, *Secret History of the American Revolution* (New York: Viking Press, 1941).

Dale Van Every, *A Company of Heroes. The American Frontier, 1775–1783* (New York: William Morrow and Company, 1962).

Baron Friedrich Adolph Von Riedesel, *Letters and Journals Relating to the War of the American Revolution* (Albany, NY: Joel Munsell, 1867). (Translated by William L. Stone). (Reprinted, New York: New York Times & Arno Press, 1968).

John G. Waite and Paul R. Huey, *Herkimer House. An Historic Structure Report* (New York: 1972).

Christopher Ward, *The War of the Revolution* (New York: The Macmillan Co., 1952) (Volumes I–II).

George Washington, *Papers of George Washington* (Virginia: University of Virginia Press, 1983). Edited by W.W. Abbot.

————, *Writings of George Washington from the Original Manuscript Sources, 1745–1799* (Washington, DC: Government Printing Office, 1931–1944), 39 Volumes. Edited by John C. Fitzpatrick.

William H. Watkins, "Slavery in Herkimer County. African Americans Were Here in the Valley From the Beginning" in *Legacy. Annals of Herkimer County* (New York: Herkimer County Historical Society, 1990). (Issue Number 3).

Richard Wheeler, *Voices of 1776* (New York: Thomas Y. Crowell, Co., 1972).

David C. Whitney, *The People of the Revolution: The Colonial Spirit of '76* (1974).

C. Keith Wilbur, *The Revolutionary Soldier, 1775–1783* (Conn.: The Globe Pequot Press, 1969.

William B. Willcox, *Portrait of a General. Sir Henry Clinton in the War of Independence* (New York: Alfred A. Knopf, 1962).

William M. Willett, *A Narrative of The Military Actions of Colonel Marinus Willett, Taken Chiefly From His Own Manuscript* (New York: G.&C.&H. Carvill, 1831).

T. Harry Williams, *The History of American Wars. From Colonial Times to World War I* (New York: Alfred A. Knopf, Inc., 1981).

John E. Wilmot, ed., *Journals of the Provincial Congress of New York* (Albany, 1842), Vol. 1.

Thomas G. Wnuck, "The Last Offensive of the American Revolution" in

The Dispatch (Summer '80) (Oswego, NY: Fort Ontario Archives).

James Albert Woodburn and Thomas Francis Moran, *American History and Government.*

A Text-Book on the History and Civil Government of the United States (New York: Longmans, Green, and Co., 1907).

Wallace F. Workmaster, *The Forts of Oswego: A Study in the Art of Defense* (Oswego, NY: Fort Ontario Archives).

Esmond Wright, ed., *The Fire of Liberty. The American War of Independence seen through the eyes of the men and women, the statesmen and soldiers who fought it.* (New York: St. Martin's Press, 1983).

George M. Wrong, *Canada and the American Revolution. The Disruption of the First British Empire* (New York: Cooper Square Publishers, Inc., 1968).

Karen Zeinert, *Those Remarkable Women of the American Revolution* (Connecticut: The Millbrook Press, 1996).

Index

Abercromby, Gen. James, 81, 189, 339n

Acland, Lady Harriet, 19, 286, 291–292, 388n

Acland, Maj. John Dyke, 19–20, 123–124, 130, 236, 267, 270, 272, 284

Adams, Abigail, 145, 152, 340n

Adams, John, 6, 62–63, 142, 145, 152, 208, 340n, 359n

Adams, Samuel, 62, 208

Adirondack Mountains, 7, 47

African-Americans, 7, 156

African-American Institute, 312

Albany, New York, 25, 30, 36, 47–48, 57, 64, 73, 84, 96, 105, 130, 134, 146, 156, 159, 166–168, 173–174, 177–178, 235, 255, 264, 287, 303, 324n

Allen, Capt. Ebenezer, 229–230, 307–308

Allen, Col. Ethan, 61, 117–118, 339n, 348–349n

Allen, John, 135

Allen, Rev. Thomas, 60, 104, 186, 191, 355n

American loyalist volunteers, 59

Anburey, Lt. Thomas, 65–66, 72–73, 124, 157, 233, 252, 261, 362n, 372n

Anstruther, Lt. Col. John, 248

HMS *Apollo*, 28, 320n

Armstrong, Maj. John, 275, 281, 387–388n

Arnold, Gen. Benedict, 14, 49, 61, 100, 117, 151, 223, 246, 356n, 358n; at war with Gates, 257–258; Bemis Heights, Battle of, 271, 273–275, 279–281, 283–284; capable commander, 378n; Freeman's Farm, Battle of, 238–239, 241, 243–245, 247, 382n; removed from command, 258–260; returns to Washington, 307; sent to Fort Ticonderoga, 95

Bach, Lt. Michael, 372n

Bailey, Col. John, 223, 247

Balcarres Redoubt, 262–263, 268, 277–279, 281, 383–385n

Baldwin, Col. Jeduthan, 53, 55–56, 61, 88–89, 214, 216–217

Ball, Capt. Robert, 279

Barner, Maj. Von (?), 44, 188, 195–196, 198–199

Batten Kill River, 158, 167, 169, 171, 178, 188, 217, 284–286, 288, 364n

Batty, John, 68–70

Baum, Lt. Col. Friedrich, 44, 176, 365n, 367–368n, 373n; Bennington, Battle of, 183–191, 193–194, 196, 199, 200; death of, 195–196; departs Cambridge, 180–181; ordered to capture supplies at Bennington, 177–179;

405

borough, movement to, 103
Frederick the Great, 22
Freeman, John, 216, 238, 241, 262
Freeman, Thomas, 241
Freeman's Farm, Battle of, 236–240, 242–247, 249–250, 252, 254–258, 262, 382–385n
French Lines75–79, 81, 88, 91–92, 101, 231, 334n, 339n, 342n
French and Indian War, 2, 27, 44, 49, 51, 72, 75, 95, 189, 319n, 323n, 337n, 341n, 363n

Gage, Gen. Thomas, 42
Gall, Gen. Walther R. von, 43, 226
Garrick, David, 42
Gates, 86, 104
Gates, Gen. Horatio, 13–14, 19, 55–56, 208, 215, 217, 224, 266, 296, 336n, 355–356n, 376n; arrives at Albany, 209–210; arrives at Bemis Heights, 223, 235; at war with Arnold, 257–258; Bemis Heights, aftermath, 284, 287–290; Bemis Heights, Battle of, 268–275, 281; brutality toward prisoners, 220; Burgoyne written off in Montreal, 174; Burgoyne's surrender, 301–305, 388–389n; digging in, 257; feud with Schuyler, 62–63; final British retreat, 298; Freeman's Farm, Battle of, 237–239, 243, 245–247, 252, 254, 256, 383n; Lady Harriet Acland, 286; letter to Burgoyne, 291; letter to Hancock, 293–294; message from Burgoyne, 29; moves to better ground around Saratoga, 214; ordered to command the Northern Army, 63; orders Bemis Heights occupied, 219–222; postwar, 379n; recalled to Washington's army, 64; removes Arnold from command, 258–260; replaces Schuyler, 209; Stark reports to, 369n; the Highlands, 301; the Shakers, 261; transportation issues, 390–391n; troop

strength, 214, 265
Gay, Samuel, 259
Germain, Lord George, 23, 26, 31–32, 111, 210, 316–317n, 319–320n, 326n, 348n; assigns troops to Burgoyne, 42; authorized Howe to attack Philadelphia, 27; Carlton to support Burgoyne, 332n; everyone has low opinion of, 32; fails to warn Burgoyne about Howe's plan, 31; failure of communications with Howe, 211; hostile toward Carleton, 32; Howe's early letter, 24; Howe's fifth letter, 28, 30; Howe's first letter, 24; Howe's fourth letter, 26, 30; Howe's second letter, 24–25; Howe's sixth letter, 29; Howe's third letter, 25, 30; native warriors, 366n; plans, 322n; plans for Howe, 321n; Washington would march north to confront Burgoyne, 37
German Military Units, 146; 1st Brigade, 38; 2nd Brigade, 38; Brunswick Light Infantry, 126, 236, 246, 249; Brunswicker Light Jaeger Infantry, 177; Hesse-Hanau Regiment, 38, 43, 236, 262–263, 330–331n, 365n; Prince Frederick Regiment, 38, 43, 145, 229, 330n; Regiment Von Barner, 330n; Regiment Von Ehrenkrook, 330n; Regiment Von Rhetz, 38, 43, 249, 262, 329–330n; Regiment Von Riedesel, 38, 43, 330n; Regiment Von Specht, 38, 43, 262, 330n
Geyso, Capt. Karl von, 126
Gleisenberg, Capt. Gottlied Joachim von, 195–196
Glover, Gen. John, 94–95, 151, 158, 207, 223, 244, 289, 294, 307
Gordon, Gen. Patrick, 100
Grant, Maj. (?), 120–121, 130
Gray, Capt. James, 106–107, 109, 347n
Great Bridge, 53
Great Redoubt, 238, 262–263, 284,